MASS MEDIA IN THE MIDDLE EAST

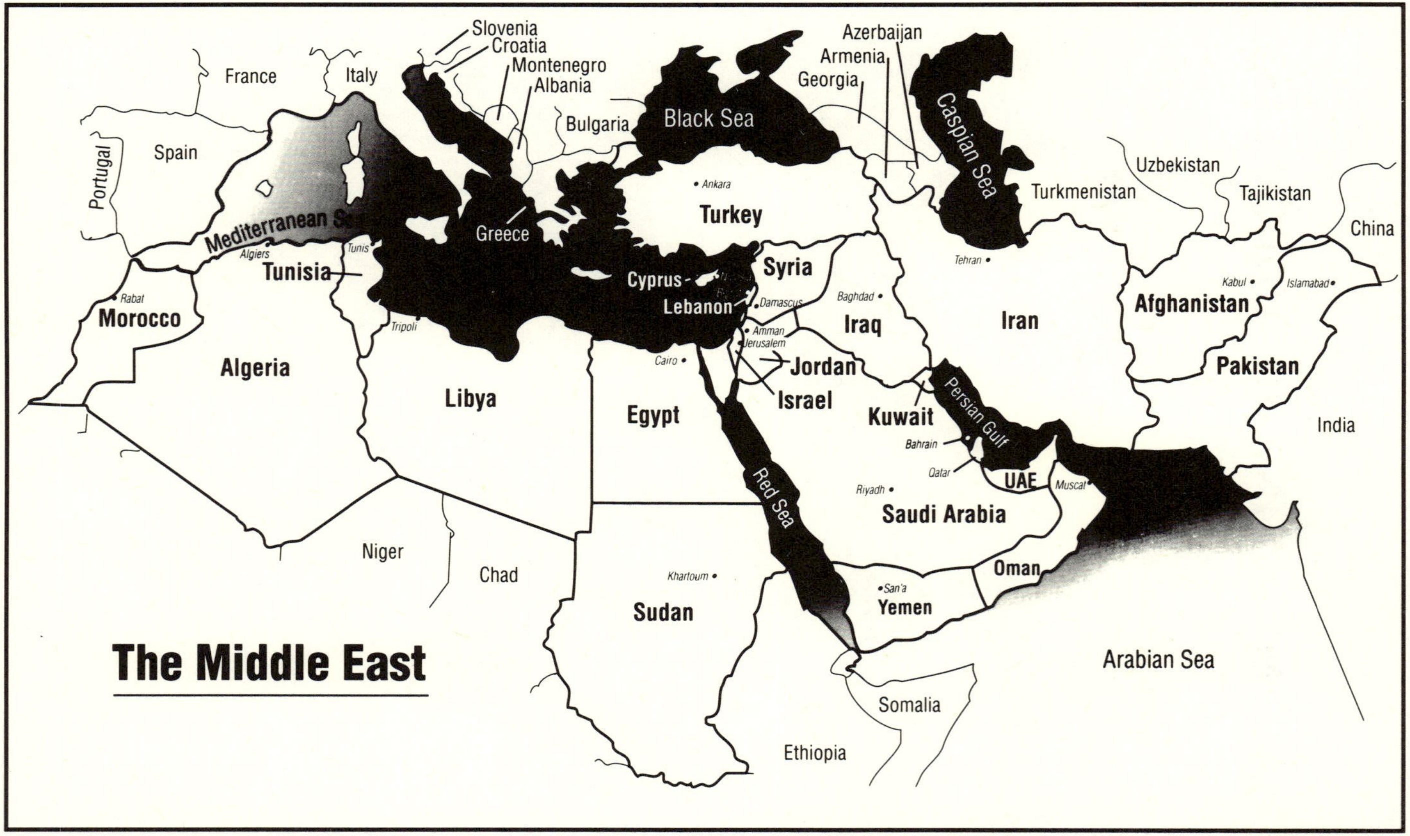

Map Graphic - Moran Design Corp.

Mass Media in the Middle East

A Comprehensive Handbook

EDITED BY
Yahya R. Kamalipour and Hamid Mowlana

Greenwood Press
Westport, Connecticut • London

Library of Congress Cataloging-in-Publication Data

Mass media in the Middle East : a comprehensive handbook / edited by
Yahya R. Kamalipour and Hamid Mowlana.
p. cm.
Includes bibliographical references and index.
ISBN 0–313–28535–7 (alk. paper)
1. Mass media—Middle East. I. Kamalipour, Yahya R.
II. Mowlana, Hamid.
P92.M5M37 1994
302.23'0956—dc20 93–50536

British Library Cataloguing in Publication Data is available.

Library of Congress Catalog Card Number: 93–50536
ISBN: 0–313–28535–7

First published in 1994

Greenwood Press, 88 Post Road West, Westport, CT 06881
An imprint of Greenwood Publishing Group, Inc.

Printed in the United States of America

The paper used in this book complies with the
Permanent Paper Standard issued by the National
Information Standards Organization (Z39.48-1984).

10 9 8 7 6 5 4 3 2 1

To my parents
my wife Mahboobeh
and my daughters Shirin and Daria
Y.R.K.

To Javad Mowlana and the family
H.M.

CONTENTS

TABLES

ACKNOWLEDGMENTS

The book you are holding in your hands is the culmination of more than two years of research and writing by 32 mass media scholars across the Middle East and the United States. We have delineated the Middle East as the Arab countries plus Afghanistan, Cyprus, Iran, Israel, Pakistan, and Turkey. This premier book is a comprehensive study of the mass communications systems in 21 Middle Eastern countries and is designed for college students, scholars, media professionals, news agencies, and the globally inclined writers, readers, and researchers. This book is also valuable to all who are committed to multicultural education.

First and foremost, we want to thank our authors, for without their genuine support, hard work, and timely contributions this project could not have come to fruition. We are grateful to all of them.

We also want to thank the institutions with which our authors are affiliated for providing financial, research, administrative, and secretarial support to our contributing authors during the course of this project.

We owe much gratitude to our respective institutions: Purdue University Calumet provided essential financial and research support during the entire course of this project. We wish specifically to thank Professor Michael R. Moore, dean of the School of Liberal Arts, and Professor William L. Robinson, head of the Communication and Creative Arts Department, for their genuine interest in this book. We are also thankful to department secretary Elizabeth Paschen for her able support.

We would like to acknowledge the grant received from the International Communication Program of the School of International Service, American University, Washington, D.C., in support of this project. We are grateful to Dean Louis Goodman of the School of International Service for his continued support and to Bill Cammack and Julia Brown for their kind assistance.

We wish to thank Jon D. Moran and Janis E. Moran of Moran Design Corporation in Hammond, Indiana, who skillfully designed the Middle East map for this book.

Furthermore, we are immensely grateful to Professor Sandra Littleton-Uetz of the English Department at Purdue University Calumet, for her expert and conscientious editorial assistance throughout this project. Most of the chapters were revised four or five times. The result is that overall this book is sharper, more concise, and easier to read than when we began editing the first drafts. Nevertheless, we wish to indicate that we worked with what was provided to us by our contributing authors. For instance, in some cases our authors have translated magazine, newspaper, book, and other titles into English, whereas in other cases only the original titles, as published in their native languages, are given. Furthermore, matters such as references or citations, or their lack of, remain the sole responsibility of the contributing authors.

Gratitude is due to the following individuals at Greenwood Press: Our editor Mildred Vasan for her interest in this project; Susan E. Badger, Copyeditor; and Nita Romer, Production Editor, for their careful attention to details and for transforming this manuscript into a skillfully designed, organized, and readable book.

Our greatest debt is undoubtedly to our families for their genuine support and love in the course of this long and, at times, painful project.

Yahya R. Kamalipour
Hamid Mowlana

INTRODUCTION

A crucial, yet unexplored, area in the study of the Middle East consists of the aspects of communication and information flow in the region. Modern telecommunications, especially space-age technology, have altered traditional notions of strategies in international and regional conflict and cooperation. Historically, transportation, navigation, and communication services have been indispensable systems of this strategic aspect of the Middle East. However, in recent times, with the development of modern communication worldwide, the region has acquired an even more vital role. Additionally, the rise of Islamic resurgence as a major revolutionary social and political force, the use of channels of communication as an important vehicle for mobilization, and the integration of modern means of communication into the old social networks—all these have further accelerated the interests and the analysis of communication systems in the Middle East.

Among the many changes that have been sweeping throughout the Middle East during the last several decades, the development of communications has been one of the most fundamental and pervasive of all in its effects on the region's diverse societies. Although there has been a geometric progression of growth in the study of mass communication systems of the Middle East during this period, individual and collective efforts of scholars and writers of this geographical area remain sporadic and unsystematic. In short, the acceleration in the output of work in international and regional studies has not been accompanied by the publication of appropriate materials that would examine the diverse mass media systems of the Middle East in a single volume. This study, therefore, arose from a recognition of the woeful lack of detailed information on the region's media systems and is designed to help fill that gap. This volume is also the first comprehensive study of the structure and functions of the mass media in the Middle East, with the hope that it will provide the reader with a review and description of the mass media in the individual countries and will fulfill the need for information regarding the communication sources and resources of the area.

The Middle East is a diverse region and frequently defies generalization. Approaching the region by looking at individual countries or political, economic, and social phenomena peculiar to a subregion provides a clearer understanding of the area's internal dynamics. It is said that change is the common denominator throughout the region, although it varies somewhat from place to place. However, it is difficult to determine with any great certainty the political and cultural changes including the processes of communication and those of the mass media in the contemporary Middle East.

For more than a century, mass media in the Middle East have been considered phenomena from the West—products, so to speak, of the impact of the West upon the Middle East. However, the mass media have been used as tools of nationalism or Islamic universalism throughout the recent history of Middle Eastern societies. In most countries of the Middle East, the spirit of independence at times became fully articulated through the combination of journalism and literature. Therefore, as the waves of anticolonialism and anti-imperialism broke upon the Middle East, journalism, literature, and politics became identified with one another. Indeed, a common characteristic noted in all the Middle Eastern countries is the historically close relationship between the mass media and political reforms.

The relationship of mass media to social and political developments in the Middle East today represents only the latest phase of a long process of transformation and change that began in the late nineteenth century and extended throughout four generations. For example, during the last two decades of the nineteenth century, two types of publications were emerging in the Middle East: the press led mainly by the Western-trained and -educated elite who were promoting European ideas of secularism, liberalism, and modern nationalism; and the press pioneered by such individuals as Seyyed Jamal al-Din Asadabadi (1838–1897), who was campaigning for a unified Islamic community throughout the Middle East, Asia, North Africa, and other Islamic lands. Born in the village of Asadabad, near Hamadan, in western Iran, Jamal al-Din (also known as Al-Afghani) was one of the most outspoken and dramatic figures of the Middle East and Islamic world. His oratory skills, combined with his influential journal *Al-Urvatul Vosgha (Indissoluble Link),* had profound impact in politically mobilizing the people in such countries as Iran, Egypt, India, and Turkey against the European powers. His influence was indeed strong in the Middle East, and his efforts resulted in altering the power base of the press. Journalism became the weapon of men and women in revolution instead of those in power. By the end of the nineteenth century, the press was transformed from a limited channel of communication to a genuine information medium of enormous impact.

The mass media of any country contains ingredients that are endemic to their local setting, characteristics that make them special products of the social milieu from which they originate. The mass media in the Middle East have developed traits that are unique to the region's social and psychological framework. In a region of explosive politics and multicultural settings, the media of the Middle East as a whole have evolved in support of independence and national development. At the same time, there has traditionally been a very close relationship between the mass media and the state in the Middle East. In fact, throughout the first decades of its existence, the press of the Middle East was restricted to official journals, the sole function of which was to communicate government announcements and proclamations and to provide certain technical information for the ruling class. Thus, the autocratic nature of the states of the region was instrumental in laying the basis for governmental media controls. Today, the media in the Middle East are a mixture of both private and governmental sectors, with the state, political parties, and the upper strata of society playing an important role.

However tremendous the growth of the mass media and modern communication technologies in the Middle East, to limit analyses of mass communication in the region to the conventional Western media models is to ignore traditional, organizational, and group channels that are unique to the region's culture—and through which modern mass media messages are filtered and legitimized. Linguistic, religious, and cultural diversity have left an important mark on the contents of mass communication in each of the political systems in the Middle East and have a pronounced impact on the structure and operation of the media. Therefore, the country chapters in this volume aim only at pinpointing several of the major issues and basic characteristics of the mass media in the recent sociopolitical and technological developments of the area. Scarcity of statistics and other data, problems associated with research in the area, and the swiftness of the processes of change all require the consideration of this work as a body of tentative conclusions and analyses rather than as a final synthesis.

Yahya R. Kamalipour
Hamid Mowlana

1

AFGHANISTAN

Mohammad Houssain Razi

INTRODUCTION

The Islamic State of Afghanistan lies in the heart of Asia, with the former Soviet Union to the north, the People's Republic of China to the northeast, Pakistan to the south and east, and Iran to the west.

The landlocked country has an area of 253,861 square miles. The land, which is barely above sea level at most points along the Oxus River, rises to peaks of over 20,000 feet in the nearby Wakhan Corridor. The Hindu Kush Mountains, which range from the northeast to the southwest, divide the country into halves and have proved a formidable barrier to communication and commercial relations between the north and the south. The estimated 1991 population was 16,450,000 (*The World Almanac and Book of Facts 1993,* 1992, p. 727).

Afghanistan exhibits great cultural diversity in terms of language, ethnic groups, religious sects, and standards of living and consequently contains many disruptive forces. All of these differences strain the country and create problems for the nation's internal communications.

Language differences are a problem. Pashtu and Dari (Persian) are the two official languages. Dari is widely spoken. There are almost 30 dialects spoken in the country (Newell, 1972, p. 13). Added to these ethnic and official languages is Arabic, the language of the Holy Quran and the religious leaders, which most Afghans have studied with their Mullahs (religious leaders), usually before they attend public schools. The actual translations and interpretations of the holy scriptures are left up to the Mullahs, who as a result have great influence and power over the people. Because of the multiplicity of the languages, schools and the communication media face tremendous obstacles.

Afghanistan is composed of several major ethnic groups. Although accurate census data are not available, the two largest ethnic groups are Pashtuns, 6.5 million, and Tajeks, 4.9 million. Other ethnic groups include Hazaras, Uzbeks, Turkmens, Aimaq, Brahui, Nuristanis, and Baluchis. Not only is Afghanistan ethnically mixed, but most of its peoples spill over the boundaries into neighboring countries (Hammond, 1984, p. 6). Among foreigners who have settled in Afghanistan are the Hindus, Jews, and Arabs.

The religion of the Afghan people is Islam (with the exception of Hindus and a smaller number of Jews). Islam permeates the entire social structure of Afghan life. About 84 percent of Afghan Muslims are Sunni, while another 15 percent are Shia, Islam's most numerous minority sect.

Afghanistan has one of the lowest levels of adult literacy in Asia. Only 23.7 percent of Afghans age 15 and over, including 38.9 percent of males and 7.8 percent of females, can read and write (*Europa World Year Book 1991,* 1991, p. 284). Although the 1964 constitution stated that education was the right of every Afghan and should be provided free of charge by the state, the government had neither the financial resources, the teachers, the textbooks, nor the facilities to implement the idea of universal education (Chohen, 1963, p. 284).

Approximately 1.3 million Afghans died fighting the Soviets in a 1979 war that produced 5.0 million Afghan refugees—the largest refugee population in history, according to the United Nations High Commission for Refugees. Following the Soviet withdrawal on February 18, 1989, and the subsequent fall of the Afghan Communist regime on April 16, 1992, Afghan society continued to suffer from further chaos and violence as rival Mujahedeen factions battled for control. The long years of war have had damaging effects on all forms of media in the country (Kaplan, 1988).

Afghanistan, like many developing countries, has formidable handicaps preventing the mass media from developing normally: a low literacy rate, a multiplicity of languages, economic underdevelopment, low per capita income (U.S.$168), and poor communication facilities. The lack of trained journalists also has been a problem. It was not until 1961 that a Journalism Department was founded in the School of Letters of Kabul University.

Afghanistan's philosophy of communications has traditionally been highly centralized and paternalistic. The media has been heavily regulated and controlled. Since most of the media is directly financed by the government, with little or no outside advertising revenue, there is little opportunity for free expression in the media, although there have been relatively brief periods in which the government relaxed its control.

PRINT MEDIA

Newspapers

The foundation of the press in Afghanistan goes back to 1873 when the first printing stone house was established as part of social reforms of the country, under King Shir Ali Khan, who established the weekly newspaper *Shams-un-Nahar.* However, the father of newspapers today is considered to be *Saraj-ul-Akhbar* (*Luminary of Chronicles*), which was founded in 1911 by Mahmud Tarzi, a great literary scholar in Afghanistan, during the reign of King Amir Habibullah Khan (Bogdanov, 1929, p. 127). The newspaper included a variety of features appealing to readers, and its influence penetrated across Afghanistan's borders. Its editorial policy included criticism of colonialism and, to a lesser extent, the government, which caused concern among the ruling elites in neighboring countries (Farhang, 1988, p. 327). The *Saraj-ul-Akhbar* was an illustrated fortnightly newspaper of 16 pages, published in Kabul, 14 by 11 inches in size, each page divided into two columns. Photozincographic art was introduced during the publication of the *Saraj-ul-Akhbar,* introducing photographs and greater visual appeal.

The *Saraj-ul-Akhbar* ceased publication after the king died but reappeared shortly under the name *Aman-e-Afghan* (named after its founder) when King Amanullah ascended to the throne. *Aman-e-Afghan* was similar in style to its predecessor and tried to enlighten the people. However, according to Bogdanov (1929), the contents of the *Aman-e-Afghan* were more varied than those of *Saraj-ul-Akhbar.* It was supported by a group of literary persons such as Abdul Hadi Dawi and Mir Sayed Qasem, who were on the editorial staff (Farhang, 1988).

The press in Afghanistan has historically been tightly controlled by the government. The Ministry of Culture and Information controls the Bakhtar News Agency, which screens and then distributes news to all media in the country. Historically, persons appointed to positions of authority in the Bakhtar News Agency and other key positions in the mass media have been selected based on their loyalty to the government in power.

Kabul dominates the press scene. Only major provinces have newspapers, which partly depend on the Kabul dailies as their source of news. According to United Nations reports in 1988, Afghanistan has 14 daily newspapers with a total circulation of 151,000 (*UNESCO Statistical Yearbook 1991,* 1990, pp. 7–101).

The Dari language press, with its appeal to the educated class of all ethnic groups and urban readership throughout Afghanistan, has retained dominance among the press.

The main daily national newspaper of Afghanistan is *Anis* (*The Companion*), an evening publication founded as a weekly on May 5, 1927, that became a daily in 1929. It is published by the Ministry of Culture and Information. The original publisher and editor of *Anis* was Muhay-ud-Din Anis, a literary Afghan scholar (Reshtia, 1948, p. 73). This newspaper, more than any other, has contributed to the awakening of the masses. Persian (Dari) is the dominant language of the newspaper, but it also contains Pashtu articles. *Anis* has a circulation estimated between 5,000 and 15,000 (Wilber, 1989). The October 10, 1992, edition of *Anis* included seven columns, with the front page devoted to national and international news; page 2 devoted to local news and opinion articles; page 3 devoted to Islamic teachings; and the back page devoted to a variety of articles about such topics as economic cooperation, world affairs, and education.

Islah (*Reform*) was founded in 1928 by King Nadir and was the descendant of a line of official newspapers. Founded as a weekly, it became a daily in 1932. It appeared in both Pashtu and Dari languages. During its early years, it was an important source of information for reformers and progressive elements of society. It first appeared in Ali-Khail, a village in Zazi in the southern Province of Paktiya (Ahung, 1965, p. 24). *Islah* continued to publish in Kabul as a national daily newspaper until a military coup on July 19, 1973. It was then renamed *Jamhuryat* (*Republic*), reflecting the change of the government from a kingdom to a republic.

Hewad (*Motherland*) is a morning Kabul newspaper founded in 1959 mainly to support the political campaign of Pashtunistan, a disputed territory between Afghanistan and Pakistan. It is published by the Ministry of Culture and Information and has a circulation of 4,600 (*World Media Handbook,* 1992, p. 2). Pashtu was for many years the only language of the newspaper; however, during the 1980s the Persian language was introduced. The August 2, 1992, edition of the newspaper included seven columns, with the front page devoted to government and international news; page 2 devoted to editorials, government news, and announcements; page 3 devoted to Islamic teachings; and the back page devoted to international news and advertising.

Kabul Times (*Kabul New Times* during Communist control) is a morning newspaper and the only English-language daily in the country. It was founded by Sabahuddin Kushkaki in 1962 for diplomatic personnel and other foreigners and has a circulation of 5,000. The July 25, 1992, edition of *Kabul Times* has seven columns, with page 1 devoted to government news and photographs of government meetings and leaders; page 2 devoted to government news and photographs; page 3 devoted to continuation of a front-page article advocating unity among Afghan factions; and the back page devoted to government news, international diplomatic news, and ads seeking bids for government purchases—including a request by the Ministry of Culture and Information for printing machines.

Enqelab-e-Saur (*April Revolution*), founded in 1979, was the official government newspaper during the years when Communists controlled the government (1978–1992). Its name was changed, under different regimes, to *Haqiqat-e-Enqelabe-e-Saur* (*Truth of the April Revolution*) in 1980; and *Payam* (*Message*) in 1988. This paper has presumably ceased publication since the fall of the Communist government to the Mujahedeen on April 28, 1992.

Independent Newspapers. For a brief time, 1949 to 1952, the press enjoyed greater freedom, the result of the election of a group of moderates to the Parliament and the approval of the 1950 press law, which led to the establishment of several privately owned newspapers. These privately owned newspapers began to question all phases of government—including mismanagement of ministry budgets and unequal treatment of various ethnic groups. These newspapers demanded the abolition of existing private monopolies and the right of people to participate in government (Akhramovich, 1966, p. 54). The four most important of these Kabul newspapers were *Watan* (*Homeland*), founded by Mir G. M. Ghobar, a great historian; *Nida-e-Khalq* (*The Voice of the People*), founded by Dr. A. R. Mahmoodi; *Angar* (*Firebrand*), founded by Faiz M. Angar; and *Ulus* (*Community*), founded by Gul Pacha Ulfat, a great Pashtu poet, published in 1951–1952 (Wilber, 1962, p. 148). The educated classes avidly read these newspapers, but the country's low literacy rate restricted their impact outside educated circles.

Despite the small impact of the independent newspapers, they were banned by the government for 14 years and returned under the protection of the 1965 Press Law. Following the adoption of the 1965 Press Law, which reduced government control, the press also enjoyed greater freedom. More than two dozen privately owned newspapers appeared from 1966 to 1973 (Nyrop & Seekins, 1986, p. 66). Most of these newspapers were antiestablishment, poorly financed, and short-lived. *Khalq* (*The Masses*)—the first major leftist weekly newspaper, founded in 1965 by Noor M. Taraki—was banned after only one month of publishing. Other banned publications were *Shula-e-Javid* (*The Eternal Flame*), *Komak* (*Help*), *Afghan Mellat* (*The Afghan Nation*), *Payam-e-Emroz* (*Message of the Day*), *Mosawat* (*Equality*), *Mellat* (*The Nation*), and *Parcham* (*Banner*).

Of the independent newspapers that survived, the best was *Karvan* (*Caravan*). Under publisher Sabahuddin Kushkaki and editor Abdul Haq Walah, both well-known Afghan journalists, the newspaper compared favorably in style, features, and professionalism with major Western newspapers. *Terjoman* (*The Interpreter*), founded by Dr. A. R. Naveen, was known for its political satire, and *Rozgar* (*Time*), founded by Yasuf Farand, focused on economic issues.

Provincial Newspapers. As a result of administrative restructuring in 1964, Afghanistan was divided into 29 provinces, some with provincial newspapers. These newspapers are generally four-page tabloids (12 by 17 inches), usually with four columns. Bakhtar News Agency is the primary source of news for the provincial newspapers, with a secondary source being broadcasts by Radio Afghanistan. Most of them have small circulations.

Bidar (*The Wakeful*) was founded in 1920 in Mazar-e-Sharif Province. Both Dari and Pashtu appear in the newspaper. According to Bogdanov (1929), the city of Mazar-e-Sharif once had two newspapers, *The Ittehad-e-Islam* (*The Union of Islam*) and the *Bidar*. The *Ittehad-e-Islam* was a weekly lithographed newspaper of four pages of two columns, each 13½ by 8¼ inches in size. This newspaper no longer exists. The *Bidar* at its early stage was a weekly lithographed newspaper of the same shape and size as the *Ittehad-e-Islam.* In April 1927, the editor of *Bidar* was Gulam Hasan Ghaznavi (Bogdanov, 1929).

Tulu-e-Afghan (*The Afghan Sunrise*) was a weekly founded in 1921 in Qandahar. In 1926, it became biweekly, publishing on Wednesdays and Saturdays. Its first editor was Abdul Aziz. Pashtu is the predominant language, with a little Dari. Circulation is around 1,500 (*Europa World Year Book 1992,* 1991).

Ittifaq-e-Islam (*Concord of Islam*) was founded as a weekly newspaper in 1920 in Herat. Its first editor was Salahuddeen Saljuqi, a great Afghan scholar. Circulation is around 5,000, and the language is mostly Dari (Persian) with some Pashtu.

Wolangah (*Beam of Light*) was founded in 1943 as a morning daily in Gardayz, Paktia Province. The language of the newspaper is predominantly Pashtu.

Sanayee (*Brightness*—named after a great Dari poet of the province) was founded in 1952 as a weekly in Ghazni. Circulation is around 1,000.

Parwan (named after its province) was founded in 1953 in Charikar in Parwan Province.

Magazines

There were 71 periodicals and magazines published in 1988 in Kabul, the center for periodical publishing in Afghanistan, which serve a variety of special interest groups (*UNESCO Statistical Yearbook 1991,* 1991). Most of the Afghan periodicals are supposed to appear weekly, monthly, or quarterly. Instead, often two or three numbers of them are joined under one cover and appear at irregular intervals, which consequently disappoints their special readers. In 1979, when the Communists took control, several publications were introduced in the languages of minority groups, something previous governments had never done. These minority-language publications include *Yulduz* (Uzebeki language), *Gorash* (Turkmani language) and *Sob* (Baluchi language). A sampling of some of the leading periodicals includes the following:

Aryana, founded in 1943, is published by the Historical Society of Afghanistan. Published quarterly predominantly in Dari, it focuses on cultural and historical issues of Afghan society.

Pashtun Zhagh (*Pashtun Voice*), which was recently renamed *Awaz* (*Voice*), was founded in 1940. It is published in both Pashtu and Dari by Radio Afghanistan and features information about radio, television, and artists.

Erfan (*Education*), founded in 1923, is published by the Ministry of Education every two months.

Kabul, originally founded in 1931 by Anjoman-e-Adabi Kabul (The Literary Society of Kabul), was the first publication sent abroad to introduce Afghanistan to foreigners. It attracted the attention of international scholars, leading some to visit Afghanistan. The Literary Society, through this publication, provided leadership for the advancement of journalism and literary work in the country. Today it is published monthly by the Afghanistan Academy of Sciences and Research

Centre. It features articles about literature, language, and culture. The original language was Dari, with Pashtu recently introduced.

Payam-e-Haq (*True Message*) was founded in 1953 by the Afghan Press Department to advocate that Islam and progress are compatible.

Zhwandoon (*Life*), founded in 1944 by the Ministry of Information and Culture, is published weekly. Featuring a variety of general interest articles, its circulation is 1,400.

Urdu (*Army*), founded in 1922 by the Ministry of Defense's printing house, focuses on military subjects but also includes general interest articles.

Adab is a literary journal published by the School of Letters of Kabul University and printed quarterly.

Mermun (*Lady*) is a magazine published by the Women's Institute in Kabul. It has long advocated the participation of women in Afghan society, encouraging their struggle for emancipation, and has led to the improvement in the status of women in Afghan society. Its circulation is 3,000.

Kar (*Work*) was founded by the Central Council of the National Union of Afghanistan, under the Communist government.

Muhasel-e-Emroz (*Today's Student*), founded in 1986, is a monthly magazine for youth. It was published by the Communist government to attract youth to its ideologies.

Haqiqat-e-Sarbaz (*The Reality of Army*), founded in 1980 by the Ministry of Defense, was distributed primarily among the Afghan Communist government army and youth.

Printing Facilities. The history of Afghan printing began with the introduction of lithographic printing (stone printing) in Kabul in 1870 when King Shir Ali Khan was promoting his social reforms (Haqshenas, 1989, p. 18). Movable type was not used in Afghanistan until 1913. In 1926, modern printing machines and new types were brought from Germany. The new printing machines became operational in 1927 (Ahung, 1965, p. 7).

Afghanistan has three main printing houses in Kabul, which are administered by government ministries. Although each of them has a specialized purpose, all of them do more generalized printing as well, depending on the needs of the government. In each of these printing houses, one can find a combination of modern and old machines. In all these printing houses, most type is set by hand. The Government Printing House is equipped with a few linotypes. Most of these printing houses are capable of four-color work. The Education Printing House is equipped with offset printing machines.

The Government Printing House, known as Matba-aye-Dawlati, established in 1936, prints most newspapers, magazines, books, and governmental forms. Administratively, it falls under the Ministry of Culture and Information.

The Education Printing House, known as Matba-aye-MaAref, owned by the Ministry of Education, prints the bulk of school textbooks and other educational publications. The Education Printing House is affiliated with the Franklin Printing Institution.

The Defense Printing House, known as Matba-aye-Defa, owned by the Ministry of Defense, meets the printing needs of the Afghan Army and related military forces.

ELECTRONIC MEDIA

Radio

Radio Afghanistan, founded in 1927 as Radio Kabul, is the country's most important mass medium of communication and education due primarily to the low literacy rate. Like print media, radio is financed and controlled by the government. Because of its greater influence with the people, the government monitors radio more closely than print media.

In the early years, the 20-kilowatt radio station only broadcast two hours each day at the frequencies of 454.5 and 660 kilocycles. To produce a better transmission within and outside the country, two shortwave transmitters of 10 and 50 kilowatts were installed in 1958–1959 at Yakatut (northern part of Kabul). Antennas were directed toward Southeast Asian countries and Europe. In 1964, when a more powerful shortwave transmitter and new Radio Afghanistan studios were constructed, broadcasting improved significantly (Anzur, 1991, p. 211). Today it broadcasts 17 hours each day from 6:00 A.M. to 11:00 P.M.

There are 34 radio transmitters and 104 radio receivers per 1,000 people in the country (*World Media Handbook,* 1992). The number of radio receivers has increased significantly since the late 1960s when it was reported that there were only 16 radio receivers per 1,000 people (Wilber, 1989, p. 251).

Traditionally, domestic radio broadcasts were in the two official languages of Afghanistan (Dari and Pashtu). The exception to this was the broadcast of the Baluchi language from 1950 to the late 1970s as part of a one-hour political program of Pashtunistan, a disputed territory between Pakistan and Afghanistan.

Radio Afghanistan's medium-wave band of 145 kilowatts and the shortwave band of 160 kilowatts make it possible to transmit to all parts of the country as well as to Europe and the Middle East. Radio Afghanistan, with its three broadcast channels, leads all mass media in reaching the greatest number of people. In 1986, there were an estimated 1.67 million radio receivers in Afghanistan (*World Media Handbook,* 1992). It should be noted, however, that most families are without radios and are isolated from the news about provincial, national, and international affairs. In addition to Radio Afghanistan's 34 radio transmitters, the government has also installed, in the main cities and provinces, loud speakers with radio receivers for broadcasts in public areas.

Although music is the main broadcast item of Radio Afghanistan, it also broadcasts news, government announcements, special events, and educational programs.

In 1965, 1967, and 1971, for the first time Radio Afghanistan broadcast entire parliamentary debates concerning the approval of prime ministers and their cabinets. Hearing these debates awakened a great political consciousness among previously silent masses—evidence of the power of radio (Dupree, 1971, p. 12).

In 1985, new radio stations were commissioned in the provinces of Qandahar, Herat, Jalalabad, Ghazni, and Asadabad, in addition to existing main stations in the provinces of Kabul and Nangarhar. Additional radio stations were to be established in the provinces of Paktia, Farah, and Badakhshan (*Europa World Year Book 1991,* 1990, p. 302).

Television

Television does not have a long history in Afghanistan. Television broadcasting in color began in 1978 with a transmission range of 50 kilometers (about 31 miles). Originally it was broadcast only two hours each day, later doubling to four hours and, by 1988, to ten hours (*Europa World Year Book 1991,* 1990).

Its growth primarily took place under the Communist government. According to the government, television substations have been established in Mazar, Herat, Qandahar, Konar, and Jalalabad provinces and broadcast in either Pashtu or Dari languages.

Programs include news, government activities, and entertainment. In the absence of locally produced movies, the television station primarily broadcasts Indian and Russian films. Recently, satellite stations have been used to expand television broadcasting.

The television stations were targets during the Afghan Mujahedden factional fighting and suffered considerable damage, including a series of rocket attacks in August 1992.

MOTION PICTURES

Afghans are primarily consumers of motion pictures rather than producers of them. In 1985, only three motion pictures were produced (*UNESCO Statistical Yearbook 1991,* 1990, pp. 4–8). Movie theaters are located in the principal cities, with at least one dozen theaters located in Kabul. Before the Russian invasion, most movies were from India and Western countries and were popular with Afghans. During the 1980s, Russian movies dominated the film scene.

The Ministry of Culture and Information has established a Department of Afghan Film, and later the Aryana Film Department, to produce news reels about government activities that are shown in movie theaters and on television.

MEDIA REGULATION

Regulation of the media has vacillated from strong government control to comparative freedom. Of the three press laws of 1922, 1950, and 1965, the 1965 Press Law was the first to provide guidelines under which a free and responsible press could develop. The law was drafted to safeguard the fundamentals of Islam, constitutional monarchy, and other values enshrined in the constitution.

During the late 1970s and 1980s, the media came under much stronger government regulation as war, invasion, and civil strife overcame the society. Several constitutions came and went (1977, 1985, 1987) during these years, providing little protection for free expression in the media (*Europa World Year Book 1991,* 1990, p. 289).

According to the constitution as it stood in May 1990, the following are among the rights guaranteed to the people: the right (1) to participate in the political sphere, (2) to freedom of speech and thought, (3) to security of residence, and (4) to privacy of communication and correspondence. The reality of the 1980s was that such guarantees were frequently ignored. Until stability returns to Afghan society, these lofty ideals, however, cannot be guaranteed. Even when stability is achieved, the policy of the new leaders of the Islamic State of Afghanistan will hold the fate of freedom of the media in their hands.

Copyright law is not observed in Afghanistan. Writings are not protected; therefore, copies are freely made of writings found in journals and newspapers.

EXTERNAL MEDIA SERVICES

Afghanistan, founded in 1948, is published by the Historical Society of Afghanistan. The magazine is in English and French, and it is distributed to embassies and foreign countries.

Radio Afghanistan also has external foreign-language broadcast services in Urdu, German, English, Arabic, French, and most recently, Russian.

NEWS AGENCIES

The Bakhtar News Agency, the only news agency in the country, was established in 1939 under the auspices of the Government Press Department (Snider, 1968). It directly controls mass media by screening all foreign and domestic news before distributing it to the media. Bakhtar exchanges international news with several news agencies such as UPI (United Press International—United States), Tass (Telegrafnoe Agentsvo Sovetskovo Soyuza—Russia), and CTK (Czechoslovak News Agency—Czechoslovakia). The Bakhtar News Agency in 1992 added an English news bulletin to keep diplomatic personnel informed of Afghan news (*Hewad,* 1992, p. 2). Bakhtar monitors news broadcasts from the British Broadcasting Corporation (BBC), Voice of America, Tass, Radio New Dehli, and others. Bakhtar offers news, photos, and features to Afghan media.

THE ROLE OF MEDIA IN NATIONAL DEVELOPMENT

The media has made some contribution to the education of the Afghan people; however, its potential has not been utilized effectively. Considering the vast need in society for educational programming, particularly considering the low literacy rate, radio and television are the logical means of extending education widely. Too often television and radio have emphasized entertainment and propaganda rather than education. The media has been more successful in mobilizing Afghans behind national events, particularly since the government owns the mass media.

CONCLUSION

Despite formidable obstacles such as censorship, cultural, linguistic, ethnic, technical, and financial problems confronting the mass media in Afghanistan, it has continued to expand its influence throughout society. The media's influence is strongest in Kabul, the center for Afghan media, but it has also increased in other parts of the country.

The future of the mass media in Afghanistan depends foremost on the establishment of peace in this war-torn country and improved economic and technical development, educational and social transformation, and a mutual respect between the people and those controlling the media.

Although the long war has had many negative effects on the media, it has also raised the political maturity of the people and increased expectations of the media. Never before in history have so many Afghans been exposed to media coverage of Afghan events, including foreign broadcasts such as the BBC and Voice of America. The turmoil of war has created a great hunger for unbiased news, which unfortunately Afghans have to look beyond their borders to find. This exposure will have long-term effects on the expectations of the media in Afghanistan for many years.

REFERENCES

Ahung, M. K. (1965). *The press system of Afghanistan.* Ann Arbor: Michigan University Press.

Akhramovich, R. T. (1966). *Outline history of Afghanistan after the Second World War* [English translation from Russian]. Moscow, USSR: Nauka Publishing House, p. 54.

Anzur, Z. (1991). History of radio in Afghanistan. *Farday-e-Afghanistan-e-Islami* [The future of Islamic Afghanistan]. Peshawor, Pakistan: Cultural Council of Afghanistan Resistance.

Bogdanov, L. (1929, January). Islamic culture. *Hyderabad Quarterly Review,* p. 127.

Chohen, M. D. (1963). Baffling questions abroad. *Childhood Education, 40,* 29.

Dupree, L. (1971). *A note on Afghanistan.* American University Field Staff Report: South Asia Series, *15,* 12.

The Europa world year book 1991. (1990). London, England: Europa Publications Limited.

Farhang, Mir M. S. (1988). *Afghanistan dar panj qern-e-akhir* [Afghanistan in the last five centuries]. Herndon, VA: American Speedy.

Hammond, T. T. (1984). *Red flag over Afghanistan.* Boulder, CO: Westview Press.

Haqshenas, S. N. (1989). *The USSR conspiracy and crimes in Afghanistan from Amir Dost Mohammad to Babrak* (2nd ed.). Peshawor, Pakistan.

Hewad. (1992, October 11) [Mizan 19, 1371]. Kabul, Afghanistan.

The Kabul Times annual. (1970). Kabul, Afghanistan, p. 133.

Kaplan, R. D. (1988, May). Why the Afghans Fight. *Reader's Digest,* p. 128.

Newell, R. S. (1972). *The politics of Afghanistan.* Ithaca, NY: Cornell University Press.

Nyrop, R. F., & Seekins, O. M. (1986). *Afghanistan—a country study.* Washington, DC: American University, p. 66.

Reshtia, S. Q. (1948). Journalism in Afghanistan. *Kabul* (Historical Society of Afghanistan), *3*(2), 73.

Snider, P. B. (1968). The route of international news, to press of Afghanistan through Bakhtar. *Gazette, 14*(1), 41.

UNESCO statistical yearbook 1991. (1990). Paris, France: UNESCO.

World media handbook. (1992). New York: United Nations.

Wilber, D. N. (1989). Afghanistan in *Encyclopedia Americana.* Danbury, CT: Grolier Inc.

———. (1962). *Afghanistan.* New Haven, CT: Human Relation Area File Press.

The world almanac and book of facts 1993. (1992). New York: World Almanac.

2

ALGERIA

Laid Zaghlami

INTRODUCTION

Algeria is located in North Africa and possesses 800 miles of land bordering the Mediterranean Sea facing southern Europe and the Sahara Desert. Algeria among the Maghrib states stretches 2,384,542 square kilometers and has open borders extending to seven countries: in the east with Tunisia and Libya; in the south with Niger, Mali, and Mauritania; and in the west with Western Sahara (former Spanish colony) and Morocco. According to a 1992 census, Algeria has a population of 25,942,000 inhabitants: 51 percent female and 49 percent male. The age distribution ranges from 0 to 14 years old (43.9 percent) to 15 to 59 years old (50.3 percent) and over 60 years old (5.8 percent). The population distribution represents 27 inhabitants per square mile. About 80 percent of the population resides in the northern region of the country.

Approximately 75 percent of the Algerian people are Arabs and 25 percent are Berbers. Approximately 35.8 percent of the Algerian population can read and write both Arabic and French. 33.6 percent of the population is illiterate, and 58 percent of those who are illiterate are female.

Foreign languages such as English, Italian, German, Spanish, and Russian are taught in colleges and universities. However, the local languages of Berbers—including Kabyle, Mozabite, Chawi, and Targui—are spoken in some regions of Algeria.

Islam is the state religion. Ninety-nine percent of the Algerians are Sunni, and less than 1 percent are Shiite Muslims and Christians.

The Algerian economy is mainly based on public enterprises established as Economic Public Enterprise (EPE). However, eased by the market economy orientation and new legislation aimed at encouraging foreign investments, private enterprises flourish throughout the country. Nonetheless, social and political problems (unemployment, housing crisis, inflation, lack of raw materials, and foreign debt of $26 billion) constitute handicaps for foreign investments and the reactivation of the economy.

Algeria has heavy and light industries in Annaba, Setif, and Skikda in eastern Algeria, and in Arzew, Oran, Sidi Bel Abbes, and Mostaganem in western Algeria. Factories are located in central Algeria in Tizi Ouzou and Boumerdes; whereas in the southern part oil and gas installations are implanted in Hassi Messaoud, Hassi R'mel, and Amenas.

The monetary unit of Algeria is the dinar. Gross national product (GNP), according to recent data, is $53.1 billion, and the GNP per capita equals $2,170 (*World Almanac and Book of Facts 1993*, 1992).

Algeria, being a developing country, is a pioneer in spending heavily on education. For instance, since 1987, about 25 percent of the budget ($21.3 billion) has been devoted to education. In the 1991–1992 academic school year, there were 7.2 million pupils (28 percent of the population) enrolled in schools: 6,275,387 were in elementary and secondary schools, 745,745 in high schools, and 275,000 in colleges/universities. Both elementary and secondary education in Algeria are free and compulsory up to age 17.

In February 1989, the Algerian voters approved a new constitution that paved the way for a multiparty system that guaranteed fundamental rights and individual freedoms. In December 1991, general elections were held. The results of the first round gave the Islamic Salvation Front (dissolved in February 1992) an overall majority of 188 seats. The next round of the electoral process was halted for political, national security, and vote-rigging reasons. Afterward, a state of emergency was declared. A new structure, called the High Council of State, was created, and Mohamed Boudiaf was appointed as the new president in January 1992. In June 1992, he was assassinated in Annaba, east of Algeria, and Ali Kafi became the new president.

COMMUNICATION PHILOSOPHY

The communication policies of Algeria are regulated through a number of decrees and information bills. From 1962 until 1982, the Algerian governments adopted a series of measures to control the mass media. In February 1982, a bill of information was promulgated that was considered to be a turning point in the Algerian information and communication philosophy regarding the mass media. The bill was based on the principles of national sovereignty and citizens' rights to information—although these rights have to meet the ideological orientation and moral values of the nation (Marcuse, 1964). Thus, the media exclusively depended on the political authority of the state and were considered the means for cultural and institutional information (McQuail, 1987).

Another bill, the Information Bill of 1990, brought more freedom of expression and opinion than previously allowed in Algeria. Generally, researchers consider the 1990 bill as a transitory code, whereas professionals see it as a penal code (Brahimi, 1990). Nevertheless, following the passage of the Information Bill of 1990, the mass media have flourished, and many new newspapers and magazines have emerged.

PRINT MEDIA

Newspapers

Before 1990, there were only 31 newspapers; two years later, more than 160 newspapers and magazines were being published in Algeria. For instance, in December 1991, 18 dailies, 69 weeklies, 27 bimonthlies, 50 monthlies, and some irregularly published newspapers were disseminating news and information to the Algerian people. In terms of language, 84 titles are published in Arabic and 85 titles in French. In terms of ownership, 37 newspapers belong to the public sector (state), 28 titles belong to different associations, 96 have private ownership, and 8 newspapers belong to political parties. Thus, press ownership is divided into public, private, and political parties.

Newspapers are distributed throughout the country by three public enterprises known collectively as National Press Distribution Enterprise (ENAMEP) and several private companies including Trans Com Express, Group Media Diffusion, and Ets Bensahnoun. However, it has been difficult to distribute periodicals to 48 districts *(wilaya)* and 1,541 boroughs *(commune)* smoothly and on a regular basis in a country whose transportation system and roads are not yet fully developed. Consequently, people living in the remote parts of the country, particularly in the south, do not have access to periodicals.

The Algerian newspapers can be divided into local, regional, and national categories. There are approximately 10 local newspapers with a small circulation number and an irregular distribution pattern. There are 6 regional newspapers in the east, 4 regional newspapers in the west, and 2 regional newspapers in the south. There are 18 national newspapers published daily—8 in Arabic and 10 in French. Table 2.1 shows the 10 top national newspapers, including their circulation and ownership patterns.

The circulation of the national dailies, in 1992, is estimated at 815,708 copies, of which 330,893 (41 percent) copies belong to public press and 484,815 (59 percent) copies belong to private sector and political parties. Daily newspapers published in Arabic have a circulation of 261,591 copies, while daily newspapers published in French have a circulation of 554,117 copies.

No observations are made for readership because the only parameter to determine readership is the approximate number of unsold newspapers. According

Table 2.1
The Top Ten Algerian National Dailies

Title	Circulation	Ownership
A* *Ach Chaab*	52,000	Public
A *As Salem*	33,300	Public
A *Al Khabar*	53,708	Private
A *El Massa*	84,000	Public
A *Djazair Youm*	35,384	Private
F* *El Moudjahid*	158,267	Public
F *Horizons*	115,788	Public
F *El Watan*	120,000	Private
F *Le Soir d'Algerie*	145,000	Private
F *Le Matin*	100,500	Private

A* Arabic
F* French

Source: Algerie Actualites, 1992.

to ENAMEP estimates, the unsold newspapers fall within the 24 percent range, which represents a loss of $18 million per year (*Report,* 1992).

The general contents of the Arabic and French newspapers consist of general information, current affairs, national and international news, satire, culture, sports, feature stories (investigative reporting), opinion, and special interest items.

Magazines

A total of 22 magazines are periodically published in Algeria; however, only 8 of them are published on a regular basis. They cover a wide range of interests such as the following: *El Ardh (agriculture), International Sport, MediaSud (media and culture), l'Unite (youth), la Radio Algerienne (radio and television), Revolution Africaine (politics and current affairs), Praticien (medicine)* and

Ounoutha (women). Other magazines specialize in such areas as media, cinema, women's interests, education, science, and publishing the television schedule. Prior to the Information Bill of 1990, some private groups, including professional organizations and cultural associations, began publishing their own magazines.

Circulation and readership data for magazines are not available. Furthermore, owing to high production costs, limited resources, the high price of paper, high distribution costs, and the high cost of color reproduction, many of the Algerian magazines are not readily available, nor are they attractive to the general public.

ELECTRONIC MEDIA

Prior to 1986, the broadcast media in Algeria was operated by Algerian Radio and Television (RTA), which was inherited from the colonialization period. In 1986, the RTA was restructured to form four public enterprises: the National Radio Broadcasting Enterprise (ENRS), the National Television Enterprise (ENTV), the National Audio-Visual Production Enterprise (ENPA), and the National Telediffusion Enterprise (ENTD). They all function under an umbrella called the Industrial and Commercial Public Institution (EPIC).

Although the four enterprises enjoy a public status, their autonomy in terms of financial and administrative matters is marginal. In business terms, they hold a double accountancy of public and private status. Thus, on one hand, they have to provide public services; and on the other hand, they can invest in private initiatives, such as advertising, marketing, concerts, and other activities.

Radio

Radio in Algeria is owned and operated by public institutions through the National Radio Broadcasting Enterprise, which is headquartered in Algiers. Radio stations in Algeria can be divided into three categories: national, regional, and local.

There are three national radio stations: Channel One, Channel Two, and Channel Three. Channel One broadcasts 24 hours per day, in Arabic, over AM (amplitude modulation), including long wave, medium wave, and shortwave. Channel Two broadcasts, in Tamazight, from 6:00 A.M. until 1:00 A.M. Channel Three broadcasts, in French, from 6:00 A.M. until 1:00 A.M.

There are also four regional stations: Constantine Radio in the east, Oran Radio in the west, Ouargla Radio in the southeast, and Bechar Radio in the southwest. These stations transmit their programs nationally, six hours a week, through Channel One. In addition, Ouahat Radio (Oasis Radio in Ouargla) and Saoura Radio (the name is related to the area of Bechar) broadcast programs within their own regions six to eight hours a day.

Local stations include Mitidja Radio, which broadcasts four hours daily on medium wave; Quran Radio broadcasts religious programs and verses from the Quran four hours daily; and Bahdja Radio, recently inaugurated, transmits music and cultural programs on FM (frequency modulation). In addition to Algiers, there are local radios in Tlemcen (west), Tamanrest (in the extreme south), Laghouat (north of the Sahara), and Setif (east). All these local stations broadcast programs on FM.

All radio stations are noncommercial, though legislation may allow private and commercial radios in the future. The existing stations broadcast a wide range of programs, including news and information, music, sports, religion, and sciences.

Channel One broadcasts programs around the clock, and its signal covers 98 percent of the Algerian territory on both long and medium waves; hence, it is enjoyed by a huge audience. Channel Two and Channel Three broadcast various cultural programs, 19 hours a day, in Tamazight and French.

In addition, the Continuing Training University (Open University) operates an educational radio station. The university rents studio facilities from the National Radio Broadcasting Enterprise and broadcasts educational programs (academic affairs, student affairs, music, current affairs) four hours a day during the academic year.

The National Radio Broadcasting Enterprise regulates and coordinates broadcasting at international, national, regional, and local levels. Although the National Radio Broadcasting Enterprise tries hard to transmit its programs to the public on a regular basis, it often faces various technical difficulties due to the lack of technical support, old transmitters, and natural obstacles. For instance, in the northern portion of Algeria, which is hilly and mountainous, people often cannot pick up the radio signals.

The National Telediffusion Enterprise (another public enterprise) provides technical expertise for existing stations, including maintaining broadcast facilities and building sites. The Post and Telecommunication Ministry, on the other hand, provides telephone lines for long-distance radio coverage and networking.

To ensure total national coverage, the National Telediffusion Enterprise plans to install two powerful 2,000-kilowatt transmitters in eastern (Ain Beida) and western (Sidi Bel Abbes) Algeria.

Television

Much of the foregoing information about radio applies to television broadcasting in Algeria. The first television station in Algeria went on the air in 1957 during the French colonization. Currently, Algeria has a single national television channel called ENTV, including four regional stations: Constantine TV, Oran TV, Ouargla TV, and Bechar TV. Although the Information Bill of 1990 gives opportunities to private companies and to individuals to establish television channels, there are no privately owned stations.

The official data indicate that television signals reach 96 percent of the Algerian population (National Audio-Visual Council Report, 1990). As in the case of radio, some of the northern inhabitants cannot, because of the mountainous terrain, pick up television signals. In other regions, along the Mediterranean Sea, the neighboring countries' (Spain, Italy, and Morocco) broadcast signals interfere with the Algerian television signals. In the south, television programs are broadcast through satellite facilities but face reception difficulties.

Domestic television production is weak and remains a source of criticism from Algerian viewers. According to *Algerian Weekly,* 7 million viewers have access to foreign programs through satellite dishes. This phenomenon is quite evident in towns and cities where satellite dishes have mushroomed on the rooftops of houses and buildings. The foreign broadcasts transmitted via satellite include French (TF1, France2, M6, Canal+), European (Eurosports), Arabic (Middle East Broadcasting Corporation [MBC], MBC London), and Cable News Network (CNN). Increasingly, the Algerian national television channel finds it difficult to match satellite programs in terms of production quality and entertainment. Consequently, an increasing number of Algerians tune in to foreign programs rather than watch the domestic broadcasts (Djezairi, 1992).

Broadcast programs on the Algerian national television channel include current affairs, sports, films, series, documentaries, and so on. The national television channel, on the average, broadcasts about 14 hours a day. Normally, broadcast hours vary from weekdays (10 hours daily) to weekends (13 hours daily). Television programming sources (see Table 2.2) include both domestic and foreign productions. Domestic sources represent 50.67 percent of the total broadcast hours consisting of news, debates, sports, music, and documentary productions (Statistics and Analysis Department, 1993).

Foreign television programming sources include 24.04 percent produced by the Arab countries (mainly Egypt, Jordan, Lebanon, Syria, and some Gulf States) and 25.29 percent produced by the European countries (primarily France, Italy, and England) and the North American countries (the United States and Canada). The foreign productions consist of soaps, films, and documentaries.

Algeria is an associated member of the European Broadcasting Union (EBU), the International Radio and Television Organization (IRTO), the Arab States Broadcasting Union (ASBU, in Tunis), and the African National Radio and Television Union (URTNA, Senegal).

Media research and broadcast rating services on public opinion and audience analysis have not yet been launched. Hence, the Algerian television, radio, and print media lack substantial information concerning public opinion and public attitudes. Nevertheless, a 1992 survey, using a sample of 1,503 respondents, was conducted by the National Center for Applied Economic Studies. The results show that 85.6 percent of Algerian households have a television set, viewers spend three to four hours daily watching television, and 31.73 percent of the

Table 2.2
Algerian TV Programs, Hours, and Sources, January 1992–December 1992

Programming	Hours/Min	Rate %	Programming Sources D*	AW*	F*
News	549 30	10.76	549 30	/	/
Debate	122 17	02.39	122 17	/	/
Sports	395 29	07.74	395 29	/	/
Soaps	716 56	14.03	18 57	434 55	263 04
Films	1048 22	20 52	102 32	195 17	750 33
Theater	31 24	00.61	15 57	15 57	/
Music	403 54	07.90	276 06	79 51	47 57
Documentary	867 14	16.98	442 48	223 24	201 02
Children	384 03	07.52	123 18	234 35	26 10
Religion	148 01	02.90	103 16	44 45	/
Games & Quiz	58 13	01.14	54 56	/	03 17
Education	108 55	02.13	108 55	/	/
Ad/Weather	220 33	04.32	220 33	/	/
Telethon	54 00	01.06	54 00	/	/
Total Hours	5108 51	100%	2588 34 (50.67%)	1228 14 (24.04%)	1292 03 (25.29%)

D* Domestic AW* Arab World F* Foreign

Source: Statistics and Analysis Department, 1993.

urban population have access to foreign television channels (National Office of Statistics, 1992).

NEW TECHNOLOGIES

New communication technologies such as satellite, computers, and fiber optics are being utilized in Algeria. Satellite is used for communications to the south of Algeria and other parts of the world. Computers, fax machines, and cellular telephone facilities are also available to the Algerian media.

Table 2.3
Number of Imported Films: Algeria

Year	1987	1988	1989	1990	1991	1992	Total
Number	262	224	76	54	09	04	629

Source: Production Department, 1992.

MOTION PICTURES

In 1897, during the French colonization, the movie industry came into existence in Algeria. Some of the films produced were *The Funny Muslim,* in 1897, and *Ali Parrot,* in 1907. These movies portrayed racial and discriminatory attitudes toward Algerians. In 1957, the Algerian National Liberation Front created the first school in film production. In 1958, movie producers began making films on the Algerian Revolution.

Algeria gained its independence from France in 1962. During the first few years of independence, the movies dealt with socialist, revolutionary, and nationalist issues. In the early 1970s, the process of conception, production, and distribution of films had to follow the government policies. Films produced during this period were mainly for domestic consumption and did not meet international standards (Aib, 1992).

By the mid-1970s, Algerian films won distinctions, decorations, and Oscars in international festivals. For instance, at the 1975 Cannes Festival, producer Lakhdar Hamina won awards for his film *Chronicle of Fiery Years.* Those years were the heydays for the Algerian movies.

However, the 1980s marked a shift in the political system. Upon becoming a multiparty system, a cinema crisis was induced by the partial disengagement of government financing from the movies. As a consequence, the public enterprise of movie production faced bankruptcy.

The absence of a clear government policy contributed to fewer films being domestically produced. In 1987, 262 films were imported from France; 80 percent of them were produced by U.S. companies based in Paris. Since then, the number of imported films has drastically decreased (see Table 2.3).

In terms of domestic film production, between 1981 and 1990, a total of 37 motion pictures were produced; 6 of these were coproduced with France, Tunisia, and Morocco (Production Department, 1992).

The Algerian Television channel also annually imports an average of 200 television and motion pictures from France and the Arab World, including Egypt, Lebanon, Jordan, and some Gulf States.

The number of movie theaters in the early years of independence was 458. In 1966, 250 movie theaters were nationalized; among them, 106 are still closed.

By 1992, this number had gradually decreased to 200 officially registered movie theaters. Only 17 movie theaters are run by local authorities, 8 are managed by the Algerian Center for Movies and Arts Industry (CAAIC), 105 are run privately, and the rest converted to other activities. Most of the movie theaters are located in the big cities of Algiers, Annaba, Constantine, and Oran.

Imported films are previewed by a television panel who determine whether or not a movie meets the country's moral codes before it is scheduled for broadcast or release to the theaters. However, it should be noted that political censorship, in its traditional form, does not exist. Some movies containing romantic scenes may be shown, but erotic films are forcefully censored.

MEDIA OWNERSHIP

The Information Bill of 1990 offered opportunities for private ownership of media, particularly newspapers. Hence, the number of newspapers rapidly increased from 31 titles before the 1990 act to 160 titles in December 1991. To encourage private ownership, the government issued an announcement inviting journalists working in the public sector to establish their own print and electronic media outlets. This invitation sparked private initiatives and ignited a new era of press freedom and media pluralism.

The print media are owned by both government and private enterprises, while the electronic media are still under governmental ownership. Independent or private radio and television stations are still waiting for authorization.

FINANCIAL SUPPORT PATTERNS

In 1990, the government set up a special fund to finance and promote the print media. In the first installment, the government contributed $10.4 million to public press, $7.9 million to the private press, and $300,000 to private audiovisual companies. In 1992, the fund provided $22.9 million to help the independent press (Ferchichi, 1993).

Owing to their EPIC status, the Algerie Presse Service (APS), the Agence Photographique d'Information et de Presse (API), and the National Radio, Television, and Telediffusion enterprises receive financial assistance from the public revenue office. Also, a fund for the development of movies, arts, and culture is set up to help public and private audiovisual enterprises.

The privately owned print media are allowed to carry advertisements, but the revenue from this source is not sufficient to meet production, distribution, and other related expenses. Therefore, the print media are supported financially by government, advertisers, and readers.

However, the public press is established as a sharing society (Societe par Actions). Shares are held by public participatory funds.

The High Council of Information set up criteria to help the press, based on the number of copies sold daily by a given newspaper, incomes from publicity, promotion of the national culture, language, and local information (High Council of Information, 1991). In December 1992, a commission of representatives from different ministries and print media was created to establish and review financial support patterns as well as to control the proper use of the finances.

MEDIA REGULATION

In February 1989, new media regulations were prompted by an evolving democratic process. The High Council of Information (promulgated in the 1990 Information Law) and the National Audio-Visual Council were established to deal with the media regulations. However, their specific roles are restricted by the Ministry of Communication and Culture (*Algerian Communication Review,* 1991).

Existing rules are neither clearly defined nor fully observed, though public and private media have to comply with principles of national sovereignty and national interests. Furthermore, public media have to meet the schedule of conditions that defines the public service requirements.

With regard to state emergency and restrictions of the High Council of Information activities, the media are regulated by both the Ministry of Interior and the Ministry of Communication and Culture. Newspapers may face interruption or suspension; journalists can be laid off for "threat to national interests and security" (Messaoudi, 1992).

EXTERNAL MEDIA SERVICES

External media services are almost nonexistent. Foreign newspapers and magazines are not available because of the economic crisis and financial difficulties in Algeria. However, the Ministry of Communications has decided to import technical and scientific magazines in the near future.

Radio Algeria is the only medium that has external services and broadcasts one hour daily in each of the following four languages: (1) Arabic programs for the Maghrib, southern Europe, and Middle East regions; (2) French programs broadcast to Europe and African French-speaking countries; (3) English programs to African English-speaking countries; and (4) Spanish programs to Spain and Latin American countries. Programs deal with Algerian news, culture, arts, Arab people, and Islam. These programs are aimed at promoting the image of the Algerian culture and society at the international level.

NEWS AGENCIES

There are two news agencies in Algeria: Algerie Presse Service (APS) and Agence Photographique d'Information et de Presse (API). Nationally, news is gathered by reporters throughout the country who are employed by the news agencies, then it is transmitted to the main offices in Algiers. In the process, different editors (gatekeepers) at the news agencies review, analyze, translate, dispatch, and print or broadcast news according to the established standards.

The Algerie Presse Service, established as a commercial public institution, is the official news agency. The agency has 48 offices and nine regional newsrooms in Algeria. Abroad, it has eight bureaus in France, Britain, Ethiopia, the Arab World, and the United States. The agency furnishes news in Arabic and in French.

Some media do gather their own news via their regional reporters. Obviously, no media could cover all national events alone; hence, the media do subscribe to the national news agencies for expanded coverage. They also subscribe to API for photographic images (facsimiles). In addition, the media also subscribe to several international agencies such as the Maghrib Arab Press (Morocco), Tunis-Afrique-Presse (Tunisia), Agence France Presse (France), and Reuters (United Kingdom).

THE ROLE OF MEDIA IN NATIONAL DEVELOPMENT

Educational media programs are absent in schools and colleges. Only the University of Algiers offers classes in information and communication sciences, and there is only one audiovisual center in Algiers.

The mass media have participated in the national development of the country through various educational and awareness campaigns. Of course, their role is dictated by social and economic conditions as well as by political demands.

The electronic media provide various programs aimed at reducing the high rate of illiteracy (33.6 percent) and deal with competition games between colleges, as well as furnish a series of courses for students taking exams. The public press also publishes pages of courses and exercises on different disciplines. The periodical *l'Ecole* specializes in education matters.

The economic and social development in Algeria has brought a similar level of development in the communication and information fields. According to the Minister of Communication and Culture (Staff, 1992), the media infrastructures and facilities have achieved an acceptable degree of development. However, mismanagement and political turmoil have, so far, led to a deadlocked situation. Lack of human expertise, ongoing technical problems, and misuse of facilities have hindered mass media's potential in playing a constructive role in the political, educational, economic, and social development of the country.

CONCLUSION

Despite the existing infrastructures and regulatory structures, the future of mass media in Algeria remains uncertain. Ultimately, as the political environment changes and the turbulent democratic process settles, the mass media must respond and adjust themselves accordingly.

For instance, the articles in the 1990 Information Act have not yet been fully implemented because the government has decided to revise it. Furthermore, the nature of the revision and the directions that the bill will take are not known. Responsibilities of the High Council of Information and the Audio-Visual Council have been restricted, if not frozen.

The television channel is often criticized in the press for partiality in news reporting and poor quality programs. Also, because of political instability, economic crisis, and shortage of frequencies, prospects for having more private radio and television channels appear remote.

In the print media, despite the short experience of the Algerian press, the private press has managed to secure a great deal of impartiality and credibility in its content. The public press, however, faces organizational and financial problems. The mass media have realized a degree of liberty and impartiality in spite of recent political events surrounding the democratization process.

REFERENCES

Aib, H. (1992, June). *Algerian cinema 1970–1990.* Algiers: Institute of Information and Communication Sciences (ISIC).

Algerian Communication Review. (1991, Spring–Autumn). Algiers: Institute of Information and Communication Sciences.

Algerie Actualities. (1992, May). Algiers: Institute of Information and Communication Sciences.

Audio-Visual Council Report. (1990). Algiers: High Council of Information.

Brahimi, B. (1990). *Le Pouvoir: La Presse et les intellectuels en Algeria.* Paris: Ed Harmattan.

Djezairi, R. (1992, July). 30 Ans de medias. *Horizons,* pp. 2–4.

Ferchichi, K. (1993, January). Presse: Le Cordon ombilical. *El Moudjahid,* pp. 12–14.

High Council of Information. (1991, December). *Annual report.* Algiers: High Council of Information.

Marcuse, H. (1964). *One dimensional man.* London: Routlege and Kegan Paul.

McQuail, D. (1987). *Mass communication theory.* London: Sage Publications.

Messaoudi, M. T. (1992, December). L'Information. *El Watan,* p. 24.

National Office of Statistics. (1992). Algeria.

Production Department. (1992, October). Algiers: Algerian Arts and Industry Movies Center.

Report. (1992, January). Algiers: National Communication Conference Algiers.

Staff. (1992, November). Interview with Minister of Communication and Culture. *Horizons,* pp. 10–12.

Statistics and Analysis Department. (1993). Algiers: National Television Enterprise.

World Almanac and Book of Facts 1993. (1992). New York: Scripps Howard.

3

BAHRAIN

Afaf Hamod and Elise K. Parsigian

INTRODUCTION

The State of Bahrain is an archipelago of 35 largely desert islands situated midway in the Arabian Gulf at nearly equal distances between the west coast of Qatar and the east coast of Saudi Arabia. Most of the population lives on the principal island of Bahrain, which occupies 586 of the total 692 square kilometers of the Bahrain land area. In relative terms, the principal island is smaller in size than New York City. The seat of the Bahrain government is at Manama, the capital.

The modern state of Bahrain came into existence in 1971 when full independence from over a century of governance under a British protectorate became official. Traditionally a sheikhdom, the state has been governed by the al-Khalifa family since 1783. Today, the amir of Bahrain is Sheikh Isa bin Sulman al-Khalifa, who succeeded his father to the throne in 1961 and took the title of amir in 1971. He is assisted by a cabinet of 16 ministers. In December 1992, an amiri decree instituted the Shura Council in order to broaden the democratic base of the government. To that end, the amir appointed a 30-member council to give opinions and advice on issues submitted to them by the cabinet regarding state policy on political, cultural, social, and administrative matters. An active member in the United Nations and the League of Arab States, Bahrain is also a founding member of the Gulf Cooperation Council (GCC), a joint body formed in 1981 by the governments of Bahrain, Saudi Arabia, the United Arab Emirates (UAE), Qatar, Kuwait, and Oman. The GCC considers and rules on affairs regarding the economy, politics, foreign policy, and defense as these concern the participating members.

Islam is the state religion of Bahrain, and 85 percent of the population is Muslim. Residents also include Christians, Hindus, and small minorities of Jews and Zoroastrians; each enjoys a climate of religious tolerance that enables open practice of faith.

At the last count in 1991, the records at the Central Statistics Organization for Bahrain show a total population figure of 508,037 persons, 323,305 of whom are Bahraini nationals. Other ethnic groups include those from Asia, other Arab countries, and Iran. In 1993, the annual growth rate of the national population stands at approximately 29.2 per thousand, and more than half (50.9 percent) of the national population is under 20 years of age. With 731 inhabitants to the square kilometer, Bahrain has the highest population density among the Arab Gulf states, and owing to the process of rapid urbanization in Bahrain, population density in its urban centers is especially high, particularly in Manama. In 1990, the estimated resident population at Manama totaled 138,784 in comparison with the estimated resident population at another principal city, Muharraq Town, 75,906 (*Europa World Year Book,* 1992). The expatriate population consists primarily of imported laborers. A recent population census indicates expatriate labor from the Asian countries constitutes more than two thirds of all expatriates in Bahrain (Central Statistics Organization, 1991). Arabic is the official language of the State of Bahrain.

Since early times, Bahrain has acted as a center for trade and communication. The traditional economic structure was based on trade, pearling, subsistence fishing, and subsistence agriculture. With the discovery of the first oil well in 1932, Bahrain entered a period of steady development and economic growth. Oil revenues during the 1960s and 1970s financed rapid growth in the construction sector and in the commodities and service markets. However, oil reserves began to dwindle in the 1980s, oil prices dropped, and the economy suffered heavy losses. In 1988–1989, revenues from oil and oil products represented 51 percent of the total revenue. The anticipated share in total revenue in 1989–1990 dropped to 46 percent, and in 1990–1991 the anticipated share rose to 57 percent (*Middle East and North Africa,* 1992).

To defend against fluctuating returns and recognizing oil resources would not last beyond the twentieth century, the state set out as early as the 1970s to diversify the economy by broadening the industrial sector (aluminum, shipbuilding, interindustry products, consumer goods) while capitalizing on its stable banking sector and centuries-old trade experience. Through the 1980s and 1990s, Bahrain moved steadily toward a service economy based mainly on the banking, trade, and entertainment industries. During this period, the liberal economic policies of Bahrain attracted capital from investors throughout the Middle East. For them, Bahrain proved to be an alternative financial center to that of war-stricken Beirut.

Advances in education kept pace with the strengthening economy. The government introduced its public school program as early as 1919. By 1986, 139 government schools had been established; now there are 158 public schools in Bahrain. The amount spent by the state for education since the 1970s has averaged about 13 percent of the government's total expenditure.

Education is not compulsory in Bahrain, yet 1991 records show that the net enrollment ratio for Bahraini students between 1989 and 1989 was 88.1 percent at the primary level, 74.5 percent at the intermediate level, and 55.5 percent at the secondary level (*Educational Statistics 1989–1990,* 1991). The state's ambitious educational program has translated into a marked increase in the literacy rate. By 1990, the literacy rate for those aged 15 and older had risen from 59.8 percent in 1971 to 77.5 percent (*World Education Report,* 1991).

Although Arabic is the official language in Bahrain, English is widely used at the market, in business, and by the media. The study of English as a second language is required at the primary level. Students acquire a level of competency that enables them to read English newspapers and periodicals by the time they graduate from the secondary level. The Bahraini elite who attend private schools become fully functional in English by graduation from high school.

Dramatic advances in mass media development took place in Bahrain following independence from British protectionism in 1971. Development was nurtured by government initiatives and its regard for mass media as a valued public service and an important means of communication in all areas of human activity (*Al-Bahrain,* 1991). On the occasion of recent telecommunication expansions, the Minister of Information, Tariq Abd ar-Rahman al-Moayed, explained that the state encourages the introduction of new media technologies because the state believes that a variety of resources delivering comprehensive, timely, and accurate news coverage provides the opportunity for media consumers to draw their own conclusions instead of being indoctrinated to any one view (*Khaleej Times,* 1991).

PRINT MEDIA

Newspapers

Considering the size of Bahrain and nearly a century of media suppression by the British, the growth of Bahrain's press industry in just the last two decades is impressive. Beginning with virtually zero press representation under the British, about 45 to 50 print media products are now published in Bahrain. Although the nation's principal daily newspapers number only three, its periodical industry is active and demonstrates a sensitivity to a variety of public needs and trade interests. The private press in Bahrain is primarily loyalist in nature, but it operates independently of government support and is commercial in structure (ad space sales, subscriptions, and newsstand sales). The government ministries publish, as well, but that output represents a minor portion of the total press industry, and only a numbered few are distributed commercially; the rest are available to the general public on request and without charge.

Of the three national dailies published in Bahrain, two are published in the Arabic language (*Akhbar al-Khaleej* and *Al-Ayam*). Together they share the largest portion of the daily and weekly newspaper readership. The third daily, *Gulf Daily News,* is published in the English language. All three are morning editions; each one reports the local, regional, and international news, and each contains editorials and articles of general interest. *Akhbar al-Khaleej* holds the largest share of the daily readership with a circulation of some 22,000. *Al-Ayam* is not far behind, with a circulation of 21,565, while *Gulf Daily News* claims a circulation of 9,812.

Among the weekly Arabic newspapers, which number only a few, *Al-Adhwaa' (The Spotlight)* is the oldest and claims a circulation of 7,000. It reports mainly news and includes topics of general interest. Two other weekly newspapers, one in the Arabic language, *Akhbar BAPCO,* and another in English, *BAPCO News,* are published by the Bahrain Petroleum Co. (BAPCO). They are employee newspapers but hold some appeal for nonemployees interested in the industry.

Magazines

The periodical industry is particularly active and includes a variety of weeklies. A few weekly magazines are specific to a particular industry, but most publish news and topics of current interest. However, the majority of less frequently published magazines address a readership involved in the oil, construction, manufacturing, and shipping industries; the professions, business, banking, and commerce; and those interested in current affairs, travel, and social topics. Magazines published in Arabic and other languages and designed specifically for children, teens, and women are available at the newsstands, but none are produced by Bahraini publishers.

It must be noted that access to the industry's record of circulation figures for either the daily, weekly, or periodical publications is mainly restricted, and figures available in references are usually based on print representatives' claims and often fail to show agreement. However, Table 3.1 does provide circulation guesstimates derived from various reference sources on a select number of newspapers and periodicals in Bahrain.

While most of the periodicals publish in the Arabic language, a good portion of the publications are published, as well, in both Arabic and English and in English only, indicating the accommodations made not only to the regional audience but to the English-speaking audience as well, many of whom make up the international membership of the commercial, financial, banking, and media populations operating out of Bahrain.

Table 3.1
Selected Newspapers and Magazines Published in Bahrain

Newspapers/Daily	Since		Language	Circulation	Publisher
Akhbar al-Khaleej (Gulf News)	1976		Arabic	22,000 (morning)	Akhbar al-Khaleej Press
Gulf Daily News	1978 (morning)		English	9,812	Akhbar al-Khaleej Press.
Al-Ayam (The Days)	1989		Arabic	21,565 (morning)	Al-Ayam Establishment
Newspapers/W'kly					
Al-Adhwaa' (The Spotlight) (news/gen'l interest)	1965		Arabic	7,000	Arab Print'g & Publ.
Akhbar BAPCO (BAPCO News) (house newspaper)	1981		Arabic	8,000	Bahrain Petroleum Co.
BAPCO News (Sun & Wed.) (house newspaper)	1981		English	1,000	Bahrain Petroleum Co.
Magazines		[Frequency]			
Al-Hayat al-Tijariya (Commerce Review)	1965	monthly	Arabic & Engl.	17,032	Bahrain Chamber of Commerce
Sada al-Usbou' (Weekly Echo) (news/gen'l interest)	1969	weekly	Arabic	25,000 (in various Gulf states)	Ali Sayyar (owner & ed.)
Al-Mujtamaa al-Jadid (The New Society) (news/gen'l interest)	1970	weekly	Arabic	(unlisted)	(unlisted)
Al-Muhandis Assoc. (The Engineer)	1972	quarterly	Arabic & Engl.	(unlisted)	Bahrain Engineeers
Al-Mawaqif (Attitudes) (political/social)	1973	weekly	Arabic	6,000	Al-Mawaqif Press
Bahrain Medical Bulletin	1979	quarterly	English	1,750	Bahrain Medical Assoc.
Panorama al-Khaleej (Gulf Panorama) (gen'l interest)	1983	monthly	Arabic & Engl.	15,000	Al Ayam Press
Al-Musafir al-Arabi (Arab Traveler)	1984	alternate months	Arabic	24,000	Falcon Publishing

Sources: Benn's (World) Media Directory, 1992; *Middle East and North Africa,* 1992; *Willings Press Guide,* 1992; *World Media Handbook,* 1992.

Note: All are published at Manama except *Akhbar BAPCO* and *BAPCO News,* published at Awali.

Arabic Private Press Under the British Protectorate

During the British occupation of Bahrain, the private Arabic press passed through a series of openings and closings, due mainly to economic and political pressures. Opportunity for long-term survival came only after the movement for independence gained momentum in 1969 and government initiatives were launched.

The appearance in 1939 of a weekly newspaper published by a Bahraini and entitled *Al-Bahrain* was a novelty. However, the weekly is not considered the debut of the press industry in Bahrain because the publication was primarily the organ of British propaganda through the years of World War II. Publication of the newspaper ended with the close of World War II in 1945.

Brave starts and quick stops characterize the introduction of private press in Bahrain. In 1950, another weekly newspaper, *Sawt al-Bahrain (Voice of Bahrain),* appeared and displayed a noticeably nationalistic orientation that led to its closing by the British in 1955. *Al-Qafila (The Caravan),* a weekly newspaper first published in 1953, was also shut down by the British in 1955, then reopened under the name *Al-Watan (The Homeland)* and shut down again within a year. *Al-Mizan (The Balance),* a relatively moderate weekly that concentrated on objective news coverage, began publishing in 1954, only to end publication two years later.

The press of the 1950s was short-lived. Nevertheless, the papers produced in that decade commanded a wide readership and were among the first to address the British presence in Bahrain and to raise nationalistic feelings.

It was well into the 1960s before Bahraini publishers attempted to function again. Among the first was the publisher of the weekly newspaper *Al-Adhwaa'* (*The Spotlight,* 1965). Then a weekly magazine appeared, *Sada al-Usbou'* (*Weekly Echo,* 1969). Another weekly magazine followed soon after, *Al-Mujtamaa al-Jadid* (*The New Society,* 1970). To avoid censure, editors of these publications reported only hard news and soft editorials, avoided discussing controversial matters, and resisted taking a stand on any one issue. The strategy enabled them to continue operation under British rule.

Arabic Private Press After Independence

The government offered starter subsidies to encourage press enterprise following independence. The first Arabic publication for a general audience to appear in this period (1973) was a weekly magazine entitled *Al-Mawaqif (Attitudes).* Three years later, the first independent newspaper in the Arabic language was published, a daily entitled *Akhbar al-Khaleej (Gulf News).* For nearly a decade, *Akhbar al-Khaleej* held an undisputed monopoly as the only domestic Arabic daily. Not long after, 1989, a second Arabic daily newspaper, *Al-Ayam (The Days),* appeared. Now an independent, *Al-Ayam* was the only publication to begin operation on a government subsidy. Together these publications provide a variety of feature articles, editorials, and international, regional, and local news. They are widely read on the island, especially as a source for local news and events.

English Private Press After Independence

In 1971, press production in the English language began with the publication of the *Gulf Mirror,* a weekly newspaper produced by a Bahraini publishing agency and staffed with English-speaking expatriates. Operations ended in the late 1980s due to financial difficulties and drop in circulation. A new independent daily, the *Gulf Daily News,* produced by the publishers of *Akhbar al-Khaleej,* had come on the scene in 1978 and won over many of the *Mirror*'s readers. The *Gulf Daily News* remains the only English-language newspaper published in Bahrain today. Its audience includes mostly British, Indian, and other English-speaking expatriates and nationals. The newspaper differs from its Arabic sister *Akhbar al-Khaleej* in that the latter devotes primary attention to Arab and regional events and issues, while the former covers more British and Asian events and matters.

Government Publications

Government publications encompass a wide variety of categories and topics and are available without charge to Bahraini residents who request them; some are sold at the newsstands. State publications are produced by personnel in the various government ministries and printed under the management of the Directorate of Publications. Topics vary from sports, laws, decrees, and commercial registrations to general information across a number of public interest areas. The following is a representative list of publications as they appeared for distribution:

- 1957: *Huna al-Bahrain (This Is Bahrain),* a monthly magazine published by the Information Ministry, commanded a wide readership mainly because it was one of the few sources of information at that time.
- 1957: *Al-Jarida al-Rasmiya (The Official Gazette),* a weekly newspaper published in the Arabic language by the Information Ministry, contained mainly new laws, decrees, ratifications, commercial registrations, and the like. It is available free of charge on request to individuals and institutions.
- 1975: *The Statistical Yearbook* is an annual published by the Ministry of Interior. It includes statistical updates on internal affairs and is free upon request.
- 1976: *Al-Riyada (Sports)* is a weekly magazine published in the Arabic language by the Supreme Council for Youth and Sports. It includes sports announcements, event results, sports features, and the like for about U.S.$0.40 at the newsstands.
- 1977: *Al-Quwwa (The Force),* a monthly magazine published in the Arabic language

by the Defense Ministry, is distributed without charge to those who wish to keep informed about defense developments.

- 1978: The Information Ministry decided to transform the 1957 *Huna al-Bahrain.* Now a weekly magazine with a shortened title, *Al-Bahrain,* the magazine followed the practice of the privately published press in terms of its content, format, and mode of distribution. Published in the Arabic language, content includes articles on political, educational, cultural, financial, and other informational subjects. For about U.S.$0.60 at the newsstands, its circulation is 3,000 (*Benn's [World] Media Directory,* 1992).
- 1978: *Al-Hidayah (The Guidance)* is a monthly magazine published in Arabic by the Ministry of Justice and Islamic Affairs and includes religious topics of interest. For about U.S.$0.60 at the newsstands, its circulation is 5,000 (*Europa World Year Book,* 1992).
- 1982: *Al-Wathiqa (The Document)* is a semiannual journal published by the Historical Documents Center. The articles appear in both Arabic and English and are prepared at the center, attached to the Amiri court. The journal contains historic information and documents concerning Bahrain, Islamic, regional, and Arabic history. The cost is about U.S.$0.60 at the newsstands.
- 1983: *Afaq Amniya (Security Outlook),* a quarterly magazine published in Arabic by the Interior Ministry and distributed free of charge, includes topics related to national security.

In addition, various periodicals are published by the Ministry of Education.

ELECTRONIC MEDIA

Electronic media began modestly while Bahrain remained under British protectionism. After independence, government-sponsored initiatives generated rapid growth, particularly after conflicts in the Gulf region escalated, and the area once again drew world attention. From the start, all of Bahrain's radio and television facilities have been, and still are, a government-owned and managed operation. The broadcast stations, except for their English services, do not air commercials. However, there is a program under way to make the telecommunication arm of the government less dependent on state support.

The move toward commercialization was launched in January 1993 when a decree by the amir initiated establishment of the Bahrain Radio and Television Corporation. The corporation is an autonomous organization attached to the Ministry of Information, but the corporation's financial structure is such that it aims to become completely independent of government support, yet still responsible in other respects to the Ministry of Information.

While expenditures for television come under a budget that is shared jointly by Radio Bahrain, Bahrain Television (BTV), the Gulf News Agency, and the marketing unit of the corporation, the largest share of that budget goes to BTV. The budget for all these services, in Bahrain dinars, totaled 6,023,450 in 1990; 8,294,600 in 1991; and 9,125,900 in 1992. The budget for local television productions (again, in Bahrain dinars) was set at 400,000 in 1990 and 500,000 in 1991 and 1992. Over those same years, television commercials brought in revenues (in Bahrain dinars) of 1,426,202 (1990), 1,583,921 (1991), and 2,211,473 (1992).

The organizational structure of the corporation includes a chairman, appointed by the amir, and nine members appointed by the prime minister, one member from the Finance Ministry, four members from the Directorate of Broadcasting and Television, and four members from the public sector involved in activities concerning the youth, sports, family, children, and science. The corporation is described as a system dedicated to the purpose of providing the public with better programs and more options and of conducting the corporation's activities on a financially self-sustaining basis.

Prior to the establishment of the corporation, the Directorate of Television and the Directorate of Broadcasting were sections in the Information Ministry, and the affairs of both were supervised by the assistant undersecretary for Broadcasting and Television. Allocations to each directorate were assigned from the total budget of the ministry by the Directorate of Financial Affairs in the Information Ministry and subject to approval by the Ministry of Finance and National Economy. Revenues derived from radio and television commercial services went to the State Treasury. During those early days, commercials aired by area businesses on radio and television were placed through and processed by the Advertising Section of the Directorate of Administration and Financial Affairs, which determined advertising rates.

The newly established corporation, under its stated purpose and divisional operations, represents a major change in the management of Bahrain's broadcasting industry, a change that is best understood within the context of its operational advance from government-sponsored beginnings to expanding commercial enterprises.

Radio

The first radio signals transmitted from Bahrain were sent in 1940 when the British established a station, but operation ended at the close of World War II. Some 15 years later, the government-owned and -operated broadcasting station Radio Bahrain was established. It broadcast on 2 kilowatts over medium wave and aired daily programs in the Arabic language for 2 hours. In the 1970s, transmission power was increased to 20 kilowatts, and in 1977, English-language programs and commercials were instituted. In the 1980s, transmission power and broadcast hours rose again—120 kilowatts, 18 hours daily. Radio Bahrain reaches audiences in neighboring Gulf states and the eastern region of Saudi Arabia and has proved to be a drawing card for commercials sponsored by businesses throughout the Gulf region. In 1991, shortwave broadcast was instituted in order to reach audiences in Europe and other Arab countries.

Today, Radio Bahrain continues to broadcast in both Arabic and English on medium wave and shortwave from a single station. The Arabic service features news, music, religious programs, drama, and sports coverage. The English service continues to air commercials for local and international businesses and features mainly pop music, news, and a few dramas and talk shows.

During and after the Gulf War, newscasts understandably increased in number. Regular news bulletins on the Arabic and English services were supplemented by a news brief on the hour, and news specials were aired when important news broke.

In addition to local radio broadcasts, audiences in Bahrain listen to programs on medium wave and shortwave from neighboring Gulf states: Iraq, Iran, Jordan, Egypt, Syria, Lebanon, Libya, and Israel. Programs aired by the Middle East Broadcasting Corporation (MBC), Radio Monte Carlo, Radio America, and the British Broadcasting Corporation (BBC) and programs from other sources depend on weather conditions and available airwaves.

Most radio receivers on sale in Bahrain have AM (amplitude modulation), FM (frequency modulation), and two or three shortwave bands. Today there are some 260,000 radio receivers in use, or 525 per 1,000 population (*World Media Handbook,* 1992), and the estimate does not include car radio ownership. At last count in 1989, registrations showed there were 90,000 passenger cars and 8,000 commercial vehicles in use in Bahrain (*World Almanac and Book of Facts 1993, 1992*).

Television

Television had a late start in Bahrain, nearly 20 years after the introduction of state radio. However, once the government undertook sponsorship for its development, Bahrain television advanced rapidly, particularly through the 1980s and 1990s, so that now Bahrain is regarded as a vital telecommunication center in the Gulf area (*Al-Hayat,* 1993). Beginning in the 1970s with only 35 hours per week on one channel, Bahrain television now broadcasts a total of 540 regularly scheduled hours per week on five channels.

Aside from BTV's local broadcasts, Bahrainis can pick up programs from two regional and two international satellite networks. Since 1975, BTV's original channel, Channel 4, has broadcast Arabic programs, local and imported, while its Channel 55 has broadcast English programs, local and imported, since 1981. The local audience also receives programs delivered by two regional satellite services, Egyptian Satellite Television (ESTV) on Channel 44 and MBC on Channel 46. Both satellite services provide newscasts, documentaries, dramas, talk shows, and family and children's programs in the Arabic language. Two international satellite networks bring in additional English-language programs via the British Broadcasting Corporation/World Service Television (BBC/WST) on Channel 57 and the Cable News Network (CNN) on Channel 55.

Bahrain television became a reality in 1972 when the government entered into a semiprivate enterprise with the American-based International Radio and Television Corporation (IRTC). However, BTV as an enterprise associated with IRTC succumbed to financial difficulties in 1975, prompting the government to step in and buy the facility that year. In the beginning, BTV broadcast a mix of Arabic and English programs on a weekly schedule of 35 hours, delivering mainly live coverage of local sports and cultural events. By 1980, the station had added 17 hours to its weekly schedule, again delivering mainly coverage of local sports and cultural events.

In 1981, a second channel (Channel 55) was added to accommodate the English-language programs and to handle the addition of commercials broadcast in English. This commercial channel was added partly in response to viewer demand, partly in compliance with state policy regarding telecommunications development, and partly because of the commercial success of English radio. In addition to reaching audiences in Bahrain, BTV also extends into eastern Saudi Arabia, Qatar, and the UAE. When the station first began broadcasting, it was a small 25-kilowatt transmission station. Still, geographic advantages and atmospheric conditions—namely, the flat land and high humidity level—enabled BTV to reach audiences throughout Bahrain and some neighboring areas.

Long before a television station was established, however, residents of Bahrain who owned television sets were able to receive signals from Saudi Arabia, Kuwait, Abu Dhabi, Iran, and Iraq. When BTV began broadcasting in the early 1970s, there were about 13,000 receivers in Bahrain. Those numbers rose to 90,000 in 1980, or 257 TV receivers per 1,000 population, then to 198,000 in 1988, or 402 units per 1,000 population (*World Media Handbook,* 1992). Today the presence of two or more units in one household is not uncommon.

BTV underwent several changes in the mid-1980s. One of those changes was the appointment of a woman, Hala al-Umran, as director of Radio and Television, now undersecretary of Radio and Television. When she took charge in 1986, average weekly transmission totaled about 105 hours weekly. As additional programs were developed, those weekly hours grew to 483, and imported programs displayed better quality and more recent production. In 1987, the Television Advisory Committee for Family and Youth Programs was established in order to address audience needs, preferences, and suggestions. The committee includes scholars and experts in education, sociology, child psychology, and communications. One of the committee's tasks at the outset included a pilot survey in order to discover viewer preferences. Results were presented to administrators, who then approved a 13-episode series for family viewing under production in 1993. BTV contracts a specialized marketing research agency to conduct ongoing and comprehensive audience surveys. Previously, the only means of obtaining audience feedback were through informal studies, personal contacts with television administrators, and examination of ''readers' corners'' in local newspapers.

During the 1990s, other channels were added to local Channels 4 and 55 to accommodate addition of the regional and international satellite services. The aim was to increase program choices and provide on-location coverage of the events unfolding in the Gulf region in the 1990s. For a summary of television development in Bahrain since 1975, see Table 3.2.

Broadcasts that originate locally include a variety of programs. About one third are locally produced; others are imported from Arab or Western countries. Arabic imports come from Egypt (60 percent), the Gulf countries (25 percent), Jordan, Lebanon, and Syria (10 percent), and other Arab countries (5 percent). English imports come from the United States (60 percent) and England (20 percent), with the remainder from other European countries and Australia. BTV classifies the types of programs offered locally in the following manner: Channel 4—information, 24 percent; education, 38 percent; entertainment, 38 percent; Channel 55—entertainment, 44 percent; education, 36 percent; information, 20 percent. Of the total programming on Channel 44, 41 percent is locally produced, and the rest (59 percent) is received via satellite. The largest portion of local programming (Channel 44) includes live coverage of sports events, 78 percent; the remainder is live coverage of cultural events and information (*Al-Bahrain,* 1992).

Cable Television

Plans to expand the first cable service of CNN International on Bahrain's multichannel distribution system are under way in 1993. The distribution of CNN's International Service to hotels, businesses, and private residences is the task of Bahrain's Radio and Television Corporation (BRTC), but other details, including information on the number of subscriptions obtained to date, have not yet been released by BRTC (R. Ciccone/CNN, personal communication, May 1993).

NEW TECHNOLOGIES

For such a relatively small state, Bahrain enjoys a modern telecommunication system that supports the service industry and promotes its growth. In 1968, Bahrain became the site for the first satellite earth station of Intelsat's satellite network in the Middle East. Then in 1985 when the first Arab satellite, ARABSAT (Arab Satellite Communications Organization), became operational, Bahrain was the first to use it on a commercial basis.

Opportunity for the expansion of electronic media came in 1981 when the Bahrain Telecommunications Company (BATELCO) was formed in which the government held a 60 percent ownership interest. Within five years, BATELCO became the forty-fifth member of the London-based International Maritime Satellite Organization (INMARSAT) (*Middle East and North Africa,* 1992).

Home videocassette recorder (VCR) units followed close on the heels of television set ownership in Bahrain, and although the number of VCRs in use is unknown, their popularity may be measured by the number of theater closings in recent years. In 1981, there were six privately owned movie theaters patron-

Table 3.2
Television Development in Bahrain*

Year	Channel	Broadcast Service	Total Hours per Week	Language	Program Source
1975	4	BTV	35	Arabic & Engl.	Local & imports
1980	4	BTV	52	Arabic & Engl.	Local & imports
1981	4	BTV		Arabic	Local & imports
"	55	BTV		English	Local & imports
		(1981 total)	91		
1985	4	BTV		Arabic	Local & imports
"	55	BTV		English	Local & imports
		(1985 total)	105		
1990	4	BTV		Arabic	Local & imports
"	55	BTV		English	Local & imports
"	44	ESTV		Arabic	Satellite
		(1990 total)	117		
"	57	CNN		English	Satellite
		(57 added after Iraqi invasion of Kuwait, Aug. '90, 24-hour live coverage daily).			
1991	4	BTV		Arabic	Local & imports
"	55	BTV		English	Local & imports
"	55	BBC/WST		English	Satellite
"	44	ESTV		Arabic	Satellite
"	44	MBC		Arabic	Satellite
"	57	CNN		English	Satellite
		(following end of Gulf war, CNN satellite hours reduce to 18 per day).			
		(1991 total)	483		
1992	4	BTV		Arabic	Local & imports
"	55	BTV		English	Local & imports
"	55	BBC/WST		English	Satellite
"	55	CNN		English	Satellite
		(CNN moves from 57 to 55 due to introduction of CNN cable service which results in reduction of daily CNN satellite hours from 18 to 3, except when events warrant, then 18-hour daily schedule returns: cable subscriptions open to hotels, businesses, and private residences).			
"	44	ESTV		Arabic	Satellite
"	57	BBC/WST (BBC/WST moves from 55)		English	Satellite
"	46	MBC (MBC moves from 44)		Arabic	Satellite
		(1992 total)	540		

Sources: Benn's (World) media directory (1992); Television and Cable Fact Book (1987); and Bahrain Ministry of Information.

*Indicates channel additions and hourly growth as television consumer services increased in volume.

ized by nearly 1.5 million moviegoers. Today, only three movie theaters remain, patronized by about half that number. The popularity of VCRs in Bahrain may be attributed to factors not uncommon in other areas: convenience and reduced cost of home viewing for family members and guests. However, in Bahrain, VCRs also permit home viewing by women for whom attendance in public places, including movie theaters, is restricted. The proliferation of pirated films on videocassettes is still another factor for the popularity of VCRs. Although the percentage of pirated films on videocassettes is unknown, the common wisdom is that the figure runs quite high, which may be due partly to the fact that no copyright laws exist in Bahrain. However, the government is moving to take action in that regard.

MOTION PICTURES

The motion picture industry is the least active arm of Bahrain's media industry. Only two privately produced films have been made in Bahrain since independence, both social dramas and both filmed in Bahrain but processed abroad. The first came out in the 1970s under the title *Bas Ya Baher (The Sea)* and was about pearl diving. The second, entitled *Al Hajez (The Barrier),* came out in 1989 and was about the cultural alienation of the youth. The two films were well received by local reviewers, but critical acceptance failed to encourage continued private enterprise.

Domestic films are mainly produced by the various government ministries. These number about a dozen yearly and are screened periodically on BTV. Most are educational documentaries concerning the religious, historic, cultural, and geological heritage of Bahrain.

The first movie theater in Bahrain opened its doors at Manama as early as 1937. By the 1950s, there were four theaters. During the 1960s, viewers filled the theaters to watch Egyptian and American films; going to the movies was a favorite pastime. However, with the introduction of television in the 1970s and widespread ownership of VCRs, the cinema industry soon felt the loss of its audience. Furthermore, relaxed copyright laws throughout the Middle East permitted extensive marketing of pirated copies of Arabic and Western films. More often than not, these copies reached the Bahrain video market long before the films were released to movie theaters. Movie audiences quickly demonstrated their preference for home video entertainment over theater attendance. Bahraini women, faced with traditional restrictions on their social activities, especially welcomed television and video technology.

Still, the theaters did not perish. By 1981, there were six privately owned cinemas in Bahrain, offering a total seating capacity for 4,039 persons. In that year alone, more than 1.3 million persons went to the movies and saw a total of 314 films, all imports.

Today, cinema houses are frequented mainly by Asian expatriates, particularly laborers from India and Pakistan for whom the theater remains an affordable leisure activity. Among members of the national population, it is the young, mainly teenage males, who attend the movie theaters, particularly to see American films. Theater owners show fewer Arabic films due to the lack of a national audience. By 1991, just three theaters remained operative, reducing seating capacity to 2,301 and securing an attendance that had dwindled down to 619,000 from nearly 1.5 million in 1981 (Central Statistics Organization, 1991).

In 1981, when theater audiences numbered far more than they do now, a total of 314 imports were approved for public viewing. The greatest number came from India, 145; American imports followed, 86; then Italy, 33; Pakistan, 11; Hong Kong, 9; Egypt, 8; Great Britain, 5; and other countries, 17. Although three of the six theaters had closed and film audiences had dwindled to less than half their number in 1981, imports totaled more in 1991 (334) than in 1981 (314). That is not too surprising since the highest number of film imports in 1991 came from India (225) to serve Asian expatriates, who are Bahrain's most frequent moviegoers. Other 1991 imports included films from the United States, 73; Egypt, 6; Pakistan, 1; and other countries, 29 (Central Statistics Organization, 1991).

All imported films must be previewed before a public showing in order to ensure that they conform to the criteria listed in Chapter 5 of the Press Law of 1979. This law prohibits the showing of, or reference to, any film or commercial without the authorization of the Monitoring Committee for Films and Publications. The committee monitors films for offenses against religious, social, health, moral, and political values. Judgment on any of these offenses is left to the authority and discretion of the committee. Their responsibility includes banning pornographic materials and anti-Islamic and pro-Zionist materials and deleting film scenes that display infringement on any constituents of the state or breach of the state's social and moral principles and values. Productions that fail to meet censors' criteria are denied public distribution.

MEDIA OWNERSHIP AND FINANCIAL SUPPORT PATTERNS

The private press represents a considerable portion of the total print output in Bahrain, and the government press does not lag far behind. As noted earlier, the private press operates independently of the government, while the government press, radio, and television are state owned and operated.

The private press is primarily commercial and obtains all of its income from public sales and newspaper space sold to commercial clients; however, information regarding total percentage income from sales versus ads is not available. Nor is information available concerning revenues obtained from the sale of government publications or space sold in some government publications that are sold or distributed free of charge.

MEDIA REGULATION

All media products are subject to regulations written into the Press Law of 1979 and are evaluated by the Monitoring Committee for Films and Publications. Print publishers in the private sector must abide by the following rules:

- To own and operate a press, prior authorization and a license must be obtained from the Department of Publications in the Ministry of Information.
- Any change in the ownership or the senior editorial staff must be approved by the Minister of Information. All editors, journalists, caricaturists, and other professional staff must obtain a license from the Ministry of Information authorizing them to work at a newspaper house.
- A written approval by the Department of Publication is required for the publication of special supplements to the regular issue. The limitation of two supplements per week for dailies and two per month for weeklies must be observed.
- Written materials must be signed by the author, and pictorial materials must be signed by their originator. In case a pseudonym is used, the real name of the author, editor, photographer, or caricaturist must be revealed when requested by the Ministry of Information.

The Press Law of 1979 also includes a list of publication offenses that are punishable as crimes against the state, such as:

- Critical or offensive treatment of the official religion of the state.
- Criticism and blame addressed to the amir.
- Agitation and incitement to murder, theft, arson, or civil unrest.
- Provocation of sectarian strife and social divisiveness.
- Material offending public morals or encroaching on the privacy of people or their honor.
- Anything that shames or faults the head of state of a country enjoying normal diplomatic relations with Bahrain.
- Offensive or degrading content addressed to any legislative or government official or tribunal.
- False information or falsified or forged documents maliciously attributed to others, the publication of which might present a threat to public security or harm the public interest.
- Announcements of secret official contacts and communications or any unauthorized communique concerning the defense forces.
- Announcements of closed session legal proceedings or announcements about crime that investigative authorities have deemed inappropriate for publication.

The regulations under the 1979 law also apply to imported radio, television, and film productions. Like the print publishers, Bahraini film producers must obtain a license to produce and distribute their films. Violations of established laws under the 1979 law result in a ban on public distribution. While the government moves toward correcting the absence of a copyright law, other protective measures are in place and acted upon. For example, a group of 13 government censors continually reviews locally produced media and media entering Bahrain for compliance with the press law, and weekly reports go to the Minister of Information. The committee's evaluation process also includes a weekly review of some 300 to 400 videotape imports. Telecommunication operations, on the other hand, are state-owned monopolies.

EXTERNAL MEDIA SERVICES

No non-Bahraini services, radio or television, broadcast out of Bahrain to other countries in a language familiar to the receiving country. Channels are reserved for delivery of local broadcasts to local and regional areas and reserved for reception from regional and international satellite services (Monitoring Committee for Publication, 1993).

However, numerous newspapers and magazines published elsewhere in the world are readily available at the newsstands.

NEWS AGENCIES

Aside from Bahrain's own national news agency, the Gulf News Agency (GNA), a number of major international news agencies operate regional offices out of Manama. The international news agencies at Manama include the Associated Press (AP), Reuters, Agence France-Presse (AFP, French Press Agency), Deutsche Presse-Agentur (DPA, German Press Agency), and the Press Trust of India (PTI).

The GNA is administratively part of the Ministry of Information. It staffs 60 resident journalists and editors in addition to ten stringer correspondents located throughout the world. The GNA is a prime source for local and government news. The agency also monitors radio broadcasts and news releases from around the world and reports items of public interest.

Press presence in the Gulf region increased noticeably during the 1990–1991 Gulf War and has since remained active. Most correspondents reported the events of the Gulf War from Manama. At the height of the war, the Ministry of Information established two press centers, one at the ministry and the other at the Gulf Hotel, where most correspondents resided and where U.S. press briefings took place.

THE ROLE OF MASS MEDIA IN NATIONAL DEVELOPMENT

Although newspapers and periodicals may have some application in the classroom, particularly in the study of English, their actual use or extent of effect if used is not known. Aside from informational programs on radio and television schedules, telecommunication does not play a significant role in classroom instruction. Media are more likely to have an educational influence on both the young and adult population through individual use of available media.

The role of Bahrain's mass media in national development is primarily played out through announcements and coverage of ceremonial and traditional events. According to Rugh (1987), the private press in Bahrain, not unlike other loyalist press in the Gulf region, is not inclined toward social advocacy that runs contrary to national interests. Activities to develop national awareness are mainly the domain of the government, and part of that task is accomplished through informational publications that document the state's historical, cultural, and religious history, and that provide updates on state activities such as defense, industrial, financial, and commercial development.

Media consumers in Bahrain generally have faith in the accuracy and substance of both the private and state media, particularly because choice of media and the opportunity for measurement against external media products remain unrestricted.

CONCLUSION

Little headway in mass media development was possible during Britain's century-long rule of Bahrain. Since independence and within the short span of three decades, mass media development in Bahrain moved swiftly from a primitive and controlled media environment under British rule to state-of-the-art communication technologies and a comparatively liberal media policy. Following independence, the private print industry advanced rapidly, aided in part at the outset by government subsidy. Meanwhile, the government creates initiatives that nurture the growth of local telecommunications and conducts successful negotiations with international networks in order to give Bahrain access to the world and to bring the world to Bahrain.

REFERENCES

Al-Bahrain. (1991, December). The National Day and the course of development.

Al-Bahrain. (1992, December). The National Day and the course of progress.

Al-Hayat. (1993, January 20).

Benn's (world) media directory (140th ed.). (1992). Kent, England: Benn Business Information Services, Ltd.

Central Statistics Organization. (1991). State of Bahrain Commerce Statistics Department. Unpublished 1991 population census.

Educational statistics 1989–1990. (1991). Bahrain: Ministry of Education.

Europa world year book (Vol. 1). (1992). London, England: Europa Publications, Ltd.

Gulf Daily News. (1993, January 7).

Khaleej Times. (1991, November 28).

Middle East and North Africa (38th ed.). (1992). London, England: Europa Publications Ltd.

Monitoring Committee for Publication. (1993). *Publication Report.* Bahrain: Information Ministry.

Rugh, W. A. (1987). *The Arab press: News media and political process in the Arab World.* Syracuse, NY: Syracuse University Press.

Television and Cable Fact Book. (1987). Washington, DC: Television Digest, Inc.

Willings Press Guide (Vol. 2). (1992). Windsor Court, England: Red Information Services, Ltd.

World almanac and book of facts 1993. (1992). New York: World Almanac.

World education report. (1991). Paris: UNESCO.

World media handbook. (1992). New York: United Nations.

4

CYPRUS

John E. Keshishoglou

INTRODUCTION

The island Republic of Cyprus is situated in the eastern part of the Mediterranean Sea, southeast of Greece, north of Egypt, and west of Syria. Turkey lies to the north of Cyprus. Its location at the crossroads of three continents and its proximity to the traditional trade routes have been major factors in shaping its history and development.

Cyprus is the third largest island in the Mediterranean. It covers an area of 3,572 square miles, which makes it comparable in size to the state of Connecticut. Its length from east to west is approximately 150 miles, and it has a maximum width of 62 miles from north to south.

The population of Cyprus is estimated at 700,000. Roughly 80 percent are Greek Cypriots, 18 percent are Turkish Cypriots, and the rest of the population is comprised of various minorities. Greek and Turkish are the official languages. English is widely spoken, and it is the language of commerce and government.

The olive groves and vineyards of Cyprus produce an abundant variety of olive oil and wines. Exporting grapes, olives, potatoes, citrus, and vegetables earns the island much needed hard currency. Other principal crops include wheat and barley. Sheep and goats are raised in many parts of the country.

The annual per capita income is over $7,000. A report from the Central Bank of Greece states:

Considering other socioeconomic indicators such as infant mortality, life expectancy, housing conditions, and the crime rate, as well as per capita number of hospital beds, passenger cars, telephones and television sets, one may conclude that the standard of living on the island is better than that reflected by per capita income alone. (*Cyprus,* 1989)

The same report indicates that Nicosia, the capital of Cyprus, ranks as the ninth least expensive city among the leading 52 business centers in the world.

Cyprus has adopted a democratic form of government most commonly found in the West. The president of the republic, who is elected for a five-year term, normally appoints the various ministers. The Council of Ministers is the executive arm of the republic. Legislative power lies with the House of Representatives, each elected to office for five years. There is a multiparty system based on proportional representation. The judiciary system is modeled after that of England. The administration of justice is exercised by the Judiciary, which is a separate and independent body. It includes the Supreme Court, the Assize courts (for serious crimes), and the District courts (for minor offenses). The Supreme Court, which consists of 13 judges, is the final legal authority on constitutional, administerial, and administrative law.

The educational system of Cyprus is highly centralized and controlled by the state. This system controls teacher appointments, promotions, transfers, and of course, salaries. The state also prescribes, to a large extent, curricular matters, such as course requirements, course contents, and textbooks to be used. Primary education is state supported, compulsory, and free.

Higher education includes both private and public institutions. The University of Cyprus, established recently by the government, offers programs in the traditional disciplines. The School of Humanities and Social Sciences includes the Departments of Philosophy, History, Greek and Turkish studies, Languages, Education, and Political Science. The School of Pure and Applied Sciences includes the Departments of Mathematics, Computer Sciences, Physics, and Engineering. The School of Economics and Administration offers degree programs in economics, public, and business administration. There are six other public institutions of higher education. These include the Pedagogical Academy, which offers a three-year course of study in teacher education, and the Higher Technical Institute, which offers a number of three-year majors in engineering, the School of Nursing, the College of Forestry, the Hotel and Catering Institute, and the Mediterranean Institute of Management. Some two dozen private schools and colleges offer programs ranging from one to four years in various disciplines such as secretarial studies, banking, computer programming, electrical, mechanical, civil engineering, and others.

COMMUNICATION PHILOSOPHY

The mass media in Cyprus operate under a combination of libertarian and social responsibility systems. There is a dual system of media ownership. While most of the media (newspapers, radio stations, magazines) are in private hands, the state owns and operates, through Cyprus Broadcasting Corporation (CyBC), two television channels (Channel 1, and Channel 2) and a number of radio stations. There are no restrictions to the publication of newspapers and magazines and no censorship. Freedom of the press is guaranteed by the press law enacted in 1989. On the other hand, the mass media accept their responsibility to society.

With regard to the broadcast media, the law allows the establishment of private radio, television, and cable TV stations, thus breaking up the monopoly that CyBC enjoyed since the 1950s under the old quasi-authoritarian system.

Foreign correspondents (there are close to 100) stationed on Cyprus operate under the same set of rules. While some countries view foreign correspondents with suspicion, even hostility, Cyprus accords them the same privileges enjoyed by native journalists.

Cyprus has developed through the years a cultural mix that is a reflection of its geographical position, ethnic makeup, and historical background. The mass media are expected to play a dual role of informing, educating, and entertaining the public, on one hand, and preserving and promoting its culture, on the other.

PRINT MEDIA

Newspapers

The development of the print media in Cyprus was influenced by certain historical facts. The Ottoman Empire ruled Cyprus (and for that matter, the entire eastern Mediterranean basin including the Balkans) until 1878. In Cyprus, they were prompt to stifle freedom of speech. Accordingly, they did not look favorably upon the publication of newspapers or magazines.

The occupation of the island by the Ottomans was succeeded by British rule in 1878. It was not until then that newspapers made their appearance. The British tolerated, to a certain degree, freedom of speech and of the press. The first newspaper, *Cyprus,* was published in the city of Larnaca in 1878. Although it was short-lived, a number of other newspapers emerged later. In fact, Larnaca seems to be the city where the early press flourished (Sophocleous, 1991).

Greek Cypriot Press

The most important milestone in the development of the mass media in general, and the print media in particular, came in 1960 when Cyprus gained its independence from the British. After independence, the media began to play an important role in the development of the republic. Several newspapers and magazines representing a variety of opinions and political affiliations began publication. One of these, *Eletheria (Freedom),* continues to publish today (Sophocleous, 1991).

Table 4.1
Greek and English-Language Dailies in Cyprus

Title	Ownership	Circulation
Agon (*Struggle*) Independent-Center-Right	N. Koshis	8,000
Alithia (*Truth*) Right-Wing	Socratis Hassikos	8,000
Apogevmatini (*Afternoon*) Independent/Moderate	A.Hadjiefthimiou, A. Stavridis, and A.Lykavkis	10,000
Eleftheria Tis Gnomis (*Freedom of Opinion*) Center-Right	Tassos Antoniadis	2,000
leftherotipia (*Free Press*) Center-Right/Democratic	Center/Right Democratic Party	7,000
Simerini (*Today*) Right-Wing/Democratic	Kostas Hadjikostis	13,000
Phileleftheros (*Liberal*) Independent	N. Pattichis	19,500
Haravgi (*Dawn*) Communist	Telegraphos Co., Ltd	13,000
Cyprus Mail (English Language Daily) Independent	Cyprus Mail Co., Ltd.	3,500

Source: Cyprus Press and Information Office (PIO), 1993.

Since the publication of the first newspaper, *Cyprus,* some 300 newspapers and magazines have been published. Many had a short life. Nevertheless, the large number of periodicals in proportion to the total population points to the fact that the Cypriots are avid readers with a keen interest in news and politics.

According to the Cyprus Press and Information Office (Dailies, 1991), nine daily newspapers are published in Greek, and one daily is published in English (see Table 4.1).

In addition to the dailies, four weekly newspapers are published in Greek and one in English. Their daily circulation ranges from a low of 3,000 to a high of 15,000 copies (see Table 4.2).

Table 4.2
Greek and English-Language Weeklies in Cyprus

Title	Ownership	Circulation
Proina Nea (*Morning News*) Socialist	Socialist Party	3,000
Paraskinion (*Behind the Scenes*) Independent	D. Michael	4,200
Ergatiki Phoni (*Worker's Voice*)	Workers Confederation	8,850
Ergatiko Vima (*Worker's Tribune*)	Cyprus Labor Federation	15,000
Cyprus Weekly (English Language) Independent	G. der Parthogh, A. Efthymiou, and G. Hadjipapas	15,000

Source: Cyprus Press and Information Office (PIO), 1993.

Western newspapers circulate freely on the island. Newspapers from Greece, Turkey, and the Arab states compete with the *International Herald Tribune, USA Today, The New York Times, Il Giornale* (Italy), *Le Monde* (France), *The Times, The Sun,* and *The Daily Express* (United Kingdom).

Magazines

The number of Greek-language magazines published on the island exceeds 30 titles. These can be categorized as general interest, special interest, and children's magazines (see Table 4.3). Like newspapers, the newsstands display magazines from all over the world, including *Time, Newsweek, Cosmopolitan,* and *Playboy.*

Turkish Cypriot Press

The development of Turkish Cypriot newspapers was somewhat slower compared with the Greek Cypriot newspapers. One reason for this is the fact that it proved difficult to find movable type of the old Turkish script with its Arabic characters. Printing equipment was lacking as well. It thus appears that the first Turkish newspaper was published on the island more than 100 years after the emergence of the Greek press, in 1878.

In World War I, Great Britain and Turkey fought on opposite sides. Following

Table 4.3
Leading Magazines in Cyprus

Title	Ownership	Circulation
To Periodiko (*The Magazine*)	Dias Co., Ltd.	20,000
Cypria (*Cypriot Woman*)	Maro Karayanni	6,000
Katanalotis (*Consumer*)	Consumers' Union	3,000
Paediki Chara (*Children's Play*)	Organization of Greek Cypriot Teachers	14,000
Trapezikos (*Bank Employee*)	Bank Employee Union	6,000
Cyprus PC	Pericles Varnavas	2,000
Selides (*Pages*)	A. Michaelidis	21,000
Gynaika ke Enimerosi (*Woman and Briefing*)	Nikos Koshis	2,000

Source: Cyprus Press and Information Office, (PIO), 1993.

the war, Great Britain declared Cyprus a Crown colony. From 1915 to 1919, no newspapers were published to meet the needs of the Turkish Cypriots, who were isolated from Turkey. Economic conditions, lack of technical expertise, and high level of illiteracy were also obstacles in the development of the press following World War I.

In the early 1930s, Turkey changed its script from Arabic to Latin. This change made it possible for the existing presses to publish newspapers in Turkish. Since then, several Turkish Cypriot newspapers have emerged; some are shown in Table 4.4.

Turkish Cypriot newspapers continue to support the Turkish occupation of the island, which took place in 1974, and are closely aligned with Turkish domestic and foreign policies.

ELECTRONIC MEDIA

Radio

In 1952, the Broadcasting Corporation Law established the Cyprus Broadcasting Corporation for the purpose of ''operating by sound or television a public broadcasting service for reception by the public'' (*Cyprus,* 1990).

Table 4.4
Turkish Cypriot Daily Newspapers

Title	Ownership	Circulation
Birlik (*Unity*)	Ramiz Manyera	4,500
Halkin Sesi (*People's Voice*)	Peter M. Turgud	6,000
Kibris Postasi (Cyprus Post)	Ismet Kotak	2,500
Yeniduzen (*New Order*)		2,000
Ortam (*Political Environment*)	Toplumcu Ltd.	1,250

Source: World Media Handbook. (1992).

The administration of CyBC is in the hands of the board of directors, appointed by the Council of Ministers. Their term of office is limited to three years. The Council of Ministers appoints one of the directors to serve as the chairman of the group. The operation of CyBC rests in the hands of the director-general, who is also appointed by the Council of Ministers.

CyBC is a nonprofit institution responsible for providing cultural and entertainment programming to the public. It derives its income primarily from licensing fees imposed on the public and from advertising revenues.

A public law enacted in March 1979 mandates all consumers of electricity to pay a fee to CyBC, added to their electricity bills every two months. The Power Authority of Cyprus collects the fee and passes it on to CyBC. The amount of the fee depends on the amount of electricity consumed by a given household. There is no charge for the first 40 kilowatts of consumption during a two-month period, and according to the law, the fee cannot exceed $70 per year. Advertising revenues come from commercials and program sponsorship. Since CyBC is a government-owned and -operated monopoly, it may also receive financial support from the government of Cyprus.

On October 4, 1953, the first official radio station went on the air in Cyprus under the auspices of CyBC's predecessor, the Cyprus Broadcasting Service (CBS). At that time, there were approximately 14,000 radio receivers on the island. Prior to 1953, the British operated a radio station in Cyprus, which was then a British colony.

The first postcolonial radio station in Cyprus carried its programming in three languages: Greek broadcasts on every Monday, Wednesday, Saturday, and Sunday; Turkish broadcasts every Tuesday and Friday; English broadcasts on Thursday and Sunday. In 1955, CyBC introduced a second station devoted to Turkish programming.

Radio broadcasting ceased operation during the Cypriot uprising and the ensuing struggle for liberation against the British, which began in 1955 and ended with Cyprus gaining its independence in 1960. CyBC was the first target of the freedom fighters, since it was a government-operated entity and therefore a symbol of colonial rule. Consequently, listeners tuned to radio stations from Greece, Turkey, and neighboring countries in the Middle East.

FM (frequency modulation) radio was first introduced in Cyprus in 1973. It soon gained more popularity, when CyBC began broadcasting in stereo FM.

The Turkish invasion of Cyprus in 1974 and the subsequent occupation of some 40 percent of the island brought about the loss of land, studio, and transmitting equipment and disrupted CyBC's operation. The FM transmitter on Mount Sinal in the Kyrenia range was confiscated by the Turks.

In 1993, CyBC operated three radio networks: Program 1, Program 2, and Program 3. They include AM (amplitude modulation) as well as FM stations. In addition, the corporation operates a shortwave station located near Limassol that broadcasts to Cypriots overseas.

Program 1 broadcasts an average of 126 hours of weekly programming in Greek. Program 2 averages the same number of hours of programs in three languages: Turkish, English, and Armenian. During the tourist season, it broadcasts a program called *Welcome to Cyprus* for visitors to the island in seven languages: Arabic, English, French, German, Swedish, Danish, and Finnish. Program 3 was introduced in 1990 as a way for CyBC to compete with the wave of new independent privately owned radio stations that were allowed for the first time to operate legally on the island.

All three radio programs offer the usual mix of music, talk shows, sports, and news. The corporation subscribes to seven news agencies. It also employs its own correspondents and stringers. Approximately 600,000 inhabitants listen to Radio Cyprus.

Private radio stations are relatively new to the island. In June 1990, the House of Representatives passed a law that allows the establishment of independent radio stations, thus effectively ending the monopoly that CyBC enjoyed. Following this ruling, independent radio stations went on the air in every part of the island (see Table 4.5). For the first time in the history of Cyprus, the public gained access to the airwaves, something that had been restricted under the old laws. In addition, independent radio stations implemented 24-hour programming, while the CyBC operated its stations about 10 to 12 hours a day.

The new era of radio necessitated drastic changes on the part of CyBC, which saw the number of its listeners shrink to an all-time low of 7 percent. Program 3 was introduced at this time to compete with the independents. Its 24-hour operation and programming format was clearly designed to make it regain its share of the listeners.

Table 4.5
Independent Radio Stations in Cyprus

Sattion	Frequency/MHz	Location
Radio Astra	92.8	Nicosia
Radio Proto	99.3	Nicosia/Limassol
Radio Proto	105.7	Paralimni/Paphos
Radio Fredrick	103.0	Nicosia
Radio Kyniras	95.7	Paphos
Radio Paphos	92.5	Paphos
Radio Epistrophi	104.3	Nicosia
Radio Astra	92.8	Nicosia
Radio Napa	90.8	Agia Napa
Radio Logos	101.5	Nicosia
Radio Top	99.9	Nicosia
Radio One	106.0	Nicosia
Radio Kronos	95.7	Nicosia
Radio Genesis	101.4	Nicosia
Radio Intercollege	99.0	Larnaca
Radio Magic	101.0	Larnaca
Radio Castro	100.3	Larnaca
Radio Larnaca	96.0	Larnaca

Source: Cyprus Press and Information Office (PIO), 1993.
MHz = Megahertz.

Television

October 1957 is given as the date when the first television broadcast took place in Cyprus. At the start, the CyBC station offered a two-hour program twice a week from 6:00 P.M. to 8:00 P.M. Gradually, the number of broadcast hours increased to its present level. The station's weekday program commences at 5:00 P.M. and ends at midnight. During the weekends and on important holidays, the hours are extended.

Programming includes locally produced as well as syndicated shows procured primarily from Europe and the United States. Local shows account for approximately 30 percent of total programming. Greek soaps and other types of serials usually carry Turkish subtitles. The three daily newscasts are in Greek, Turkish, and English. Turkish programming also includes a daily newsreel that is viewed by a sizable number of Turkish Cypriots. A weekly program outline is likely to include the following:

Local productions	**Percent**
News, talk shows, culture, education, and entertainment	32
Station breaks and announcements	5
Commercials	10
Programs from Greece	6

Entertainment, cultural news, and information	
Foreign-produced programs	47

Instructional television received a boost in 1966 when CyBC signed an agreement with the Ministry of Education to produce and broadcast lessons in geography and biology. Other subjects were added later.

CyBC's main television transmitter, located on Mount Olympus, uses 35 transponder stations to reach the various parts of the island. It has two-way links with Eurovision (of the European Broadcasting Union), and it produces *Euronews* for the European television channel. Following an agreement between Cyprus and Greece, there has been a direct link, since November 1990, between CyBC and the Greek (state-owned) television channel ET-1. Viewers in both countries may now watch both channels.

Ever mindful of the Turkish Cypriot minority on the island, CyBC broadcasts Turkish programming and shows with Turkish subtitles. The introduction of a second television channel in 1992 helped in this regard. It offers some eight hours of programming and news in Turkish, approximately six hours in English, and three hours in Armenian.

Equally mindful of the large number of visitors in Cyprus, CyBC offers daily newscasts in English. It also programs feature films from various countries in the original language but with Greek subtitles.

Independent television arrived in Cyprus following the passage of a new law by the Cyprus legislation in early April 1992. The law empowers the Council of Ministers to issue licenses to private television stations. This brought to an end some 30 years of monopoly enjoyed by CyBC. Hence, the first independent station commenced broadcasting in late April 1992. The church-owned LOGOS (the Word) made its inauguration on Easter Day. It offers news and, in general, educational programming suitable for family and children's viewing. The station's weekday program lasts about 11 hours: from 7:00 to 9:00 A.M., from 12:30 P.M. to 2:00 P.M., and from 5:00 to 11:00 P.M.

The first cable television network commenced operations in Cyprus in 1992. The privately owned Lumiere Television Network is attempting to lure subscribers by offering feature films, sports, cultural, educational, and children's programming. With its headquarters located in Nicosia, the cable network plans to distribute its signal via coaxial cable and later via satellite. With the introduction of independent radio and television stations and cable television, Cyprus followed the pattern that has been adopted throughout Europe and other parts of the world.

MOTION PICTURES

There is virtually no production of feature films in Cyprus. Since 1983, only four feature films have been produced. However, the government has encouraged and periodically supports the production of documentaries. With the advent of television, a number of independent production companies were established, specializing in the production of commercials and documentaries.

Most of the feature films shown on Cyprus come from the United States. Few come from Greece. A total of 47 feature films were imported in 1990: 42 from the United States and 5 from Greece. The number increased to 65 in 1991.

There are a total of 12 motion picture theaters on the island. Of these, 6 are found in Nicosia, 2 in Limassol, 1 in Larnaca, 2 in Paphos, and 1 in Paralimni.

Motion picture attendance has also increased during the last two years. For 1993, it is estimated that 160,000 people will go to the movies in Nicosia, 50,000 in Limassol, and 25,000 in Larnaca. The majority of moviegoers are in the 15 to 30 age group.

MEDIA OWNERSHIP AND FINANCIAL SUPPORT PATTERNS

Virtually all newspapers and magazines, except the official government publications (such as *Cyprus Bulletin, Cyprus View,* and a few others), are privately owned. Newspapers derive their support from direct sales to the public from newsstands, advertising, and direct contributions by the political entities with which they are affiliated. Unlike the Western countries, the concept of newspaper subscription by mail has not been successful in Cyprus.

Although political contribution is a crucial source of revenue, many newspaper and magazine publishers operate their own printing presses/businesses, which provides added financial support for the survival of their papers. This is particularly important in the case of magazines, which do not benefit as much from political contributions as do the newspapers.

The electronic media, including CyBC stations, are supported by both licensing fees and advertising revenues. When approving CyBC's 1992 operating budget, the Cyprus House of Representatives approved a 50 percent increase in the license fee based on electricity consumption. This increase became necessary to fund the operation of CyBC's Channel 2 (Cyprus News Agency [CNA], personal communication, March 21, 1992).

The financial state of the independent broadcaster remains tenuous. Radio Super, which was the first independent radio station established in Cyprus, ceased operation a year later due to financial difficulties. Another independent, Radio Astra (Stars), is also struggling to survive. Other independent stations face similar difficulties. In the final analysis, it will be the listeners and the marketplace that will determine how many stations the island supports.

The fate of the independent television station is not certain. Whether and to what extent it will be able to compete with CyBC remain to be seen. If what happened in other countries serves as an example, independent television survived and even prospered in several nations when the state-owned broadcasting monopoly was broken. The main difference is that Cyprus is a small country with rather limited resources. A similar argument may be advanced for the fate of cable television. Would enough households subscribe in order to ensure the system's survival?

MEDIA REGULATION

On August 2, 1989, the Cyprus House of Representatives enacted the Press Law of 1989, which modifies and unifies all laws pertaining to the freedom of the press and the publication and circulation of newspapers, magazines, and other types of printed material.

The law also offers guidelines for the establishment and operation of printing presses and publishing houses. The Press Law of 1989, which replaced the existing law, proposed the establishment of a Press Council that would be responsible for safeguarding the freedom of the press and the rights of journalists and, in general, would monitor the profession. It promoted investigative journalism and protected the rights of journalists to keep their sources secret.

The Press Law of 1989 established a special service, Archi Typou (Press Headquarters), to advise the Minister of the Interior on issues pertaining to the granting of permits for the establishment of newspapers, news agencies, and press circulation agencies to Cypriot and foreign nationals. It set the price for newspapers and the fees to be paid to those selling newspapers and magazines.

On June 20, 1990, the House of Representatives updated the laws pertaining to radio broadcasting. The law established the Radio Consulting Committee to study and make recommendations for new (independent) radio station licenses, the renewal of existing licenses (every three years), enforcing the proper use of radio frequencies as determined by the International Telecommunication Union (ITU), and dealing with all issues pertaining to broadcasting.

The law prescribes two types of broadcasting licenses: local and national. A local license is for the operation of a radio station by a municipality or a group within a municipality, provided its members are Cypriot nationals. National licenses (both AM and FM) are given to stations that reach other parts of the island.

The law sets limits for commercials that must not exceed 10 percent of the total broadcasting time nor ten minutes per hour. Cigarette commercials are banned. Commercials for children's toys may also be banned on CyBC stations (Law pertaining to Radio Stations, 1990).

EXTERNAL MEDIA SERVICES

CyBC broadcasts three times a week (Friday, Saturday, and Sunday) to Cypriots living abroad. Using a shortwave transmitter located at Zygi, near the city of Limassol, the 30-minute program includes news from and about Cyprus and also music. The broadcast, *I Kypros Konta Sas (Cyprus Near You)* begins at

10:15 P.M. Greenwich mean time (GMT), and it is broadcast on 9695 Kilohertz and 7230 kilohertz.

CyBC AM radio offers regular newscasts in four languages: Turkish, English, Armenian, and Arabic. An estimated 30 million nationals who reside in Greece, Turkey, Egypt, Jordan, Syria, Lebanon, and other countries in the region tune in to Radio Cyprus.

Cyprus television Channel 1 is received in Greece since the exchange agreement, in 1990, between the two countries. In turn, Cyprus receives Greek television channel ET-1.

CyBC is studying the feasibility of providing regular two-way television connection between Cyprus, Egypt, Syria, Israel, and Lebanon. A new fiber optic submarine network, scheduled for completion in 1994, will make such interconnection possible by 2020 (Sophocleous, 1991).

NEWS AGENCIES

The Press and Information Office (PIO) of Cyprus disseminates information and interprets government policy, especially with regard to mass media. It also serves as the government's own publisher, and it is responsible for all governmental publications. The PIO issues press releases and produces photographs and a variety of audiovisual material, interpreting and promoting the government's work, both in Cyprus and overseas.

The Cyprus News Agency (CNA), established in 1976, is an independent and autonomous corporation that gathers and disseminates news taking place on Cyprus and from overseas about Cyprus. To a lesser extent, it covers events in the Middle East.

An unusually large number of foreign correspondents are stationed in Cyprus. They represent news organizations from all over the globe because Cyprus is viewed as the news hub, located strategically at the crossroads of Europe and the Middle East. Locating a correspondent in Cyprus makes sense both from a financial point of view as well as for the accessibility to developing stories in a wide region. The existing situation in Lebanon is another reason. It is considered no longer safe to station Western correspondents in Beirut, and Cyprus proved to be a safe alternative.

Owing to its favorable climate and geographical location, 70 media and news agencies, representing 25 nations around the world, have their own bureaus in Cyprus. Major news agencies or wire services such as Associated Press (United States), Reuters (United Kingdom), Agence France Presse (France), Tass (Russia), ANSA (Agenzia Nazionale Stampa Associata, Italy), Xinhua (China), Sofia Press News Agency (Bulgaria), DPA (Deutsche Presse-Agentur, Germany), Southam News (Canada), Kyoto News Service (Japan), and others have stationed their own offices and correspondents in Cyprus.

THE ROLE OF MEDIA IN NATIONAL DEVELOPMENT

Turkey's invasion and occupation of approximately 40 percent of Cyprus mandated a revision of the guidelines in the operation of the broadcast media, CyBC in particular. Although these guidelines were enacted in 1974, they remain in effect while the occupation of the island continues. The guidelines call upon CyBC to:

- Inform, educate, and entertain, as well as to maintain the morale and spirit of the Greek Cypriots.
- Participate, in conjunction with the state, in enlightenment of world opinion.
- Maintain continuous contact with and enlighten the Turkish Cypriots and the Turkish population of southern Turkey.
- Inform and entertain Armenian Cypriots in Cyprus and in the Arab countries as well as the English-speaking listeners in Cyprus and the Middle East.
- Maintain free flow of information with Cypriots living overseas.
- Actively participate in the cultural life of the island.
- Preserve on film and on tape the history of the island (''CyBC Launches Second Channel,'' 1991).

CyBC has been, to a large extent, successful in carrying out the state's mandate. Its programming over the years clearly reflects its effort to address these guidelines.

The corporation publishes some 12 different publications to supplement its programming. These range from monthly *Radioprogramma*, with the radio and television listings, to such diverse publications as *Pre-Socratic Philosophers, Introduction to Byzantine Painting, Topics and Views, Elements of Psychology, Learn Greek, The Years of Adolescence,* and many others.

Documentaries, produced by CyBC, deal with every aspect of life on Cyprus, ranging from history (including the series on the Turkish invasion), education, culture, and development to recent issues about the environment, the disintegration of the Soviet Union, and developments in the Middle East. CyBC and the print media in general have been contributing forces to the rapid development of the island.

CONCLUSION

Considering the fact that Cyprus gained its independence in 1960, it is easier to understand the magnitude of the growth of the mass media. This is particularly true about the print media. Newspapers and magazines flourish on the island. Freedom of the press emerged following World War II. To be sure, while private ownership of radio and television stations was allowed recently, the broadcasting media under CyBC made considerable progress over the years.

Satellites, cable, data communications, and events in the Middle East propelled Cyprus into an international communications center. A variety of news agencies and other mass media have established offices in Nicosia. Newspapers and magazines from several countries have their own correspondents in Cyprus. In addition to its strategically placed location, Cyprus offers modern facilities and technology for gathering and disseminating news.

Cyprus recognized early on the importance of mass media and has resolved to remain in the forefront of developing technology, promptly implementing innovations in this field.

REFERENCES

CyBC launches second channel. (1991, March 12). *Cyprus News Agency.*

Cyprus. (1990). Nicosia: Press and Information Office, Republic of Cyprus.

Cyprus, a center for international business. (1989). Nicosia: Central Bank of Cyprus.

Cyprus: The way to full EC membership. (1991). Nicosia: Press and Information Office, Republic of Cyprus.

Cyprus Press and Information Office. (1993).

Dailies. (1991). Nicosia: News release by the Press and Information Office, Republic of Cyprus.

Law Pertaining to Radio Stations. (1990, July 9). *Official Newspaper of the Republic of Cyprus.*

Sophocleous, A. C. (1991). *Mass media in Cyprus.* Nicosia: Press and Information Office, Republic of Cyprus.

World media handbook. (1992). New York: United Nations.

5

EGYPT

Sonia Dabbous

INTRODUCTION

Egypt is located on the northeast corner of the African continent. One of the most densely populated countries of the Middle East, its population has rapidly increased: 16 million in 1933; 38 million in 1976; 52 million in 1987; 56 million in 1990.

Geographically, Egypt extends from the Mediterranean Sea on the north to Sudan on the south, and from the Red Sea on the east to Libya on the west. Even though the total area of Egypt is around 1 million square kilometers, less than 5 percent of the land is inhabited. Administratively, modern Egypt is divided into 26 governorates. Four of these governorates are major metropolitan areas (Cairo, Alexandria, Port Said, and Suez), 9 are located on the Nile Valley, and 5 are frontier governorates. Around one-fifth of the Egyptian population is found in the urban governorates. The majority of the population is rural: in lower Egypt (72 percent) and in upper Egypt (68 percent). Islam is the religion of the state, and Arabic is its official language.

Education is officially compulsory for the 9 years between 6 and 15 years of age. Primary education starts at 6 years and lasts for 5 years, reduced from 6 in 1989; secondary education begins at the age of 11 and lasts for 6 years. In 1989, total enrollment at primary and secondary schools was equivalent to 89 percent of the school-age population. There are 13 universities. Education at all levels is available free of charge. However, there are several private schools and some private universities: The American University in Cairo and, in 1994, the national universities.

The Egyptian economy follows a system of a mixed economy under government supervision. The fundamental difficulty confronting the Egyptian economy is the pressure on resources, owing to one of the world's highest ratios of population to habitable and cultivable land. Egypt's formerly unmanageable foreign debt has been alleviated by the cancellation of obligation to the United States and to Arab creditors in return for its support of the multinational forces in the 1991 war with Iraq and by the conclusion of restructuring agreements with international organizations. The activities of the private sector are increasing.

The system of the republican government is headed by President Hosni Mubarak, who came to office on October 14, 1981. The president of Egypt, who must be of Egyptian parentage, is nominated by one-third of the members of the people's assembly, approved by at least two-thirds, and elected by popular referendum. President Mubarak is the third elected president after the 1952 revolution, preceded by the late Presidents Gamal Abdel Nasser and Anwar el-Sadat.

Egypt has a People's Assembly, consisting of 350 members, that is elected for five years and is the legislative body that approves general policy. Egypt also has a Shura Council, which consists of 210 members. The Shura Council is an advisory council that started in 1980. Members are chosen by election, and 70 of the members are chosen by the president.

The current constitution was approved by referendum on September 11, 1971. In June 1977, the People's Assembly adopted a new law on political parties. The law was passed in accordance with Article 5 of the constitution, which describes the political system as a multiparty one with five main parties: the ruling national Democratic Party, the Socialist Worker's Party, the Liberal Socialist's Party, Union Progressive, and the New Wafd Party established in 1984.

PRINT MEDIA

Newspapers

The history of the Egyptian press is the history of Egypt. Every political event and reform had its influence on the press. The Egyptian press was the first voice calling for independence, demanding education for the masses, and introducing Western thought and ideas.

The press in its modern sense was introduced to Egypt by Napoleon Bonaparte in 1798. He was also the first to issue the first publication's legislation on January 14, 1799, which was followed by another legislation on November 26, 1800, under General Mino. Mohammed Ali issued the first Egyptian newspaper in 1882, called *Al Waqai al-Misreya,* or the *Egyptian Events.*

A new era of the Egyptian press started in 1881, when the first Egyptian press law was formulated. The law consisted of 23 articles, the most important Article 13, which stated that "government authorities had the right to close down or confiscate a paper for violating public order, religion or morals." During this period, freedom of the press became a political issue of concern in Egypt, and the government attempted to protect the freedom of the press. With the beginning of the British Occupation, in 1882, the Egyptian press developed and flourished. During the time of the British Occupation, the Egyptian national press emerged. It started with the publication of *Al-Liwa'a* by Mustafa Kamil in 1900 and was followed by *Muayyad* and *Al-Garida* with their subsequent parties emerging. These papers continued emerging as a response to the British Occupation until 1914, when World War I began and brought along restrictions on the Egyptian press through martial laws. Many papers had to close down, and others lost their national spirit.

When, in 1919, some of the restrictions were lifted on the press, the press became a strong tool in encouraging the nationalist spirit of the revolution, in the same year asking for Egypt's independence and a constitution. In 1920, a press syndicate was established under King Fouad. The members of the syndicate were mainly publication owners, and it was generally inactive.

In 1923 Egypt saw its first constitution; the general scheme of the Egyptian Constitution, promulgated by a Royal Prescript in 1923, was that a cabinet drawn from the majority in Parliament would hold office as long as it retained the confidence of that majority. Such a state of affairs gave obvious scope for the creation and functioning of parties on the European model and for each to have a newspaper propagating its ideas.

During this period of parliamentary democracy between 1923 and 1952, power was distributed between the king, the Wafd, and the British. In some cases, minority parties and foreign interests came into the picture. There were many different points of view about the terms reached with Britain for Egypt's first constitution. The press participated fully in these discussions. Each party took its own line; each had newspapers publishing its news and views.

From 1923 until 1939, the Egyptian press largely enjoyed freedom. With the beginning of World War II, martial law was reimposed, which led to the disappearance of several papers. Those who survived could not express their opinions freely; censorship was imposed on all publications. Nevertheless, it was during this period that the anti-Wafd government *Black Book* was issued. Shortly after the end of World War II, in June 1945, censorship was lifted and martial laws abolished. Press censorship was reimposed in 1948 during the Palestine War. Several papers were suspended, but their editors soon came up with new papers through simply replacing the titles. This period of turmoil lasted until 1950, when martial laws were once again removed (El Bishiri, 1950).

The lifting of the censorship in 1950 led to a rapid growth of the radical and extreme nationalist press. The press for the following two years is characterized by some of the strongest press attacks against the government and the king. At the end of 1951, a united Egyptian press front had emerged. At the end of September 1951, the press openly called for a revolution (Janokouwski, 1975).

The second phase in the history of the Egyptian press, from 1952 to 1954, is marked by an unstable relationship of the political leaders to the press. During this period, censorship was imposed and lifted several times. The imposition of censorship was assigned to the Ministry of National Guidance. Censors were appointed for every newspaper. Whenever censorship was lifted, the press called for the restoration of freedom of the press and for the end of military control (Peretez, 1959). In 1954 the Revolutionary Command Council ordered the resolution of the Press Syndicate and appointed a ministerial committee headed by Salah Salem (Naguib, 1955).

From 1954 to 1960, several measures were taken by the government to integrate the press into the regime. In 1956, the Revolutionary Command Council was resolved, and a new constitution emerged. Article 25 of this constitution stated that the freedom of the press publications and copyright are safeguarded in the interest of public welfare and within the limits of law. In 1957, the Office of Censorship of Publications was established, and the government issued its own publications. In 1960, the press was nationalized under the Press Organization Law. The press was owned by the Arab Socialist Union, which after 1962 appointed a board of directors to control and manage the publication houses. Each paper had a board of directors, half of whom were appointed and half elected. The role of the media at this stage was to fully support the ideology of the state. The final breakdown in the credibility of the press occurred in 1967, when the press completely overestimated the military power in the Egyptian-Israeli War (Mansfield, 1963).

The latest era dates from the takeover of Sadat in 1970. The press during Sadat's reign could be categorized into two periods: before 1976, where every step taken by Sadat was reported in a positive view, and after 1976, when the opposition press emerged.

In the period before 1976, Sadat attempted to make up for the mistakes of Nasser. He tried to rebuild the people's faith in the army by raising their morale in the media. In 1973, Sadat introduced a set of policy reforms, including an opening toward the West. The 1971 constitution gave freedom to the press; he lifted the physical newspaper censorship. In 1974, Sadat removed all Soviet experts and Mohammed Heikal, the former confidant of Nasser and editor of *Al-Ahram,* Cairo's most influential newspaper. In 1975 the Supreme Press Council was established (Dabbous, 1985).

In 1980, Law 148 was issued, dealing with the authority of the press and the rights and responsibilities of the reporters. Sadat failed to provide the democratic atmosphere for the political parties to operate. By September 1981 all the opposition papers were closed, and many leaders of the opposing parties were imprisoned. The press in this period lost the degree of freedom it had enjoyed, turned instead into a state-controlled instrument for managing public opinion.

Mubarak has set free all the imprisoned leaders and given the opposition parties the freedom to operate again. There are now five major parties in Egypt, each publishing its own newspaper with circulations of 100,000 or more: Al-Ahrar (*Al-Ahrar,* weekly), Al-Wafd (*Al-Wafd,* daily), Al Tagamo'a (*Al-Ahali,* weekly), Al-Watani (*Mayo,* weekly), and the Socialist Labor Party (*Al-Sha'ab,* weekly). Because of a more efficient distribution network, the official newspapers—*Al-Akhbar, Akhbar al-Yom,* and *Al-Ahram*—sell many more, between 400,000 and 1 million copies a day. Other small party papers appear irregularly (Dabbous, 1992).

Although the political parties agree on the desire to see something done to solve the problems in Egypt, agreement is limited on the practical means of accomplishing it. Every party has its own program, and this difference is reflected in the way each party paper discusses aspects and incidents taking place in Egyptian society.

As of 1993, 263 licensed newspapers are published in Egypt: 38 by national publishing houses, 38 by government organs, 11 by political parties, 24 by unions and companies, 79 by individuals and professional societies, 12 by universities, 18 by social clubs and youth centers, 30 by provincial governments, 7 by the United Nations Educational, Scientific and Cultural Organization (UNESCO), and 6 by news agencies and embassies in Cairo.

ELECTRONIC MEDIA

Radio

Radio broadcasting in Egypt started in the 1920s with several private commercial stations, mostly located in Cairo. Some of them were named after the Royal family of Egypt, for example, Radio Farouk and Radio Princess Fawzya. Others had more general names such as Radio of Free Egypt or Egyptian Radio Magazine.

However, these stations were not very highly developed since they were set up in rooms or small flats. They were owned by groups of businessmen and financed by commercials. According to Douglas Boyd (1989), there were over 100 amateur wireless stations operating in this period. In addition, the merchants found themselves losing money because there were few radio sets at that time. Hence, radio stations in Egypt stopped operating on May 29, 1934. The government's stations began broadcasting on May 31, 1934.

The history of Egyptian radio can be divided into four stages:

Stage I (1934–1947). This stage is characterized by a ten-year renewable contract between the Marconi Coclea Company of the United Kingdom and the Egyptian government. Marconi Coclea then became responsible for operating it, on the condition that the programs would be free of direct or indirect commercials unless the government saw it necessary.

The system was financed by a license fee on receivers, with 60 percent to Marconi for the station's operation and the remaining 40 percent for the government. Although financially most of the country couldn't buy radio sets, listening increased in Egypt because merchants or owners of coffeeshops would have a set to attract customers. During this time, radio was run by the Ministry of Transportation. In 1939, it shifted to become the Ministry of Social Affairs with the operation of the Marconi Company.

However, under Marconi, Egyptian radio was largely influenced by Britain. During the Marconi stage, there were two main stations and the local European station. The main stations started with 14 hours of daily programming, while the local European station broadcast 4 hours daily, mainly entertainment programs in English and French for foreigners living in Egypt. The contract broke up in 1947 because Egyptians disliked the British policy for presenting news.

Stage II (1947–1952). The end of the Marconi contract marked the beginning of this stage. In 1947, the government took control of radio and the Ministry of Social Affairs became in charge of the broadcast operations. A major characteristic of this period is *Law 98* of 1949 which stated the rights and duties of Egyptian radio to include: monitoring of all broadcast stations, permitting new studios to open, encouraging program exchange among stations, allowing businesses to advertise products, and forming musical groups.

The law also stipulated that the language of the radio broadcasts be Arabic, Egypt's national language. This is in view of the fact that the earlier broadcasts, dating back to 1934, were in Arabic, French, and English. In 1950, the Egyptian radio inaugurated its first Arabic news department and introduced regularly scheduled news bulletins daily.

Stage III (1952–1981). Broadcasting greatly developed since the Revolutionary Command Council realized the importance of radio as a communication medium. Immediately after the revolution, radio was placed under the control of the Free Officers. After the Ministry of Information was established, broadcasting became autonomous by the formation of the Egyptian Radio and Television Federation. Nevertheless, control on TV and radio, as stated by Boyd (1989), "alternated, depending on political circumstances, between the Ministry of Information and the Office of the President."

An authorized study of radio programs during the first months after the revolution showed that Egyptian radio broadcast 51 interviews, 35 special programs, and 37 poems, supporting the revolution (Egyptian State Information Service, 1988). Group listening to radio was great in Egypt during the 1950s, especially among the lower classes. Radio listening became more popular because of the inexpensive battery-operated radios. According to UNESCO, 144 out of 1,000 people own radios. This is the highest ratio in Africa and an average ratio for the Middle East.

Stage IV (1981–). A new phase started in April 1981 with the application of a new specialized system called the Broadcasting Network System. With this network, Egyptian broadcasting consists of seven networks that broadcast about 85,033 hours during 1985–1986, with an average daily of 235 hours and 42 minutes (*Egyptian Radio and TV Yearbook, 1986–87*). The existing radio broadcasts in Egypt include:

- General Arabic or Main Program: Started May 31, 1934, it broadcasts programs in Arabic for both domestic and external (mainly the Arab World) audiences. The program is noncommercial and airs a wide range of programs including entertainment, cultural, educational, religious, and dramas.
- People's Program (Al Sha'ab): Started July 25, 1959, it is mainly an educational/instructional program intended for the working classes, addressing their problems and concerns, including illiteracy.
- Alexandria Program: Started July 26, 1954, as the first regional station in Egypt, it broadcasts a variety of entertainment, cultural, and educational programs for local audiences.
- Youth and Sports Program: Started September 1974, it broadcasts live coverage of sports and light cultural programs for the youth.
- Greater Cairo Program: Started April 1, 1981, it broadcasts programs, four hours daily, for mainly the residents of the Greater Cairo area.
- Middle Delta Program: A regional station, it broadcasts 54 hours per week for the residents of Delta towns: Monofia, Gharbeya, Dakahlia, Kafr, El Shiekh, and Domiata.
- North/Upper Egypt Program: This regional broadcast airs 28 hours per week for the residents of the rural areas.
- North Sinai Program: Started April 25, 1984, it serves the Sinai residents by broadcasting programs that help this previously Israeli occupied territory to be abreast of events in Egypt.
- Local European Program: Started in 1934, this cultural broadcast airs programs in six languages, including English and French, for the foreign residents in Egypt.
- Second Program: Started May 5, 1957, it is the main instructional station, offering a wide range of educational and cultural programs.
- Musical Program: Started March 1968, it broadcasts classical, light music, and folk songs.
- Holy Quran Program: Started March 29, 1964, it features readings from the Holy Quran, including discussions, interpretations, talks, and commentaries.
- Middle East Program: Started in 1964, it is a commercial station with a variety of programs intended for the Arabic-speaking countries in the Middle East.
- Voice of the Arabs: Started July 4, 1953, with the aim of strengthening Arab nationalism, and also reflecting Egyptian politics, it broadcasts programs, on two shortwave frequencies, 21 hours daily.
- Palestine Program: Started October 29, 1960, its programs, intended to deal with the Palestinian issues and problems, are carried by the Voice of the Arabs.
- Nile Valley Program (Wadi al-Nil): It originally began as Sudan Corner, in 1949, and was carried by the Main Program for half an hour per week. In 1954, it started broadcasting daily programs, in Sudanese, on a separate frequency from Cairo. By 1976, it

was broadcasting 22.6 hours daily. In 1984, the station changed its name to Nile Valley Program. The program is run as a joint venture by Egypt and Sudan.

Television

In 1959, the Egyptian government accepted an offer by the Radio Corporation of America (RCA) to establish a television broadcast facility. Hence, on July 21, 1960, at 7:00 P.M., the station (First Channel) went on the air with readings from the Quran, followed by a speech by President Gamal Abdel Nasser. After five broadcast hours, the station signed off at midnight.

The Second Channel began broadcast in July 1961. This channel presents cultural, informational, and instructional programs including programs about foreign cultures and civilizations.

Color television was introduced in Egypt in 1976, and by 1980, most Egyptians could receive the First Channel and Second Channel TV broadcasts clearly. Reportedly, in 1980, for a population of 45 million people, there were 2,971,545 TV sets. By 1983, there were 4,252,982 TV sets.

In terms of hours, in 1990, the First Channel's broadcasting reached 5,178 hours and 58 minutes, or about 14 hours and 11 minutes per day. This channel airs a variety of programs such as news, specials, religion, serials, and films aimed at a national audience.

On October 6, 1985, the Third Channel went on the air, broadcasting mainly locally produced programs in Cairo, Kalioubia, and Giza. In October 1988, the Fourth Channel was introduced to serve Port Said, Suez, and Ismailia; and in October 1990, the Fifth Channel opened to serve Alexandria. In addition to news, religion, cultural, and entertainment programs, these stations broadcast informational and instructional programs addressing local problems and issues.

In 1992, the total time of TV broadcasting reached 15,497 hours and 28 minutes, or about 44 hours and 28 minutes daily.

NEW TECHNOLOGIES

Satellite broadcasting in Egypt started as a cooperative venture between Egyptian TV and ARABSAT (Arab Satellite Communications Organization); hence, the Egyptian Satellite Channel (ESC), covering Africa, the Arab World, and the Mediterranean coast, went into operation, for the first time, in November 1990.

Egypt has established two new Earth Stations. The first, located in Maadi, receives six hours of programming daily from other countries—some of which are chosen for broadcast on Egyptian TV. Moreover, the first Egyptian satellite news station for receiving the Cable News Network's (CNN) programs, from the United States, was also established.

Although the main goals of ESC were to reach the remote areas within Egypt, it now serves the newly developed tourist areas and villages as well as companies, army, mining, and petroleum sites scattered throughout the nation. In fact, the Egyptian Radio and Television Union is negotiating an agreement with European Cable Television to receive its programs for broadcast on ESC *(Egyptian Radio and TV Yearbook, 1989–90).*

ESC also rebroadcasts the programs of the First Channel, including selected programs of the Second, Third, Fourth, and Fifth channels.

The second station, located in Moqattam, receives programs transmitted by the French channel CFI (Channel France International). The main purpose of this service is to increase the sources of foreign enlightenment. At the same time, it is a step toward a future plan for direct broadcasting to homes.

The Satellite News Service feeds the CNE (Egyptian News Channel). Egypt has joined the world of international news through an independent news channel operated by CNE, through the American CNN, transmitting news 24 hours daily via the International Telecommunication Satellite Consortium (INTELSAT). The CNN programs are broadcast on UHF and can be picked up by any TV set equipped with a decoder.

MOTION PICTURES

Historians have not agreed on the exact date when the first Egyptian movie was produced. Some say it was on January 27, 1896; others say it was on January 19, 1897. The first movie, according to cinema historians, was made by a foreigner known as Schneider. But some have declared that Egyptian movie history was started in 1900 at the Santy Cafe near Azbakia by two foreigners, Mr. and Mrs. Franschisco Botivily.

On November 16, 1927, the first Egyptian silent film, *Laila,* was shown. It had starred famous actress Aziz Amir together with a group of Egyptian theater stars. This film is generally considered to be the real starting point of the Egyptian cinema.

The most successful venture in the history of the Egyptian cinema was the silent movie *Zenab,* directed by Mohamed Karim—Egypt's most famous film director. *Zenab* was a great success when it was shown in the Metropole cinema on April 12, 1930.

The first film with voice was *Awlad al-Zawat,* shown on March 14, 1932. This film attracted many new audiences who were mostly illiterate and unable to read subtitles in silent film. One of the most successful films in the early years of spoken cinema was *Al Warda Al-Bida,* also directed by Mohamed Karim and starring Mohamed Abdel Wahab—Egypt's most famous singer. It was shown in the movie theaters for many years. In fact, its profits exceeded a quarter of a million Egyptian pounds of what was spent on producing the film.

In 1934, Talaat Harb, an Egyptian businessman, formed Misr Company for Acting and Cinema, which later became known as the Studio Misr. This was an important development in Egyptian cinema. The first film shot in this fully equipped studio was *Wedad,* starring Om Kalthoum—Egypt's most famous female singer. Several other musical films followed.

In 1945, a new era began in the history of the Egyptian cinema with the postwar films. Movie production increased because many producers were in pursuit of making profits and wealth; hence, they turned the art of moviemaking into a commercial venture. It was quantity and not quality that they looked for. For instance, the number of films produced in 1945–1946 jumped to 67 from 28 in 1944–1945 and from only 16 in 1943–1944 (Sharaf Al Din, 1990).

On August 8, 1952, Mohamed Naguib, the president of Egypt, issued a declaration for the film industry that included the following statement: "The cinema is a source of education, knowledge and entertainment. We must consider this because if we do not take this into consideration it will affect the young and make our standard go down." Therefore, from 1952 to 1962, the film industry entered a critical stage in its history. In this ten-year period, nearly 600 films (60 films per year) were produced. The most famous of these were *Allah Maana* (1955) and *Roda Qalby* (1957). Also, to encourage better-quality films, the Ministry of Culture held several film competitions, the first in 1955.

In 1963, a public sector film production known as the Cinema Institute was created. However, unable to compete with the local and international market, the institute failed to gain revenues and profits to cover its expenses; it folded in 1969. "The Egyptian cinema produced during the period of public sector 416 films, 50% of which were public sector productions, 40% private sector financed by the public sector, 10% produced by private sector financed by Lebanese and distributed by Arab companies" (Sharaf Al Din, 1990).

In the early 1960s the films focused on poverty, importance of education, the necessity of a socialist society, and abolishing class differences. By the late 1960s, the Egyptian cinema produced only 33 topical films. Among them were: 1 film about the problems of adolescence, 8 films about social and marital problems, 6 films about the everyday problems of actors and artists, and 4 mysteries, which were mostly failures.

After the 1967 war with Israel, Egyptian films turned their focus to entertainment, thereby assisting viewers in overcoming their losses and dealing with the country's defeat. The 1960s were known as the period of "Fear" (Sharaf Al Din, 1990). Censorship was so strong that Nasser himself had to watch the film *Some Fear* and approve it for public showing.

Under President Anwar el-Sadat, the movies soon forgot the war and began dealing with other subjects that were more profitable. The open-door period in the mid-1970s included a number of films, most of which were commercial and purely fictional or unrealistic. This was followed by films against the open-door policy. They were against economic and social practices and wanted to warn people about the corruption that was going on under the name of the open-door policy. Thirteen such films were shown in Egypt between 1975 and 1981.

Under President Hosni Mubarak, cinema has become a business depending on supply and demand. Also, a new social class has appeared, demanding a different taste in almost all arts. Since profit making is a very important aspect of the cinema business, producers tailor their films to meet the demands of this new audience. In general, this narrow perspective has contributed to the deterioration in many recent films (El-Fowal, 1990).

MEDIA OWNERSHIP AND REGULATION

The Egyptian media in general, and the press in particular, has undoubtedly had a long history of struggling to maintain its power and influence on policy-making, especially during its nationalization under Nasser's regime. Although, according to the existing rules, political parties as well as religious and private persons are free to publish newspapers in Egypt, the press still faces major problems such as state ownership; state control of a large number of the national newspapers, including the broadcast media; and the problem of differing interpretations of the laws and regulations concerning the media.

Radio became government owned and operated, and power was passed into the hands of the Ministry of Social Affairs in 1947. This stage is mainly characterized by Egyptian control of radio. A major characteristic of this stage is Law 98 of 1949 that stated the rights and duties of Egyptian radio as monitoring all Egyptian stations, permitting studios to open, exchanging programs, allowing parties, selling its products, and forming musical groups.

In 1963, Presidential Decree 2958 was issued, putting the Egyptian broadcasting organization under the control of the Ministry of National Guidance. This was followed by three laws that transferred the Egyptian broadcasting organization to the Radio and TV Union, an apparatus theoretically independent from the government.

EXTERNAL MEDIA SERVICES

External broadcast services began in 1953 to propagate the Egyptian viewpoints around the world. A variety of political, cultural, and entertainment programs are aired, via shortwave, on a number of radio stations, including the Voice of the Arabs, General Arabic Programs, Second Program, Middle East Program, Quran Program, and People's Program. Broadcasts are in 34 languages, including Albanian, Arabic, Bengali, English, French, German, Hindi, Indonesian, Italian, Persian, Portuguese, Pushtu, Spanish, Thai, Turkish, and a number of other languages (*World Radio-TV Handbook,* 1992, p. 145). Program content consists of news, music, and cultural and informational items. In addition, Egyptian radio has established an Arabic news department for the dissemination of news and information throughout the Arab World.

NEWS AGENCIES

The Middle East News Agency (MENA) is the major news provider in Egypt responsible for the dissemination and control of national news. MENA is owned by the government and is a semiofficial enterprise under the jurisdiction of the

Ministry of Information. MENA started functioning February 28, 1956. In 1978, the ownership of MENA was moved to the Shura Council. In 1980, a board of directors was chosen to run the organization.

Before MENA was established, the Arab News Agency (ANA) was founded in 1936. But ANA only translated news from Reuters into Arabic. MENA was first established as a private organization in which Egyptian subscribers bought shares. "In January 1962, the agency became the property of the state, and it became part of the General Egyptian organization for news and publications" (Dajani, 1980). Although MENA originally started with only 40 employees, today it employs over 1,200, 400 of whom are journalists (Middle East News Agency, [MENA] 1989).

MENA exchanges news with approximately 25 news agencies and relays 40,000 words on its local Arabic report; 35,000 words on its overseas Arabic report; 25,000 words on its English report; 15,000 words on its French report; and 44,000 words on its economic cast in English (MENA, 1989). Several Arab news agencies relay their reports, in Arabic, through MENA. These are the Qatary News Agency, the Omani News Agency, and the Saudi News Agency (Dajani, 1980). MENA has an agreement with all Arab countries to transmit to them, and while MENA has Arab subscribers, no fees are charged to the information service of any other Arab country (Dajani, 1980).

MENA started publishing the *Cairo Press Review* on April 9, 1956. This review provides a daily image and translation of the most important editorials and articles appearing in the Egyptian press. The review is published in English in order to make it possible for diplomats and foreign correspondents in Egypt to be up-to-date with the news published in the Egyptian press. MENA also publishes the *Party Press Review,* which translates into English the news published by the opposition party papers that appear in Egypt.

MENA offers training programs for those interested in journalism. It also has training courses for wireless staffers, administrators, engineers, accountants, maintenance, and operators. MENA is supposed to earn an annual budgetary allocation from the Ministry of Information, but the agency tends to rely more and maintain itself through contracts with Agence France-Presse and Reuters in addition to its television service and photo exchange service (MENA, 1989).

CONCLUSION

The stages of the evolution of the Egyptian media reflect the turbulence, the changes, and the different landmarks the rulers of Egypt have left behind. Egypt has moved from a kingdom to a republic, and from a most liberal regime to an autocratic leadership followed by attempts by both Presidents Sadat and Mubarak to allow a spark of freedom to ignite. With the fast technological revolution in media, the flow of information knows no cultural, political, and national boundaries.

Under President Hosni Mubarak, the opposition press is probably at its highest level of freedom since the fall of the monarchy in 1953 (*IPI Report,* July 1983). Mubarak was responsible for restoring the limited liberalization suspended by Sadat in 1981 and allowed the opposition press to publish. Mubarak even allowed the New Wafd to be readmitted to the legitimate party system, showing real signs of strength and flexibility to the nation (Hinnenbusch, 1985).

The circulation of the opposition press has rapidly grown during Mubarak's period. The present situation of the Egyptian press shows a substantial improvement in freedom but not an unlimited one, as the constitution states: "an independent popular authority, performing its duties in the manner prescribed by law."

However, Mubarak has restored to the media a moderate code of liberation that can be seen as the starting point for a long-term perspective on media development in Egypt. The relationship of the mass media with political power has always, in almost every country, been looked upon with the utmost importance. All news travels through these channels, and without an open channel, a country's political stability cannot be fully guaranteed.

REFERENCES

Boyd, D. (1989). *Broadcasting in the Arab World: A survey of radio.* Philadelphia, PA: Temple University Press.

Dabbous, S. (1985, November). *The role of the press in Egypt's democratic experiment.* Paper presented at the Middle East Studies Association meeting, New Orleans, LA.

Dabbous, S. (1992). Comparisons of national and opposition press coverage. In R. E. Weinsenborn (Ed.), *Media in the midst of war: The Gulf War from Cairo to global village.* Cairo, Egypt: Adham Center Press.

Dajani, K. F. (1980). *Egypt's role as a major media producer, supplier, and distributor to the Arab World: A historical descriptive study.* Unpublished doctoral dissertation, University of Michigan, Ann Arbor.

Egyptian Radio and TV Yearbook. (Various years). Egyptian State Information Service Mass Media in Egypt (1988). *Yesterday, today and tomorrow.* Egypt: State Information service.

El Bishiri, T. (1950). *Al Harakah Al Syasiah fi Masr: 1945–1952.* Cairo Egypt.

El-Fowal, N. (1990). *Gomhour el-cinema* [A study of cinema audience in Egypt]. Cairo, Egypt: State Information Office.

Hinnenbusch, R. A., Jr. (1985). *Egyptian politics under Sadat.* Cambridge, England: Cambridge University Press.

IPI Report. (1981, December–January). Cairo, Egypt: State Information Service.

IPI Report. (1983, July). Cairo, Egypt: State Information Service.

IPI Report. (1986, December). Cairo, Egypt: State Information Service.

Janokouwski, J. (1975). *Egypt's young rebels.* Stanford, CT: Stanford University Press.

Mansfield, P. (1963). *Nasser's Egypt.* London: Penguin African Library.

Middle East News Agency (MENA). (1989). *MENA report 30 years in the media.* Cairo, Egypt: MENA.

Naguib, M. (1955). *Egypt's destiny.* London: Victor Gollancz Ltd.

Peretez, D. (1959, Winter). Democracy and the revolution in Egypt. *Middle East Journal, 13.*

Sharaf Al Din, D. (1990). *The history of the Egyptian cinema.* Cairo, Egypt: State Information Service.

State Information Service. (1992). *Press in Egypt: Laws and regulations.* Cairo, Egypt.

World radio-TV handbook. (1992). Amsterdam, The Netherlands: Billboard AG.

6

IRAN

Abbas Malek and Mehdi Mohsenian Rad

INTRODUCTION

Iran, or Persia until the early twentieth century, is one of the oldest nations in the world, having been founded more than 4,000 years ago by a group of Aryans who settled Asia Minor. Since its establishment, Iran has witnessed a succession of great dynasties including the Achaemenids (500–330 B.C.), the Sassanians (A.D. 226–650), and the Safavides (1500–1722). Under the Achaemenids, the Persian government ruled over a vast portion of the civilized world, including territory from eastern India and South Asia to North Africa, the shores of the Balkan Sea, and the entire Balkan area to Greece. At the time, the empire managed to maintain a functional communication system across its vast territories (Safa, 1976, pp. 1–6). Presently, however, Iran covers 1,648,195 square kilometers of Middle Eastern territory and is bordered by two former Soviet republics (Azerbaijan and Tajikistan) and the Caspian Sea in the north, Afghanistan and Pakistan in the east, Turkey and Iraq in the west, and the Persian Gulf and the Gulf of Oman in the south. The country is divided into 24 *ostan* (provinces), 195 *shahrestan* (districts), 513 *shahr* (cities), 602 *bakhsh* (towns), 2,100 *dehestan* (villages), and 104,000 *abadi* (hamlets). Tehran, with nearly one-fifth of the country's population, is the capital city, and Mashhad, Isfahan, Tabriz, Shiraz, Kermanshah, Ghom, Oroomieh, and Rasht are among the most populous cities in Iran (*Salnameh Amari Iran,* 1991).

As part of a mountainous region, Iran's average altitude is 1,200 meters, with its highest point being Mount Damovand (4,000 meters); however, it also possesses elevations as low as only 56 meters above sea level. Iran consists of two major mountain ranges in the east and the west surrounding the central plateau deserts of Dasht-e-Kavir and Dasht-e-Lut. Although Iran is known for its moderate Mediterranean weather, the various regions demonstrate the diversity of the Iranian climate. In the north, along the Caspian Sea, the climate is moderate and humid, while the central areas of Dasht-e-Kavir and Dasht-e-Lut are mostly dry with warmer temperatures. The western and eastern parts of the country, however, experience the four seasons with warm to hot summers and cool to cold winters (Mahmoodi, 1991).

According to the 1991 census, Iran is the most populous Middle Eastern country, with a population of 58,110,227. The population is 57 percent and 43 percent urban and rural, respectively. In addition, Iran has one of the highest ratios of young people in the world, as 45.5 percent of the population are under the age of 15 (*Salnameh Amari Iran,* 1991, pp. 42–43).

Public education and literacy are old features of Iranian society, illustrated by the numerous ancient libraries currently being discovered in the country. Before A.D. 1219, for instance, there were 144 libraries in Iran, of which 56 were purely educational, while the rest were for public use. There also existed an extensive court library system, one of which consisted of over 162,400 volumes. Most of these libraries, however, were destroyed by invaders such as Genghis Khan and the Arabs (Pasargard, 1970).

Iranians are predominantly Shiite Muslims, and one of the unique characteristics of the Iranian culture is its religious practices and the role of public places, such as mosques, and the influence they have on public interaction and communication. Traditionally, it has been in mosques that members of the public engaged in both religious practice and social discourse. Indeed, architecturally, mosques were designed for large numbers of people to participate in ceremonies. In 1612, for example, there was a mosque in Isfahan architecturally designed for a speaker to reach more than 1,000 audience members at a time. Religious leaders used these forums to disseminate their religious and social messages. For that purpose, mosques still play a central role in social communication, since they can easily accommodate large audiences at any time (Mohsenian Rad, 1990).

In a 1979 national referendum, the overwhelming majority of Iranians voted in favor of adopting an Islamic republic form of government and thus brought more than 4,000 years of a monarchical system of government to an end. The 1979 constitution divided the government into three branches: executive, legislative, and judicial. The executive branch is headed by the president, elected by universal adult suffrage for a period of four years. The legislature consists of 170 representatives (deputies) elected directly by the people—males and females—over 16 years of age for a period of four years. The deputies serve in the Majlis (congress), which is required by the constitution to broadcast all of its sessions by at least one national radio network. The judicial branch, composed predominantly of religious leaders, monitors all laws and regulations in order to ensure compliance with Islamic laws. All three branches of the government function under the leadership of one grand ayatollah, Velayat-e-Fagih, who is the commander in chief and the highest authority in the country (*Ghanoon Asasi Jomhoori-e-Islami-e-Iran,* 1992).

PRINT MEDIA

Traditionally, the Iranian culture has been an oral culture. Most of the literature and traditions have been transmitted from generation to generation through readings in public and private places. This tradition continued even after the invasion of Iran by the Arabs and imposition of Islam on the Iranian society. Some classical works (the *Shahnameh,* which is almost a thousand years old) are still being recited by orators in public teahouses in many parts of the country. Despite a strong oral tradition, there is some evidence that writing in some form has been practiced in Iran for over 3,000 years (Mohsenian Rad, 1990, pp. 496–497). As recently as 1992, in an ancient southern city, Zabul (referred to as "The Burned City" in Persian literature), archeological discoveries are providing evidence of the practice of writing in ancient Iran (*Kayhan,* 1992).

The first book in Iran to use modern print technology was printed in 1638 and was the first book ever published in the Middle East (*Majaleh Sanaat,* 1991, p. 2). The printing machine, which used copper letters, was built by Iranian artisans who designed it solely based on what they had heard about the printing press that was first developed in Europe. The book was a 570-page religious book published by an Armenian church in Julfa, Isfahan, in the Armenian language. It was not until 1818, however, that the first book in Farsi was published in Iran (*Majaleh Sanaat,* 1991, p. 59).

Newspapers

The newspaper in Iran is a nineteenth-century phenomenon, with the first newspaper being published in 1837 in Tehran (Mowlana, 1978, p. 45). Since the beginning, newspapers have been vital tools, due to their utility to Iranian leaders in the dissemination of political and social opinions. Newspapers played an influential role in Iran's two major revolutions: the Constitutional Revolution of 1906 and the Islamic Revolution of 1979. During and after both revolutions, the newspapers in Iran enjoyed tremendous popularity and growth. In the 1906 revolution, newspapers played a very active and important role in social and political mobilization through their use by revolutionary leaders (Mohsenian Rad, 1992). During the Islamic Revolution and immediately after, the country witnessed an unprecedented freedom in what newspapers could publish and growth in their number. For the first time, after more than a half century, newspapers felt free to publish without prior restraints or fear from the government. In short, the country witnessed a major growth in number, diversity, and freedom in newspapers, and to some extent, if not the freedom, the number and diversity

Table 6.1
Publication Places for Newspapers: Iran

Place	No.of Newspapers
Tehran	55
Isfahan	7
East Azerbaijan (Tabriz)	6
Khorasan (Mashhad)	4
Markazi	4
Gheelan (Rasht)	3
Mazandaran	3

Source: Compiled based on data in Mohsenian Rad, 1992.

continue today. Some newspapers in Iran have been in existence for over 60 years, though the majority have come into existence within the past 10 years. In fact, 86.5 percent of all existing newspapers were born after the Islamic Revolution of 1979.

Currently, 85 newspapers are in publication in Iran, of which 20 are dailies. The largest circulations belong to the two major dailies, *Kayhan* and *Ettela'at,* with circulations of 500,000 and 400,000, respectively. Both are published in Tehran and distributed nationally. Other major nationally distributed papers include *Salam, Abrar,* and *Resalat,* which are also published in Tehran. In general, over 68 percent of the country's newspapers are published in Tehran. After Tehran, the largest numbers of newspapers in the country are published in Isfahan, East Azerbaijan, Khorasan, Markazi, Gheelan, and Mazandaran (see Table 6.1).

Although Farsi is the official language in Iran, 15 percent of all newspapers are published in other languages, such as Arabic, English, Armenian, Turkish (Azari, Istanbully, and Russian), and Urdu. In addition, there are a few bilingual newspapers printed in Farsi/Arabic, Farsi/Turkish, and Farsi/English.

Iranian newspapers enjoy a relatively high readership in major cities. One recent survey in Tehran found that 14.5 percent of the surveyed people 16 years and older mentioned that they read newspapers regularly, while 20.8 percent read most of the time, 28.8 percent sometimes, and 21.9 percent rarely (several times in a month); only 14 percent of the surveyed population mentioned that they never read newspapers. In addition, the survey found a direct correlation between the level of education, age, and sex of the reader and the degree of

Table 6.2
Iranian Magazine Subject Categories

Subject	Percentage
Human and social affairs	28.5
General scientific	13.0
Vocation	12.4
Popular	10.6
General health & Medicine	7.7
Children and adolescents	5.8
Arts	5.8
Religion	4.1
Sports	3.6
Women	2.3
Agriculture	2.3
Funnies	1.7
Specialized	1.7
Ethnics	.5

Source: Compiled based on data in Mohsenian Rad, 1992.

newspaper readership. For example, the more educated, male, and older the audience, the more frequently newspapers are read (Sohrabzadeh & Asadi, 1990, pp. 29–31).

Magazines

Presently in Iran, 345 magazines are being published. They are divided into several categories based on the subjects they cover (see Table 6.2). The largest share belongs to the category of human and social affairs (covering subjects

Table 6.3
Top Iranian Magazine Circulation

Title	Circulation
Sports	153,000
Popular	132,000
General scientific	82,000
Women	70,000
Agriculture	70,000
Children	60,000

Source: Compiled based on data in Mohsenian Rad, 1992.

such as literature, law, political economy issues, and history). The second largest category of magazines is targeted at the upper middle class with relatively high educational backgrounds and covers issues such as general scientific subjects. The third highest percentage of magazines are mostly technical and vocational magazines. The fourth largest category is popular entertainment. After these, magazine subjects in publication may be broken down as follows: general health and medicine, children and adolescents, the arts, religion, sports, women, agriculture, funnies, specialized magazines for the armed forces, and finally, magazines dealing with ethnic topics for different tribal and minority groups.

Sports magazines, although only composing 3.6 percent of all Iranian magazines, have the largest circulation; the second largest circulation belongs to the popular magazines, while the third largest includes more general scientific and informational magazines. Women's magazines have a circulation of 70,000, as do the agricultural (farmer) magazines written for inhabitants of villages and hamlets. Children and adolescents magazines have the smallest circulation among all general magazines with large circulation in Iran (see Table 6.3). In general, the more highly specialized magazines usually publish around 1,000 copies per issue.

As is the case with newspapers, Tehran remains the major publication center, since over 90 percent of all magazines are published in the nation's capital. In contrast, however, the history of Iranian magazine publication appears to be shorter than that of newspapers. The average age for a magazine in Iran is about seven years. While 81 percent of all newspapers are in Farsi, only 74 percent of magazines are published in Farsi. Eighteen percent of all the magazines are in Farsi/English, 1.4 percent are in English, and the remainder are in French, Arabic, Kurdish, and the special languages for visually handicapped people.

In the previously mentioned survey in Tehran, 17 percent of the people stated that they read magazines regularly, 30.1 percent read them often, and 31.4 percent read them occasionally (Sohrabzadeh & Asadi, 1990, p. 38). Therefore, less than half of the surveyed population in Tehran rarely or never read magazines. Unlike the case of newspaper readership, a negative correlation exists between age and magazine readership. Magazines seem to be more popular among younger Iranians than any other age group, while newspapers attract an older audience. However, the older the readers, the higher the interest level in more scientific and technical magazines (Sohrabzadeh & Asadi, 1990, p. 68).

ELECTRONIC MEDIA

Radio

Prior to the establishment of the first radio station in Iran in 1940, only a very narrow segment of the economic and political elite owned radios and were able to listen to foreign broadcasts. At the time, the only signals that could be received in Iran were from the British Broadcasting Corporation (BBC), Germany, France, Italy, Egypt, and the Soviet Union. In 1938, one of the major newspapers in Iran, *Ettela'at,* even began to list the BBC's nightly schedules and promised its readers that soon it would list other foreign broadcasts such as Radio Berlin, Paris, Rome, and Cairo (Mohsenian Rad, 1990, pp. 501–502).

By 1938, however, the government also began the process of establishing an Iranian radio system, with the main objective of creating a system that could handle national communication needs, as well as provide radio programs to the public (*Majaleh Radio Iran,* 1964, p. 1). The first Iranian radio station was inaugurated on August 24, 1940. The first series of transmitters consisted of 10 and 20 kilowatts and 2 kilowatts shortwaves/medium waves. Between 1940 and 1942, Iranian radio was able to stay on the air only four hours a day (*Majaleh Radio Iran,* 1963, p. 26).

During the early stages of operation of radio (1940–1942), the Ministry of Post, Telephone, and Telegraph (PTT) supervised the operation of the radio system in Iran (*Tamasha,* 1976). After undergoing some shifts and changes in supervision and operation, it later came under the Director General of Publications and Propaganda, attached to the Prime Minister's Office. In 1946, after the establishment of a new Ministry of Information and the incorporation of the old department of the General Director of Publications and Propaganda, Radio Iran was placed under the supervision of the new ministry (*Tamasha,* 1976).

In 1971, the government formed an independent national organization to run the Iranian Television (ITV) system. The same organization in 1975 was expanded to include the national radio system and was given a new name, the

National Iranian Radio and Television (NIRT). NIRT was the sole governmental institution in charge of broadcasting in Iran until the Islamic Revolution in 1979. After the victory of the Islamic Revolution, the NIRT was restructured and renamed the Voice and Profile of the Islamic Republic (VPIR). It is an independent governmental institution that operates under a broad body consisting of representatives of all three branches of government. In other words, the electronic media system is an intergovernmental agency.

After its introduction, it did not take long until radio became a popular medium that occupied a very important place within Iranian society. Among the reasons for radio's fast popularity and growth in Iran was its entertainment potential. But probably the most important reason was the convenience of radio as a means for the government to disseminate news and information. "[I]n a country as vast and heterogeneous as Iran, radio was clearly the most effective means for reaching the people and soon became an indispensable instrument for political struggles for power" (Tehranian, Hakinzadeh, and Vidale, 1977, p. 258). Tabriz, in the northeastern part of Iran, was the first city after Tehran in which radio broadcasting became operational in 1946. By 1971, there were 30 radio broadcasting stations in 30 different cities in Iran (*Ettela'at,* 1976, p. 14). The extent of the radio's popularity was so high that, as one writer put it: "If the radio doesn't broadcast one day, the people feel that they have lost one of their closest relatives" (*Tamasha,* 1976).

Until 1950, all radio programs in Iran were live broadcasts. As a result, broadcasting was limited to several hours daily. After 1950, when recorded programs became available, broadcasting hours were expanded. By 1960 Iranian radio was broadcasting 24 hours a day (*Majaleh Radio Iran,* 1964). In 1991, there were 138 operational radio broadcasting centers, of which 70 broadcast on an AM (amplitude modulation) medium band (12 high-, 14 medium-, and 44 low-power stations) and 68 broadcast on an FM (frequency modulation) band (26 high-, 8 medium-, and 34 low-power stations) (Ravabeteh Omoomieh Seda va Symayeh Iran, 1991, p. 56).

The government needs radio to reach the public, especially in isolated areas. This fact has been a dominant factor in the growth of radio. Geography, the size of the country, and the socioeconomic status of the majority of the population are among the factors contributing to this phenomenon. For example, in 1962 there were 70 radio receivers for every 1,000 individuals, while the number of newspapers per 1,000 did not exceed 15 (Elahi, Motamed Nezad, and Mohsenian Rad, 1973, p. 12). In 1981, there were 155 radio sets for every 1,000 population, and the ratio increased to 224 per 1,000 by 1985 (Mohsenian Rad, 1990, p. 504). It is estimated that in 1992 there exists at least 1 radio set for each family in Iran.

There are two major national radio networks in Iran, the First and the Second National Radio networks. In 1990, the Iranian radio system broadcast a total of 49,124 hours of programming. The First National Radio Network broadcast 8,842 hours, and the Second National Radio Network broadcast 982 hours, while

Table 6.4
Programming in the First National Radio Network: Iran

Type of Programs	%	Type of Programs	%
Cultural and Social	16.8	Music	12.9
News	12.9	Islamic Education	11.3
Arts and Literature	8.4	Entertainment	6.3
Sports	6.1	Koran and call prayer	5.6
How to do Programs	4.8	Economics	4.0
General Informational	3.0	Political discussions	3.8
Historical discussions	2.1	Defense	1.3
Friday Prayer	.7		

Source: Ravabeteh Omoomieh Seda va Symayeh Iran, 1991.

the rest, 39,300 hours, was broadcast by 27 other broadcasting centers across the country (Ravabeteh Omoomieh Seda va Symayeh Iran, 1991).

The First National Radio Network broadcasts widely diverse programming, as shown in Table 6.4. In contrast, the main responsibility of the Second National Radio Network, as is required by the constitution, is to directly broadcast parliamentary sessions, whether live or taped. Out of 981 hours of programming on this network, 481 hours (49 percent) revolved around the debates in Parliament. The rest were: 24.5 percent religious education, 16.2 percent direct broadcast from the Friday Prayer ceremonies, and 10.3 percent music (Ravabeteh Omoomieh Seda va Symayeh Iran, 1991, pp. 6–9).

Of the programming broadcast on the Iranian radio networks during 1990, more than 18 percent was directed to minority ethnic groups. Of this, 4.7 percent was news, while the remainder was on a variety of issues concerning each target group. The majority of these programs were in Arabic, especially in the south. Other minority programs were directed to and broadcast for the Kurds in the western provinces, including Kermanshah Kurdish, Oroomieh Kurdish, Turkoman in the north, Baluchi in the east, and other minority groups. Even among one ethnic group, such as the Kurds, several languages of programming are required to accommodate everyone (Ravabeteh Omoomieh Seda va Symayeh Iran, 1991).

There are three radio stations that broadcast nothing but recitation from the Holy Book, the Quran. One major new characteristic of Iranian radio programming after the revolution is that two kinds of music are forbidden: (1) any kind of music sung by a solo woman singer, not a group, since this is considered against Islamic rules, and (2) Western popular music. This exclusion of Western music has resulted in the growth and reintroduction of traditional Iranian music with emphasis on male singers. All in all, the new characteristic of the Iranian radio is one of ''Islamization'' of its broadcasts. This new format, not surprisingly, is very religious oriented and almost free of all foreign programs.

Television

In contrast to radio, television in Iran was introduced as a private enterprise. Television in Iran was established as two low-power stations using ten- and three-kilowatt transmitters in Tehran (1958) and Abadan (1960). These two stations were privately owned, commercial ventures of a wealthy Harvard-educated Iranian entrepreneur, Iraj Sabet, who had also introduced Pepsi-Cola to the country and later an RCA (Radio Corporation of America) television manufacturing industry (Mowlana, 1989).

Commercial television in Iran, however, did not last long. In 1971 a newly established governmental organization, Iranian Television, nationalized the television industry and ended commercial television operation in the country. By 1975, ITV expanded to include the national radio operation in a governmental body called the National Iranian Radio and Television. After the revolution in 1979, the NIRT further evolved to reflect, both structurally and functionally, the new sociopolitical structure of the new Iranian society. The NIRT was changed to Voice and Profile of the Islamic Republic as the first step in the process.

Before the revolution, television in Iran, as in many developing countries, was dominated by imported programs from the West, especially the United States. Western music, for example, occupied 13 times as much airtime as traditional Iranian music (Asadi & Mehrdad, 1975, p. 49). Western soap operas and sitcoms were the main part of prime time every night. In 1976, for instance, for every show produced domestically, there were three imported shows being broadcast on television. Ninety-nine out of 100 movies shown on television were imported and dubbed (Aminpour, 1976, p. 9). Overall, television was filled with American movies, soap operas, and sitcoms. ''There were no religious programs on television and the Shah's so-called 'White Revolution' was designed to make Iran a secular society modelled on Europe and the United States'' (Mowlana, 1989, p. 17).

The change in political and social thinking after the Islamic Revolution of 1979 began to appear in other media, newspapers and even radio, much sooner than it did in television, primarily because it was financially and technically harder and more complex to alter than other media. For television, these changes needed time, organization, and extensive financial and human resources. After all, for over a quarter of a century, the NIRT had accumulated an extensive archive of foreign material. The new VPIR had to replace the entire collection, in addition to implementing changes in thinking and production needed to reflect an Islamic philosophy. As a result, in the early days of the revolution, the only alternative for television was a drastic reduction in broadcasting hours until appropriate programming could be produced. Furthermore, eight years of war with Iraq added to the difficulties and even impeded this restructuring process. A combination of these factors resulted in a very slow start for Iranian television during the first decade following the revolution.

Although the transition was slow, the new Iranian television emerged with a new type of programming that is very different from the type that existed prior to the revolution. The difference can be seen not only in domestic versus foreign programs but in the type of programs as well. In 1990, Iranian television broadcast 12,262 hours of programming from two major national networks and 21 local stations across the country. Some 2,948 hours of these programs (24 percent) were broadcast from the First National Radio Network, 2,398 hours (19.5 percent) were broadcast by the Second National Radio Network, and 6,915 hours (56.4 percent) were from local production that was produced and broadcast by 21 television stations in the country (Ravabeteh Omoomieh Seda va Symayeh Iran, 1991, pp. 30–40).

Considering the number of stations in the country, 21 broadcasting centers, it should be noted that an average local production did not exceed 329 hours (54 minutes daily) per television station in 1990. Therefore, the dependency on, and the importance of, centralized network programming is obvious. In short, except for the time when local stations are broadcasting a locally produced program, which is less than an hour per day, they carry signals from one of the two major networks.

Presently, 85.3 percent of all television programs are produced domestically (Ravabeteh Omoomieh Seda va Symayeh Iran, 1991, p. 62). This change is significant in the orientation of broadcasting in the country. Before the revolution, the trend was the reverse with an imported to domestic program ratio of 3:1. As one writer put it, "It was precisely this sort of program that was contributing, among other things, to the alienation of the Iranians, thereby sowing the seeds of the revolution" (Mowlana, 1989, p. 37).

In 1990, 81.3 percent of all television shows were recorded on film or video, while the rest were live programs. Seventy-three percent of all broadcast shows were first-run, and the rest were repeated shows. Movies and concerts compose the majority of reruns on television. Almost all television programs in Iran were produced in color (Ravabeteh Omoomieh Seda va Symayeh Iran, 1991, p. 80).

Like radio, television programming and production are prepared within the framework of Islamic intent. There are no movies or programs with love scenes such as the ones that are commonly shown in the West. All the imported programs are closely monitored and reviewed for "un-Islamic" scenes, which are edited out or not shown at all if they cannot be "corrected."

Table 6.5 summarizes the types of programming produced and broadcast on Iranian television during 1990.

The most watched television programs are movies. Fifty-six percent of the

Table 6.5
Domestic TV Program Productions, 1990: Iran

Program Type	Percentage
Children and adolescents	16.4
Social and cultural	14.9
News	14.4
General educational	10.4
Islamic education	8.7
Sports	8.4
Skill and how to do	5.1
Koran and call for prayer	4.9
Entertainment	3.7
Arts and literature	3.4
Political	2.1
Defense	1.3
Economics	1.1
Advertising	1.0
Historical	.4
Others	3.8

Source: Ravabeteh Omoomieh Seda va Symayeh Iran, 1991.

viewers in Tehran mentioned that they always or most of the time watch movies on television. The next most watched programs on television were popular sitcoms (entertainment) and the news, with 34 percent and 31 percent of the audience, respectively (*Salam,* 1992).

As far as imported programs are concerned, the Islamic government has made a conscious effort to avoid reverting to the old, prerevolutionary types of programming. ''Gone are the US- and Western-style products. *Dynasty* and *Dallas* are unknown names to the Iranian audience. Hollywood products in general are scarce in the electronic media'' (Mowlana, 1989, p. 38). Therefore, the United States has almost completely disappeared as a major provider and source of programming for Iranian television. Japan, England, and Germany are now among the major sources of imported programming. As a matter of fact, one Japanese show, *Oshin,* became one of the most popular shows in Iranian television.

As a member of the International Telecommunication Satellite Consortium (INTELSAT), Iran has access to major international events. In the summer of 1992, for example, some of the Olympic Games were broadcast both live and taped. However, certain events such as women's swimming and gymnastics were kept off the air, due to their incompatibility with Islamic codes.

MOTION PICTURES

The introduction of still photography to Iran is credited to one of the Qjar kings, Nasser-al-Din Shah (1831–1895) (Estayn, 1989, p. 13). In the king's personal documents, 20,000 still pictures are believed to represent the first practice of photography in Iran during the late nineteenth century. Nasser-al-Din Shah's son and successor, Mozaffar-al-Din Shah, observed scenes being filmed with the newly developed cinematograph during a trip to Contrexeville, France. The shah ordered his personal photographer, Mirza Ebrahim, to purchase the equipment and learn how to operate it. After returning home, the photographer was ordered to film the lions in the royal zoo. This filming is believed to be the first shot in Iran (Gaffary, 1990). Among the first screening, exclusively for members of the court and royal family, were films about a carnival (filmed in France) and a religious ceremony (filmed in Tehran).

The first public demonstration of the newly imported kinescope came in 1906. It was installed in a dark area where people could insert a coin to watch a two- to three-minute action film. In 1908, two years later, the first public theater capable of seating 200 was inaugurated (Mehrabi, 1983, pp. 14–15). Regularly scheduled short film screening, however, did not occur until 1913. Almost all the movies shown were French movies. As a part of an entertainment package, ''on busy days the performances were accompanied by a piano and a violin, and refreshments appropriate for the season were served'' (Gaffary, 1990).

In 1921, the first long and still silent film was produced in Iran. Twelve years later (1933), the sound movie entitled *Dokhtar-e-Lur* was presented, and a new film industry was born. From the beginning, the newly born domestic industry, however, had a difficult time competing with the more technically advanced and better-produced imported films. At the same time, the public appetite for imported films seemed to reduce the incentive to produce domestic movies. Therefore, the majority of theaters screened foreign films. This trend continued for over a half century. In 1947, for example, the industry produced only 2 films;

Table 6.6
Number of Theaters in Iran

Year	Number
1963	112
1968	122
1973	432
1978	453
1979	198
1986	247
1990	273

Source: Compiled based on data in Asadi & Mehrdad, 1975; Mohsenian Rad, 1992.

the number increased to 20 in 1952, 30 in 1962, and 88 films in 1971. Even this very slow growth, however, was not sustained, since by 1977 the total number of domestic films dropped to 50, while movie theaters showed 504 foreign films during the same period (Asadi & Mehrdad, 1975, p. 85).

Despite this slow growth in the film industry, there was a steady growth in the number of theaters in Iran. As is illustrated in Table 6.6, in five years (1968 to 1973) the number of theaters more than tripled. This growth continued until 1978, when the revolutionary movement began to act against and hinder the existing motion picture structure.

During the uprising of 1978–1979, movie theaters were perceived as a symbol of Western domination responsible for the moral decay of Islamic society. Theaters were among the first targets of mobs of demonstrators across the country. As a matter of fact, the burning of a movie theater in a poor neighborhood in southern Tehran on March 27, 1978, became a turning point in the public uprising. It started a chain reaction that resulted in the destruction of more than 120 theaters, or 26 percent of all existing theaters in the country (Mohsenian Rad, 1979, p. 16). In short, the people perceived movie theaters as a center for the dissemination of an alien culture and Western value systems that were incompatible with indigenous Islamic values.

Immediately after the revolution, the new Islamic government required that movie theaters, along with other social institutions in the country, adjust to the new political environment. The new revolutionary government therefore:

Table 6.7
Film Audience in Iran

Year	Domestic %	Foreign %
1986	62.6	4
1987	67.1	32.9
1988	74.9	25.1
1989	73.3	26.7
1990	80.0	20.0

Source: Salnameh Amari Iran 1369, 1991, p. 167.

instituted a four-step monitoring procedure to ensure full control over the content of each film, as well as final determination of who is ''fit'' to work on it. The script must first be approved. Then the producers must submit the names of the proposed cast and crews in order to receive a production permit. When the film is finished, it is reviewed by a board, and if approved, the producers may apply for a screening permit. (Akrami, 1987, p. 139)

These restrictions naturally resulted in a drastic decline in the number of films produced domestically, as well as the importation of foreign films. Akrami (1990), on the other hand, found:

One positive result of the government's film policies [for domestic production] has been to put an end to the production and screening of so-called *film farsi,* which had dominated the Persian film industry for fifty years. Films no longer contain elements of gratuitous sex and violence or mandatory musical numbers. Instead, they are oriented to issues and to attracting audiences through the appeal of story lines and production values. Another positive development has been the decentralization of film making. Before the revolution, Tehran was the sole production center in Iran. Now films are made in major cities in several provinces, with local talent and local facilities which has made the medium more accessible to a greater range of potential talent and opened the way to a new generation of film makers. (p. 577)

As a result, the film industry began to witness a major increase in production and audiences. In 1990, for example, out of 80.5 million moviegoers, 80 percent saw domestic films. As Table 6.7 shows, the upward trend in the success and popularity of domestic movies is recognizable.

MEDIA OWNERSHIP AND REGULATION

The Iranian Constitution explicitly states that the economic structure of the country consists of three sectors: public, cooperatives, and private. The broadcasting industry must be within the public sector (Ghanoon Asasi Jomhoori-e-Islami-e-Iran, 1992). Therefore, there are no private/commercial broadcasting stations, radio or television, in Iran. Print media, on the other hand, bear no limitations as far as ownership is concerned. Participants in all sectors—private, cooperative, or public—can own and operate the print media. As a matter of fact, the majority of newspapers and magazines are private enterprises operating commercially. At the same time, there are several newspapers or magazines that are owned and operated by the government or political parties. The two largest dailies in the country, *Kayhan* and *Ettela'at,* for example, are owned by a foundation that is a governmental agency that functions only as the owner, not the operator. In short, there is a mixed private/public ownership of the print media in Iran.

Immediately after the revolution, the Islamic government created a foundation to oversee all of the businesses belonging to the shah's close associates who had left/escaped the country. As it happened, the owners of the two largest dailies were among the escapees. Therefore, the foundation confiscated their newspapers, among other things. Although these two major newspapers are "nationalized" papers, they operate under independent management similar to other privately owned newspapers. Overall, 88 percent of all newspapers in Iran are owned by private enterprises.

The share of governmental ownership in the magazine industry is somewhat larger than its share of the newspaper industry. Excluding universities and research institutions, which are all parts of the public sector, 24.3 percent of all magazines are owned by the government. The armed forces own and operate 2.9 percent, and the private sector owns 44 percent of all the existing magazines. The remainder belong to research and educational institutions that may or may not be in the public sector. Overall, the majority of print media in Iran is privately owned.

Regardless of the type of ownership in the media industry, the government maintains an influence in the operation of the media, as it does in other major industries in the country. To import or set up any kind of media business, like any other industry, requires governmental permit (license) and, in most cases, includes subsidies. The major materials needed for almost any industry, imported or not, are distributed by the government through public agencies. In short, although private ownership of the media is allowed and in some cases even encouraged, the government's influence is felt in almost every aspect of the production process.

The legal basis for media ownership policy, in general, is found in the constitution. In the introduction of the constitution, it is clearly stated that the media in general, and radio and television in particular, must be utilized to enhance and propagate Islamic values (*Rooznameh Rasmi,* 1980). In addition, there are seven clauses in the constitution (3, 15, 24, 44, 69, 168, 175) that outline the responsibilities of the mass media. General education, use of all spoken languages in the country, and the dissemination of all congressional debates are among the duties assigned to the media by the constitution. To accomplish these, the constitution grants the needed freedom to the media to perform their duties in Clause 24. However, this freedom exists only as long as all Islamic principles are observed.

EXTERNAL MEDIA SERVICES

The Iranian radio services began their broadcasts beyond national boundaries in 1961. The main targets of these broadcasts were mostly neighboring countries and few European countries. Initially, international broadcasting was limited to five languages—French, Arabic, English, Turkish, and Russian. However, when broadcast centers were expanded, so were the international broadcasting capabilities. In fact, by the 1970s, Iranian external radio had expanded its foreign broadcast languages to include Armenian, Ashoori, Kurdish, and Baluchi.

The Islamic government has afforded a great amount of attention to external broadcasting. Since the revolution,

> Iranian external radio broadcasting has increased from about 170 hours a week in 1978 to 323 hours in 1986, in 13 languages and ranking 18th in the world's top 20 major broadcasters. These include the United States (2,368 hours), the [former] Soviet Union (2,259), China (1,411), Taiwan (1,098), West Germany (821), and Egypt—including the Middle East radio (820). (Mowlana, 1989, p. 35)

In 1990 Iranian radio broadcast more than 19,125 hours of external programming in 17 different languages. Seventy-five percent of all external broadcasting was from Tehran, while the remaining 25 percent was accounted for by other stations throughout the country (Ravabeteh Omoomieh Seda va Symayeh Iran, 1991).

Being surrounded by Arab nations, and sharing the same religion, Islam, the Iranian external broadcasting services have paid special attention to Arab populations. Over 31 percent of all external radio broadcasts are in Arabic, while the rest is divided among 16 other languages, as shown in Table 6.8.

An emphasis on the Arabic language was not exclusive to radio but was evident in television external broadcasting as well. In 1990, for example, Iranian television produced and broadcast 1,094 hours of programming for external broadcasting, of which 86 percent was in Arabic. In short, Iran is one of the most active nations in the region for broadcasting to Arab Middle Eastern countries. "In terms of weekly programme hours to the Middle East, Iran ranks fourth among major international broadcasters with 233 hours/8 languages, following Egypt (495 hours/3 languages), the [former] Soviet Union (371 hours/

Table 6.8
Foreign Radio Language Programs in 1990: Iran

Language	%	Language	%
Arabic	31.6	Kurdish	9.5
Urdu	7.5	Turkish(Gafgazi)	6.7
Turkish(Istanbully)	6.0	English	5.7
Spanish	5.7	Pashtoo	4.7
Turkamani	3.9	Russian	3.8
French	3.3	Armenian	2.9
Ashoori	2.0	Dari	1.9
Bangali	1.9	Baloochi	1.4
German	1.4		

Source: Public Relations Office of SPIR, 1991.

11 languages), and the United Kingdom (250 hours/4 languages)'' (Mowlana, 1989, p. 35).

Politics and programs on political issues were among the top priorities in Iranian external broadcasting in 1990, as close to half of all broadcast radio programs (43.5 percent) were political in nature. Religious (23.8 percent), cultural (15.2 percent), literary and artistic (8.6 percent), economic (3.7 percent), and historical (2.2 percent) programs were among other types of programming externally broadcast by Iran in 1990 (Ravabeteh Omoomieh Seda va Symayeh Iran, 1991).

NEWS AGENCIES

The Pars News Agency was the first news organization established within the Foreign Ministry in 1934. The main task of this office was to collect and disseminate international news among media outlets in the country. Utilizing telegraph lines, the Pars News Agency produced two daily bulletins in Farsi and French. In 1943, the first teletype machine capable of receiving news from the French news agency was installed. Thus, the news-gathering activities of the Pars Agency were limited to two channels: (1) direct from the French news agency using a teletype machine or (2) from other international sources through telegraph lines.

In 1963, the Pars Agency Office was expanded to a new department within the Foreign Ministry and given the title of the Pars News Agency. In 1975, with the creation of the Ministry of Information and Tourism, the Pars News Agency was placed under this new ministry. Following the Islamic Revolution, the Pars News Agency was further changed to the Islamic Republic News Agency (IRNA), which falls within the jurisdiction of the Ministry of Culture and Islamic Guidance (Khabar Gozarieh Jomhoori-e-Islami, 1981, pp. 16–17).

In addition to its membership in the major Western international news agencies, IRNA is an active member of many smaller news agencies around the world. IRNA is in constant contact and interaction with regional news agencies, such as the Non-Aligned News Agency Pool (NANAP), the International Islamic News Agency (IRANA), and the OPEC (Organization of Petroleum Exporting Countries) News Agency (OPECNA) (Khabar Gozarieh Jomhoori-e-Islami, 1990). Aside from IRANA, almost every media institution operates its own news-gathering department. The Center for News and Information within the VPIR is one such institution's specific news-gathering center worthy of mention (National Iranian Radio and Television, 1972, p. 82).

CONCLUSION

The long history of public communication in Iran may be classified into three distinct periods: the old or ancient period, the modern period, and the contemporary period.

In the old or ancient period, strong evidence supports writing as a means of communication present in ancient Persia. The history of communication over distances, employing the use of horse carriage posts, may be traced back to a thousand years B.C. The existence of a sophisticated library system, about 4,000 years ago, for public and private use across the land has also been well documented. Therefore, Iran is considered one of the pioneering countries in regard to the different media systems initiated and utilized in the early part of human civilization.

Modern communication, however, did not begin until the late part of the seventeenth century. In 1683, Iranian artisans imitated the newly developed European press. Modern publishing, such as the first book (1683), first newspaper (1837), and first magazine (early 1900s), introduced Iran to the era of modern communication. The period continued to prosper with the introduction of electronic media, such as motion pictures, radio, and television, in the early to mid-twentieth century.

From the very beginning, modern communication was an open system with its roots firmly planted abroad. It began with technological imitation of foreign sources and continued with duplication or direct importation of foreign software to fill the existing hardware. Such a trend continued in increasing fashion through the 1960s and 1970s, resulting in frequent cultural clashes.

The third period, the contemporary era, is characterized by the Islamization of the country as a whole and the media of mass communication in particular. There are several characteristics that distinguish the contemporary era. First, and the most important, is the role of religion as the dominant aspect of Iranian society, specifically in the media. The present regime demands that the media observe all Islamic values as defined by the Islamic government. The government has even appointed Islamic legal experts to the boards of the state news and broadcasting agencies in order to advise the staff on Islamic laws. These government experts regard information and entertainment as social goods and ensure that whatever goes out is compatible with Islamic values and ethics.

Second, there exist limitations on imported media content, especially from Western countries. The new Islamic government, unlike any other previous regime in Iran, is quite serious about protection of the Islamic culture and values of the country and would not allow the importation of any media software that is considered incompatible with these values and ethics. In short, there is a system of control in place that monitors the entire import, export, and movement of media material to and from Iran. This by itself demonstrates the dedication of the Iranian Islamic government to the protection of the Islamic value system and its recognition of the importance of media content in the maintenance of these values.

The third characteristic of the contemporary period is the process by which the government is attempting to encourage self-sufficiency for media products and, to some degree, succeeding. This policy and all the incentives that the government provides have resulted in a new generation of media producers and professionals. The new generation is dedicated, not only to the preservation of Islamic values but to the propagation of such Islamic systems. Iranian-made movies that reflect the Islamic value system are being distributed and received around the world. Iran is one of the major participants in international film festivals, and its films always portray the dominant Islamic thinking and practice of the Iranian society at large.

Fourth, the government is committed to Islamic ideology and thinking through the use of media institutions. The extent to which the present government in Iran attempts to propagate Islamic ideology is unprecedented in the long history of the country. It is considered a religious duty for an Islamic regime to disseminate Islamic ideology.

Iran has become one of the major countries in the world as far as international broadcasting is concerned. Iran is one of the few countries that also maintains a very specific and distinct cultural and media policy. The source of such a policy is the constitution of the Islamic Republic of Iran.

REFERENCES

Akrami, J. (1987). Persian cinema and politics in Iran. In J. D. H. Downing (Ed.), *Film and politics in the Third World.* New York: Praeger.

Akrami, J. (1990). Feature film in Persia. In *Encyclopedia Iranica.* Costa Mesa, CA: Mazda.

Aminpour, M. (1976). *Barrasi mohtavayeht barnameh-hayeh television meli Iran: 1351–55* [Content analysis of Iranian national television programs: 1351–55]. Unpublished thesis, College of Social Communication, Tehran.

Asadi, A., & Mehrdad, H. (1975). *Nagsheh rasaneh-ha dar poshtibani toseaeh farhanghi* [The role of media in support of cultural development]. Tehran: Iran Communication and Development Institute.

Elahi, S., Motamed Necad, K., and Mohsenian Rad, M. (1973). *Barrasi mohtavayeht barnameh-hayeh radio Iran* [Content analysis of Iranian radio programs]. Tehran: College of Communication.

Estayn, D. (1989). *Saraghaze akkasi dar Iran* [Introduction of photography in Iran] (E. Hashemi, Trans.). Tehran: Esperk.

Ettela'at (1976). No. 14689.

Gaffary, F. (1990). History of cinema in Iran. In *Encyclopedia Iranica.* Costa Mesa, CA: Mazda.

Ghanoon Asasi Jomhoori-e-Islami-e-Iran [The Constitution of the Islamic Republic of Iran]. (1992). Tehran: The Ministry of Culture and Islamic Guidance.

Khabar Gozarieh Jomhoori-e-Islami. (1981). Jozveheh moarphyeh Khabar Gozarieh Jomhoori-e-Islami [Introduction to the Islamic News Agency]. Tehran: Sazeman Khabar Gozarieh Jomhoori-e-Islami.

Khabar Gozarieh Jomhoori-e-Islami. (1990). Jozveheh moarphyeh Khabar Gozarieh Jomhoori-e-Islami [Introduction to the Islamic News Agency]. Tehran: Sazeman Khabar Gozarieh Jomhoori-e-Islami.

Mahmoodi, F. (1991). *Geography-e-Iran* [Iranian geography]. Tehran: Sherkat Chap va Nashr Iran.

Majaleh Radio Iran [Iranian radio magazine]. (1963). No. 87.

Majaleh Radio Iran [Iranian radio magazine]. (1964). No. 91.

Majaleh Sanaat. (1991). Aghaze chap dar Julfa: Anchenankeh bood, anchenankeh hast [The beginning of printing in Julfa]. No. 104.

Mehrabi, M. (1983). *Tarikh cinemayeh Iran* [History of Iranian cinema]. Tehran: Enteshharat Mahnameh Cinemaie Film.

Mohsenian Rad, M. (1979). *Barresi cinemayeh gabl az Englab-e-Islami* [Investigation of Iranian cinema prior to the Islamic Revolution]. A report prepared for Center for Social Communication Research, No. 3.

Mohsenian Rad, M. (1990). *Ertebatshenasi* [Communicology]. Tehran: Soroosh.

Mohsenian Rad, M. (1992). *Engelab va degar gooni arzeshha* [Revolution and the development of values]. Tehran: Soroosh.

Mowlana, H. (1978). *Sayer ertebatat ejtemai dar Iran* [Social communication in Iran]. Tehran: College of Communication.

Mowlana, H. (1989). The Islamization of Iranian television. *Intermedia, 17* (5).

National Iranian Radio and Television. (1971). Tehran: NIRT Publications Department.

National Iranian Radio and Television. (1972). Tehran: NIRT Publications Department.

Pasargard, B. (1970). *Chronology tarikh Iran* [The chronology of Iranian history]. Tehran: Ishraghi.

Ravabeteh Omoomieh Seda va Symayeh Iran [Public Relations Office of the Voice and Profile of the Islamic Republic of Iran]. (1991). *Gozaresh salaneh 1369* [1991 annual report]. Tehran: Author.

Rooznameh Rasmi [official newspaper]. (1980). No. 11286.

Safa, Z. (1976). *Tarikh syasi, ejtemaai, va farhanghi-e-Iran as aghaz ta payan ahd Safafi* [Political and cultural history of Iran from its beginning to the end of the Safavied period]. Tehran: Amirkabir.

Salam. (1992, September 22). No. 384.

Salnameh amari Iran 1369 [Iranian statistical yearbook of 1369]. (1991). Tehran: Center for the Census.

Sohrabzadeh, M., & Asadi, A. (1990). *Bahremandi shahvrandan Tehrani as matbooat* [Media use of Tehran's urban dwellers]. Unpublished manuscript, Ministry of Culture and Islamic Guidance, Center for Communication Research and Studies, Tehran.

Tamasha. (1976). No. 56.

Tehranian, M., Hakinzadeh, F., and Vidale, M. (1977). *Communication policy for national development.* London: Routledge and Kegan Paul.

7

IRAQ

Khalid Serhan Hurrat and Lisa Isabel Leidig

INTRODUCTION

The Republic of Iraq is roughly the size of the state of California, 175,000 square miles, has a population of approximately 18 million, and is located in the northeastern part of the Arabian Peninsula. Modern Iraq is a secular heterogeneous society consisting of many ethnic groups, including, among others, Kurds, Turkomans, Assyrians, Armenians, and Jews, with the majority being Arabs. Arabic is the official language and is spoken by 80 percent of the population. Kurdish, Turkoman, a dialect of Turkish, and Syriac are officially recognized. Islam is the predominant religion in Iraq, but religious freedom is granted to all citizens and protected by law.

The Arab Ba'th Socialist Party (ABSP), which secured power through two coups, one on July 17 and the other on July 30, 1968, is the ruling party in Iraq. This party has stressed nationalism rather than Islam as a basis of unity and has promoted the principles of socialism in the political system. Legislative and executive powers in Iraq are vested in four authorities: the Revolutionary Command Council (RCC), the president, the Council of Ministers, and the National Assembly. The RCC, headed by the president of the republic, is the supreme legislative authority. The National Assembly of some 250 members, which are nationally elected, works with the RCC to enact legislation. The Council of Ministers, which is responsible for carrying out the decisions of the legislature, is composed of the heads of the following ministries: Foreign Affairs, Interior, Defense, Finance, Justice, Education, Labor and Social Affairs,

Health, Culture and Information, Agriculture and Agrarian Reform, Military Industries, Housing and Developments, Planning, Trade, Industry and Minerals, Oil, Transport and Communications, Higher Education and Scientific Research, Religious Trusts and Affairs, Irrigation, and Local Rule. The country is divided into 18 governates, of which 3 in the north are administered autonomously (Embassy of the Republic of Iraq, 1992, p. 2).

Since 1968, the government's economic focus has been to utilize natural resources to diversify the economic base and to increase self-sufficiency in manufactured goods and foodstuffs. The government typically adopts five-year economic development plans. Agricultural and industrial development projects receive the highest priorities (Embassy of the Republic of Iraq, 1992). Oil, nationalized in 1972, is Iraq's largest industry, and oil exports provide for approximately 95 percent of its foreign exchange earnings (*CIA World Factbook,* 1991, pp. 148–149). In addition to petroleum, Iraq exports agricultural goods, sulfur, fertilizers, and textiles. Principal imports include food, semifinished and finished raw materials, machinery and equipment, motor vehicles, and consumer goods. Although the economy is largely centrally controlled, some small-scale industries and services and most agriculture is left to private enterprise (Embassy of the Republic of Iraq, 1992, p. 2; *CIA World Factbook,* 1991, pp. 148–149).

Education, including university, is free and compulsory to the age of 15. The education system is coeducational. Schooling begins in kindergarten and runs through six primary grades. Three intermediate grades follow as part of the secondary curriculum. There are nine Iraqi universities where studies are conducted up to the B.A. and Ph.D. levels in the arts and sciences (Embassy of the Republic of Iraq, 1992, p. 3). The Department of Journalism at the University of Baghdad, established in 1964, is the only school of journalism in the country. This school offers degrees in print, photo, and radio and television journalism. As of October 1992, the school had approximately 300 undergraduate students, 11 M.A. students, and 4 Ph.D. students (Personal communication, University of Baghdad, October 1992).

COMMUNICATION PHILOSOPHY

The ABSP regards the media as a tool of development that is responsible to society. Sabah Yassin (1981, Editorial. Ath-Thawia), a member of the ABSP and editor in chief of the leading Iraqi daily *Ath-Thawra,* summarized his party's view of the media: "The mass media is entrusted with the task of enlightening the masses with the democratic and socialist approach, enhancing the trends of the public opinion to rectify the democratic march, reinforcing the socialist structure . . . to help build a perfectly revolutionary society." For example, the ABSP believes that it is better to show a program about the benefits of oral hydration than a soap opera since many children suffer from chronic diarrhea.

Iraq's communication philosophy emerged from the political report of the eighth ABSP Regional Congress, referred to as the "Party Platform," held in 1977. In this report, the Ministry of Information and Culture (1977) defined the Iraqi media as:

- A disseminator of ABSP principles and of the president's ideologies.
- A reinforcer of the faith in the revolution and its future.
- An instructor of Iraqi development achievements.
- A supporter of Iraqi national unity and physical and spiritual harmony among different social classes.
- A combator against destructive dogmas and rumors targeted at the revolution and the ABSP in general.
- A creative inspirer of youths.

This report also provided for the creation of a National Communications Bureau to serve as Iraq's senior committee for communication. The main functions of this bureau are to ensure that party ideology, principles, policies, and everyday matters are spread throughout the population, using all media (Arab Ba'th Socialist Party [ABSP], 1977).

PRINT MEDIA

Newspapers

There are approximately six daily newspapers and 20 magazines of various subjects published in Iraq. The number and quantity available of news dailies and other print media tends to fluctuate for political and economic reasons. Iraq's daily newspapers include: *Ath-Thawra (The Revolution), Al Jumhuriya (The Republic), Al Qadissiya, Al Iraq, The Baghdad Observer,* and *Babil.* There is general consensus among Iraqi researchers of mass communications that the first newspaper ever published in the country was in 1869 when the Ottoman Wali (Arabic for mayor) first published *Al-Thawra* in Baghdad in Arabic and Turkish (Bakr, 1966, p. 3).

These newspapers generally serve as mouthpieces for different state institutions and organizations and for the ABSP. *Ath-Thawra,* a political daily founded in 1968, is the official voice of the ABSP. It has a daily circulation of approximately 150,000 copies, and an international edition is published in London. *Al Jumhuriya,* also a political daily published by Al-Jamaheer House for the Press, was founded in 1976 and has a daily circulation of 150,000 copies. *Al Iraq* is a Kurdish newspaper that specializes in reporting news from and of interest to the Autonomous Rule Region. This paper circulates about 27,000 copies a day. *Al Qadissiya,* named after the battle in A.D. 637, in which the Muslims defeated the Persians and expelled them from Iraq, is a political and military daily published by the Ministry of Defense, Department of Political Education. Its articles focus on political and military issues with special reports on the armed forces. It has a daily circulation rate of approximately 130,000 copies. *The Baghdad Observer* is an English-language daily, with a circulation ranging from 5,000 to 20,000 copies daily. It was founded in 1967 by the Ministry of Information and Culture's publishing house, Dar Al-Ma'mun for Translation Publishing, to serve the foreign community in Iraq (*Official Handbook,* 1990, pp. 112–115). *Babil,* established in 1990, is an independent daily that reports on issues, events, and national politics. It has a daily circulation rate of 40,000 copies. Since the editor in chief of this paper is Uday Hussein, the eldest son of Saddam Hussein, many readers regard this newspaper as the inner voice of the ruler (Personal communication, December 1992).

Magazines

The nondaily press includes a number of weekly, biweekly, and fortnightly general interest publications and monthly periodicals published by various ministries. The majority of these publications are in Arabic, but some are in French, Turkoman, and Kurdish. Examples of these types of publications include *Alif Ba',* a weekly magazine published by the Ministry of Information and Culture that covers a wide range of subjects of general interest; *Howkari,* a weekly Kurdish paper published by the Department of Kurdish Culture, Ministry of Information and Culture; *Yurd,* a weekly paper in Turkoman published by the Department of Turkoman Culture, Ministry of Information and Culture; and *Hurras Al-Watan,* a Department of Political Education, Ministry of Defense, publication that covers political and cultural affairs, emphasizing articles of a military nature (*Official Handbook,* 1990, p. 115). In addition to these government publications, an independent editor publishes *Al Rasid,* a weekly comic magazine of four pages that makes fun of daily life and politics through sarcastic cartoons (Personal communication, December 1992).

Some monthly magazines include *Autonomous Rule,* a political and cultural review, published in both Arabic and Kurdish by the Secretariate General for Culture and Youth, Autonomous Rule Region; and *Baghdad,* a French-language monthly published by Dar Al Ma'mun for Translation and Publishing. Professional journals published by trade unions and popular organizations are other important aspects of Iraqi publishing. Their publications range in frequency from weekly to monthly. The principal ones include: *Al Mur'a,* voice of the General Federation of Iraqi Women; *Sawt Al Fallah,* voice of the General Federation of the Peasant Cooperative Society; *Sawt Al Talaba and Shabab,* voice of the National Union of Iraqi Students and Youth; *Waii Al Ummal,* voice of the General Federation of Trade Unions; and *Al Itihad,* voice of the General Federation of the Chambers of Commerce and Industry (*Official Handbook,* 1990, pp. 115–116).

ELECTRONIC MEDIA

The Television and Radio Administration is responsible for providing television and radio services throughout the country. This centralized broadcasting administration ensures that organization and program content do not contradict ABSP policies but serve the government and the ABSP's political, social, and economic goals. This administration is headed by two director generals, one for TV and one for radio, who report to the Ministry of Information and Culture. These director generals are responsible for managing all aspects of radio and television broadcasting, including program production and expenditures.

Radio

Radio broadcasting, which began in 1936, covers the entire country. There are three national radio stations: two AM (amplitude modulation) stations (Radio Baghdad, called the First Program, and Sawt al-Jamheer, the Voice of the Masses, called the Second Program), and one FM (frequency modulation) station (Radio Baghdad). All of these stations are government owned. The First Program is on the air for 21.3 hours daily. In addition to music programming, this station serves as the official voice of the government, informing the public of current political events and government ideology. Prior to the 1991 Gulf War, the First Program broadcast programs in local and foreign languages, including Arabic, Assyrian, English, French, German, Hebrew, Turkish, Persian, and Russian. The First Program is intended to reach audiences in and outside of Iraq. Examples of broadcasts designed for international audiences include a 3-hour English broadcast to Europe, a 2-hour English broadcast to Asia, and two daily 4-hour Persian broadcasts (Baghdad Radio, personal communication, December 1992). The Second Program is on the air for 12 hours daily, and its programming largely consists of music and cultural programs.

The First and Second programs both do some broadcasting in Turkoman and Assyrian. These two stations typically air programming in Turkoman for 3.3 hours daily and programming in Assyrian for 4.3 hours daily. There is also a Kurdish radio station that services the Autonomous Rule Region in northern Iraq. This station is on the air for 17.3 hours daily. Kurdish radio was suspended from January 17 to July 1, 1991. The other radio stations were on the air during this period but were subject to interruption (Baghdad Radio, personal communication, December 1992).

The first FM station went on the air in 1980. This station typically broadcasts for six hours daily and nine hours on Fridays. Broadcasts are in English, except for news broadcasts in other foreign languages. Programming emphasizes talk over music and is targeted toward young and foreign audiences. European and American pop music along with classical music can be heard on this station. In addition to English, this station provides news broadcasts in German, French, and Russian. Commercials are permitted on this station, but all revenues earned through advertising are submitted to the Finance Ministry and are not used by the station for budget expenditures (Statistics and Planning Section, 1992).

Television

There are 11 sections to the General Establishment of TV Administration, including administration, coordination, executive, children's programs, development programs, decor and props, films and serials, drama, cultural programs, entertainment programs, and youth and sport sections. The director general appoints a provincial director for each local television station. These directors serve as agents of the Iraqi broadcasting establishment and are responsible to the director general in Baghdad.

Baghdad Television, which went on the air in 1956, was the first television station in Iraq and in the Middle East. Baghdad Television is government owned and comprises two national stations (Channel 1 and Channel 2) and five local stations, one for each province, including Kirkuk, Mosul, Basrah, Missan, and Al-Muthana. Channel 1 is on the air for nine hours a day, and its programming is a mix of general information, political, and entertainment formats.

Channel 2 broadcasts six hours a day. The programming on this channel is of a more cultural and educational nature and includes foreign programming (see Table 7.1 for a breakdown of programming material for both channels for November 1992). Channel 2 broadcasts news in both French and English. Programming from the BBC (British Broadcasting Corporation, United Kingdom), ITV (United Kingdom), RAI (Radio Televisione Italiana, Italy), France 2 (France), the United States, and other Arab countries frequently appears on this channel. Except for cartoons, foreign-language programming is generally accompanied by subtitles and is not dubbed. Any revenue earned from advertising on these two channels, as for radio, is submitted to the Finance Ministry.

Baghdad Television and the Ministry of Education produce approximately 50 percent of all television programming. The government promotes national culture by instructing writers and creators of programming to produce domestic programming that reflects government ideology and policy. Iraq's five local television stations typically broadcast nine hours a day to local communities. The majority of the programming shown on these channels comes from the two national stations in Baghdad; however, for two hours a day, local programming, usually produced by the station itself, is aired. Programs are primarily in Arabic except for the Kirkuk station, which, for the most part, produces its local programming in Kurdish (S. Rassam, personal communication, July 1992). The programming content of these local channels is tightly censored.

The absence of a large menu of entertainment programming produced in Iraq forces television authorities to accept some foreign programming. Imported programming comes primarily from other Arab countries. The majority of non-Arab sources of programming comes from the United Kingdom, Russia,

Table 7.1
Content of Iraqi Television Programming, November 1992

Type of Program	Channel 1 # of hours	Percent of total hours	Channel 2 # of hours	Percent of total hours
Political/News	66	17.16	41	19.5
President's Activities	10	2.6	--	--
Religious	35	9.1	7.55	3.5
Cultural	10	2.6	12.5	5.95
Children	35	9.1	19.34	9.71
Province Activities	4.5	1.17	--	--
Sports	20	5.2	6.5	3.09
Educational	20	5.2	--	--
Scientific	8	2.08	19.47	9.27
Music	34	7.94	16.2	7.71
Guidance	20	5.20	25	11.01
Iraqi Serials	18	4.68	3.3	1.57
Arabic Serials	31.5	8.19	12	5.71
Foreign Serials	8	2.08	13	6.19
Arab Movies	22	5.72	8	3.81
Foreign Movies	17	4.42	18	8.57
National Songs	4	1.04	--	--
Commercials	8	2.08	--	--
Plays	--	--	8	3.81
Other	13.5	3.38	--	--
TOTAL	384	100%	209.86	100%

Sources: Radio and TV Administration, 1992; *Iraqi TV Guide,* 1992.

Germany, and France. Foreign programming, including Arab, is subject to tight censorship.

Iraqi television is connected with Atlantic and Indian Ocean satellites via reception in Dujail, east of Baghdad. Iraq is also linked with Kuwait and Syria by a microwave network. These connections enable Iraq to receive and transmit television news daily from around the world. There is a thriving video black market in Iraq that supplies consumers with the latest videocassettes from Europe, the United States, and other Arab states. As of December 1992, cable television was still unavailable in Iraq.

MOTION PICTURES

The Television and Radio Administration and the Cinema and Theatre Administration, which are state owned and operated, are the primary program producers in Iraq for both motion pictures and television serials. Documentary films are the most common type of film production in Iraq due to the high technical standards and costs required for entertainment programming. For the first half of 1992, Baghdad TV produced 3 serials and 22 individual programs. In 1989, a more representative year of the industry, the Television and Radio Administration and the Cinema and Theatre Administration produced 20 short films, 13 documentaries, and 5 feature films (Central Statistical Organization, 1992).

In recent years, a number of private and also semiprivate production companies that produce entertainment programming have emerged. Babil Corporation, founded in 1980 and headquartered in Baghdad, is the most successful of these production companies. Four other private companies have established themselves in the entertainment industry but, so far, have produced a limited amount of programming (Personal communication, July 1992). In 1990, Babil Corporation, which is 52 percent government owned and 48 percent privately owned, produced 1 motion picture, 3 movies for television, and 7 plays. In 1991, it produced 5 television movies and 1 television serial. For 1992, Babil produced 1 motion picture, 3 movies for television, and 14 units of a children's serial (Babil Corporation, personal communication, December 1992).

In 1990, the Television and Radio Administration exported film programming to Qatar (6 hours), Abu Dhabi (14 hours), and Saudi Arabia (34 hours), for a total of 54 hours (Statistics and Research Unit, 1990). For the same year, Iraq imported a total of 913 hours of film programming from Arab countries consisting of 36 melodramas, 3 religious serials, 15 children's serials, 2 cartoon films, 6 historical and cultural serials, 15 various serials, 39 varieties and plays, 17 motion pictures, 8 children's movies, 5 science serials, and 10 soap operas from non-Arab countries (Statistics and Research Unit, 1990). Import figures for film programming in 1992 are considerably lower than in 1990, while film exports increased slightly. In 1992, Iraq imported 6 soap operas (66 hours), 3 religious serials (40 hours), 2 cultural serials (36 hours), and 2 children's serials (4 hours), for a total of 146 hours, and exported 9 TV series and 1 motion picture, for a total of 69 hours (Television and Radio Administration, personal communication, December 1992).

Iraq has 35 theaters, 14 in Baghdad and 21 scattered throughout the provinces. These theaters are mainly used for plays, and there are few motion picture showings since most motion pictures that are available in Iraq are shown on TV. For these reasons, statistics on patterns of cinema attendance are negligible (Cinema and Theatre Administration, personal communication, November 1992).

MEDIA OWNERSHIP AND FINANCIAL SUPPORT PATTERNS

Most media in Iraq are owned by the government. The government does not permit independent broadcasting; however, there are some private programming film production companies and publishers. The Iraqi broadcasting budget is primarily drawn from the annual funds allocated by the Ministry of Finance and to a minor extent from fees for services rendered by the organization such as commercials, programs, parties, bulletins, and publications. Expenditures for broadcasting typically exceed annual budget allocations, but the government makes good the difference. Revenues earned from commercial advertising are from the public or mixed sector. The private sector is not allowed to transmit advertisements, in order to avoid contradictions with government policy. Advertising prices are very low; consequently, revenues earned from advertising are negligible (Personal communication, July 1992).

The government controls all radio frequencies, and there are no license fees for television or radio. There were radio license fees following the establishment of radio broadcasting in 1936, but because of license evasion, the government abolished this tax in the late 1940s. Viewers are not charged for broadcasting services.

MEDIA REGULATION

Censorship is an important element of Iraq's communication philosophy. The Ministry of Information and Culture guides, directs, and shapes the content of the media to ensure that ideas or images do not clash with the ABSP ideology, principles, or policies. The director of the Office of Censorship at the Ministry of Information and Culture is responsible for ensuring that programming and information that is explicitly sexual in nature, excessively violent, or objectionable for political reasons be avoided. Obscene language, explicit romantic scenes, nudity, and action-thrillers are all prohibited. Films promoting capitalist ideals are also forbidden, while programming material that portrays the struggle of developing countries against colonialism is highly visible (Office of Censorship, personal communication, November 1992).

There are two approaches to censorship in Iraq: direct censorship by experts employed or contracted by the ministry and self-censorship on the part of journalists and program producers. Direct censorship is used for all imported programming, including other Arab productions. Journalists and Iraqi program producers generally apply self-censorship when reporting news or when producing programming material for the public. That is to say, these journalists make a conscious effort to screen and to produce materials that do not clash with party ideology or cultural values (Office of Censorship, personal communication, November 1992).

EXTERNAL MEDIA SERVICES

Baghdad Radio transmits several programs on shortwave intended for external audiences. For example, the Europe program, an English-language broadcast, targets audiences in East Asia and Europe. This program is on the air for five hours daily and is designed to inform listeners about progress achieved in Iraq, in all areas, and to explain significant regional and international political issues from Iraq's perspective (Statistics and Research Unit, 1990). The Europe program also includes news bulletins in French, Spanish, and German and can be picked up in North America and Japan. Other programs intended for external audiences include a one-hour daily broadcast in Turkish and Russian and a three-hour daily broadcast in Arabic intended for Europe and North and South America. A two-hour daily broadcast in Arabic is also available for listeners in the Arab countries of North Africa, Egypt, Sudan, and the African Horn countries. In addition to radio broadcasts, the Iraqi News Agency (INA) provides external news bulletins daily in English and Arabic.

The government of Iraq strictly prohibits the free flow of information across international borders and attempts to jam unwanted foreign broadcasts. However, Iraq's geographical location enables its citizens to receive a large variety of foreign programming from neighboring countries in spite of the government's efforts to restrict it. In Basrah, for example, viewers can receive programming from Iran, Kuwait, Bahrain, Qatar, and Saudi Arabia. Furthermore, since foreign entertainment programming generally tends to be of a higher quality than Iraqi programming, it attracts large numbers of Iraqi viewers. A survey done by the Iraqi broadcasting establishment in the 1980s found that 88.4 percent of Basrah viewers tuned into foreign television stations (Al-Rawi, 1983, p. 247). Iraqi viewers generally watch foreign television broadcasts in secret since they are not approved by the government. This is especially true for Iranian broadcasts, which are strictly prohibited.

Prior to Iraq's 1990 invasion of Kuwait and subsequent UN-sanctioned economic embargo, most popular foreign magazines and newspapers could be purchased in Iraq (Personal communication, July 1992).

NEWS AGENCIES

The government provides a large percentage of national and international news to national newspapers and broadcast stations through the Iraqi News Agency. The INA was founded in November 1959, is headquartered in Baghdad, and has ten international and five domestic bureaus. Its international bureaus are located in Cairo, Moscow, Sanna, Beirut, Tunis, London, Amman, New York, Paris, and Geneva. The INA has both commercial and exchange agreements for news and photos with foreign news agencies. It has exchange and cooperative agreements with Bulgaria, Czechoslovakia, Vietnam, Poland, Germany, Hungary, Romania, Cuba, China, Italy, Pakistan, Portugal, Bangladesh, France, Spain, Senegal, Turkey, Iran, Japan, India, Malaysia, Indonesia, Syria, United Arab Emirates, Libya, Tunisia, Yemen, Qatar, Jordan, Algiers, Morocco, and Palestine. In addition, the INA typically subscribes to Reuters, Agence France-Presse (AFP), United Press International (UPI), Agence Photographique d'Information et de Presse (API), Deutsche Presse-Agentur (DPA), Telegrafnoe Agentsvo Sovetskovo Soyuza (Tass), and Middle East News Agency (MENA). In 1991, the INA issued 61,202 news items to local and national subscribers and 24,236 news items to international subscribers. These 1991 figures are significantly lower than 1989 figures (112,308 for local subscribers and 83,790 for foreign subscribers) (Iraqi News Agency, personal communication, December 1992).

THE ROLE OF MEDIA IN NATIONAL DEVELOPMENT

The ABSP uses the mass media to communicate its social economic development goals to the Iraqi population and to provide instruction regarding the required labor and skills needed to realize these goals. In 1968, the Seventh Congress of the ABSP determined that it was necessary to reshape national culture in accordance with party ideology. This congress stressed the importance of spreading new cultural concepts and scientific methods and preparing a comprehensive campaign to eradicate illiteracy. The mass media's role in this process has been to document and spread awareness of the development process, to challenge old values and practices in society, to spread the values and practices of the ABSP, and to encourage the masses to participate in the development process (Al-Rawi, 1983, pp. 192–194).

In 1972, according to *Radio and Television Magazine* ("Communication Apparatus and Current Phase," 1972), the National Communication Bureau identified broadcasting as the most important apparatus in the state for its ability, via television and radio, to directly inform and convince the masses of the state's achievements and goals in the development process. The ABSP uses broadcasting to visually display successful development projects in order to convince the population of the benefits of its economic achievements (Al-Rawi, 1983, p. 208). Broadcasting is also used to promote the idea of a nationalist culture by stressing Iraq's Arab heritage and by spreading awareness of Iraq's achievements in poetry, literature, theater, and cinema (Al-Rawi, 1983, p. 210).

Television is perhaps Iraq's most highly valued communications medium for socioeconomic development. The state uses television to transmit educational programs (Channel 2 was originally established in 1972 for this purpose) to serve a wide range of students and to motivate illiterates to overcome language and math difficulties (Al-Rawi, 1983, p. 212). A massive literacy campaign, beginning in the 1970s and promoted through television, resulted in an increase in adult literacy from 42 percent to 93 percent (Embassy of the Republic of Iraq, 1992, p. 1).

Increases in oil revenue after the government nationalized the oil industry in 1972 made it possible for the state to spend resources on improving social economic conditions. A primary ABSP objective was to supply all citizens with electricity. Once this was achieved, the government provided television sets, free of charge, to popular organizations and societies. For example, TV sets were initially provided to all coffeehouses in a large number of villages so that the general population would be kept informed of the state's development policies (Al-Rawi, 1983, p. 367). According to recent statistics made available by the Central Statistical Organization for the Ministry of Planning (1992), 86 percent of the population possess television sets.

CONCLUSION

Since 1968, when the ABSP assumed power, the role of the mass media in Iraq has primarily been to serve as a tool of government. The ABSP uses the media to inform, educate, and indoctrinate the masses with its programs and ideologies. The presence of entertainment programming is limited. Furthermore, the fact that the government is the primary producer of programming material for broadcasting and owner of mass media entities and apparatus further limits the degree of diversity both in content and type of media available in Iraq.

REFERENCES

Al-Rawi, K. H. A. (1983). *Television and development in Iraq: Aspects of government policy with special reference to the effect of television on two Iraqi villages.* Unpublished doctoral dissertation, University of Keele.

Arab Ba'th Socialist Party (ABSP). (1971). *The internal constitution.* Baghdad: Ministry of Information and Culture.

Arab Ba'th Socialist Party (ABSP). (1977). *The party platform.* Baghdad: Ministry of Information and Culture.

Babil Corporation. (1992). *Production statistics.* Baghdad: Babil Corporation.

Bakr, M. (1966). *Ath-Thawra: Inception and development.* Baghdad: Al-Jumhuriya Printing House.

Central Statistical Organization. (1992). *Iraq: Figures & indicators 1992.* Baghdad: Ministry of Planning.

CIA world factbook. (1991). Washington, DC: United States Government Printing Office.

Communication apparatus and current phase. (1972, July 1). *Radio and Television Magazine,* p. 60.

Embassy of the Republic of Iraq. (1992). *Iraq: The people; education & tourism series.* Washington, DC. Embassy of the Republic of Iraq.

Official handbook, Iraq 1990. (1990). Baghdad: Ministry of Information and Culture.

Statistics and Planning Section. (1990). *1990 annual plan.* Baghdad: TV and Radio Administration.

Statistics and Planning Section. (1992). *1992 annual plan.* Baghdad: TV and Radio Administration.

Statistics and Research Unit. (1990). *1990 annual report.* Baghdad: TV and Radio Administration.

8

ISRAEL

Sam Lehman-Wilzig and Amit Schejter

INTRODUCTION

The State of Israel, established in 1948, lies on the eastern coast of the Mediterranean, bordered on the north by Lebanon, on the northeast by Syria, on the east by Jordan, and on the southwest by Egypt. Its population is approximately 5.2 million, of which 82 percent are Jewish—split almost equally between those originating from the Levant and those from Euro-America. Of the minorities, 14 percent are Arab Muslims, a bit over 2 percent are Christians (Arab and others), and somewhat under 2 percent are Druze and a small number of others (black Hebrews, Vietnamese, Samaritans, Bahai). The country's two official languages are Hebrew and Arabic, although English is employed in virtually all government ministries and the economy. As a result of mass immigration over the decades, 70 different languages are in use among the Israeli population.

The country has a unicameral parliamentary form of government (120 members in the Knesset), with a democratic, national, purely proportional election system of competing party lists (about 30 parties usually run, with 10 to 15 gaining seats for the four-year term). In 1996, direct election of the prime minister is scheduled to take place, with mounting public pressure to reform the Knesset system to half district and half proportional (similar to Germany). Municipal elections are held every five years, with direct elections of the mayor and proportional elections for the council. However, the degree of local autonomy is limited, as the Interior Ministry oversees most functions while providing grants amounting to 50 percent of the municipal budget.

Israel's economy historically has been quasi-socialist, with the government employing about 25 percent of the national work force and the giant labor federation Histadrut employing another 25 percent through its own conglomerate Hevrat Ovdim and subsidiary companies. As a result of the economy's near collapse in the mid-1980s, significant liberalization has taken place in the Israeli economy through reduced taxation, reform of the stock market, ongoing privatization of government corporations (including the national phone company), and removal of foreign currency restrictions. Today, Israel's economy is decidedly mixed, and the trend clearly points toward more free market policies.

The state's school system has traditionally been divided into a secular and a religious strand, as well as an ultrareligious "independent" system. More recently, greater curricular and organizational variety have been introduced. The same holds true for higher education. Lately, in addition to Israel's seven major universities, several types of academic and vocational colleges have evolved.

Israel's communications organizational framework was also originally highly centralistic and paternalistic, but here, too, significant changes have come about due to public pressure (Lehman-Wilzig, 1992, pp. 85–95). Much of the country's media philosophy was drawn from the British, who supervised the Mandate prior to 1948. The British impressed upon the Jewish authorities a philosophy of communications as cultural uplifter and agent of political socialization. This approach is still dominant today in Israel's public radio and television, which are under the auspices of the Ministry of Education and Culture. Only recently have the authorities begun to accept the concept of mass media as pure entertainment, grudgingly establishing a commercial "second channel."

Owing to Israel's ongoing serious security problems, an army censorship apparatus still has the authority to censor national security–related material, for by law, all editorial matter must be sent to the censor prior to publication. However, distinct evolution over time in the media's relationship to the governing authorities is discernible.

From 1948 until the early stages of the 1973 Yom Kippur War, Israel's press had basically echoed the government's overall line, especially regarding national security and foreign policy. After the war, with the national consensus breaking down in these matters, the press became ever more critical and probing. The 1982 Lebanon War marked another watershed with extremely critical reports appearing as a matter of course (Negbi, 1986). By the time the Intifada commenced in late 1987, Israel's journalists felt free to publicly discuss virtually all issues, while growing economic competition between several of the mainstream dailies further heightened this trend.

In short, Israel's media philosophy today is closer to being "libertarian," that is, unfettered in its journalistic practices, as compared with the pre-1973 approach of "social responsibility," which demanded self-restraint on the part of the media. Many citizens and most politicians, however, do not fully accept this evolution, leading to occasional strong attacks against the media for overstepping their bounds.

PRINT MEDIA

Newspapers

For a small country, Israel has a very robust and diverse daily press, which reflects the fact that over 85.5 percent of the adult population reads a newspaper on a daily basis (Gallup Israel, 1992). There are 11 Hebrew dailies. *Yediot Akhronot (Latest News)* is by far the most popular paper, with 51.7 percent of the country's daily readership during the week. Its popularity stems in part from ideologically neutral reporting, a wide variety of commentators over the entire political spectrum, as well as colorful writing and graphics. Since the late 1970s, the leading paper *Ma'ariv* (from the root "evening") commands 14.6 percent of the readership. Its ownership changed hands in 1992, whereupon it became somewhat more right wing as well as closer in popular style to *Yediot Akhronot.*

Ha'aretz (The Land), Israel's most erudite daily with a strong intellectual and dovish/laissez-faire slant, holds 5.5 percent of the market. *Hadashot (News),* a recent addition specializing in color, graphics, and short news items, sells to 8.8 percent of the market. The smaller papers include *Globes (The Globe),* a relatively new economic daily; *The Financial Times,* with 2.5 percent market share; *Telegraph,* another economic daily scheduled to commence publication in mid-1993; *Dauar (Mailman),* the organ of the giant labor federation Histadrut (2.1 percent); *Al Ha'mishmar (On Guard),* the organ of the socialist Mapam Party (approximately 1 percent); and *Ha'tzofe (The Viewer),* the organ of the National Religious Party (0.8 percent). The latter three papers are in danger of closing as a result of their declining readership and the lack of willingness or ability on the part of their party sponsors to continue heavily subsidizing them. Somewhat out of the mainstream are three ultra-Orthodox dailies, each an organ of a different camp: *Ha'modiah (The Announcer), Yeted Ne'eman (Loyal Stake),* and the recently established *Yom Le'yom (Day to Day).* The ultra-Orthodox community (about 10 percent of Israel's Jewish population) also has a fully developed alternative mass media system consisting of wall posters for socio-political communication and synagogue newsletters for religious indoctrination.

Aside from the ultra-Orthodox dailies with their own strict standards of what cannot be published (no pictures of women; no reporting on crime, television, sports), Israel's Hebrew press is of generally high quality and extremely comprehensive in its coverage, with the larger dailies publishing magazine supplements almost daily on such matters as sports, economics, consumerism, and culture. Investigative reporting came into its own during the 1980s, mostly in the political and economic realms. Somewhat lagging behind is international news coverage, except when there is an Israeli slant or anything interesting having to do with the United States. However, none of these papers can be considered purveyors of "yellow journalism," although *Yediot Akhronot* and *Ma'ariv* have become somewhat more sensationalist over time.

Israel also has several Arabic-language dailies emanating from East Jerusalem and a few other cities. *Al-Ittihad* is based in Haifa, while *Al-Kuds, Al-Fajr, Al-Shaab,* and *Al-Nahar* are published in East Jerusalem. A few Arabic weeklies and monthlies also appear. The former include *Al-Sinnara,* with the largest readership, *Kul al-Arab,* and *Al-Bayadir Assiyasi;* among the latter is *Al-Usbu'.* The Israeli-Arab press in general is highly unstable, given severe economic problems and stricter press censorship than that found among the Israeli-Jewish publications.

The Jerusalem Post is the only English-language paper issued daily. It attracts about 2.5 percent of local Israeli readership including tourists and diplomatic personnel stationed in Israel. Until the early 1990s it had a moderate leftist slant, but under new ownership (followed by the exodus of most of the paper's veteran editorial staff), it has taken a very hawkish stance in the area of national security, peace, and the territories. *The Jerusalem Report,* commencing in 1990, is a biweekly news and analysis magazine for local and overseas consumption with a relatively dovish slant. *Link* is a bimonthly economic magazine. All the dailies listed above are distributed nationally.

Several national weekly papers in Hebrew are also published, serving Israel's ultrareligious communities: *Yom Ha'shishi (The Sixth Day), Erev Shabbat (Sabbath Eve), Sha'arim (Gates),* and *Ha'makhaneh Ha'kharedi (The God-Fearing Camp).* The weekly *Sha'ar La'matkhil (Beginner's Gate)* is an easy Hebrew daily newspaper for new immigrants (youth and adult), while *The Jerusalem Post* publishes three easy English monthly papers for different age levels.

Beginning in the early 1980s, local and regional weekly newspapers began to attract a growing readership. In the lead are Tel Aviv's *Tel Aviv* (of the *Yediot* chain), which has captured 63.7 percent of area readership; *Ha'ir (The City),* with 43.4 percent; and Jerusalem's *Kol Ha'ir (The City's Voice),* with 65.7 percent. There are three major newspaper chains, each with several local weeklies apiece: the Schocken chain (owners of *Ha'aretz* and *Ha'ir*) and the *Yediot Akhronot* and *Ma'ariv* chains. Other local papers are independent, with many cities having more than one paper competing for local readers.

Altogether, 63 local and regional weeklies were in operation as of mid-1992; this is a large number given the country's overall population of slightly over 5 million. In the three large metropolitan cities, only about 20 percent of the adult population do not read the local papers; in the smaller cities and towns, a mere 10 percent do not read them. As the political system continues the gradual trend toward greater decentralization, the local press should increase in importance even if growing competition cuts back the actual number of papers in print.

Magazines

The number of Hebrew-language magazines is no less impressive, although the variety is somewhat less broad than found in most Western democracies. Still, here, too, readership is quite high, for only 26 percent of both the adult and the youth population do not read any weekly magazines. As Israel entered the postindustrial age only in the last decade or so, with a concomitant rise in standard of living, certain types of magazines, such as comics and consumerism, have not yet become popular. Still, there are enough magazines to satisfy most tastes.

Topical. Ha'olam Ha'zeh (2.0 percent adult national readership) is the oldest weekly magazine dealing with current events and is also the only one that fits into the "yellow journalism" mold. After having recently changed owners several times, the magazine is now published as a supplement of *Globes*. *Monitin* (0.8 percent), on the other hand, is a very slick, glossy biweekly magazine devoting attention to both hard issues as well as life-style subjects.

Women. La'isha (17.1 percent), a weekly, is Israel's largest-selling magazine for women, owned by the *Yediot* conglomerate. *Att* (5.6 percent) and *Olam Ha'isha* (4.9 percent) are monthlies. *Na'amat* (0.9 percent) is a monthly published by Israel's largest women's organization. *Olam Ha'ofnah* is a fashion-oriented monthly.

Military. Ba'makhaneh (6.0 percent) is the Israeli Army's biweekly magazine, read by civilians and soldiers alike. Its subject matter ranges widely, in line with numerous nonmilitary functions, such as education, with which the army is involved. *Skirah Khodsheet* is a more serious monthly, covering topics well beyond the military. *Biton Khail Avir* (2.7 percent) covers air force matters.

Juvenile. Israel boasts 15 different weekly, biweekly, and monthly magazines for youth aged 4 to 18 years old. Of these, a *Ma'ariv* publication for ages 12 to 18 (39.4 percent) is the most widely read weekly, while *Rosh-1* (11.1 percent), *P'nai Plus* (11.1 percent), and *Ma'shehu* (6.8 percent) also have a wide readership.

Political. Unsurprisingly, this category forms the largest group of magazines reflecting the entire political spectrum. On the Left, the biweekly *Politikah* deals with sociopolitical issues from a dovish and socially progressive perspective. On the Right, the monthly *Nativ* takes a hawkish perspective on the administered territories and the Arab-Israeli conflict and a neoconservative approach to socioeconomic matters. *Nekudah* is the monthly organ of the settlers in the territories, ideologically linked with the extraparliamentary movement "Emunim."

Sectoral. Four kibbutz- and moshav-related magazines are published: *Kibbutz* (weekly), *Ha'daf Ha'yarok* (monthly), *Moshav* (monthly), and *Kav La'moshav* (biweekly).

Hed Ha'khinukh is a monthly put out by the national teachers union. Other trades and professions also publish their magazines, including:

Computers and Technology. Among the leading magazines covering these topics are weeklies such as *Anashim U'makhshevim* (1.3 percent) and *Reshet Makshevim;* the monthlies *Mekhonot, 32 Bit,* and *Technologiyot;* and the quarterly *Khimiyah.*

Management and Labor. As a former Socialist country moving in a free market direction, Israelis have an abiding interest in marketplace-related publications. The major ones are *Hamifal* (monthly), dealing with factory matters; *Mashabei Enosh* (monthly), covering utilization of labor; *Va'adim* (monthly), reporting on trade union activities; *Nihul* (biweekly), for managers; and *Ta'asiyah Ve'nihul* (quarterly), for industrial management.

Publishing and Advertising. The most distinguished monthly in this field is *Otot,* put out by the Israel Advertising Association. In 1993, the monthly *Tikshoret* began publication, covering much the same areas of journalism, marketing, advertising, and public relations, albeit from a more personal and less professional or academic perspective. Other magazines dealing with more technical aspects, such as printing, are also published.

Culture and the Arts. Studio (monthly) and *Mishkafayim* (quarterly) are the two leading art and culture magazines.

Miscellaneous. Horim Ve'yeladim (3.2 percent) is a parents' monthly. *Ha'khodesh Ba'meshek* (monthly) deals with economic matters. *Eretz Ha'yaal, Teva Ve'aretz* (1.4 percent), *Masah Akher* (monthly; 30,000 subscribers), and the quarterly *Eretz Magazine* (English; 20,000 subscribers, 75 percent overseas) are travel and nature magazines. Other fields in which magazines appear are building and construction, farming and agriculture, accounting, insurance and finance, car driving and racing, medicine, tourism, and sports.

ELECTRONIC MEDIA

Radio

Since Kol Yisrael, Israel's governmentally run radio network, was transformed from Kol Yerushalayim (which commenced broadcasting in 1936) to Kol Yisrael (The Voice of Israel) with the establishment of the state, Israel's radio scene has expanded enormously. From the perspective of number of listeners, hours of daily broadcasting, and number of channels, Kol Yisrael ranks as the fifth largest radio station in the world.

In 1993, Kol Yisrael consisted of seven channels. Five broadcast AM (amplitude modulation) and FM (frequency modulation): Channel A broadcasts cultural programs (4.4 percent adult audience); Channel B emphasizes news and current events along with popular music (26.8 percent); Channel C is youth oriented, a rock music station (28.6 percent adults, 43.7 percent youth); Channel D carries Arabic-language news and entertainment programming; and there is also the classical music channel (3.4 percent). Two others appear on AM only: The foreign-language channel provides mostly news and some music for non-Hebrew-speaking groups and broadcasts primarily in English, French, and Russian but also in nine other languages such as Yiddish, Rumanian, and Spanish. All of Kol Yisrael's channels together broadcast 112 hours daily. Funding for all these channels comes both from an annual broadcasting fee paid by the listening public and from commercial advertising.

The most popular adult station in Israel in Galei Zahal (38.3 percent audience share), an Israeli Army radio station founded in 1950 under the British Mandate. Since 1973, Galei Zahal has increased its broadcast time and fare in order to offer troops and civilians a broad range of round-the-clock programming, including news, rock, jazz, talk shows, and even over-the-air university lectures. The army is not interested in continuing its support of this station, and an alternative setup is being sought.

In 1973, peace activist Abie Nathan's Voice of Peace (3.1 percent) began broadcasting as Israel's first offshore ''pirate'' radio station. Despite many financial problems, it continues to broadcast, even adding news programs in 1992. In 1988, Channel 7 (6.5 percent), a second offshore pirate station emphasizing religious and nationalist themes, began operation. These stations are heard on AM and FM.

Israel's radio programming tends to be very eclectic, which is in line with the sundry population sectors and the diverse ethnic and cultural backgrounds of its citizenry. The one constant feature throughout all programming is news. Because of Israel's security problems and ongoing peace negotiations, all Israelis are news junkies. Thus, almost all the stations, including the pirate channels, carry Kol Yisrael's 5-minute news spot every hour on the hour. Full-hour news programs are also broadcast on Galei Zahal and Channel B at least three times a day, and both offer scheduled news updates every 30 minutes throughout the day. These two major stations have their own reporters for party, parliamentary, military, economic, and political affairs coverage. Other programs such as call-in talk shows, satire, and interview shows have a heavy news component. Israeli journalists do not stick to one medium. Many reporters and commentators appear steadily in the printed press, radio, and television, even though only one of these media generally serves as their salary base.

Television

Israel's first prime minister, David Ben-Gurion, refused to countenance the idea of television, considering the medium a culturally corrupting force. Nonetheless, television was introduced in 1965 as the Educational TV Channel under government auspices. Known as Reshut Ha'shidur, the Israel Broadcasting Authority (IBA), it is controlled by a board of directors composed of political appointees. Three years later, regular prime-time programming was instituted on the same channel, Israel Television (ITV), but proved to be a disappointment. The reasons for dissatisfaction included political pressure regarding content, perceived overly critical news coverage, and lack of sufficient funding for original programming. Hence, most entertainment programs are American or British; very few locally produced comedy or dramatic series have succeeded in Israel.

With increasing television competition in the late 1980s, Israel TV began to seek other sources of funding beyond the annual license fee paid by each viewing family as dictated by law. ITV began to invite corporate sponsorship of selected programs. Consequently, paid public service ads have been running from the start, with the definition of *public service* used rather broadly.

Overall, for the first 20 years of Israeli television, Israelis had only one local channel. During the daytime, its broadcast fare included educational programs (math, science, foreign language), juvenile material (cartoons, children's movies), and an occasional satirical entertainment program before 6:00 P.M. The evening hours of 6:00 to 8:00 were slotted for Arabic-language programs, especially news, sports, and drama series. Prime-time programming has emphasized current events and news; the most popular program in Israel is the 30-minute news show *Mabat* (65.8 percent adult viewership) at 9:00 P.M. Entertainment programs such as sports, talk shows, quiz programs, and foreign series (*L.A. Law, The Cosby Show*) run until approximately midnight. Due to the relatively narrow fare, Israelis began to tune in to neighborhood pirate cable TV stations in the mid-1980s, and as a result of this growing pressure, several changes and reforms occurred.

In the late 1980s, a half-hour news program, *New Evening* (37.9 percent), was introduced at 5:00 P.M., followed by a 15-minute English-language news show. Late-night Hebrew programming was extended to run well past midnight. *Good Morning Israel,* a light news and feature program, aired from 6:30 to 8:00 A.M., began in 1992. More important, a Second Channel was experimentally established in the mid-1980s and slowly grew in popularity and sophistication. Despite severe lack of funding, it reached about 20 percent viewership overall. The Second Channel finally turned commercial in 1993, with the expectation of reaching at least parity with Channel One within a short time. Also, legislation was enacted setting up privately owned cable television franchises throughout the country. Depending on where Israelis live, many receive several external channels: Egypt TV, Jordan TV, and the Christian Broadcasting Network's Middle East TV emanating from Cyprus.

Israeli television and radio traditionally did not have a sophisticated ratings system, but recently semiannual surveys have been inaugurated on a steady basis—at this stage, more for advertising purposes than for changes in programming. Once advertising comes on stream in the Second Channel and perhaps later in cable television, ratings should become a much more important factor in Israeli broadcasting.

Finally, until a few years ago, the major radio and TV studios were to be found within the walls of Kol Yisrael and the IBA in Jerusalem and Tel Aviv, plus one or two independents such as Herzliya Studios. With the onset of the Second Channel and its statutory requirements for local production, the competing companies have established several highly sophisticated television studios around the country, which will form the basis of increased production for local origination programming on cable TV and the Second Channel, as well as for export.

Cable Television

Cable television is regulated under the Bezek Law of 1982. The law privatized, to a limited extent, all telecommunications services in Israel. The Cable Television Council was formed to develop policies concerning cable TV broadcasting and to oversee their execution.

The council divided the country into 31 service areas and started awarding franchises in 1988, with actual broadcasting beginning in January 1991. The service areas were awarded in blocs, which enabled the council to impose a less attractive area on a contractor bidding for an area with more commercial potential. Bloc awards ensured service to the entire population. In practice, once adjoining areas were awarded to the same bidder, those areas were combined into one, at least for the initial 12-year life of the franchise. Legislation is pending that would limit any one franchise company to maximum 33 percent ownership of the whole country's potential market.

Twenty percent of all broadcasting must be of local production. Every franchise must carry all legal over-the-air regular TV broadcasts; this includes a future satellite channel. A special channel has been allotted to the instructional television center at the Ministry of Education. Cable broadcasts currently include local theme channels (children, science, family, sports, and movies) and imported channels from around the world.

The success of cable television in Israel is overwhelming, by Western standards. By the summer of 1992, about ten areas had their infrastructure installed and had commenced broadcasting, mainly within their urban sectors. In these areas, the first wave of signed-up subscribers passed the 50 percent mark of all households, and up to 60 percent in areas where additional marketing efforts were made. Installation and monthly subscription rates are regulated by the council.

NEW TECHNOLOGIES

Videocassette recorders became very popular in the 1980s. Some 49.5 percent of Israelis viewed at least one video feature film a month in 1987, with 26.5 percent viewing four video films or more.

A cellular phone network was established in Israel in 1984. This network is operated jointly by Bezek (Israel Telecommunications Corporation) and Motorola (Israel), covering all populated areas in the country.

Bezek also operates two satellite stations for the broadcasting of telephone and television signals to satellites over the Atlantic and Indian oceans. Israel is the supplier of satellite services to the Republic of Kazakhstan. Future expansion of these services is expected. While Bezek's satellite dishes broadcast 98 percent of the time, many satellite dishes are used for reception by other bodies such as the Israel Broadcasting Authority, the various cable television companies, and many private households.

Isranet, a national fiber optic data network, serves all major media, research institutes and universities, major banks, and insurance companies. Both national and international data bases are accessible through this network.

MOTION PICTURES

The first Hebrew cinematograph production can be traced to 1911 (Gross & Gross, 1991); organized forms of the Israeli film industry can already be identified in the 1920s (Shir-Ran & Zimmerman, 1988). In 1927 the first film review appeared in Hebrew, in *Ha'aretz* (Zimmerman, 1988). The first Hebrew films produced were of two genres: feature films and newsreels. By the time the state was established, two film labs were operating, and two movie magazines were being published on a regular basis. But modern Israeli film is not a continuation of the Hebrew films during the British Mandate, neither in organization nor in substance, as new studios were established and the content began to reflect the new Israeli sociopolitical reality (Gross, 1974).

A decline in movie attendance and subsequently in the number of films screened occurred between 1970 and 1990. In 1970 a total of 417 movies were screened in Israel, compared with 229 in 1990. According to the *Statistical Abstract of Israel* (1991), while 62.9 percent of the population attended a movie theater at least once a month in 1969, only 41.5 percent did so during 1986–1987. By 1993, as an Israel Advertising Association (IAA) poll found (IAA, 1993), the percentage had dropped further to 35.8 percent of the total population testifying to visiting a movie theater during the previous month and 56.2 percent in the previous six months. A much higher proportion of youngsters up to the age of 18 (84.9 percent) visited a movie theater than that of the general population (51.4 percent).

The total number of movies, screened in 130 movie houses, grew from 180 in 1989 to 231 in the summer of 1992. This growth is due to the popularity of multiplex movie theaters, some with as many as nine screens, built inside the growing number of modern shopping malls throughout the country. Israel's first Omnimax giant screen theater is scheduled for completion by 1994 in the central region city of Rishon Le'Zion.

Israel is generally perceived as being beset by three ongoing conflicts—between Jews and Arabs; between secular and religious Jews; and between new immigrants and old-timers, which is mainly a conflict between Middle Eastern and European Jews. These same conflicts have been the raw material for Israeli films since the first productions in 1950 and have continued. Shohat (1989) claims that both Palestinians and Oriental Jews were denied serious representation in Israeli film, an industry dominated by European Jews, just as in daily political life in the country.

More than 500 full-length Hebrew films were produced in Israel between 1911 and 1991 (Gross & Gross, 1991). These films included made-for-television movies. Nearly 400 films were produced by Israelis in Israel between 1948 and 1989 (Vert, 1989). Since the 1960s, from 10 to 19 films have been produced in Israel every year. Israeli films have received international awards at the Cannes Film Festival, Berlin Festival, and Academy Awards (1971 and 1984).

The first attempts to support Israeli film production were embodied in the Support of Israeli Film Law of 1954, in which movie theaters were required to show a certain number of Israeli films annually. More substantial support came with the establishment of the Foundation for the Advancement of Quality Israeli Films in 1980. The foundation has so far invested between $50,000 and $150,000 each in 46 original productions. Furthermore, the amount of government support to the film industry was tripled in January 1, 1993, laying a more solid foundation for the production of Israeli documentaries.

Of the 229 films screened in Israel in 1990, only 12 were local productions. The rest were imported from a variety of countries, especially the United States (141 films). Unlike 1970, when 54 of the 417 imported films originated in Arab countries, none were imported from those countries during 1990. All foreign films are subtitled in English and, occasionally, Arabic.

Monitoring of films in Israel is as old as cinematography in British Palestine. The Cinematograph Films Ordinance of 1927, which was subsequently incorporated into Israeli law, creates a supervising council whose license is required before public screening of any films. Disregarding the council's orders is a criminal offense. Until the 1989 suspension of the Public Performances Ordinance, the council was also charged with licensing plays. It is a common practice of the council to rate movies according to the major categories "for adults only" and "for general viewing." This practice is self-enforced by the movie theaters.

MEDIA OWNERSHIP

As long as the print media were under private ownership and the broadcast media were government monopoly, the question of media ownership was a nonissue in Israel. The introduction of two commercial electronic media in the early 1990s brought to the attention of policymakers the full-blown dilemmas of cross-ownership.

The first debate concerned the Second Network for Television and Radio. The network provides three franchises each with the right to broadcast two days a week and Saturday, on a rotation basis. A seventh of broadcast time is allotted to Educational Television, a government enterprise. In mid-1992 the auction for the franchises took place, but potential bidders refused to participate because of two limitations. First, the agreement with Educational Television as a fourth partner receiving income without any investment was seen as unfair government interference in a commercial enterprise. More significant was the fact that the groups formed to compete for the franchises consisted mainly of print media owners, and the fear of cross-ownership engendered strong opposition to these partnerships within the Knesset, academia, and among government officials. A revised agreement was reached only in March 1993 (two years after the Second Network began the bidding process), providing the print media with a maximum 30 percent share ownership of a franchise, but only up to 24 percent in voting power. The compromise paved the way for seven groups to put in bids by the deadline of March 31, 1993.

Simultaneously, legal procedures have been undertaken concerning the cartelization of the cable industry. All seven cable franchisers formed a conglomerate known as Israel Cable Programming (ICP). The conglomerate purchased all the local cable channel programming that the franchises broadcast. Complaints regarding lack of competition led to the antitrust commissioner taking the ICP to court on charges of an illegal cartel.

The commissioner offered a compromise that would allow the cartel to exist for three years since the commencement of cable broadcasting (January 1991), after which a new settlement would be agreed upon. The idea behind the compromise was to let the cable industry penetrate Israeli homes in its initial period as a legal cartel. The ultimate structure opening the cable market to competition is unknown.

MEDIA REGULATION

The 1933 Press Ordinance regulates the printed press. The Broadcast Authority Law of 1965 and the Second Network for Radio and Television Law of 1990 regulate the broadcast media.

The Press Ordinance states that no newspaper in Israel can be published without previously receiving a license signed by the Ministry of Interior Affairs. The ordinance enumerates the eligibility requirements of a person wishing to serve, for example, as a newspaper editor, such as a minimum age of 25 and a high school matriculation diploma.

The ordinance empowers the Minister of Interior to close a newspaper when it has published either a news item that might jeopardize the public's safety or a false account that causes panic or despair. This provision was given a restrictive interpretation by the Supreme Court in 1953, subjecting it to the 1948 Proclamation of Independence as the quasi-constitutional basis for such an interpretation. The court ruled that enforcement of Section 19 of the Press Ordinance should be carried out only if there was a "near certainty" of danger to public safety.

The right to close publications is also granted to the military censor under another British regulation, the Emergency Defense Regulations of 1945. This regulation is one of four powers given to the censor. The other three powers are (1) the right to request a review for all material intended for publication ("prior restraint"), (2) the administrative penal authority to confiscate printing presses used for printing forbidden materials, and (3) the authority to forbid publication of material that might jeopardize the security of the state (Segal, 1990).

In a 1988 ruling of the High Court of Justice, the same legal construction adopted for interpreting the extent of the civil authority's power to close newspapers was applied to the military authorities. The court ruled that the British military regulation should be interpreted within the context of its new democratic environment.

The reason the military censor's actions were not questioned until 1988 is due to the existence of the self-regulatory body known as the Editors' Council. The council is a joint body of all the Hebrew dailies (except *Hadashot,* which refused to join), the Israeli Broadcasting Authority, Galei Zahal, and ITIM (Hebrew acronym for the Associated Israel Press Service). The council operates under an agreement in which issues concerning national security are brought by the government for discussion in informal briefings and will not be published in the Israeli media. The council has a procedure for appealing any decisions by the Israel Defense Force's chief of staff. The legal significance of this agreement is that the regular military censorship procedures do not apply to the media participating in the council. This presumed positive discrimination in itself has not been challenged in court (Segal, 1990).

Another self-regulatory body is the Press Council, which was formed in 1963 by the National Organization of Israeli Journalists, the Editors Council, and the newspaper management union (Strassman, 1986). The Press Council oversees the ethical conduct of journalists in Israel with its published ethical code applying to all media, including nonmembers of the council. According to the Press Council's own declaration, the ethical code only deals with how to report. The right to decide what to report, though limited within the boundaries of elementary etiquette, is up to the editors of the respective media.

Notwithstanding all these regulations, laws, and institutional bodies, the operating environment for Israel's Arabic-language press is far more stringent than for the Jewish press (Hebrew and foreign language). First, the former are not part of the Editors' Council. Second, given Israel's sensitivity to its security situation, the Arabic press is held to stricter standards of political ''incitement'' and discussion of military-related issues. As a result, Arabic-language newspapers have been closed down for limited periods of time and on a few occasions have been forced to go out of business permanently.

Regulation of broadcast media has been revolutionized in 1990 with the adoption of the Second Network for Television and Radio Law. Until then, all broadcasting was regulated under the Broadcasting Authority Law of 1965. The main difference between the two networks is that broadcasting in the Second Network's TV channel is given to commercial franchises for a term of four years, while the IBA's broadcasts are supervised by the government. Both networks are overseen by government-appointed councils.

The commercial nature of the Second Network led to special attention being given to broadcast content. The programs may not include incitement to racism, other forms of prejudice, or political broadcasting. Similar provisions concerning content are applied in the Bezek Law of 1982 concerning cable broadcasting. The Second Network council has the power to enact a fairness doctrine (Barak, 1987).

In addition to the franchises' share, instructional television has been apportioned one-seventh of broadcast time on the Second Channel. At least one-third of all broadcasts must be locally produced, while at least half of these must be purchased, and not produced by the broadcasting franchises, from independent studios. These two provisions were instituted in order to strengthen Hebrew/Israeli culture in the face of foreign-language dominance, as well as to ensure that independent local producers continue to survive as a counterforce to the full-time production staffs within the various channels. The Second Channel is allowed to broadcast news, but no commercials are permitted during the news program. Broadcasting of commercials in general is limited to 10 percent of all television and 15 percent of all radio broadcast time.

The appearance of the Second Channel and the drift of viewers to cable's huge variety of programming after years of broadcast monopoly have led to a rethinking of the role and status of the IBA. A ministerial committee appointed by the Ministries of Justice and Education was to present a new structure for the IBA by May 1993. The committee's charter seeks to redesign the legal, economic, and organizational structure and status of the IBA.

EXTERNAL MEDIA SERVICES

Other than the two hours devoted to Arabic programming and a quarter-hour evening news show in English, all Israeli over-the-air television is in Hebrew (or accompanied by Hebrew subtitling). However, depending on their location, Israelis can receive signals from Cyprus, Syria, Jordan (two channels), and Egypt as well as several foreign channels via cable.

Foreign-language radio fare is more diverse: BBC (British Broadcasting Corporation) World Service, Voice of America, and Monte Carlo are the dominant three, but with minor effort, Israelis can hear radio programs from virtually the entire Middle East and most of Europe.

Conversely, for a small country, Israel has a large presence in the world's overseas airwaves by broadcasting shortwave radio programming during the hours 3:00 to 22:00 GMT (Greenwich mean time) to every continent in Hebrew (regular and simple), English, Russian, Yemenite, Bucharian, Georgian, Persian, Yiddish, Rumanian, Hungarian, French, Spanish, Ladino, and Arabic. The primary audience is world Jewry, although a large number of non-Jews tune in as well, owing to their interest in the State of Israel.

In addition to broadcasting, Israel provides a wide array of foreign-language publications due to its polyglot origins. Altogether, there are 29 locally produced dailies and weeklies in the following tongues: 11 Russian, of which the leaders are *Vremya, Vesty, Nasha Strana,* and *Novostz'* (Milner, 1992); 5 Rumanian; 2

French; 2 Spanish; 2 Yiddish; and 1 each in Polish, Bulgarian, Georgian, German, Hungarian, Turkish, and Ladino (Israel Government Press Office, 1992).

Over 1,000 different foreign-language publications are imported by the giant Steimatzky bookstore chain. About half are in English, with the rest mostly in French, German, and Russian. The main foreign-language newspapers are *International Herald Tribune, Wall Street Journal, Financial Times;* weekly topical magazines—*Time, Newsweek, Der, Speigel, L'Express;* and general monthlies—*Burda, Byte, Cosmopolitan.*

NEWS AGENCIES

Israel has one news agency, ITIM, which is composed of representatives of all the major newspapers (plus stringers). The agency distributes material domestically and overseas, as well as translating selected overseas material for domestic use. In addition, the Israeli press uses foreign agencies, primarily Associated Press (AP), Reuters, and Agence France-Presse (AFP).

Within Israel, there are three official bodies that distribute information to the press. The Government Press Office is attached to the Prime Minister's Office; it services local and foreign reporters (foreign press authorization, translated abstracts of the Hebrew press, official statements, and documents of the various government ministries). Reporters can and do go directly to specific ministries for information as well. The Foreign Ministry Press and Information Departments transmit detailed information to local and visiting journalists alike, provide tours for the latter, and offer daily press briefings. Overseas, the Israeli embassies and consulates provide much the same information to the foreign media. The Israeli Army Press spokesman is attached to the Office of the Chief of Staff; this unit provides information regarding military matters to the local and foreign press, arranges and authorizes interviews with high-ranking officers, and offers periodic briefings.

THE ROLE OF MEDIA IN NATIONAL DEVELOPMENT

The important role of Israel's mass media in national development is demonstrated in institutions formed for that purpose, as well as in the media's participation in ceremonial and traditional events. Instructional television started broadcasting in Israel in 1966, two years before the beginning of regular TV broadcasts. It broadcasts daily on the IBA's channel from 8:00 A.M. to 5:30 P.M., except Saturdays. The morning programs are geared for the schools. From a predominantly instructional medium, the service changed its character in the 1980s to become more family oriented, especially in the afternoon hours. New programs include entertainment and news. Concurrently, it also changed its name to Israel Educational Television (IETV). As noted earlier, IETV is allotted one-seventh of the Second Channel's broadcast time and one channel in the cable TV system. So far, both options have not been exploited. Indeed, the restructuring of Israel's broadcast system has led to a rethinking of the role of educational television. A plan to privatize the enterprise is being debated.

Fortunately, the role of media in education and national development is not limited to formal institutions. As a rule, the media are mobilized to support national efforts and to participate in national events. Examples of this support can be seen in the context of the country's main national efforts as defined by the state: the absorption of immigrants and national security issues. During the massive waves of immigration during the early 1950s and the late 1980s, the electronic media made a special effort to broadcast programs aimed at teaching Hebrew to the immigrants, broadcasting in their own language or adding subtitles to television broadcasts. During the Gulf War of 1991, all the radio stations, including Galei Zahal, combined to broadcast as one. Participation in national events and ceremonies is most evident during the special broadcasts on Independence Day, Memorial Day, plus the lack of, or limited broadcasts, on Jewish holidays such as Yom Kippur (the Day of Atonement) and Tisha B'av (commemorating the destruction of the temples at Jerusalem).

The commercial print media has also joined in the national effort. The Histadrut has owned a chain of newspapers in various European languages since the 1950s, while the Hebrew dailies began publishing special editions and supplements in Russian to help the several hundred thousand immigrants arriving from the former Soviet Union in the late 1980s and early 1990s.

CONCLUSION

Israel has always had a variegated and strong free press, circumscribed somewhat by its serious problems of national security. Per capita newspaper readership is among the highest in the world, with the number of printed press venues far beyond what one would expect from such a small country.

On the other hand, until very recently its electronic media fare has been quite limited due to governmental control of all official radio and TV channels. Public pressure and the citizenry's development and support of alternative media venues have forced the government's hand, and Israel is now in the process of a complete media revolution that by the mid-1990s should bring it in line with most Western democracies.

A more educated citizenry, new communication technologies, as well as a gradual reduction of national security tensions are all increasing the pressure on the authorities to lessen censorship and other communications regulations. In line with greater liberalization of economic policy, the Israeli media scene attitudinally, philosophically, and organizationally is steadily becoming more open to private ownership of the electronic media and even greater freedom of expression among the print media.

REFERENCES

Barak, D. (1987). The individual's access to the media: Balance of interests and freedom of speech [In Hebrew]. *Tel Aviv University Law Review, 12*(l), 183–204.

Gallup Israel. (1992, February). *Survey of mass media consumption, 1992* [In Hebrew]. N.P.: Advertisers' Association.

Gross, N. (1974). The Israeli film 1948–1950 [In Hebrew]. *Kolnoa, 74* (1), 93–103.

Gross, N., & Gross, J. (1991). *The Hebrew film: Chapters in the history of cinematography and film in Israel* [In Hebrew]. Jerusalem: Maor Velech.

Israel Advertising Association (IAA). (1993). *The media poll.* [In Hebrew]. Tel Aviv: Israel Advertising Association.

Israel Government Press Office. (1992). *National list of publications* [In Hebrew]. Jerusalem.

Lehman-Wilzig, S. (1992). *WILDFIRE: Grassroots revolts in Israel in the post-socialist era.* Albany, NY: SUNY Press.

Milner, I. (1992, July 27). The owner wasn't interested [In Hebrew]. *Ha'aretz,* p. B2.

Negbi, M. (1986). Paper tiger: The struggle for press freedom in Israel. *Statistical Abstract of Israel.* (1991). Jerusalem: Government Publications. *Jerusalem Quarterly, 39,* 17–32.

Segal, Z. (1990). Military censorship: Its authority, judicial review over its activities, and a proposal for an alternative agreement [In Hebrew]. *Tel Aviv University Law Review, 16*(2), 311–342.

Shir-Ran, S., & Zimmerman, M. (1988). In the beginning there was the cinematograph [In Hebrew]. *Cinematheque, 40,* 10–13.

Shohat, E. (1989). *Israel cinema: East/West and the politics of representation.* Austin: University of Texas Press.

Strassman, G. (1986). *Media laws and journalistic ethics* [In Hebrew]. Tel Aviv: Tel Aviv University, Carlebach Chair for Journalism.

Vert, D. (1989). Full length Israeli films [In Hebrew]. *Cinematheque, 49,* 34–43.

Zimmerman, M. (1988). The Hebrew cinema learns to talk [In Hebrew]. *Cinematheque, 41,* 14–18.

Zimmerman, M. (1989). The phoenix [In Hebrew]. *Cinematheque, 41,* 30–31.

9

JORDAN

Muhammad I. Ayish, Mohamed Najib El-Sarayrah, and Ziyad D. Rifai

INTRODUCTION

The Hashemite Kingdom of Jordan is an Arab Middle East country with an area of 89,000 square kilometers inhabited by about 4 million people, more than 80 percent of whom are concentrated in one-eighth of the total land area. Ninety-six percent of Jordanians are Muslims, while 4 percent are Christians (Zou'bi, Poedjastoeti, & Ayad, 1992). Jordan shares borders with Syria to the north, Saudi Arabia to the southeast, Iraq to the east, and Palestine to the west.

Founded in 1921 as the Trans-Jordan Emirate, Jordan gained independence from British Mandate in 1946 and became a constitutional monarchy, the Hashemite Kingdom of Jordan. After the 1948 Arab-Israeli war, two areas of Palestine, known as the West Bank and East Jerusalem, were united with the Hashemite Kingdom of Jordan following a national conference in Jericho in 1950. However, in June 1967, the West Bank and East Jerusalem fell under Israeli occupation, and in 1988, Jordan cut off legal and administrative links with the occupied territories to enable Palestinians to develop their future national political identity and independence.

The Jordanian economy follows a free market system in which the private sector employs about 70 percent of the country's labor force. In 1991, the gross national product (GNP) totaled JD2,586.3 million, equal to $4 billion, with agriculture, trade, manufacturing, and financial/insurance services accounting for the major part of GNP. In that year, per capita income totaled $1,050 (Central

Bank of Jordan, 1992). Since the beginning of 1992, the Jordanian economy has started to show promising signs of growth after three years of stagnation.

In the area of education, the number of students attending school in the academic year 1989–1990 totaled 1,016,777, while over 200,000 students are enrolled in various state and private universities and community colleges. According to recent statistics, the rate of illiteracy in Jordan was estimated at 28 percent.

As a constitutional monarchy, Jordan has evolved its own democratic system of governance. In November 1989, a national Parliament was freely elected, and in June 1992, a national charter defining important aspects of political life in the country was endorsed by a national conference held under the patronage of King Hussein. In August of the same year, martial law was abolished, and political parties were legalized in Jordan, opening the way for a greater degree of pluralism in the country's political outlook. One of the immediate outcomes of the democratization process in Jordan has been a set of press laws that seem to have provided print media with the freest environment in their history. As for broadcast media, they remain under government control and are thus not subject to the provisions of the new press law. Perhaps for reasons rooted in the historical primacy of government control of broadcasting in the Arab World, the Jordanian Minister of Information once put it, "Broadcast media are the property of the Nation as a whole" (M. Sharif, personal communication, October 18, 1992).

PRINT MEDIA

Newspapers

The first Jordanian newspaper appeared in 1920 under the title *Al-Haq Yalo* (*Right Is Superior*), during the temporary stay of Prince Abdullah, founder of Jordan, in the southern city of Maan. A year later, Prince Abdullah moved north to the capital city of Amman to establish the Trans-Jordan Emirate (Mousa, 1988, p. 85).

In the post-Emirate foundation period, the first newspaper was *Al-Sharq al-Arabi* (*The Arab East*) in 1923 as a government publication. In its first six years, *Al-Sharq al-Arabi* published literary and political articles, national and international news, and official announcements. In 1929, this paper became the official bulletin of the government of Trans-Jordan (Ministry of Information, 1978, p. 11).

Three weeklies were established in 1927 in Jordan: *Jazirat al-Arab* (*Arab Peninsula*), *Al-Sharia* (*Islamic Law*), and *Al-Urdan* (*Jordan*). In 1939, the daily *Al-Jazirah* (*The Peninsula*) appeared in Amman. With the forced influx of hundreds of thousands of Palestinians to Jordan following the 1948 Arab-Israeli war, two daily newspapers, formerly published in Jaffa, *Filestin* (*Palestine*) and

Al-Difa'a (*Defense*), moved to Jerusalem. The two papers continued publication until the June war of 1967, when they were forced to move to Jordan.

In the 1940s, several newspapers and magazines appeared in Jordan, such as *Al-Jihad* (*Holy War*) (1947); *Al-Nesser* (*Eagle*) (1947); *Al-Haq* (*Right*) (1947); *Al-Ahed* (*Pledge*) (1947); *Al-Horeih* (*Liberty*) (1948); *Al-Baath* (*Resurrection*) (1948); and others. These publications were unable to function for long mainly due to financial troubles (Arab House, 1980, pp. 18–19).

During the 1920s, 1930s, and 1940s, the press in Jordan was characterized by some historians as courageous in handling social and political issues. It was especially keen in creating national awareness with respect to important issues of concern to the country, particularly independence from British colonial rule (Jordan Press, 1980, p. 20).

The 1950s witnessed a mushrooming of publications with mostly political orientation as a result of a growing liberal atmosphere in the country in that decade. About 40 newspapers and magazines appeared in Jordan in that period, but most of them could not survive long for financial and later for political reasons. Most prominent among these publications were *Al-Jihad* (*Holy War*) (1953) and *Akhbar Al-Usbu* (*News of the Week*) (1959). The latter continues to publish to date. Newspapers were known in the 1950s for their party affiliations, and their advocacy of foreign interests and ideologies seemed to have prompted the government to revoke their licenses (Jordan Press, 1980, p. 30).

The year 1967 marked the first attempts by the Jordanian government to place limits on the number of publications and on the margin of freedom accorded to them. In that year, six newspapers, five in Arabic and one in English, were dominant: *Filestin* (*Palestine*), *Al-Difa'a* (*Defense*), *Al-Manar* (*Minaret*), *Al-Jihad* (*Holy War*), *Al-Urdun* (*Jordan*), and the *Jerusalem Star.* Following newspaper criticisms of the Jordanian Army's responses to Israeli border raids, an executive order was issued to reorganize the press. The June 1967 war disrupted the reorganization process and led to the transfer of the Jerusalem newspapers to Amman as a result of the Israeli occupation of the West Bank and the Holy City (Rugh, 1979, p. 78).

In 1968, the government issued new newspaper licenses on condition that the four Jerusalem dailies merge into two, ostensibly to improve the quality of the press, but the move was widely perceived as an attempt to win more support for the government through this step (Rugh, 1979, p. 78). Two dailies emerged in Amman in the meantime: *Al-Dustour* (*Constitution*) (1967) and *Al-Difa'a* (*Defense*) (1968). Almost immediately after these two papers went into publication in 1970, they became directly involved in the confrontation between the government and the Palestinian commando movement. As a result, the government closed down *Al-Difa'a* and established the state-run *Al-Rai* (*Opinion*) in 1971 (Rugh, 1979, p. 76).

During the 1970s, three additional daily Arabic newspapers operated in Jordan: *Al-Sabah* (*Morning*) (1971); *Al-Akhbar* (*News*) (1975), and *Al-Shaab* (*People*) (1976). The three papers published for a few years before disappearing.

In 1980, the Jordanian press consisted of three dailies: *Al-Rai* (50,000 copies), *Al-Dustour* (30,000 copies), and the *Jordan Times* (10,000). Both *Al-Rai* and *Al-Dustour* increased their circulation to 65,000 and 55,000 copies, respectively, by 1983. Early in that year, a new daily newspaper, *Sawt Al-Shaab (People's Voice),* appeared at the newsstands in Amman (El-Sarayrah, 1984, p. xiii).

In 1988, the government, through the Economic Security Commission, issued an executive order dissolving the boards of directors of the three Jordanian newspapers. According to the order, temporary commissions were formed to administer work at the three newspapers, including those of the editors. The government said the move was necessary to protect the interests of investors. However, the measures were widely regarded as another attempt to limit freedom of the press in Jordan. The order was made void in 1989.

During the 1970s and early 1980s, the press in Jordan was characterized as loyalist, though it had some features of a free press such as private ownership (El-Sarayrah, 1984, p. xv). On the other hand, Mousa (1988, pp. 81–110) suggested in his study of the Jordanian press that "the private newspaper closely falls under the social responsibility model in certain aspects, like its commitment to society and its independence in handling international news." As first developed in the mid-1950s, this model had two premises: Freedom carries concomitant obligations, and the press is obliged to be responsible to society for carrying out certain essential functions of mass communication (Sibert, Peterson, & Schramm, 1963, p. 74).

According to Badran, government-press relationships in Jordan in the 1980s may be better understood by examining the country's official information policy (Badran, 1988, pp. 335–340). In his 1986 address to the government-appointed National Consultative Council, King Hussein stated that press freedom should not be conceived of separately from press responsibility. However, successive Jordanian governments have given different interpretations to the king's viewpoint, adopting several approaches in dealing with the press.

After the democratization process was launched in November 1989, a new journalistic atmosphere began to take shape in Jordan. In his Letter of Designation addressed to the prime minister entrusted with forming a new government in April 1989, King Hussein stated: "With respect to the field of communication, emphasis should be placed on fostering the relationship between officials and citizens within the framework of a quiet dialogue, either through interpersonal or mass communications." (Badran).

By the end of 1992, print media published in Jordan consisted of 4 dailies, 20 weeklies, and 6 magazines. The 4 dailies published in Jordan are the Arabic-language *Al-Rai, Al-Dustour,* and *Sawat Al-Shaab* and the English-language *Jordan Times. Al-Rai* was established initially by the government in 1971 to propagate its viewpoints and policies before it became privately owned by the Jordan Press Foundation. Sixty-two percent of the paper's shares are owned by several public institutions and 38 percent by the private sector. Classified as an independent Arab political daily, *Al-Rai* is believed to be the most influential publication in Jordan, with a daily circulation of 90,000 copies. During the 1970s and 1980s, the paper was suspended several times by the government in connection with publishing information relating to the Syrian intervention in Lebanon and to the Jordanian Armed Forces.

According to a study conducted in 1986, *Al-Rai* provided its readers with a varied outlook regarding local, Arab, and international issues. Half of its space was devoted to local news coverage and editorials. Local coverage was not completely balanced with respect to rural and urban issues and to official and unofficial events. *Al-Rai* also relied on international news agencies for foreign news (Mousa, 1988, pp. 81–110), something that seems to be consistent with another finding by El-Sarayrah (1983, pp. 363–365) with regard to the Jordanian newspaper's dependence on Western news agencies for their international news coverage. According to El-Sarayrah (1983, pp. 363–365), *Al-Rai* devoted 41.49 percent of its space to foreign news.

As for advertisements, Mousa noted that 25 percent of *Al-Rai* space was devoted to commercial and private messages, and in 1992, moreover, the percentage of space allocated to advertising in the paper jumped to 51.2 percent. A study by El-Sarayrah indicated that *Al-Rai* had 58.5 percent out of total advertisement space in the three Arabic daily newspapers (El-Sarayrah, 1992). The newspaper appears in 40 pages in two sections.

Al-Dustour, a politically independent daily published by the Jordan Press and Publishing Co., was established in 1967. It is owned by both the private sector (60 percent of shares) and public institutions (40 percent). According to *Al-Dustour* sources, the newspaper's circulation ranged between 75,000 and 80,000 copies in the year 1992. *Al-Dustour* was suspended several times by the government in the predemocracy era for different reasons, such as calling for a general amnesty for all political prisoners in the country (Rugh, 1979, p. 78).

According to El-Sarayrah (1983), *Al-Dustour* devoted 58 percent of its foreign news coverage to the Middle East and heavily relied on Western news agencies for foreign news. In 1992, this newspaper devoted 32.9 percent of its space to advertisements, and the paper gained 32.5 percent of overall advertisement space used by the three Arabic dailies (El-Sarayrah, 1992). The paper is published in 28 pages.

Sawat Al-Shaab is a political daily, established in 1983 and owned by several public institutions (67 percent of shares) and the private sector (33 percent). With a circulation ranging between 25,000 and 30,000 copies a day, this newspaper is facing financial hardships. According to El-Sarayrah (1992), *Sawat Al-Shaab* devoted 11.5 percent of its space to advertisements and ranked third (9 percent) in terms of the ratio of space devoted to advertisement in all Jordanian newspapers. Low advertising income seems to be partly responsible for this paper's financial troubles.

The *Jordan Times* is the only political English-language daily newspaper in Jordan. Established in 1975 by the Jordan Press Company, publisher of *Al-Rai* newspaper, the *Times* has a circulation of no less than 12,000 copies and is read mainly by diplomats and foreigners in addition to university staff. It is published in eight pages. According to Badran (1988, pp. 325–340), the *Times*'s staff was found to be well exposed to a number of U.S. and British publications such as the *International Herald Tribune, The Guardian,* and the *Washington Post.* The study also revealed that more than half of the *Times*'s stories (51.5 percent) had originated in foreign capitals. The paper also relied heavily on Western news agencies, especially for regional and international news coverage.

Weekly newspapers published in Jordan prior to the endorsement of the new Press and Publications Law include *Akhbar Al-Usbu* (*News of the Week*), *Al-Sahafi* (*The Journalist*), *Al-Liwa* (*The Banner*), *Shihan* (a town in southern Jordan), *Sahafat Al-Yarmouk* (*Yarmouk Press*), and in English, *The Star.*

Launched in 1959, *Akhbar Al-Usbu* is owned by Al-Reemoni Press and Publishing Co. With a 20,000-copy circulation, this weekly is classified as a popular publication.

Al-Sahafi is a political weekly established in 1964. With a low 1,000-copy circulation, this publication does not appear regularly at newsstands.

Al-Liwa is a political weekly established in 1973 and is published by Al-Liwa Press and Publishing House, a private enterprise. This weekly is classified as Islamic in its orientation.

Shihan represents a new journalistic phenomenon in Jordan because of its critical, satirical, and sensational approach to various social and political issues. This paper was launched as a specialized publication in 1984. A year later, the paper's license was suspended after the government had perceived it to have gone beyond its authorized mandate. Although *Shihan* migrated to Greece and Egypt, its circulation remained wide inside Jordan as a political and social weekly. In 1991, the paper was allowed to republish in Jordan. The 100,000-copy circulation paper is classified as liberal.

Sahafat Al-Yarmouk is a weekly community newspaper published by the Department of Journalism and Mass Communication/Yarmouk University. The paper is distributed free of charge and is believed to have a 5,000-copy circulation. The paper's content consists mainly of development news, especially that relating to northern Jordan.

The Star is a political economic weekly published in English by Media Services International. Originally launched in 1967 in Jerusalem as the *Jerusalem Star,* this English-language weekly appeared in Jordan in 1982, then was suspended by the Government Economic Security Commission in 1988. In 1990, it reemerged as *The Star* with a new license. The paper is believed to have a 10,000-copy circulation.

Prior to the passing of the new Press and Publications Law, the following weeklies had been published with foreign franchises: *Al-Ahaly* (*People*), *Al-Watan* (*Homeland*), *Akher Khabar* (*Latest News*), *Al-Rebat* (*Bond*), *Al-Belad* (*The Country*), *Al-Raseef* (*Pavement*), *Al-Hewar* (*Dialogue*), and *Al-Jaleah* (*Community*).

Seven party-affiliated weeklies have been granted permission to publish or are in the process of acquiring such permissions. They include: *Al-Mustaghbal* (*Future*) (Future Party), *Al-Ahd* (*Pledge*) (Pledge Party), *Al-Watan* (*Homeland*) (Progress and Justice Party), *Al-Horieh* (*Liberty*) (Al-Horieh Party), *Nidaa Al-Watan* (*Homeland Call*) (Popular Unity Party), *Al-Massera* (*March*) (Jordan Progressive Democratic Party), and *Al-Jamaheer* (*Masses*) (Communist Party).

Magazines

Al-Ufuq is Jordan's only political and economic magazine, first launched in March 1982 under the title *Al Ufuq Al Iqtisadi* (Economic Horizon). In August 1982, the magazine was suspended by the government after publishing an analysis dealing with repercussions of the 1982 Israeli invasion of Lebanon on Jordan and the Palestinians. On April 1992, *Al-Ufuq* was permitted to republish as a pan-Arab political weekly by Al Ufuq Press and Publishing House. Its editor, Tareq Masarweh, is one of the most influential columnists in Jordan.

Jordan's nonpolitical magazines include *Al-Aswaq* (*Markets*) (economic), *Al-Shebab* (*Youth*) (social), *Al-Shareea* (*Islamic Law*) (religious), *Afkar* (*Ideas*) (cultural), and *Besma* (*Smile*) (women).

ELECTRONIC MEDIA

Jordan maintains an extensive system of multilingual radio and television services operating within the Jordan Radio and Television Corporation (JRTC). In May 1992, reception of satellite transmissions by private home dish owners was legalized, and plans are being considered for introducing cable television in the greater area of the capital city of Amman on a commercial basis. On the occasion of Jordan television's silver jubilee anniversary (April 28, 1993), a satellite transmission channel was inaugurated.

Radio

Radio broadcasting in Jordan started as early as 1936 with the establishment of the Palestine Broadcasting Service by British Mandate authorities in both Jordan and Palestine (Boyd, 1982, p. 85). Studios for the Palestinian radio station were based in Jerusalem, while the transmitter and tower were situated in the nearby town of Ramallah in the Israeli-occupied West Bank. The station used a 20-kilowatt power transmitter to broadcast its Arabic/English programs, which were designed to establish communication channels with Arab and Jewish communities in Palestine and to counter Italian propaganda in the Middle East.

Following the 1948 Arab-Israeli war, the station's transmitter and tower were taken over by the Jordanian forces, giving rise to a new radio service known as the Hashemite Broadcasting Service (HBS) (Jarrar, 1986, p. 12). In 1956, another radio station began transmitting from Amman by using a 20-kilowatt power transmitter to respond to anti-Jordanian government radio propaganda,

Table 9.1
Radio Jordan's Arabic Programs

Programs	Percentages
Service-oriented	43.29
News and political	14.08
Religious	11.44
Music and songs	10.32
Cultural	10.17
Family and children	3.80
Sports and youth	3.79
Specials	1.07

Source: Jordan Radio and Television Corporation, 1992.

emanating mainly from Cairo. The current Hashemite Broadcasting Service was inaugurated on March 1, 1959, by King Hussein, who described the station as Jordan's "vivid voice, energetically defining Arabism and Islam" (Boyd, 1982, p. 86). With the loss of the West Bank in the June 1967 war, HBS was operating totally from Amman, as the Jerusalem studios were taken over by Israeli occupation forces.

By the end of 1992, radio broadcasting in Jordan was carried in three languages: Arabic, English, and French, broadcast on FM (frequency modulation) medium, short-, and long waves. Topics of HBS Arabic programming and their percentages are listed in Table 9.1.

The dominance of service-oriented programs, especially talk shows involving a two-way communication between listeners and officials via radio, indicates innovative programming by HBS. In one of these call-in programs, it was noted that such a format has provided citizens with ample access opportunities to take part in discussions of daily life problems in the country (Ayish, 1990). This programming format is a practical implementation of longtime calls for harnessing mass media in the service of national development. But this developmental role, more or less, seems to be constrained by existing government policies on the various issues of development. A study of development-oriented programs on Jordan radio and television indicated that absence of explicit and declared government policies on the issues of family planning and population control in general seems to have inhibited direct discussions of the two issues by broadcasters (Ayish & Shalabieh, 1991).

Broadcasts on the main Arabic program start at 5:30 A.M. with readings from the Holy Quran, a tradition followed by Arab, Islamic, and even some international broadcasters in Arabic, and end at 1:30 A.M. Jordan's keenness in maintaining strong contacts with Jordanian expatriates abroad (especially in the Gulf states) has motivated the government to upgrade the transmission power of its broadcasts, especially on shortwave. A newly introduced talk program, *Good Morning Homeland,* seems to underscore interest in capturing Jordanian and Arab listeners residing in countries as far away as the United States and Australia.

A two-hour daily FM broadcast was launched in early 1992 to help motorists move around in the congested streets of Amman during rush hours. The broadcast includes updated information on the situation of roads and crowded spots. It also includes music and interviews. In January 1993, local community broadcasting was introduced for the first time outside Amman with the launching of an FM station in the northern city of Irbid. Broadcasting for six hours a day, the station carries national newscasts, talk shows, and development programs.

Television

Unlike radio, television was a latecomer to Jordan, whose neighbors were already using the medium for broadcasting (Batayneh, 1988). Jarrar noted that Jordanian officials became fully convinced of the vitality of television for the country in 1964 (Jarrar, 1986, p. 18). Funds were allocated for conducting a feasibility study that was carried out by a team of international consultants (Boyd, 1982, pp. 90–91). The final report submitted by the international consultants called for establishing a television station to cover initially the Amman area before being expanded to include such cities as Irbid and Nablus. The proposals, which also called for financing the station from advertising revenues and TV set fees, were rejected by the government, and so were requests by local businessmen to operate the station as a commercial enterprise along the lines of the Lebanese television system.

In autumn 1965, the Jordanian government decided to go ahead with establishing television as a government-controlled operation, and bids for equipment and furnishings were advertised in local and foreign newspapers. Although the 1967 Arab-Israeli war delayed the introduction of television, experimental transmissions were launched on February 17, 1968, for 90 minutes and consisted of minidocumentaries and music. The station was officially inaugurated on April 27, 1968, with a four-hour transmission. In 1992, Jordan Television's (JTV) Arabic channel was broadcasting for an average of ten hours a day.

Jordan Television broadcasts in four languages on two channels. The main channel is exclusively in Arabic, while the foreign channel carries programs in French, Hebrew, and English. Programs on the Arabic channel include news, drama series, music, development programs, children's programs, religious programs, sports, and movies. Jordan Television is a member of the European Broadcasting Union (EBU) and subscribes to *Eutelsat,* the European Telecommunications Satellite Organization transmissions. It receives four daily news feeds via satellite for inclusion in its nightly news bulletins in Arabic, English, French, and Hebrew (Ayish, 1983). In a recent comparative study of Jordan Television's use of international news film materials versus local items, Ayish noted a significant emphasis on local events, especially those with development components (Ayish, 1990).

Jordan is also a full member of the Arab States Broadcasting Union (ASBU) and subscribes to its satellite project ARABSAT (Arab Satellite Communications Organization), which, among other things, is used by JTV and other Arab TV stations to exchange TV news materials and other programs. Jordan Television also broadcasts weekly news briefs originating in several Arab states as part of the ASBU *Arab Forum* show.

Jordan Television's foreign channel starts transmission at 3:00 P.M. with a two-hour Arabic teletext service that was introduced in 1990. The teletext program includes public service announcements and commercial messages with music playing in the background. JTV is one of very few stations in the area with such teletext services.

Actual broadcasting begins at 6:00 P.M. with French cultural programs, then a French news bulletin at 7:00 P.M. local time. News in Hebrew is broadcast at 7:30 P.M. for 15 minutes, after which the two channels link up for the main Arabic newscast at 8:00 P.M. English-language programs start at 8:30 P.M. with British/American sitcoms, documentaries, drama series, some local talk shows, and the *News at Ten* with Arabic subtitles (see Table 9.2). The foreign channel usually signs off at midnight.

Jordan Television programming has undergone major technological developments with the introduction of modern equipment for outdoor broadcasting. Recently, Jordan Television has demonstrated its technological proficiency by transmitting live the arrival home of King Hussein after a month-long absence abroad to undergo major surgery. Millions of viewers were glued to their TV sets to watch the royal procession move through the heavily congested streets of Amman. Two weeks later, Jordan Television scored another broadcast victory by launching its first live telethon program to raise funds for a cancer medical center. The volume of incoming calls from contributors was so overwhelming that the telethon organizers decided to extend the live program till past midnight. In the midst of JTV's celebrations of its silver jubilee anniversary on April 27, 1993, King Hussein inaugurated the station's fully computerized newsroom.

Jordan Television depends for its funding on allocations from the national budget, advertising revenue, and TV set fees collected as part of utility bills. Well over 91 percent of Jordanian households are estimated to have TV sets.

The legalization of home satellite reception in Jordan and the availability of Cable News Network (CNN) programs in major hotels and at subscribers' homes

Table 9.2
JTV English-Language Programs for One Week—December 16–31, 1992

Weekdays	8:30pm	9:00	9:30	10:00	10:20
Monday	Step by Step	Fine Romance		News	The Dismissed
Tuesday	The Golden.Girls	Made in Heaven		News	Film
Wednesday	Saved by the Bell	Spotlight	Investigative	News	Taking a Stand
Thursday	The Golden Girls	Civil Wars		News	Film
Friday	Wings	Gabriel's Fire		News	Colombo
Saturday	America's Funniest Video	Perspective	Varieties	News	Film
Sunday	Family Matters	Documentary		News	Law & Order

Source: Jordan Radio and Television Corporation (1992).

in Amman create pressures on Jordan Television to stand up to their challenge. Although Jordanian officials do not seem to be too concerned about the implications of this step, the specter of a dwindling Jordan Television audience is worrisome.

Television production in Jordan is carried out by the Jordan Company for Television, Radio and Cinematic Production, and scores of private production enterprises. In the 1980s, Jordanian television programs, especially drama series dealing with Bedouin life, had been widely marketed in the Arab Gulf states where the Bedouin accent was easily understood by local viewers. After the Gulf War, however, Jordanian television program production suffered a setback in light of the embargo imposed on its importation by Gulf television systems.

MOTION PICTURES

As for film industry in Jordan, the bulk of attention seems to be focused on video production. However, there are 45 movie theaters in Jordan; half of them are located in the capital city of Amman. According to available data, Jordan imports from 700 to 1,000 films a year from other nations, especially Turkey, India, China, the United States, and the United Kingdom (Abu Saud et al., 1992). A study of imported movies concluded that films center on social issues, violence, romance, and soft pornography, while few have comic, historical, or human orientations. About 200 movies per year, on average, are not permitted to play in Jordan by the Film Censorship Council, a Ministry of Information body in charge of gatekeeping incoming visual and audio materials in Jordan.

The number of moviegoers ranges between 200 and 500 persons a day, a relatively low figure that may be explained by the widespread proliferation of home video sets in Jordan. According to a recent survey, the number of video sets in Jordan is estimated at between 60,000 and 80,000, while video rental stores total 500 in number (Abu Saud et al., 1992). Like other film materials, videotapes are screened before they are permitted to appear at rental stores in Jordan. Video materials banned from entering Jordan are those that are:

- Subject to the Arab League–sponsored boycott laws or sympathetic to Israel.
- Pornographic.
- Insulting to Arabs and to Islamic teachings.
- Instigating sectarian or ethnic divisions.
- Lacking in moral values.

MEDIA OWNERSHIP

Media ownership and control patterns in Jordan seem to reflect a mixed system of mass communications whereby broadcast media continue to serve as public, government-controlled and -operated institutions, while print media function mainly as private commercial or party-affiliated outlets.

MEDIA REGULATION

Prior to May 17, 1993, the Jordanian press had operated under Jordan's Press and Publications Law, first passed in 1953 and modified in 1973. According to this law, the government is the sole authority to license all papers and magazines and to withdraw licenses if a publication "threatens national existence" or security; infringes on "the constitutional principles of the Kingdom"; harms "national feelings"; or offends "public decency." The law specifically forbids publication of news about the Royal Family unless approved by it, of articles defaming religion or contrary to public morality, or of unauthorized military and secret information (Armouti, 1982, pp. 21–22). On many occasions, Jordanian newspaper editors did not hesitate to speak out against the law, calling for revision (El-Sarayrah, 1983 p. xv).

In April 1993, a Royal Decree endorsed the new Press and Publications Law after it had been passed by both houses of Parliament. The new law went into effect on May 17, 1993. Article 3 of the law states that "freedom of opinion is guaranteed to every Jordanian citizen" and that "Jordanians are allowed to express their opinions freely through speech, writing, photography, and printing as means of expression and information" (Jordan Press and Publications Law, 1993). The law grants the right to own or start publications to all Jordanians, individuals, and political parties. It also prohibits the closure of newspapers and other publications and makes government decisions on the press appealable.

The new legislation also calls on journalists to abide by a professional code of ethics through presenting news in an objective, comprehensive, and balanced manner by demonstrating accuracy, objectivity, and fairness in news commentaries and analyses and refraining from publishing any materials that would instigate violence, fanaticism, bigotry, hatred, racism, and sectarianism. It also provides the right of correction and response to all individuals affected by the publication of unfounded news. Yet that right is not extended to corrections that do not carry full clear names of writers and that come over two months after the publication of erroneous materials.

The law contains several controversial provisions that have prompted negative reactions from Jordanian journalists and some international organizations concerned with press freedom (Article 19, 1993). Criticisms centered on issues relating to licensing journalists, editors, and directors of publications and printing facilities; access to information; revelation of sources; and prior restraint on press coverage of certain areas.

With respect to the licensing of journalists, the definition of *journalist* originally proposed by the government was "any person who meets the conditions for membership in the Journalists' Association or chooses journalism as a profession." However, when the draft law was presented to the Lower House of Parliament in its 1992 session, deputies amended the provision and restricted the definition of a journalist only to a person who is a member of the Journalists' Association.

Article 6 of the new law declares that "any person or political party has the right to own and publish newspapers or magazines" (Jordan Press and Publications Law, 1993). But Article 18 considerably limits the enjoyment of this right by requiring an owner of a publication to be a Jordanian residing in the Kingdom of Jordan unconvicted of crime or a misdemeanor involving honor or public morals. The article fails to define the meaning of *honor* and *public morals* but more seriously denies foreigners and Jordanians living abroad the right to establish or own newspapers and periodicals.

Although Article 5(a) guarantees to the press the right to "collect information, news and statistics of concern to citizens from different sources," and although Article 7 guarantees that "officials and non-officials shall facilitate the task of the journalist or the researcher to review their programs and projects," it falls short of making such duty mandatory. In the same spirit, Article 5(d) recognizes the right of the newspaper or news agency, the editor, and the journalist "to keep secret the sources of their information except from the judiciary" (Jordan Press and Publications Law, 1993).

Article 4 states that the "press is free to operate and present news, information, and comments and to publish articles on culture and science within the limits of the law."

EXTERNAL MEDIA SERVICES

The English Service of Radio Jordan started transmission in 1973 for 1.5 hours a day on medium and shortwaves for audiences inside Jordan as well as abroad. By April 1978, transmission time totaled 14 hours and was also carried on FM. In 1981, the English Service of Radio Jordan had a transmission time of 17 hours a day. Programs carried by the service include news, Western and Arabic music, cultural programs, talk shows, and drama. The *Jordan Radio and Television Yearbook* (Jordan Radio and Television Corporation, 1992) defines the objectives of the service as including:

1. Presenting Jordan's political viewpoints regarding Arab and international issues.
2. Acquainting Western listeners with Islamic teachings and values.
3. Promoting tourism.
4. Marketing Jordan among foreign investors.
5. Highlighting the country's democratic practices.

A French service has been recently introduced to Radio Jordan after an information and cultural agreement was signed between Jordan and France during the November 26, 1992, state visit to Jordan by French President François Mitterand. Broadcasting for two hours a day on FM, the station carries news and other programs in French in addition to French music.

NEWS AGENCIES

The Jordanian News Agency (Petra) was established on July 16, 1969, to serve as a collector and distributor of local and national news to media in Jordan and abroad. Petra has a 154-person staff—about half of them work as reporters and editors and are members of the Jordan Press Association. Petra transmits three bulletins a day: a general bulletin, a restricted bulletin (to government officials), and an external bulletin. Until 1990, the agency had correspondents based in Damascus, Baghdad, Cairo, Tunis, Beirut, London, Madrid, and Moscow. Austerity measures, however, led to the closure of these bureaus. The agency looks forward to upgrading its performance through acquiring institutional and financial autonomy, replacing its shortwave transmission facilities with satellite linkups, and having access to international information banks.

THE ROLE OF MEDIA IN NATIONAL DEVELOPMENT

The developmental role of mass media in Jordan has always been recognized. In response to United Nations Educational, Scientific and Cultural Organization (UNESCO) calls for harnessing mass media in the service of national development, Jordan was one of the few countries to establish a Development Communication Department at the Ministry of Information in the mid-1970s. The department produces television and radio documentaries as well as short messages relating to the environment, public sanitation, agriculture, vocational training, and safety at home and at work.

Mass media in Jordan often carry programs and messages on health, the environment, child care, and birth spacing. The materials are usually produced by the Ministry of Health or some other nongovernmental organizations like Noor Al-Hussein Foundation to raise public awareness of the issues. The Health Education Project carried out by the Ministry of Health with funding from the U.S. Agency for International Development (USAID) from 1981 to 1986 sought to educate mothers and the public at large via television on basic child care and protection against dehydration (Hamzeh, 1990). Another health communication project was carried out in the late 1980s by Noor Al-Hussein Foundation with funding from USAID and in cooperation with the American Academy for Educational Development on breast feeding and birth spacing in Jordan. The project utilized television spots to educate mothers on both topics (Bahous & Abu Laban, 1990).

Jordan Television also cooperates with the Ministry of Education to produce and broadcast educational materials to be viewed by students at schools on subjects like geography, English, physics, chemistry, and the like. These educational programs are directed to morning and afternoon classes and are intended as supplemental materials to formal classroom lectures.

The most interesting experiment in the use of communication for education was carried out by the Department of Journalism and Mass Communication (DJMC) at Yarmouk University. The project, implemented from 1986 to 1990, and funded by both UNESCO and the United Nations Fund for Population Activities (UNFPA), sought to educate residents of a northern Jordanian rural community on the population problem and family planning. Although the whole project was designed to serve as an educational experiment for the DJMC staff and students, field research indicated that communication does play a role in educating the general public on the sensitive issue of family planning and in modifying attitudes and practices relating to that issue (Population Communication Project, 1990).

CONCLUSION

Mass media have always been shaped by the social, political, and cultural milieu in which they operate, and the Jordanian media are no exception. Since the launching of the first newspaper in the early 1920s, Jordanian newspapers have evolved in tandem with the country's development, echoing national concerns and ambitions. In its 70-year history, Jordan has espoused a mixed system of governance in which private enterprise worked along parallel lines with the public sector in an atmosphere of cooperation and reciprocity. As a result, mass media in Jordan have always taken on this mixed system outlook with newspapers and other print media falling in the private sector domain, while broadcasting remains a government concern.

Although the Jordanian press enjoyed a considerable degree of freedom in the 1950s, it was not until 1989 that Jordanian media were presented with genuine opportunities for practicing their free handling of public affairs in a democratized environment. Three years later, democracy in Jordan withstood a multitude of challenges, the most formidable of which was the Gulf crisis and war. By demonstrating a high degree of responsibility, both the media and the public have proven their maturity and concern over safeguarding a democratic Jordan.

With the abolition of martial law and the legalization of political parties in Jordan, the media are expected to increase in number and exhibit a greater degree of pluralism, reflecting a wider array of political orientations. This development is likely to put more pressure on already established nonpartisan publications to strive to maintain their audiences in order to ensure the flow of advertising revenue.

Another challenge facing the press in Jordan relates to the application of the provisions of new Press and Publications Law. After the law has been endorsed by Parliament, the specter of putting it into effect would appear uncomfortable to journalists as the law would potentially be used by the government to curb press freedom. A national drive has been mounted to introduce amendments that would make the new law conducive to freedom of speech and the press. In May 1993, the Minister of Information replied to criticisms of the new press law by saying that Jordanian democracy derives from the peculiarities of the country's distinguished Arab and Islamic character, and press legislations are not enacted to stay unchanged (Sharif, 1993).

Jordanian television's launching of a satellite transmission channel seems to reflect JTV's international ambitions to join the global club of satellite broadcasters. In his inaugural speech on April 27, 1993, King Hussein said the medium will serve as a pan-Arab voice committed to and working toward enhancing freedom and enhancing Arab unity. The limited territorial expanse of Jordan has made it vulnerable to television transmissions from neighboring countries, and the problem has been aggravated by the recent legalization of home satellite reception equipment. In radio broadcasting, Jordanian listeners are already exposed to scores of Arab and international radio stations transmitting political, cultural, and even educational programs in Arabic to listeners in the Middle East. More quality radio and television programs could lessen the negative impact of competition, but it would not be possible to eliminate its effects.

REFERENCES

Abu Saud, A., Innab, Z., Al Hoar, M., & Rifai, Z. (1992, May). *Communication and culture sector.* Paper presented to the National Conference on Children, Amman.

Arab House for Encyclopedias. (1980). *The Jordan press.* Beirut: Arab House for Encyclopedias.

Armouti, M. (1982). *Communication development and society.* Irbid, Jordan: Yarmouk University Press.

Article 19. (1992, December 4). *Jordan: Critique of the draft press and publications law.* London: England.

Ayish, M. (1983). *The flow of newsfilm to Jordan television via Eurovision.* Unpublished master's thesis, University of Minnesota, Twin Cities.

Ayish, M. (1989, Fall). Newsfilm in Jordan Television's Arabic nightly newscasts. *Journal of Broadcasting and Electronic Media, 33*(4), 453–460.

Ayish, M. (1990). Media access in the Third World: A case of a Jordanian radio program. *Gazette, 45,* 173–187.

Ayish, M., & Shalabieh, M. (1991). Population communication in Jordanian radio and television [In Arabic]. *Abhath Al-Yarmouk, 7,* 1. Jordan.

Badran, B. (1988, Summer). Press-government relations in Jordan: A case study. *Journalism Quarterly,* pp. 335–340, 346.

Bahous, S., & Abu Laban, A. (1990, March). *The health communication project at Noor Al-Hussein Foundation.* Paper presented at the National Symposium on Communication, Population and Development, Irbid, Jordan.

Batayneh, A. (1988). *An investigation of the news selection criteria of Jordan television.* Unpublished doctoral dissertation, Florida State University.

Boyd, D. (1982). *Broadcasting in the Arab World: A survey of radio and television in the Middle East.* Philadelphia: Temple University Press.

Central Bank of Jordan. (1992, November). *Monthly Analytical Bulletin.* Amman, Jordan.

El-Sarayrah, M. (1984). *Foreign news in two Jordanian newspapers.* Unpublished master's thesis, Ohio University.

El-Sarayrah, M. (1986). Foreign news in two Jordanian newspapers. *Journalism Quarterly, 36,* 363–365.

El-Sarayrah, M. (1992). Advertising in Jordanian daily newspapers [In Arabic]. *Abhath Al-Yarmouk.* Irbid, Jordan.

Hamzeh, M. (1990, March). *The role of health education in the areas of childhood and maternity care.* Paper presented at the National Symposium on Communication, Population and Development, Irbid, Jordan.

Jarrar, F. (1986). *Television, satellites and communication* [In Arabic]. Amman: Shukair & Akasheh.

Jordan Press and Publications Law. (1993). Amman, Jordan.

Jordan Radio and Television Corporation. (1992). *Jordan radio and television yearbook.* Amman: JRTC.

Ministry of Information. (1978). *Mass communication in Jordan.* Amman: Ministry of Information Press.

———. (1980). *Jordan Press.* Amman: Ministry of Information Press.

Mousa, I. (1988). Characteristics of the modern Jordanian press as represented by the daily *Al-Rai* newspaper. *Abhath Al-Yarmouk, 4*(1), 81–115.

Population Communication Project. (1990). *Effects of IEC campaigns on family planning practices: A practical model.* Department of Journalism and Mass Communication, Yarmouk University, in cooperation with UNESCO and UNFPA.

Rugh, W. (1979). *The Arab press: News media and political processes in the Arab World.* Syracuse, NY: Syracuse University Press.

Sharif, M. (1993, May 10). The new press and publications law. A lecture at Yarmouk University, Irbid.

Sibert, F., Peterson, T., & Schramm, W. (1963). *Four theories of the press.* Urbana: University of Illinois Press.

Zou'bi A., Poedjastoeti, S., & Ayad, M. (1992). *Jordan population and family health survey.* Columbia, MD: IRD/Macro International, Inc.

10

KUWAIT

Fayad E. Kazan

INTRODUCTION

Kuwait is one of the Arab states of the Gulf region, bound to the north by Iraq, to the east by the Gulf coast, and to the south by Saudi Arabia. Located in southwestern Asia with an area of 6,877 square miles, Kuwait's topography mainly consists of flat desert interspersed with low hills. Kuwaiti coastal waters are shallow in the northern part, where a number of islands lie, the biggest of which is Babiyan Island.

Waves of Arab nomads, who were mainly hunters, settled in the Kuwait Bay area in A.D. 1700. In the second half of the eighteenth century, Kuwait attracted many tribes from the Arabian Peninsula, including the Al-Sabah tribe who ruled Kuwait since the beginning of the nineteenth century and laid the foundation for modern Kuwait.

Before the discovery of oil, Kuwaiti people depended on the sea and on trade for survival. This was true of the Arab nomads who settled Kuwait Bay in A.D. 1700. At that time and up until the discovery of oil, Kuwait occupied a central place in Gulf trade and pearl diving, and the Kuwaitis traded not only with neighboring countries but also with the ports of East Africa and South Asia as well. Kuwait managed to establish a boat-building industry and developed a huge commercial fleet (Bseso, 1984). By the end of World War II, Kuwait's economy declined, and it was not until after the discovery of oil that Kuwait became one of the wealthiest societies in the world. The search for oil in Kuwait began in 1936, but exporting it in commercial quantities did not occur until

1946. As a major Arab oil-producing country, Kuwait produces more than 1.6 million barrels of oil a day, which amounts to more than 10 percent of the Organization of Petroleum Exporting Countries's (OPEC) daily oil production. Kuwait's oil reserves are estimated at 94 billion barrels, which constitutes 20.5 percent of the overall oil reserve of the countries of the Gulf Cooperation Council (GCC) (*Statistical Review of World Energy,* 1992).

Because of the desert terrain, the role of Kuwait's agriculture in the economy is marginal. Thus, Kuwait's economy depends mainly on the government-controlled petroleum industry and on Kuwaiti investments abroad, which amounted to $100 billion before the Iraqi invasion of Kuwait in August of 1990.

The State of Kuwait was established as a constitutional monarchy after it gained its independence from Britain in 1961. Shortly after, it became a member of the United Nations and of the League of Arab States. Following Kuwait's independence, the Iraqi regime of Abdel Karim Qassem threatened to annex it; subsequently, British troops were called in to protect the new state. Later on, the British troops were withdrawn and replaced by a military force from the League of Arab States. The new Iraqi government that replaced the Qassem regime recognized Kuwait as a sovereign state, and the Arab League military contingent was withdrawn.

With the demise of the Iraqi threat to its national security, and the new prosperity that emerged from oil, the Kuwaiti government embarked on extensive plans for socioeconomic and political developments. In the field of health, Kuwait has managed to build scores of hospitals, clinics, and health centers that provide adequate health services to Kuwaitis and foreign nationals free of charge. These developments have, in turn, led to major improvements in the infant mortality rate, life expectancy at birth, and the mortality rate of the general population (*Human Development Report,* 1992).

In the field of education, the number of schools increased more than fourfold from 1962 to 1993; the number of enrolled students increased by about 7 times; and the number of teachers increased 13 times. Kuwait University was established in 1967, Kuwait Institute for Scientific Research in 1973, and Kuwait Foundation for the Advancement of Sciences in 1976. Meanwhile, several applied education and vocational training centers were established. Consequently, the level of education has progressed in Kuwait, bringing down the illiteracy rate from 89 percent in 1963 to 32 percent in 1990 (*Human Development Report,* 1992).

Politically, Kuwait played an active foreign policy role in the Arab and Islamic worlds in particular and in the world arena in general. Kuwait strove to preserve its neutrality in terms of the East/West conflict during the era of the cold war and played an active role in the bloc of the nonaligned states. Since 1962, when the Kuwait Fund for Arab Economic Development (KFAED) was established, Kuwait has provided hundreds of low-interest development loans to the Arab, African, and Asian countries. In 1981, KFAED activities were extended to all the developing countries, and the KFAED budget was increased from \$3.5 billion to \$7 billion accordingly. Kuwait has allocated about 5 percent of its gross national product (GNP) for development efforts in the developing countries (''Kuwait on the March,'' 1989; Ministry of Information, 1989).

Political stability along with the improvement in the quality of life in Kuwait attracted a diverse population from the Gulf region—the Arab World, Pakistan, and India—and from the Philippines. This led to a general increase in the Kuwaiti population, so that Kuwait is inhabited by about 2 million people, of whom 800,000 or about 40 percent are Kuwaiti nationals. According to the 1985 census, Kuwaitis and non-Kuwaiti Arabs formed 78 percent of the Kuwait population. The remaining 22 percent consisted mainly of South and East Asians (''Kuwait on the March,'' 1989; Ministry of Information, 1989).

Kuwaitis adhere to Islam as their official religion. Arabic is the native language of the Kuwaiti population, who are mostly Arabs with a minority of Kuwaitis from Persian origin. English is the second most spoken language.

PRINT MEDIA

Newspapers

Kuwaiti press began to emerge in 1928 (Rugh, 1979, p. 72), but it was not until the 1960s that the Kuwaiti dailies started to appear with a high level of sophistication and a wide spectrum of orientations.

The number of print media in Kuwait, their quality, diversity, competition, outspokenness, and freedom have prompted Rugh (1987) to classify them within what he calls the ''diverse'' press category, while those of Qatar, United Arab Emirates (UAE), and Saudi Arabia are classified within the ''loyalist'' press category:

> The diverse press [has as its] most significant distinguishing characteristic . . . that the newspapers are clearly different from each other in content and apparent political tendency as well as in style. They are all privately owned and reflect a variety of viewpoints. . . . [In] . . . loyalist press systems similarities outweigh any differences among papers within one country . . . [and] its most prominent characteristic is that the newspapers are consistently loyal to and supportive of the regime in power despite the fact that they are privately owned. (Rugh, 1987, p. 71)

Although Kuwaiti newspapers vary in their orientations, they do express their support for the amir (king) and the royal family regardless of their differences. The daily newspapers in Kuwait consist of *Al-Raey Al-Am (Public Opinion), Kuwait Times, Al-Siyassah (Politics), Al-Qabas (The Beacon), Al-Watun (The Homeland), Al-Anbaa (The News),* and *Arab Times.*

Al-Qabas and *Al-Watun* newspapers tend to be more outspoken and liberal

Table 10.1
Major Daily Newspapers in Kuwait, 1993

Newspapers	First Published	Circulation*
Al-Raey Al-Am (Public Opinion)	1961	40,000
Kuwait Times	1961	25,000
Al-Siyassah (Politics)	1965	50,000
Al-Qabas (The Beacon)	1972	65,000
Alwatun (The Homeland)	1974	60,000
Al-Anbaa (The News)	1976	100,000
ArabTimes	1977	50,000

*Based on publishers' estimates.

in their orientations than all other Kuwaiti newspapers. On the other hand, *Al-Siyassah* tends to be the most conservative of Kuwaiti newspapers.

Table 10.1 shows the inauguration dates and the circulation figures of the major daily newspapers in Kuwait. However, it should be noted that the circulation figures were obtained from the newspapers themselves. This may cast some doubts on the validity of those figures.

A recent readership survey of 782 respondents by the Kuwaiti-based Pan-Arab Research Center (PARC) showed that *Al-Qabas* is read by about 60 percent of the respondents, followed by *Al-Anbaa* (48.5 percent), *Al-Watun* (41.6 percent), *Al-Siyassah* (16.3 percent), *Arab Times* (11.7 percent), *Al-Rai Al-Am* (10.9 percent), and *Kuwait Times* (7.8 percent). Recent UN data indicate that Kuwait has 209 copies of newspapers per 1,000 population (*Human Development Report,* 1992).

Unlike the media of the other Gulf countries that have mainly progressed in a quantitative sense, Kuwaiti media have progressed both quantitatively and qualitatively. This is not surprising, because Kuwait is characterized by a more diversified and pluralistic demographic structure and a higher level of popular political participation than the other Arab states of the Gulf. Thus, Kuwait's structural and cultural characteristics have been reflected in the quality of its print media. Kuwait print media not only are popular at home but also are very popular in the rest of the Arab World.

In the fall of 1990, shortly after the Iraqi occupation of Kuwait, *Sawt Al-Kuwait (Voice of Kuwait)* and *New Arabia* newspapers were launched by the Kuwaiti government. In March 1991, *Al-Fajr Al-Jadeed (The New Dawn),* another Kuwaiti daily, with close ties to the Kuwaiti government, was also launched from Kuwait. Yet these three government-owned and -controlled newspapers went out of business mainly because they could not compete with the privately owned Kuwaiti newspapers.

Magazines

A number of magazines are published in Kuwait. Foremost among them is *Al-Arabi (The Arabian).* First published by the Kuwaiti Ministry of Information in 1958, *Al-Arabi* is probably the most widely read social and educational magazine in the Arab World. Like other Kuwaiti magazines, *Al-Arabi* publication was interrupted as a result of the Iraqi invasion of Kuwait. *Al-Arabi* resumed its publication on September 1, 1991.

Al-Nahda (The Renaissance), established in 1967, is a monthly magazine that focuses on sociopolitical and economic issues. *Al-Moukhtalef (Unique)* focuses on social issues. *Al-Arab (Arabs)* is the first magazine published after Kuwait's liberation. Both *Al-Arab* and *Al-Moukhtalef* magazines are monthly magazines, although they were weekly magazines before the Iraqi invasion.

Weekly magazines include *Ousraty (My Family),* which is a sociopolitical and cultural magazine; *Annas (People)* is a critical and social magazine; *Hayatana (Our Life)* is a women's magazine; *Al-Majales (Gatherings)* is a sociopolitical magazine; and *Al-Balagh (Notification)* is a mostly religious magazine. Table 10.2 shows the inauguration dates and circulation figures of the major magazines in Kuwait.

Kuwait's print media covers a wide range of viewpoints. In essence, the print media is a reflection of the relatively cosmopolitan nature of Kuwaiti society and its democratic aspirations. Kuwait's print media consist of a diverse spectrum of viewpoints—liberal, leftist, rightist, and moderate.

After the Gulf War, Kuwaiti authorities became intolerant of criticism by the press as exemplified by the recent charge directed against the Kuwaiti newspaper *Al-Qabas* for allegedly printing news that was seen as endangering Kuwait's national security. However, this government action is "viewed by many Kuwaitis as an attempt to muzzle press criticism of the [Kuwaiti] Government" ("Kuwait," 1992).

Nonetheless, the liberal and diverse content of Kuwait print media make them popular in Kuwait and in all the Arab World. Furthermore, Kuwait ranks second to Saudi Arabia with respect to the number of periodicals published in the GCC countries.

Table 10.2
Major Magazines in Kuwait, 1993

Magazine	First Published	Circulation*	
Al-Araby (Pioneer)	1958	360,000	Monthly
Al-Nahda (Renaissance)	1967	117,000	Monthly
Al-Moukhtalef	1991	27,000	Monthly
Al-Arab (Arabs)	1990	45,000	Weekly
Annas (People)	1991	40,000	Weekly
Hayatana (Our life)	1992	60,000	Weekly
Al-Majales (Gatherings)	1970	120,000	Weekly
Al-Balagh (Notification)	1969	20,000	Weekly
Ousraty (My Family)	1966	78,000	Weekly

*Based on publishers' estimates.

ELECTRONIC MEDIA

Because of the electronic media's importance as a means of control, national integration, and political persuasion, Kuwaiti electronic media (radio and television) are owned, financed, tightly controlled, and managed by the Kuwaiti government through the Ministry of Information. The ministry's role is to ensure that radio and television programs do not violate the communication policy guidelines of the Kuwaiti government.

The motivations for introducing broadcasting facilities into Gulf societies were varied. Considerations of national prestige, of sovereignty, of national identity, and of competition induced the small states of the Gulf, including Kuwait, to establish broadcasting facilities. The establishment of electronic media did not encounter any obstacles from the religious authorities in Kuwait.

Radio

Radio broadcasting started in Kuwait in 1951 from a half-kilowatt power transmitter, operated for two and a half hours daily ("Kuwait on the March," 1989; Ministry of Information, 1989). Independence in 1961 marked a turning point for Kuwaiti broadcasting. Kuwaiti radio programs, transmitters, and audience increased rapidly. A small country like Kuwait can be easily covered by a single medium wave radio transmitter. However, as a major oil exporter, and as a diversified, highly urbanized, and cosmopolitan society, Kuwait wanted to match these characteristics with a comparable broadcasting apparatus—hence, the rapid increase in the number of Kuwaiti radio facilities and the increase in the number of radio sets, which amounted to 337 sets per 1,000 population (*Human Development Report,* 1992). Before its invasion by Iraq, Kuwait had five radio stations with 21 FM (frequency modulation), medium, and shortwave transmitters ranging from 5 to 750 kilowatts of power (Ministry of Information, 1992). Those facilities enabled Kuwait to broadcast its programs through eight radio services, namely, First Program, Second Program, Quran Service, European Service, Urdu Service, Persian Service, Short Wave Service, and FM Service.

During the Iraqi occupation, Kuwaiti radio, in exile, resumed programming using 100-kilowatt medium wave transmitters, located in Saudi Arabia and Egypt, calling on the Kuwaiti people to rebel against the Iraqi occupation forces. The radio broadcast programs 18 hours daily from 7:00 A.M. to 1:00 A.M.

In 1993, Kuwait has five radio program services: First Program, Second Program, Quran Service, European Service, and FM Service. Kuwaiti radio broadcasts its programs using the following transmitters:

- Two shortwave transmitters with 500 kilowatts each.
- Ten medium wave transmitters ranging in power from 2 to 5 kilowatts.
- Four FM transmitters ranging in power from 2 to 5 kilowatts.

Additionally, the following transmitters are scheduled to become operational in 1993–1994:

- Two medium wave 600-kilowatt transmitters.
- Two shortwave 500-kilowatt transmitters.
- Three medium wave transmitters ranging from 50 to 200 kilowatts of power.
- Six FM stereo transmitters with 20 kilowatts of power each (A. Abdullah & S. Jaafar, personal interview, March 15, 1993).

Kuwaiti radio provides its fare through several programs: General Service, which broadcasts 21 hours a day; the Second Program, 6 hours a day; the Holy Quran Service, 9 hours a day; the European Service, 3 hours a day; and the FM

Table 10.3
Radio Programs and Transmission Hours: Kuwait

Category	1st Program	2nd Program
Religious	12	7
News/Public Affairs	20.2	21.4
Entertainment	54.9	56.8
Cultural	10.1	11.6
Drama	2.8	3.2

Source: Constructed from Ministry of Information, 1992.

Service, 15 hours a day. Both the General Service and the Second Program broadcast in Arabic. According to Kuwaiti Ministry of Information (1992), the General Service transmission time amounted to 624 hours per month. The Second Program transmission hours amounted to 186 hours per month. Table 10.3 lists program types and program hours for both services.

The European Program transmission time amounted to 381 hours, and the FM Program transmission time amounted to 2,760 hours throughout the first half of 1992.

Television

In 1957, Kuwait television started its monochrome transmission as a private enterprise from a 100 kilowatts of power transmitter (''Kuwait on the March,'' 1989; Ministry of Information, 1989). In 1961, when Kuwait gained its independence, television ownership was transferred to the Kuwaiti government. As in the case of Kuwaiti radio, a new era in the history of Kuwaiti television began. In 1974, Kuwait monochrome service was transformed into a phase alternate line (PAL) color system.

As was the case of Kuwaiti radio, Kuwait television studios and equipment were destroyed during the Iraqi occupation. After Kuwait's liberation, the Kuwaiti government contracted several Western companies that embarked on rebuilding Kuwaiti TV broadcasting infrastructure.

Table 10.4 shows the nine television channels in operation in 1993, including channel assignment, location, and power.

Before the Iraqi invasion, Kuwait television transmitted its programs from six transmission stations ranging from 200 to 640 kilowatts. Since Kuwait is still recovering from the effects of the Gulf War, Kuwaiti television broadcasts its

Table 10.4
Television Channels in Kuwait

Channel	Program	Location	KWT Power
5 VHF	Egyptian Satellite	Al-Mouqwaa	5
8 VHF	First Program	Al-Mouqwaa	6
10 VHF	Second Program	Al-Mouqwaa	6
12 VHF	MBC	Al-Mouqwaa	5
24 UHF	First Program	Faylaka	Being tested
38 UHF	Second Program	Al-Moujamaa	10
39 UHF	Second Program	Faylaka	Being tested
45 UHF	First Program	Al-Mouqwaa	10
47 UHF	Third Program	Al-Mouqwaa	1

Source: Compiled from information provided by Majeed Baghdadi of the Kuwaiti Ministry of Information; and from "Kuwait; TV Channels," 1993, p. 16.

KW = Kilowatt.
UHF = Ultrahigh Frequency.
VHF = Very high Frequency.

programs from two television stations with power ranging between 1 and 100 kilowatts. In addition to covering Kuwait, Kuwaiti television coverage includes certain parts of Iraq, the Eastern Province of Saudi Arabia, Bahrain, Qatar, United Arab Emirates, and Oman (Kazan, 1993). Since its early years, Kuwaiti television transmission time increased five times, from 28 hours per week in 1963 to an average of 149 hours per week in 1993. Kuwait society has a high penetration rate of television sets, amounting to about 300 sets per 1,000 population (*Human Development Report,* 1992).

In 1978 the Kuwaiti television complex was inaugurated. The complex serves as headquarters for the Kuwaiti radio and television services. The complex also houses studios that were once equipped with very sophisticated production and technical facilities second only to those of Saudi Arabia in the Gulf region.

Kuwait has several ground satellite stations, the latest of which were inaugurated in the summer of 1992. Kuwait's ground satellite stations are connected to the ARABSAT (Arab Satellite Communications Organization) and to the two satellites orbiting above the Atlantic and Indian oceans, enabling Kuwaiti au-

Table 10.5
Television Programs and Transmission Hours: Kuwait

Category	1st Program	2nd Program	3rd Program
Religious	11.6	2.6	2.6
News/Public Affairs	27.8	1.6	---
Entertainment	22.7	11.0	75
Cultural	9.4	11.4	22.4
Drama	26.5	42.7	---
Commercials	2.0	0.7	---

Source: Constructed from Ministry of Information, 1992.

diences to receive live coverage of important events from different parts of the world. This is made possible by daily dispatches from Arab States Broadcasting Union (ASBU), World-Wide TV Network (WTN), Reuter TV, British Broadcasting Corporation (BBC) TV, and Eurovision. The total duration of these daily dispatches amounts to about three hours. Meanwhile, there is an agreement between Cable News Network (CNN) and Kuwaiti TV to the effect that the latter can use certain CNN programming under certain circumstances (M. Al-Hajery, personal interview, March 20, 1993).

Television Programming. In the summer season, Kuwaiti TV First Program transmission starts at 9:00 A.M. and ends at 1:00 A.M. On the weekend, transmission starts at 9:00 A.M. and ends at 2:00 A.M. During the Holy month of Ramadan and religious holidays, transmission time starts at 1:00 P.M. and ends at 4:00 A.M. During the winter, transmission starts at 1:00 P.M. and ends at 1:00 A.M. Second Program transmission begins at 4:00 P.M. and ends at midnight during winter and summer. On the weekend, Second Program transmission begins at 4:00 P.M. and ends at midnight. During Ramadan, Kuwait Television Second Program transmission starts at 7:00 P.M. and ends at 2:00 P.M. The transmission of Kuwaiti TV First Program averages 98 hours a week, while that of the Second Program averages 51 hours a week. In addition to Kuwait TV First and Second programs, there is a Third Program, which is mainly sports programming. The Third Program transmission time averages 6 hours and 22 minutes per day (Ministry of Information, 1992). Table 10.5 shows program categories and transmission hours for the First, Second, and Third programs.

Formerly, 80 percent of the programs broadcast by Kuwaiti TV First Program were locally produced. The remaining 20 percent were imported from Arab and foreign countries. In 1993, about 25 percent of those programs are locally produced; the remaining 75 percent are imported from the Arab World. As for the Second Program, 80 to 90 percent of its programs are imported and the remaining 20 to 10 percent locally produced.

In the case of both radio and television, the First Program in Kuwait is directed at the natives, at the people of the Gulf at large, and at the entire Arab World in the case of radio. The English-language Second Program is directed at the expatriates living in Kuwait and in the Gulf region in general, and in the entire world in the case of radio.

Kuwaiti TV allows the broadcasting of commercials on both First and Second programs. The electronic media in Kuwait is staffed mainly by nationals.

Aside from the entertainment content, Kuwaiti electronic media content tends to cover political and social events from the perspective of the Kuwaiti government, which owns, finances, controls, operates, and manages Kuwaiti electronic media. Kuwaiti electronic media shy away from politically and socially controversial issues and tend to take a neutral stance concerning disputes among the Arab countries. This is not surprising, however, given the policy of the Kuwaiti government, which aims at staying on good terms with all countries. Kuwaiti electronic media, also, feature a highly diversified and cosmopolitan diet.

NEW TECHNOLOGIES

With the exception of radio and television sets, video sets are probably the most widespread communication media in Kuwait. Kuwait has perhaps the highest rate of VCR (videocasette recorder) equipment in the world, because it is completely saturated by VCRs; that is, each Kuwaiti family owns at least one VCR set. The Gulf area has the highest VCR ownership rate in the world, measuring at 50 VCRs per 1,000 population. This penetration rate far exceeds that of the United States and Western Europe (''Videocassettes,'' 1983).

Kuwait has around 200 shops for video rental and sales. About 75 percent of those shops distribute videos, in Arabic and English languages, and 25 percent distribute Indian videos. On the average, each video shop receives around 30 new programs a month. About 5 percent of those programs are pirated movies and television programs, imported or smuggled from the United States and western Europe. This situation has alarmed the Kuwaiti government as represented by the Ministry of Information. Consequently, a plan is being devised by the Kuwaiti government to enact the required laws and regulations to protect the rights of individuals and companies that produce video programs, on one hand, and the interest of Kuwaiti society, on the other.

Under the current situation, in order to be protected, video program copyrights have to be registered in the Department of Artistic Classifications of the Kuwaiti Ministry of Information. Based on this, the Ministry of Information requests that any individuals or companies that intend to buy video programs for distribution should prove their ownership of such programs through a certificate issued by the chamber of commerce of the country from which the programs were bought.

Meanwhile, the chamber of commerce certificate has to be certified by the Kuwaiti Embassy located in that particular country (S. Al-Nousf, personal interview, March 10, 1993). In addition, the Ministry of Information is in charge of licensing and inspection of video shops in Kuwait. Video shop licenses are issued for a year and renewed yearly as well. License fees amount to KD25 per year.

To get a permit for video program distribution, video shops send their video programs to the Kuwaiti Ministry of Information for review. The review lasts two to ten days, after which the Ministry of Information either approves or disapproves the distribution of those video programs. In some cases, certain parts of a video program are deleted, such as scenes in which kisses and excessive violence appear, before the permit for the distribution of that particular video program is granted. During the first half of 1992, the Kuwaiti Ministry of Information rejected 609 video programs out of 9,057 that were submitted for review (Ministry of Information, 1992).

The distribution of video programs is diminishing in Kuwait due to the diffusion of satellite dishes that are capable of picking up television signals from the Far East, western Europe, and North America. An estimated 60 to 70 percent of Kuwaiti homes own satellite dishes. The value of each satellite dish does not exceed U.S.$650. In addition to the Kuwaiti and Gulf TV programs, Kuwaiti audiences are exposed to several international TV programs such as STAR TV and STAR TV PLUS from Hong Kong, CNN International from the United States, BBC TV ASIA and Middle East Broadcasting Corporation (MBC) from London, and a channel from France, among others. Kuwaiti audiences are also exposed to an Egyptian Satellite Channel. Depending on the power and direction of the satellite dish, Kuwait viewers can pick up a large number of TV stations on their TV sets. In a recent study (PARC, 1992), 912 Kuwaiti respondents were surveyed concerning their video and television viewing habits. About 67 percent of the respondents mentioned that they had watched TV seven days per week. In contrast, only 10.1 percent of the respondents mentioned that they had watched video seven days per week.

Thus, with the mounting diffusion and increase in power of satellite dishes in Kuwait, and with the increase in the quality of television programs aired on Gulf TV stations, video program distribution is expected to decline further in Kuwaiti society.

MOTION PICTURES

The establishment of motion pictures in Kuwait dates back to the early 1950s. The birth of the National Company of Kuwaiti Cinema (NCKC) in 1954 gave a push to motion picture viewing in Kuwait. Owned by the Kuwaiti public, NCKC was licensed by the Kuwaiti government to be the sole company that has a monopoly on the construction of movie houses and the import of films within Kuwait. NCKC's monopoly on Kuwaiti cinema expires in the year 2004. NCKC is run by a board of directors elected by NCKC shareholders.

Kuwait originally had 14 movie houses, including 2 drive-in theaters. After Kuwait's liberation, NCKC rebuilt 7 movie houses. Each movie house accommodates around 700 viewers. Attendance in 1993 amounts to about 15 percent during weekdays and 40 to 45 percent during the weekend. These figures for movie attendance are down from 25 percent during the weekdays and 55 percent during the weekend.

The decline in the rate of movie attendance in Kuwait can be attributed to the following factors: (1) the quantitative and qualitative change in the demographic structure of Kuwaiti society after the liberation of Kuwait, (2) the wide diffusion of VCR equipment and video programs within Kuwait, (3) the improvement in the quality of programs broadcast by Gulf governments' television stations that reach Kuwaiti audiences, and (4) the mounting diffusion of the satellite dishes that enable Kuwaiti audiences to watch international TV stations such as CNN International, BBC TV ASIA, MBC, STAR 5, and STAR 5 PLUS television stations, among others.

NCKC imports all the films shown in its movie houses. Arabic films, which are mostly Egyptian, constitute 50 percent of the overall films shown. The remaining 50 percent consist of foreign films that are imported from the major American and European film companies through their agents in Beirut, Lebanon. For social and cultural reasons, Arab films get higher viewer attendance than foreign films.

The Cinema Censorship of the Kuwaiti Ministry of Information gets the films imported by NCKC through the Kuwaiti Customs Department. The Cinema Censorship screens the films to make sure that they conform with Kuwaiti communication policy. If they do, the Cinema Censorship authorizes showing them (A. Al-Hounayyef, personal interview, March 15, 1993).

MEDIA REGULATION

The year 1956 marked the passage of Kuwait's first publication law, which sought to regulate the relations between the Kuwaiti government and the press. The law covered all printing and publishing activities within Kuwait. Major developments within Kuwaiti society, such as gaining independence, the increase in the GNP, the growth of the literacy rate, and population increase necessitated the creation of a new press law. This need led to the passage of the 1961 Press Law, which has been amended several times to accommodate the sweeping changes that have taken place in Kuwait society since 1961.

Kuwaiti press law prohibited Kuwaiti media from criticizing their ruler, their government, the Arab heads of states, or those states considered friendly to Kuwait. Furthermore, Kuwait media were discouraged from propagating any ideas or principles that might lead to the destabilization of Kuwaiti sociopolitical order and that might negatively affect the interests of the State of Kuwait. These provisions remain effective in the 1976 Press Law, which superseded the 1961 Press Law (Kuwait Press Law, Articles 23, 24, 30, 1982).

Though Kuwaiti print media are forbidden by law from violating the above principles, the Kuwaiti "press still has considerable freedom to criticize. . . . [I]t has developed a degree of diversity, competition and outspokenness which puts it in a special category distinguishable from the press systems [of the other Gulf countries]" (Rugh, 1979, p. 105). The 1976 Kuwaiti press law amendment gave the Kuwaiti government the power to suspend or revoke the license of any newspaper for violating the Kuwaiti press law principles. A few months after the liberation of Kuwait, the Kuwaiti government abolished its censorship of the press. The Kuwaiti press, in turn, established its own rules for self-censorship. Relative to other Gulf countries, Kuwait does have a tradition of free press. With the election of a new Parliament in Kuwait, the enhancement of stability and security, and the tolerance of political opposition on the part of the Kuwaiti government, the Kuwaiti press is expected to regain the degree of freedom it enjoyed prior to 1986, the year in which the Kuwaiti Constitution was suspended.

The enforcement of communication policy in Kuwait takes place through a variety of mechanisms. Foremost among these are (1) direct governmental ownership and control, as in the case of all radio and television media; (2) control over issuing and revoking of licenses for print media and press personnel; (3) censorship; and (4) the levying of financial and/or jail penalties against recalcitrant newspapers, periodicals, or journalists. Meanwhile, the privately owned print media's need for advertising revenue and for government subsidies in the form of advertisements and subscriptions gives the Kuwaiti government additional power to ensure compliance with its communication policy. The enforcement of Kuwait communication policy takes place through court procedures.

NEWS AGENCIES

Kuwait News Agency (KUNA) was established as an independent institution by the Kuwaiti government in October 1976. Officially, KUNA started its Arabic-language transmission on February 15, 1979, and its English-language transmission on February 25, 1980. As defined by Article 2 of the decree that established it, KUNA's tasks consist of collecting and disseminating political and socioeconomic information relevant to Kuwait, both within Kuwait and abroad. In 1986, KUNA's reports and news dispatches that were transmitted to Kuwaiti embassies and diplomatic missions as well as to news organizations worldwide numbered about 50,000.

KUNA is managed by a board of directors supervised by the Minister of Information. It conducts its activities through the following six departments: the editorial desk department, the public relations and foreign offices department, the information and research department, the engineering department, the administrative affairs department, and the financial affairs department (Kuwait News Agency, 1993).

KUNA has become the leading news agency in the Arab World in many ways. For one thing, it has the greatest number of offices functioning throughout the world (22 in all); it employs around 300 staff members, including the largest number of full-time correspondents worldwide (39 in all, of which 12 are Kuwaiti nationals). It also leads the other Arab World news agencies in terms of the number of stories published per year.

CONCLUSION

Oil is the prime mover that led to the economic prosperity of Kuwaiti society, attracted a diversified population to Kuwait, led to the increase in the literacy and urbanization rates, and finally, led to progress in the levels of socioeconomic and political development. All these factors, in turn, ushered in the progress of Kuwaiti mass media.

Kuwaitis succeeded in preserving their neutrality between East and West during the cold war and managed to preserve their internal and external security in a region that was full of turmoil. Besides their high per capita income and high standard of living, Kuwaitis enjoyed relatively high levels of political and press freedom.

The Iraqi invasion has caused a lasting impact on all aspects of the Kuwaiti society. In addition to experiencing a setback, the Kuwaiti media have suffered from a sluggish economy and unfavorable demographic changes. Ultimately, a genuine democracy and a free press in Kuwait are the best guarantees for Kuwaitis to learn from their mistakes and to make Kuwait truly secure, independent, and free.

REFERENCES

Bseso, F. (1984). *Development cooperation among the countries of the Arab Gulf Cooperation Council.* Beirut, Lebanon: Institute for Arab Unity Studies.

Gulfvision. (1982). *Gulf TV handbook: The authoritative directory of TV in the Gulf states.* Milan, Italy: Dolphin.

Human development report. (1992). United Nations Development Program. New York: Oxford University Press.

Kazan, F. (1993). *Mass media, modernity and development: Arab states of the Gulf.* Westport, CT: Praeger.

Kuwait. (1992, May 1). *Washington Post,* p. A24.

Kuwait News Agency (KUNA). (1993). Kuwait: Ministry of Information.

Kuwait on the march. (1989, November 21). *Al-Arabi,* p. 12.

Kuwait Press Law. (1982). *Articles 23, 24, 30.* Kuwait: Government Publications.

Kuwaiti TV channels. (1993, March 15). *Qabas,* p. 16.

Ministry of Information. (1976). *Oanun al Matbouat wa'l Nashr, 1976* [Kuwait Press and Publication Law of 1976]. Articles 23, 24, 30.

———. (1983). *Information and statistics bulletin.* Kuwait: Ministry of Information.
———. (1989). *Information and statistics bulletin.* Kuwait: Ministry of Information.
———. (1992). *Information* and statistics bulletin. Kuwait: Ministry of Information.
PARC. (1992, November). *Media Update Kuwait.* Kuwait: Pan-Arab Research Center.
Rugh, W. (1979). *The Arab press.* Syracuse, NY: Syracuse University Press.
Rugh, W. (1987). *The Arab press* (rev. ed.). Syracuse, NY: Syracuse University Press.
Statistical review of world energy. (1992). British Petroleum Company. London: Britannic House.
Videocassettes. (1983, July 26). *Al-Reyadh,* p. 7.

11

LEBANON

Mahmoud M. Hammoud
and Walid A. Afifi

INTRODUCTION

Lebanon, which gained its independence from France in 1943, is a small country on the eastern shore of the Mediterranean. A little over 4,000 square miles with a population of approximately 4 million, Lebanon is flanked by Israel to the south and Syria to the east and has Beirut as its capital. Lebanon is characterized by a relatively educated populace (75 percent literacy rate) and great religious and cultural diversity (75 percent Muslim, 20 percent Christian, 5 percent Jewish) (*Handbook of the Nations,* 1990). Of the 17 legally recognized religious sects, the Shi'a Muslims constitute the largest community, with Christian Maronites a close second. The official language is Arabic, but French and English are also widely spoken, while Kurdish and Armenian are limited to ethnic minorities.

Lebanon, originally formed from five Turkish Empire districts, was under French Mandate from 1920 to 1941. It officially gained its independence on November 22, 1943, and French troops completed withdrawal in 1946. When the republic was established, the unwritten ''national pact'' of 1943, a time when Christians were the majority, provided that the president be a Maronite Christian, the prime minister be a Sunni Muslim, and the speaker of the Parliament be a Shi'a Muslim. It was also agreed that the executive and legislative branches of government constitute a 6:5 ratio, Christians to Muslims. In accordance with the 1990 Taif agreement (which formally ended the civil war and dissolved the militia organizations), the Parliament was increased from 99 to 108 seats, equally divided between Christian and Muslim.

Until the outbreak of civil war in 1975, Lebanon prospered, with Beirut acting as a bridge between East and West. Beirut became a major cultural and educational center with a flourishing economy, expanding press, developing universities, and increasingly sophisticated telecommunications and technological advancements.

The civil war shook the Lebanese society's foundations by weakening the authority of the central government, paralyzing economic activities, damaging infrastructures, and decentralizing all major institutions, including the mass media. Transportation became under the control of militias as illegal ports were opened, roads blocked, and the airport intermittently closed. The decision by Israel to invade Lebanon in 1982 further added to the country's instability. The economic implications of these changes, of course, have been devastating, making a once-strong Lebanese pound (*Lp*3 = U.S.$1) woefully weak (*Lp*2,700 = U.S.$1).

Although the upheavals that have gripped Lebanon since 1975 have hindered the operation of the mass media institutions, private militias, political parties, and other representatives with vested interests have subsidized the media's continued operation. In fact, the number of media outlets increased during the war, with the establishment of several television stations, more than 100 radio stations, dozens of newspapers, and many magazines. The opportunity to distribute (often biased) information illegally through mass media channels without penalty was too attractive for most political parties to ignore.

PRINT MEDIA

Newspapers

Very little extensive research, and equally little historical review, has been conducted on the development of newspapers in Lebanon. Dajani (1979, 1992), in fact, provides the only source of a systematic program of research focused on media efforts in Lebanon.

The first attempt to introduce printing into Lebanon came in 1610 when Maronite priests moved a printing press from Rome to a monastery in North Lebanon (Dajani, 1979, 1992). Owing to the low literacy rate, this effort lasted only a short period. An increase in the population's literacy (due to Christian missionaries' schools) resulted in the introduction of three Arabic printing presses between 1751 and 1848. In 1857, Khalil el-Khuri, the former director of publications in the Ottoman administration, brought to Beirut the first printing press unrelated to religious orders and published the first popular Arabic newspaper in the Arab World. Several popular Arabic newspapers soon followed. The first daily Lebanese newspaper, however, did not appear until 1894.

A special "protocol" signed by England, Prussia, Russia, France, and Austria in 1861 gave Lebanon special freedoms for the press not given other Arab countries. The prime purpose of the early Lebanese papers, however, was to spread a specific religious or ethnic-oriented message. Each paper spoke for a specific group and could make no claims to objectivity. This early characteristic of the press in Lebanon has shaped its development since.

The early twentieth century brought a new Ottoman ruler who attempted to limit the growth of the Lebanese print media (Dajani, 1992). Although often frustrated, media censorship peaked in 1916 when 16 journalists were hanged for stirring up public opinion. The occupation of Lebanon by the Allies after World War I did not improve the situation. Press restrictions continued under the French Mandate (1920–1942), with the price for editors championing the call for independence ranging from imprisonment to severe fines. By the end of the mandate, there were about 250 publications that were discontinued as a result of French actions.

Although Lebanon gained independence in 1943, authority to regulate the press was not turned over to the Lebanese until 1946. It took a change in the government in 1952, however, before press restrictions were lifted—a move that resulted in a large increase in the number of daily newspapers (each sponsored by a different leader or group). The sudden expansion led many publishers to pressure the government to control the development, an act that was enacted in 1953 with a decree banning the issuance of new licenses for publication as long as Lebanon had more than 25 dailies and 20 weeklies and periodicals. Finally, in 1962, the Lebanese press law, which remains in effect, was established. The law prohibits the publication of news that endangers the national security, or unity or frontiers of the state, or that degrades a foreign head of state. The restrictions in this law, however, have been loosely interpreted and only rarely enforced. The Lebanese press reached the apex of its development and had the most freedom during the reign of the first two Lebanese presidents (Dajani, 1992). Since then, modifications to the 1962 law and the outbreak of the 1975 civil war have resulted in a decline in both quality and freedom. Although the government announced several censorship measures between 1975 and 1990, it failed to apply these measures. In fact, the continued relative freedom of the press in Lebanon could be attributed to two reasons (Dajani, 1992): (1) Most of the newspapers that refused to comply with the decrees had backing from militant political bosses and were thus protected, and (2) the officials entrusted with censorship were not diligent. The serious deterioration of the security situation and the escalating collapse of the economy, however, were a greater threat. Between 1983 and 1990, the value of the Lebanese pound plummeted from *Lp*3/U.S.$1 to *Lp*1,000/U.S.$1. Accordingly, the price of the newspaper increased from *Lp*0.50 to *Lp*500 in three years. In addition, circulation of the papers was limited to the areas controlled by that paper's constituents.

In summary, the biggest problem of the Lebanese print media has been its financial dependence on outside sources (Abu-Laban, 1966). This dependence, in turn, has led to complete editorial commitment to the country or movement offering funding, rigid promotion of their policies, or agreement to support their positions. In instances where economic attempts to control the press failed, violent means prevailed. Numerous examples of journalist assassinations or newspaper plant destruction during the civil war may be cited, including the assassination of the Journalist Associations's head and the owner of a leading newspaper. Although the recent improvement in both security and government control has led to a decrease in overt means of influence, the structure of covert influence remains in place.

Lebanon has 105 licensed political publications (53 daily papers, 48 weeklies, and 4 monthly magazines) as well as over 300 nonpolitical publications (Dajani, 1992). Out of these publications, only 1 or 2 newspapers had a circulation of over 60,000 during their peak period, and only 2 magazines had a circulation of over 100,000 copies. By 1988, the circulation of the paper with widest distribution went down to 34,000. Circulation figures, however, are considered guarded secrets in Lebanon and, when released, are often exaggerated.

The press is almost exclusively published in the capital, Beirut, with the northern town of Tripoli a distant second. Lebanon has 28 licensed local news agencies and ten registered offices of regional and international news agencies, including Reuters, Associated Press (AP), United Press International (UPI), Agence France-Press (AFP), and Tass (Telegrafnoe Agentsvo Sovetskovo Soyuza) (Dajani, 1992). The official national agency, the National News Agency (NNA), was founded in 1964. By 1975, NNA supplied local and national news to 600 subscribers.

The serious economic crisis facing the press forced them, beginning in 1988, to appear only six times a week. Today, only two newspapers have recovered enough to allow Sunday editions. Papers are published in four to ten pages, depending on financial success. The Lebanese papers do not have specialized editorial pages and have no place for publishing letters to the editor. Opinion is usually included in the news story, and important editorials usually appear on the front page. Unlike Western conceptions of media, the Lebanese do not view the newspaper as a forum for dialogue but instead exclusively as a source of information. Their specialized pages are few and relatively weak. Most of the leading papers have specialized sports, cultural, and economic pages, however. The six leading Lebanese daily newspapers, in terms of their influence and quality are the following: *An-Nahar* is a moderate, right-of-center paper and has the highest circulation in Lebanon; *As-Safir,* a left-of-center paper, has the second highest estimated circulation, gaining prominence at the beginning of the civil war; *Ad-Diyar* gained popularity in 1987 by taking courageous stands against the militia bosses; *Al-Amal* is a rightist paper that is the organ of the Maronite Christian Phalangist Party; *Al-Anwar* is a paper with an Arab nationalist lean; and *L'Orient-Le Jour* is a French paper that is perhaps the most respected daily publication in Lebanon but is mostly read by the elite (Dajani, 1992).

A recent analysis of leading newspapers showed that 63 percent of the space was devoted to local matters. The civil war clearly contributed significantly to the fact that this proportion represents a greater percentage of local coverage than newspapers in other Arab countries. In fact, military and defense issues were by far the most common subjects appearing in the local news coverage. An analysis of readership patterns showed this trend: 90 percent of the elite group (conceptualized as people who hold influential positions in party structures, business, religious, or social organizations) regularly read a newspaper, and 63 percent regularly read three or more magazines, while only 27 percent of blue-collar workers regularly read a newspaper and 16 percent regularly read three or more magazines. Regardless of social status, newspapers were considered to be, by far, the most credible of the daily media sources.

Despite its small size and war-plagued history, Lebanon remains a leading Middle Eastern country in terms of the quality and number of its newspapers. In addition, Lebanon offers a choice of newspapers in Arabic, French, English, and Armenian.

Magazines

Like newspapers, the history of magazines in Lebanon is varied and has been shaped by the country's turbulent history. The status of political magazines, however, is considerably lower than that held by newspapers and therefore deserving of less attention than the more major media sources.

The last available records of magazine licenses and publication indicates that 47 political weeklies are licensed, but 26 of those have either stopped publication or emigrated. Similarly, records indicate 484 licensed nonpolitical magazines, of which only 50 are published. Such numbers, however, are often inaccurate owing to the large number of illegal (unlicensed) magazines that are published and/or circulated in Lebanon. In addition, the recent peace has led to the return of many foreign magazines to Lebanese store shelves and the availability of magazines in Arabic, French, English, and Armenian.

The most important political magazine (*An-Nahar Al-arabi* [*The Arab Day*]) is read by the elite and is published by the publisher of *An-Nahar,* one of the leading newspapers in Lebanon. Besides political analysis, the magazine provides arts and cultural articles. *Al-Ousbou' al-Arabi* (*The Arab Week*) has published since 1959 and has approximately 88,000 readers. It is distributed throughout the Arab World and is considered a general interest magazine. The magazine with the third highest circulation, *Al-Hawadess* (*The Events*), is published temporarily from London. It provides political analysis, features, social events, and games and has a circulation approaching 85,000 copies. In addition, other magazines circulated in Lebanon have been known to influence the political climate; for example, *Al-Shiraa* (*The Sail*) exposed the Iran-Contra affair.

The nonpolitical magazines include a variety of specialized magazines about sports, children, business and economics, and entertainment. The most important of these is *Al-Hasna* (*The Beauty*), which targets women, and *Achabaka* (*The Net*), which includes social events, entertainment updates, and feature articles and has a circulation of approximately 126,000 copies. While several other periodicals exist (focusing on wide-ranging issues), the government's loss of control over their circulation allows for discussion of only the most publicly respected magazines. In addition, the readership figures may reflect the magazine's limited circulation (imposed by militias) or specialized political interests. Most important, however, the economic conditions in Lebanon and the expansion of alternative media outlets made magazines the ignored media of choice.

ELECTRONIC MEDIA

Radio

Radio Levant, in 1938, was the first radio station established in Lebanon and was instituted by the French colonial power in Lebanon to bring together the Arab and French cultures in the area and combat Fascist propaganda beamed from Germany and Italy (Dajani, 1992). It began, as it remained until the outbreak of the civil war, under strict government control. In 1946, the station was formally handed over to the national government. A protocol allowing France 145 minutes, England 60 minutes, and the United States 30 minutes of daily use was signed. The station was renamed the Lebanese Broadcasting Station. In 1960, the British aired a pro-Zionist play, and the public uproar forced the Lebanese government to withdraw permission from the British and American broadcasters to use the station and to place the French broadcasts under supervision. A legislative decree in 1961 gave the new government radio agency a monopoly over radio transmission in Lebanon and did not allow radio to broadcast any political dialogue. Soon after, broadcasting time doubled, and programs in five languages (Arabic, Armenian, English, French, and Spanish) were broadcast regularly. Radio broadcasting on FM (frequency modulation) began in 1965, when the government received an old FM transmitter as a gift from the Arabian American Oil Company (ARAMCO).

The increasing popularity of the radio as a source of information led the government, in 1972, to adopt a new plan for the development of radio broadcasting in Lebanon (Dajani, 1992). In 1975, the first phase of development was completed and the station renamed Radio Lebanon. The civil war, however, resulted in a halt to the development project and the emergence of several illegal stations that offer a wider variety of programming, are more professionally managed, and enjoy a wider audience than does Radio Lebanon.

Radio Lebanon is Lebanon's only mass communication news medium, which is completely under governmental control and receives its budget from the Ministry of Information. No annual license fees are paid for radio sets, and no nonpublic advertising is allowed on radio. Programs introduced one day may be stopped the next if an important official so decides. Programs may be interrupted to broadcast a favorite song for an official or report favorable news.

The Voice of Lebanon, in 1975, was the first illegal station to broadcast after the beginning of the civil war. It quickly enjoyed the widest Lebanese audience. Other rebel stations quickly followed. Among the powerful stations still broadcasting are the Voice of the Nation, supporting the Muslim Sunnis; the Voice of the Mountain, supporting the Druze; the Voice of the People, supporting the Communist Party; and the Voice of Free Lebanon, supporting the Maronite Christians. During the civil war, these stations served as good sources for listeners to learn about security concerns in specific areas. Radio Lebanon, on the other hand, often focused on international events, thus avoiding reports about the country's worsening condition.

The Taif agreement began serious discussion within the government about the state of the illegal stations (*Call for the Re-Organization of Media in Lebanon,* 1991), which had grown so much, had such a vast listening audience, and had already earned a kind of de facto recognition. Their abolition, even if desired, was not a viable option. Faced with this dilemma, the Minister of Information has suggested that the pirate radio stations each pay 5 percent of their advertising revenues to the budget of Radio Lebanon in return for getting licenses by the government.

A survey of radio listening habits in Lebanon showed that Radio Lebanon enjoyed a large listening audience early in the civil war but was hurt significantly by the competition provided by the pirate stations. Currently, Radio Lebanon ranks very low in both prestige and influence. A recent survey, however, suggests that radio is doing quite well as a media source in Lebanon (Dajani, 1992). Although radio falls slightly below newspapers in perceived utility, it is considered a more useful and credible source of information than is television.

The rise of the illegal stations and the reception of several quality foreign radio stations (British Broadcasting Corporation [BBC], Monte Carlo), however, have increased radio's credibility significantly, decreasing the gap between radio and newspapers as the primary choice for information.

Television

The introduction of television to Lebanon can be traced back to two Lebanese businessmen, William Ezzeddine and Alec Arida, who first approached the government in 1954 with a proposal to operate a television station. In 1959, after delays caused by negotiations and unrest, the first television broadcasts were aired, and La Compagnie Libanaise de Te'le'vision (CLT) (The Lebanese Television Company) was founded. The station operated a transmitter in Beirut at half a kilowatt of power, with two relay stations.

Three years later, the second television station, Compagnie de Te'le'vision du Liban et du Proche Orient (The Lebanese and Near East Television Company), began operation. It was given access to three channels, two of which were devoted to Arabic programming and one to English and French programming. Both television companies adopted the Sequence Couleur a Memoire (SECAM) coloring system and used the 625 definition system. Over 50 percent of programming was imported from the United States, France, and Egypt. The newscasts were under the direct supervision of the Ministry of Information. Each station offered approximately 60 hours of television time each week. To remain profitable, the two companies began coordinating their programming through a private independent company; then, in 1972, they finally merged to form Tele-Liban, which, to this day, broadcasts Arabic programs on two channels and French or English programs on another.

The civil war caused a major blow to Tele-Liban, already suffering from inadequate funding, lack of innovations, outdated equipment, and bureaucratic governmental supervision. As is often the case in war, channels fell quickly under military control. Illegal stations (funded by various parties with vested interest) soon emerged. The first of these stations to operate was the Lebanese Broadcasting Corporation (LBC), which was launched in 1985 by the Lebanese Forces militia. In contrast to Tele-Liban's weak equipment, LBC's access to technologically advanced equipment established it as the leading station in Lebanon. Within one year, LBC overtook Tele-Liban in popularity and advertisement revenue. Its continued success since 1985 has attracted the most qualified producers of television programming in Lebanon to its staff.

Other illegal stations soon followed: Al-Mashreq TV (started in 1990), owned by Lebanese ministers, is focused on Arabic programming; and New Television (NTV) (started in 1991) is owned and operated by the Communist Party. "Programming is done to serve various age groups by carefully selecting programs including some produced by the station itself," according to the director of the station (1992). NTV also attracted well-known directors from Te'le'-Liban, like Antonne Reme. The station telecasts programs for children, women, political analysis, law (monthly), health, comedy, and soaps (30 percent of total programming). The advertising revenues are modest, but the station has managed to increase its standing to second place after LBC. The station plans to increase its local programming by coproduction with Arab producers.

The only religious station in Lebanon, besides the Middle East Television (operated by Pat Robertson, the U.S. televangelist), broadcasting from the Israeli-occupied South Lebanon is Al-Manar TV, controlled by the Party of God (Hizballah).

Other television stations broadcasting in Beirut whose signals may or may not cover all of Lebanon include Sigma TV and Kilykia Television. Both stations are based in West Beirut and offer mostly Arabic programs and songs and accept commercials but no newscasts in their programs. The latter is associated with the Al-Nahdah organization that publishes a newspaper called *Ad-Diyar* (*Home*). In a newspaper interview (March 2, 1992), Antoine Ghareeb, the political supervisor of the station, described its mission as aimed at reuniting Lebanese society around strong national foundations and confronting any attempts to normalize the relationship with Zionists. Until the summer of 1992, the station lacked a clear signal.

In East Beirut, a number of television stations are in operation. The Lebanese Forces militia also operates C33, a second television station, which broadcasts unedited and untranslated versions of Western movies, mostly French. Murr TV (MTV), described as an independent station, is owned by Michael Murr (a former defense minister), one of his sons, and a group of Lebanese businessmen. The station features French programs, but general manager Michael Murr told *Ad-Diyar* newspaper (March 2, 1992) that the station had plans to add Arabic and other Western programs to its programming. Independent Television (ITV) is owned by Henry Sfeir, who is a Maronite priest and a former candidate for the presidency in Lebanon (Dajani, 1992).

Other stations include Al-Salam TV; TV One (broadcasts music videos); Cable Video Network (CVT); and Al-Mahaba Television, established by a group of Maronite priests. These stations were still under trial period and generally telecast international programs that are received through large dish antennas or through videocassette recorders (VCRs), which are abundantly available in Lebanon. Their share of the advertisement market is still negligible, especially when compared with the big four stations. Their coverage may not reach beyond Beirut and the surrounding area, but some of them plan to extend their coverage to the rest of the country.

The latest arrival in the television market is Future Television (FTV), whose owner is a Lebanese billionaire, Rafik Hariri, who became the prime minister of Lebanon in 1992. FTV transmits from Saida in the south and through recruitment has positioned itself among the leading television stations in Lebanon.

Besides these stations, there are a number of television stations whose coverage is confined to a small broadcast area such as Arab Television and Alisar, in the south; Al-Marada TV, in the north; and Al-Amal TV, operated by Israeli-controlled militia.

The stations resist government control over newscasts and have a system to avoid competition between newscasts. These stations also broadcast news briefs throughout their transmission and cover live events. Some stations rebroadcast news from Cable News Network (CNN) (United States), TV5 (France), SKY News (Britain), BBC (Britain), and so on, without editing or translation.

Cable Television

Because of its small size, there is no need in Lebanon for cable television since few relay stations could provide coverage for the whole country. Nevertheless, a new company called Cable Television (CTV) has been advertising in the local newspapers, offering eight channels including two international stations, the BBC of London and the Middle East Broadcasting Corporation (MBC), which also broadcasts from London.

NEW TECHNOLOGIES

For its regional and international links, Lebanon relies on one inactive Indian Ocean INTELSAT (International Telecommunication Satellite Consortium) satellite earth station. Lebanon is also a member of the Arab Satellite Communication Organization (ARABSAT). During the civil war the number of VCRs increased dramatically, like television and radio sets, because of illegal ports along the Lebanese shore.

MOTION PICTURES

The history of cinema in Lebanon is long (Sadoul, 1966) and was adversely affected by the civil war. The security situation often led to a sharp decrease in movie patrons. The recent return to peace has led to a reemergence of the cinema as a source for entertainment, but movie production companies have yet to return. By 1992, the number of movie theaters (116) had increased since the early 1980s but was still considerably less than the 170 open movie theaters in 1975.

The first Lebanese film, *The Adventures of Elias Mabrouk,* was a silent comedy that appeared in 1929 (Khouri, 1966). It told the story of a Lebanese immigrant who returned to Lebanon from the United States after a long absence. In 1933, Mrs. Gargour established Lumnar Film Company, which later released the first film produced entirely in an Arab country, since the Egyptian films were sent to France for developing. The breakup and eventual dissolution of Lumnar made for a slow period of movie production between the early 1940s until the early 1950s when two new film studios were founded in Lebanon. However, it was not until the 1960s that the movie production industry truly developed. Film production, although never very large, doubled between 1963 and 1967 (from 8 to 17 films per year). This trend continued until 1975, when the dangers of the civil war led most of the production companies to move elsewhere.

An early analysis of the Lebanese film industry (Jabre, 1966) suggested four major problems that explained the industry's relative ineffectiveness. These reasons are still applicable when analyzing the current state of the industry: (1) The majority of the technical directors and producers lack a national Lebanese background (former Egyptians); (2) the differences between Egyptian and Lebanese dialect make it difficult to make movies for export that appeal to a wide Middle Eastern audience; (3) the industry lacks professional producers; and (4) the government does not provide assistance to the industry.

Since the number of locally produced films is limited, Lebanon is one of the biggest importers of foreign films (especially American-made) in the Middle East. In fact, many theaters exclusively show American films, and most American film companies have offices in Beirut. The task of movie censorship is given to the General Security division of the Ministry of Information, although movies are often accepted in their previously released format.

MEDIA OWNERSHIP AND REGULATION

The press is governed by the Press Law of 1948, which was revised in 1962. Under the terms of these laws, certain press freedoms were guaranteed, transforming the Lebanese press into a regional press addressing the concerns of a wider Arab audience. However, the liberal laws did not guarantee total freedom for the Lebanese press. Because of lack of financial self-sufficiency, these media outlets were open to control by interest groups, including those of Arab regimes and foreign embassies. According to the 1962 law, papers whose circulation remains below a minimum of 1,500 for a given period may have their licenses revoked. These terms contribute to a high increase in the price of licensed publications. Prior to the civil war, about three-fourths of the licensed publications were not publishing for financial reasons.

Because the initiative to establish television in Lebanon belongs to the private sector, the ownership of the stations was given to that sector by a license from the government. However, because of the importance of this medium, the government made sure to include provisions that assert its control over television broadcasting. According to Law No. 126 (June 12, 1959), the Ministry of Mail, Telecommunication, and Telephony bears the responsibility for overseeing the establishment, maintenance, management, and operation of communication networks. Television broadcasting is granted by a special permit from the Council of Ministers.

EXTERNAL MEDIA SERVICES

Radio Lebanon foreign service previously broadcast about two hours to Africa in Arabic, English, and French; two and a half hours to South America in Arabic, Spanish, and Portuguese; and about two and a half hours to Europe and North America in Arabic, English, French, and Spanish. Broadcasting was affected tremendously during the civil war but resumed later.

L'Orient Le Jour, published by An-nahar Publishing House, is the foremost French paper and is read by the elite. The other influential French paper is *Le Soir.* Of the 20 licensed French publications, only 2 nonpolitical publish currently: *Sport Auto* and *Le Commerce du Levant* (commercial and financial). In 1988, three new nonpolitical French magazines appeared. They are *La Coupe* (sports); *Public* (arts); and *Idea's* (fashion), publishing in Arabic and English besides its French version.

Of the 51 licensed English magazines, the only one continuing to be published is *The Monday Morning. The Daily Star,* an English newspaper, ceased publication in 1985, shortly after another English daily, *Ayk,* had closed down.

NEWS AGENCIES

Lebanon has 28 licensed local news agencies and ten registered offices of regional and international news agencies, including Reuters, AP, UPI, AFP, and

Tass. The official national agency, the National News Agency, was founded in 1964. By 1975, NNA supplied local and national news to 600 subscribers. Most newspapers and some of the radio and television stations have their own correspondents in major Lebanese cities as well as in major capitals in Europe, especially London and Paris, and in the United States.

THE ROLE OF MEDIA IN NATIONAL DEVELOPMENT

Although Lebanon is a media-rich country, the mass media institutions played a less-than-positive role in the tasks pertaining to education, training, and national development. For instance, the Lebanese press acted more as ''viewspapers'' than a platform for discussion among various Lebanese groups or opposing points of view.

The broadcasting industry also did little to contribute to education, training, or national development. Both licensed and illegal broadcasting have failed to provide Lebanese citizens with information to satisfy their real societal needs. This is more evident in television broadcasting. Since its inception, Lebanese television has relied heavily on imported programs, most of which are alien to the Lebanese culture. The small number of local programs produced are either superficial or have no educational value. The major concerns of television officials have been financial gains. The government, on the other hand, has been interested in asserting its control, particularly on news broadcasts, paying little attention to the kind and quality of the programs. Radio broadcasting, licensed and illegal, does not differ very much from that of television except that their programs are locally produced, mostly for entertainment purposes.

The Lebanese mass media, in both print and broadcast, have failed to contribute to societal development.

CONCLUSION

The early history of the media in Lebanon portrays an institution with great freedoms, great contributors, and great promise. Many have argued, in fact, that Lebanon was the jewel of the Middle East for journalists and other media professionals. The outbreak of the civil war, however, changed the Lebanese landscape in many ways, and media institutions did not escape that fate.

A careful analysis of the history of media in Lebanon reveals that its structure may have been shaped more by the civil war than by any other institution. The impact of these changes has gone relatively unexamined, yet there is clearly a need to further understand the impact of the media's reinstitutionalization on the country's populace.

REFERENCES

Abu-Laban, B. (1966). Factors in social control of the press in Lebanon. *Journalism Quarterly, 43,* 514.

Al-Aredi, W. (1992, March 2). Diversity in broadcasting did not unify the essence of the institutions. *Ad-Diyar.*

Basha, A. (1992, August 19). Television forces between the state and society: Part I. *As-Safir,* No. 6262, p. 12.

Basha, A. (1992, August 20). Television forces between the state and society: Part II. *As-Safir,* No. 6263, p. 12.

Basha, A. (1992, August 21). Television forces between the state and society: Part III. *As-Safir,* No. 6264, p. 12.

Call for the re-organization of media in Lebanon. (1991, May). Beirut: Lebanese Ministry of Information.

Dajani, N. H. (1979). *Studies in broadcasting.* London: International Institute of Communications.

Dajani, N. H. (1992). *Disoriented media in a fragmented society: The Lebanese experience.* Beirut: American University of Beirut Press.

Handbook of the nations (10th ed.). (1990). Detroit: Gale Research Inc.

Jabre, F. (1966). The industry in Lebanon, 1958–1965. In G. Sadoul (Ed.), *The cinema in the Arab countries* (pp. 172–178). Beirut: Interarab Centre of Cinema & Television.

Khouri, L. (1966). History of the Lebanese cinema. In G. Sadoul (Ed.), *The cinema in the Arab countries* (pp. 120–124). Beirut: Interarab Centre of Cinema & Television.

Rugh, R. A. (1979). *The Arab press: News media and political process in the Arab World.* Syracuse: Syracuse University Press.

Sadoul, G. (Ed.). (1966). *The cinema in the Arab countries.* Beirut: Interarab Centre of Cinema & Television.

Zgheib, E. (1992, April 3). After the decision to reorganize the illegal mass media, what is the future of private radio and television stations? *Ad-Diyar.*

12

LIBYA

Karim Mezran

INTRODUCTION

The Great Socialist People's Libyan Arab Jamahiriyya (as Libya has been known since April 1986) is an Arab and Islamic country, bounded on the north by the Mediterranean Sea, on the east by Egypt and Sudan, on the south and southwest by Chad and Niger, on the west by Algeria, and on the northwest by Tunisia. The three provinces of Libya are Tripolitania in the west, with an area of 285,000 square kilometers (110,000 square miles); Cyrenaica in the east, area 905,000 square kilometers (350,000 square miles); and the Fezzan in the south, area 570,000 square kilometers (680,000 square miles).

After the Italian colonization, which ended in 1943, Tripolitania and Cyrenaica were ruled by a British administration, while the Fezzan was administered by the French. Independence was granted by the United Nations in 1951 with the establishment of a monarchy under King Idriss.

The revolutionary government that came to power in September 1969 renamed the three regions; thus, Tripolitania became known as the ''Western Provinces''; Cyrenaica, as the ''Eastern Provinces''; and Fezzan, as the ''Southern Provinces.''

According to the 1984 census, the population was approximately 3.63 million inhabitants. The population in 1991 was estimated at 4.70 million (Economist Intelligence Unit, 1992–1993). The official language is Arabic, and while the government discourages it, English is used extensively, and French and Italian are used to a lesser extent. More than 90 percent of the population is composed of Arabic-speaking Sunni Muslims of mixed Arab and Berber ancestry. The rest is composed of Berbers, Tuaregs, and black Africans, with small Greek and Maltese communities.

In the early 1980s, the literacy rate was estimated at between 50 and 60 percent, about 70 percent for men and 35 percent for women. The 1990 estimates place these figures at 90 percent for men and 30 percent for women *(UNESCO Statistical Yearbook,* 1991). In 1986, total enrollment in Libyan schools amounted to more than 1,245,000 students, of which 54 percent were males and 46 percent females. Thus, the gap in education between genders has been narrowing (Chapin Metz, 1989). There are two universities, one in Tripoli (Al-Fateh University) and one in Benghazi (Gar Younis University), complemented by facilities at Tobruk. There is also a college of science and technology at Marsa Brega, with additional facilities at Misurata. A new university in Sabha (Fezzan) with branches in such cities as Derna, Sirte, and Zavia has also been created.

Economically, Libya is heavily dependent on oil revenues. Before the discovery of petroleum in the late 1950s, agriculture was the basis of the economy, and domestic revenue covered only about one-half of the government's ordinary and development expenditures. Between 1962 and 1968, however, national income increased from LD131 million (Libyan dinar) to LD798 million, and the gross national product (GNP) increased from LD163 million to LD709 million. Exports of petroleum during this period increased 835 percent, accounting for 51 percent of gross domestic product (GDP) in 1968. Despite massive investment in agriculture and non-petroleum-related industry, the percentage of Libya's GDP derived from oil has remained fairly constant since the early 1970s, fluctuating between 60 and 70 percent.

Libya is still critically dependent on food imports, which have made up as much as 20 percent of total imports. This dependence on imports is due mainly to the country's arid climate and poor soil. In fact, only 1.2 percent of Libya's 1.76 million square kilometers is arable land, and less than 1 percent is irrigated (Economist Intelligence Unit, 1992–1993).

The September 9, 1969, military coup d'état marked the beginning of a different economic philosophy for Libya by changing it from a Western-oriented, capitalist country to a strongly nationalist, anti-Western socialist state. Thus, state intervention in the economy increased. In 1970, distribution and marketing of petroleum were nationalized; in 1971, the government took over petroleum company assets; in September 1978, a large number of private companies were taken over by workers committees. In 1979, all direct importing business was transferred to 62 public corporations, and the issuing of licenses was stopped. In March 1981, it was announced that all licenses for shops selling clothes, electrical goods, shoes, household appliances, and spare parts were to be canceled, and that by the end of the year all retail shops would have to close and become controlled by state-administered supermarkets.

All these projects were jeopardized by the economic crisis that hit Libya in the early 1980s due to the low price of oil. In the period 1980 to 1986, GDP declined from $35,000 million to $24,000 million, and average GDP per capita fell from $10,900 in 1980 to $5,400 in 1988 (Europa Publications, 1992). The economic crisis forced the regime to introduce a series of economic and political liberalization measures in March 1988. Thus, private shops were encouraged to reopen, and measures to dismantle obstacles to trade and tourism were adopted. In December 1989, the government announced plans to reduce its budget deficit by removing subsidies on wheat, flour, sugar, tea, and salt. However, control on prices and interest and exchange rates were maintained, and all important sectors of the economy remained under the effective control of the state, which in 1990 retained 70 percent of all Libyan salaried workers on its payroll.

The current political order of Libya took shape in March 1972, when the General People's Congress (GPC) adopted the Declaration of the Establishment of the People's Authority and proclaimed the Socialist People's Libyan Arab Republic. The GPC adopted resolutions designating Colonel Muammar Qadhafi as its general secretary and creating the General Secretariat of the GPC, comprising the remaining members of the defunct Revolutionary Command Council (RCC). It also appointed the General People's Committee, which replaced the Council of Ministers.

All legislative and executive authority was vested in the GPC. Thus, Colonel Muammar Qadhafi, as general secretary of the GPC, was the main decision maker. All Libyan adults had the right and duty to participate in the deliberations of their local Basic People's Congress (BPC), whose decisions were passed to the GPC for consideration and implementation as national policy.

Until the discovery of oil, Libya had one of the lowest per capita income levels in Africa. In 1963, approximately one in four Libyan families had no housing, and many others were living in substandard dwellings (McDaniel, 1982). Both the kingdom and subsequent revolutionary governments had improvements in agriculture, electrification, transportation, industrialization, and housing as their main development objectives. Thus, the development of the media never figured very prominently in national development.

In the 1963–1968 development plan, only about $10 million was allocated to "news and guidance," a sum that amounted to only 1.5 percent of the total budget. In the development budget for 1969–1974, the Ministry of Information and Culture allocated $46.8 million, or about 1.3 percent, for information and communication (McDaniel, 1982). The development budget expenditures for 1986, 1987, and 1988 show an allocation to Information and Culture of LD12 million, LD10 million, and LD8 million, respectively (Economist Intelligence Unit, 1992–1993).

COMMUNICATION PHILOSOPHY

The regime established by Colonel Muammar Qadhafi on September 1, 1969, had many characteristics in common with those in power in other Arab countries. The one particularly related to the press system and to the mass media in general is that the ruling group is composed of a small military junta who normally prohibits any opposition or any challenge from the media. This strong ideological connotation implies that the regime cannot be content with normal acquiescence on the part of the people but, on the contrary, needs to rally it continuously to support the government's political platform, giving a high level of importance to the media.

At the end of part one of *The Green Book,* in which Colonel Qadhafi explains and describes his social and political theories, Qadhafi discusses the press: "The press is a means of expression of the society and is not a means of expression of a natural or corporate person. Logically and democratically, the press, therefore, cannot be owned by either of those"; and again, "Democratically, a natural person should not be permitted to own any means of publication or information" (Qadhafi, 1976, pp. 38–39).

Also, according to Qadhafi's theory as expressed in *The Green Book,* the problem of freedom of the press is generally the product of an incorrectly understood and applied democracy. This assumes that the role of the press and of the mass media is to educate society about democracy and to sustain efforts to fight corruption in order to achieve a just society. As a consequence, ownership of all newspapers and mass media should belong to the people as embodied by the ruling group.

PRINT MEDIA

Newspapers

The first newspaper, *Al-Munaqqib* (*The Investigator*), appeared in 1827. It was written in French and published by the foreign counsels in Tripoli, and its distribution was limited to those individuals who could read French.

On August 17, 1897, the newspaper *Al-Taraqqi* (*Progress*) came out. This four-page weekly is considered to be the first all Arabic political newspaper in Libya.

However, the first official regular newspaper to be produced according to modern methods was *Jaridat Tarabulus al-Gharb* (*The Newspaper of Tripoli of the West*), which appeared during the reign of Sultan Abdal-Aziz and, by an 1866 decree, was issued by the sultan himself. A weekly appearing every Thursday morning for 45 years, it consisted of four pages, printed in Arabic and in Turkish, and published news of Libya and the empire together with official announcements, public notices, and events of the court. It was closed on the eve of the Italian invasion of July 22, 1911, and was replaced by the Italian authorities with the newspaper *Jaridat al-ltalia al-Jadida* (*The New Italy Newspaper*), then considered as the official newspaper, appearing in both Arabic and Italian.

The New Italy Newspaper began its publication in 1912, serving as the official organ of the Italian colonial government. This newspaper was very different in ideology from the other two published in Libya by the Italian community before the invasion: *The Giornale di Tripoli* (*The Tripoli Journal*), published in 1908, and *L'Eco di Tripoli,* in 1909. They carried local news and were mainly concerned with the affairs of the Italian Community in Libya. These and other publications called for considering Libya an extension of Italy and carried a heavy ideological and cultural prejudice against the native population.

The Libyan side was represented by the Mujahiddin (Fighters) who opposed the Italian colonization. The Mujahiddins reacted to the invasion by forming a government in 1920 to run the country's administration and military affairs, called the Tripolitanian Republic. One of the members of the nationalist party, the Hizb-al Islam al-Watani (Islamic National Party), was journalist Othman al Kizzani, who was charged with publishing a paper that would represent the party and its ideas. One month after the formation of the republic, the first issue of this newspaper, *Al-Liwa al-Tarabulsi* (*The Tripolitanian Banner*), was put out. It was a weekly political, economic, and social paper in Arabic. This paper, which greatly contributed to reform and culture, was stopped by the authorities and its publisher prosecuted more than once.

One month after the British entered the country, *Tarabulus al-Gharb* (*Tripoli of the West*), the newspaper that disappeared at the start of the Italian invasion, reappeared as the organ of the British administration. The first edition, different in size and format, came out on February 8, 1943, and was published daily until 1968.

Independence in Libya was immediately characterized by a rapid expansion of journalism and printing trade. The state operated three Arabic-language dailies: In Tripoli the old *Tarabulus al-Gharb* (*Tripoli of the West*) was succeeded by the daily *Tarabulus al-Gharb* (*Tripoli of the West*); in Benghazi there was the daily *Barca al-Jadida;* and from Sebha in Fezzan Province came the daily *Fezzan.* These three newspapers appeared daily with coverage of local and overseas news, along with various articles and feature stories (Ministry of Information and Culture, 1966).

There were also privately owned newspapers, although under the monarchy political parties were suppressed; thus, newspapers could only represent personal opinions. Leading among those privately owned newspapers were the Arabic daily *Ar-Riad,* the Italian daily *Giornale di Tripoli* (*Tripoli Journal*), and the Arabic weekly *Al-Murrah.*

There were also three privately owned English weeklies: the *Tripoli Mirror,* the *Sunday Ghibli* from Tripoli, and the *Cyrenaica Weekly News* from Benghazi. Many of these newspapers were subsidized by the state, which also offered them the use of its printing plants. The Libyan News Agency, which started its regular service in 1966, supplied local and foreign news to the newspapers at nominal charges and provided training courses for journalists. Many newspapers subscribed also to Reuters and its Arabic service and to the Italian news agency Agenzia Nazionale Stampa Associata (ANSA).

Until 1972, the government did not expressly order the privately owned newspapers to shut down but slowly started to cut back the subsidies that the monarchy had given to the private press. In January 1970, only the official newspaper of the regime, *Al-Thawrah* (*Revolution*), established to explain Qadhafi's ideas and to campaign for his regime, would receive the lucrative advertisements placed by government ministries (Rugh, 1979). In January 1972, following a set of trials held by the Revolutionary Command Council to extirpate "corruption of public opinion," the suspension of all newspapers and the revocation of the publishing licenses for the papers were ordered. As a consequence of this policy, all newspapers and periodicals in Libya are published either by the Jamahiriyya News Agency (JANA), by government secretariats, by the press services, or by the trade unions.

There are seven weekly newspapers: *Ad-Dawa al-Islamiyya* (*The Islamic Call*), which treats cultural and religious issues and is published in Arabic, English, and French by the World Islamic Call Society; *Al-Riyadah al-Jamahiriyya* (*Sports of the Republic*), a sports newspaper published by the General People's Committee for Information; *Al-Muntijun* (*The Producers or Workers*), which is published by the Federation of Labor Unions and deals with the problems and issues of workers; *Al-Zahf al-Akdar* (*The Green March*), the ideological journal of the revolutionary committees; *Al-Muwadhaf* (*The Employee*), published by the General Employees' Congress, dealing with professional and public administration issues; *Al-Jamahiriyya* (*The Republic*), which started its publication in 1980, published in Arabic by the revolutionary committees and dealing with political, cultural, and ideological issues; and *As-Shatt* (*The Beach*), a local newspaper published by the municipality of Tripoli, which reports local news, information, and services.

As of 1993, there is only one daily newspaper that is the official mouthpiece of the regime, *Al-Fajr al-Jadid* (*The New Dawn*). It is published by JANA to report the news and some political comments.

There are also three biweekly newspapers: *Al-Mizan* (*The Balance*), published by the Secretariat of Justice, dealing with security and social matters; *Gar Younis,* a Benghazi newspaper published by the University of Gar Younis, dealing with cultural, scientific, and general knowledge issues; and *Jil al-Jihadi* (*Challenging Youth*), published by the educational institution's revolutionary committees and dealing with educational issues and problems of youth.

In addition, there is one monthly newspaper, *Al-Irada* (*The Will),* published by the General League for the Handicapped, which is the official organ of the handicapped, and two monthly bulletins, the *Economic Bulletin* and the *Scientific Bulletin,* published by JANA. There is one quarterly newspaper, *Al-Akha* (*The Brotherhood*), published by the General Council of the Libyan Red Crescent, dealing with issues concerning general culture, society, social problems, and health.

Among the widely read newspapers are *Al-Fajr al-Jadid* (*The New Dawn*), because it is the most complete in terms of information, and *Al-Zahf al-Akdar*

(*The Green March*), because it gives the readers a clear picture of the ideas and policies of the regime. Also *Al-Riyadah al-Jamahiriyya* (*Sports of the Republic*) is very popular, especially with the youth, because of its reports on local sports events.

Magazines

In all, the publications that appeared during the second Ottoman period (1850–1911) were about seven, including magazines, and there were at least four printing presses. Some of these publications were *Abu Qushsha,* a comic weekly (1908); *Al-Asr al-Jadid* (*The New Era*), whose publication started in 1909 and was concerned with scientific, political, and literary issues; and *Al-Raqi* (*The Observer*), a weekly in Arabic and Turkish (1915). These publications played a very important role in developing and spreading ideas of nationalism, self-determination, and political consciousness among the Libyan people (Al-Suwali, 1984).

The first magazine to appear in Libya was the *Majallat al-Funun* (*Magazine of the Arts*) in 1889. Published in Arabic, this 23-page magazine specialized in the methods and techniques of agriculture, basic science, geography, and nature.

Later, many magazines were published, such as *L'Eco di Tagiura,* a biweekly that began its publications in 1917; the *Ghibli,* a monthly magazine in 1919; *El Gerid* and *Il Piccolo* weekly magazines in 1919; *Il Rinnovamento* and *L'Unione* in 1920; and a few others.

After Libyan independence, the Ministry of Information and Culture produced a number of Arabic magazines such as the biweekly illustrated magazine *Libya al-Wahda* (*Unity*) and the monthly *Al-Maraa* (*The Woman*), a magazine for women with subjects related to them. There was also a children's magazine, *Al-Tifl* (*The Child*), and a literary monthly magazine, *Ar-Riwad,* concerned with literary and cultural subjects.

A number of magazines are published in Libya. The exact number is unknown, because some magazines have been published sporadically or only once. Among them are *Al-Musafir* (*The Traveller*), published by the Libyan Airlines; *Al-Idha'a,* which contains broadcast schedules and issues; *Ath-Thaqafa al-Arabiyya* (*Arab Culture*), which deals with the cultural issues; *Al-Hadara* (*The Civilization*), which is published in Athens and deals with general political, economic, and historical issues; *Al-Handasa* (*Engineering*), published by the Engineers Association; and *Al-Istisrar* (*Investment*), published by the Export Development Council to give information about investments. A magazine that deals with problems involving children, *Al-Tifl* (*The Child*), a magazine for the house, *Al-Manzil* (*The Home*), and a magazine for women, *Al-Mara'* (*The Women*), are also published.

In addition, many foreign newspapers and magazines, including American, British, French, and German, are also available in Tripoli and Benghazi, although not on a regular basis. Among the daily foreign newspapers readily available are the *Herald Tribune,* the *New York Times,* and *The Guardian.* The most common foreign magazines are *Newsweek, Time, The Economist, Le Monde, Le Figaro, L'Express,* and *Der Spiegel.* Also, a large number of Italian daily newspapers and magazines are frequently sold in Libya due to the existence of a large Italian community, especially in Tripoli and Benghazi, and also to the fact that many Libyans speak Italian. Among the Italian daily newspapers sold in Tripoli are *Il Corriere della Sella, La Stampa,* and *La Republica.* Italian magazines such as *L'Espresso, Panorama, Gente,* and *Epoca* are also available.

ELECTRONIC MEDIA

Radio

Under the Italian administration as well as under the British, there were no radio stations in Libya. Very few people had radio sets, and those who did felt adequately served by the Italian- and Arabic-language programs that reached Libya. Estimates made shortly after independence placed the number of radio receivers at only 5,000 for a population of about 1 million inhabitants. Only in 1957 was the Libyan Radio Service established. Programming was very limited in time and quality. The government of Libya took direct control of the Libyan Radio Service in 1962 and kept that control until the 1969 revolution.

The radical change experienced by the Libyan people in every aspect of their social lives in 1969 could not have left the important sector of the mass media untouched. The necessity for the new regime to spread its political ideology and to campaign for its ideas both within the country as well as abroad made the use and control of the media one of its primary concerns. Thus, political information and cultural services became one of the main priorities of radio and television, which had been put under the control of the newly created Ministry of Information and Culture.

The low population density of Libya as well as the vastness of the country have been the most difficult broadcasting problems to overcome. Radio service to most of Libya has taken place by transmitting to all parts of the country by means of two high-power facilities on opposite sides of Libya—in Tripoli and Sabrata in the west, and El Bayda in the east. Thus, each day a national Arabic service is broadcast covering almost the entire territory. The radio broadcasts are not considered commercial since they are financed by the government. Their programs are produced locally, and they are transmitted to most parts of the country as well as to the neighboring states of Algeria, Tunisia, and Egypt.

A main channel under the name of Libyan Broadcasting Station transmits from Tripoli from 6:00 A.M. to 1:00 A.M., and another transmits from Benghazi. They air a variety of programs, including religious, social, and historical, as well as some entertainment programs such as contemporary and traditional Arabic music. The Channel of the Holy Quran broadcasts from Tripoli. It transmits from 6:00 A.M. to 6:00 P.M. and is designed for the instruction, recitation, and exegesis of the Quran. It also covers matters of personal spiritual life, prayers, and other religious themes. The same channel transmits another program, *Voice of the Arab Homeland,* from 7:00 P.M. to 5:00 A.M. Though varied in length and content, all of its programs are characterized by a commitment to the Arab World's affairs and Arab nationalism.

Two other broadcasts, one on FM (frequency modulation) and one on AM (amplitude modulation), and one on AM are in English and French. Each broadcast includes a variety of programs and is allotted a specific number of hours every day. They generally consist of news and recorded European music shows. In 1990 there were about 1 million radio receivers and 400,000 television receivers in use (*UNESCO Statistical Yearbook,* 1991).

Television

On National Independence Day, December 24, 1968, the Libyan TV Service began regular broadcasting. Most of the technicians and the operational staff were foreigners, and most of the programs were imported from abroad. In the summer, it was possible to receive the programs broadcast by the Tunisian and the Italian stations. There were also daily telecasts from the American Wheelus Airbase in Tripoli, one of the first television stations in the Arab World. All broadcasts were in English, and the station showed a good fare of local news and coverage of local events as well as movies and shows imported from the United States. While the programs of the American base could reach only Tripoli and its vicinity, the eastern areas of Libya could receive transmissions from facilities operated by the British Forces Broadcasting Service in Tobruk.

However, television program services have improved greatly since the revolution. According to government sources, a new television relay station was installed late in 1973 at Yefren, and by the end of the year, another one was built in Tobruk. Since 1975, the three main production centers have been linked by microwave interconnection, providing a national network for television.

One main channel, the Libyan Television Station, transmits programs in Arabic from Tripoli. It signs on at 6:00 A.M. and signs off at 1:00 A.M. throughout the week except on Fridays, the weekly holiday, when it signs on at 9:00 A.M. and signs off at midnight. Another channel from Benghazi transmits various programs including health, training, instructional programs, lectures, entertainment shows, news bulletins, religious, documentaries, scientific, movies, interviews, and public discussions. The channel also airs live, religious and national celebrations.

Other specialized programs are transmitted that deal with social and economic issues pertaining to a number of secretariats such as the Social Security, Health, Internal Security, Training and Information, Industry, and Public Service secretariats. Those programs are interrupted by paid publicity spots advertising products from both the public and private sectors. Most of these programs are produced locally. In addition, Libyan television subscribes to and imports many scientific programs and documentaries, as well as shows and movies, under a cultural exchange agreement that Libya has signed with many countries, both European and Arab.

A special children's channel called "the little channel" (*Al-Qanaat al-Saghira*) is devoted to matters of education, religion, art, recreational activities, games, and cartoons. It broadcasts for two hours daily from 3:00 P.M. to 5:00 P.M. in the afternoon. In addition, there is a program from 10:00 A.M. to 12:00 P.M. devoted to education at home such as parent-child relations.

A special channel transmits in English and French for approximately three hours daily, from 7:00 P.M. to 10:00 P.M. It offers religious and social programs, as well as lectures, talk shows, documentaries, serials, films, and songs. This channel enjoys a high viewership because a good part of the population that resides in Libya is foreign, and among them French and English are widely spoken, besides the fact that many Libyans speak at least one of these two languages. The Secretariat of Information is expanding and adding more transmitters in order to cover the entire southern part of the country as well as the neighboring countries.

The television is run by a committee called the Public Committee of the Great Jamahiriyya Television. It is supervised by the People's Committee for Information, which is part of the Ministry of Information, consisting of officials chosen from the trade unions, professional categories, and the specific secretariats of such committees as the General People's Committee for Communications, Social Security, and Health.

Libyans in Tripolitania have easy access to the programs of the television stations of the neighboring states of Tunisia (both Arabic and French) and Italy. All the main channels of Italian television are within reach of everybody's television, and these programs are very popular in Tripoli, especially the extensive coverage that the Italian television provides of popular sports such as soccer and tennis.

MOTION PICTURES

Libya has more than 30 movie theaters scattered throughout the country; most of them are concentrated in the two major cities of Tripoli and Benghazi. Some of those movie theaters are sometimes used for live theater as well. In addition, Tripoli has a special theater for children.

The two ancient Roman theaters of Sabrata and Leptis Magna are sometimes used for public presentations, mainly folklore dances. Since attendance to movie houses and theaters is very high in Libya, especially among young people, there are talks among the various departments within the government to increase the number of movie theaters and shows.

The Information Services Corporation performs many tasks within the Libyan information sector. This corporation is public, thus government owned, like most of the mass media in Libya. Among its many tasks are the distribution and propagation of paid commercial spots, advertising products from both the private and the public sectors. It is also concerned with the preparation and recording, importing, and distribution of video- and audiocassettes and with the preparation of local series as well as documentaries and short and long films that are produced locally. Among the various films produced or financed by Libya are *Al-Shadiyya* (*The Splinter*), *Omar al-Mukhtar,* and *The Message.* These films have been shown in many countries in the West as well as in the Arab World. Libya also imports films for its cinematographic sector from the United States, Britain, France, Italy, India, Japan, China, Russia, and many Arab countries. All imported films must pass through a censorship department within the Ministry of Information before being shown on television or in movie theaters.

MEDIA OWNERSHIP

The ownership of all print and electronic media belongs to the government, either directly or through one of its many branches or agencies. The laws that regulate the press are (1) the Publications Law of June 17, 1972, No. 76, and (2) the Public Corporation for Publication, Distribution, and Publicity Law of September 25, 1974 (Ashiurakis, 1975).

MEDIA REGULATION

The laws that regulated mass media under the monarchy were reorganized and modified after the 1969 revolution. Mass media establishment and formation are regulated by the following laws and regulations: the General Press Corporation Law of 1972; the Publications Law of June 17, 1972, No. 76; the Public Corporation for Publication, Distribution, and Publicity Law of September 25, 1974; the General Corporation for the People's Revolution Broadcasting Station of 1973; and the General Corporation for Cinematography and the General Corporation for Theater, Music and Arts, both of 1973. Mass media in Libya, in order to ensure control of the people over this important sector, are run by the People's Committees. There are no independent or self-regulatory agencies.

The most dramatic change occurred with the cultural revolution of 1973, when after the historic speech of Zwara, Colonel Qadhafi called on the masses to seize all radio and television stations and the local news agency. As a consequence of this speech, a new broadcasting law was promulgated. This law charged the People's Revolutionary Broadcasting Corporation with achieving the following objectives: (1) to embody the Arab revolutionary objectives of freedom, socialism, and unity and to promote such objectives in the minds of the people, (2) to stress the fact that Libya is an integral part of the Arab homeland, and (3) to link the Arab struggle to liberate the occupied Arab territories with any liberation cause of the Third World.

Broadcasting was defined as a public corporation by the new law, which set also its hierarchical and administrative structure. A People's Committee was elected from within this corporation; it was headed by a general director appointed by the head of the General People's Committee, which implemented and permitted political control of radio and television by the regime. All persons employed had to be professional broadcasters, but considering the late development of television and radio in Libya, shortages occurred almost from the beginning. In order to overcome this problem, technical facilities capable of providing the necessary training have been made available at the University of Benghazi as well as in Tripoli, and many employees have been sent to Western countries to study and obtain the necessary technical skills.

EXTERNAL MEDIA SERVICES

Voice of the Great Homeland in Arabic is the external service of Radio Libya. A variety of programs are aired, via shortwave, for listeners residing outside the country. Internally, two radio stations broadcast a variety of programs in English and French, including news and European music. Also, a special television channel transmits a variety of programs in English and French for approximately three hours daily, from 7:00 P.M. to 10:00 P.M.

NEWS AGENCIES

The official Libyan news agency is Jamahiriyya News Agency, or JANA. This agency gathers, writes, and distributes news to the Libyan media as well as to foreign agencies. In addition, many other joint agencies for the mutual exchange of information, reports, and world news function within the country. Wire services such as Reuters and the Italian ANSA are also available.

In the case of broadcasting, because of the high costs of production and logistical difficulties involved in the electronic news-gathering process, very little field reporting is included in the daily newscasts. Most of the news is simply read by the anchors.

CONCLUSION

In general, a high degree of dissatisfaction exists among both the Libyan population and the large community of foreign workers and diplomats presently living in Libya concerning the nature and quality of television and radio programs. One of the main reasons is the hiring of technical and administrative personnel based on political criteria rather than on expertise or knowledge. This, in turn, has not only downgraded the quality of the programs but has also reduced the ability to develop and produce a set of programs that would be of interest to the general population. Another reason is the fact that the broadcast signals do not yet effectively reach the southern part of the country with its sparsely populated villages located at great distances from each other.

Although talks and discussions are being held in the pertinent governmental departments, the outcomes are yet unknown. As of December 1992, neither statistical projections nor economic data of any reliability have been issued by the government to indicate what amount of money and what priorities are going to be allocated to the various mass media. Ostensibly, the mass media, like many other institutions in the Libyan government's sphere of action, are kept in limbo because of the country's economic crises. Only with a softening of the economic crises and the allocation of more money to mass media will it be possible to see the revitalization of these important institutions and any future development regarding new telecommunication technologies.

REFERENCES

Ashiurakis, A. M. (1975). *Madkhal ila i'laam 'Arabi Libii* [Introduction to the Libyan Arab media]. Tripoli: Dar Al Fargiani.

Al-Suwali, A. (1984). *Fann sin'at al sahafa* [The art of the press industry]. Tripoli, Libya.

Al-Suwali, A. (1989). *Bidaiat al sahafa al Libya* [The beginning of the Libyan press]. Tripoli, Libya.

Economist Intelligence Unit. (1992–1993). Tripoli, Libya.

Europa Publications. (1991). *The Middle East and North Africa.* London: Author.

Europa Publications. (1992). *The Middle East and North Africa.* London: Author.

McDaniel, D. (1982). Libya. In D. A. Boyd (Ed.), *Broadcasting in the Arab World: A survey of radio and television in the Middle East.* Philadelphia, PA: Temple University Press.

Ministry of Information and Culture. (1966). Journalism in Libya. *The Libyan Review, 3.*

Qadhafi, M. (1976). *The green book: Democracy.* Libya: Government Publications.

Rugh, W. (1979). *The Arab press.* New York: Syracuse University Press.

UNESCO Statistical Yearbook. (1991). Paris: United Nations Educational, Scientific and Cultural Organization.

13

OMAN

Hana S. Noor Al-Deen

INTRODUCTION

The Sultanate of Oman enjoys a very strategic location at the tip of the Musandam Peninsula on the southern shore of the Strait of Hormuz. Its coastline stretches for more than 1,600 kilometers (1,000 miles), and its terrain covers an estimated 300,000 square kilometers (116,000 square miles). Topographically, the Sultanate of Oman "except for the Dhofar . . . region, consists of three divisions: a coastal plain, a mountain range, and a plateau" (Oman, 1988, p. 275). The Omani people, who number about 2 million, can be categorized into four groups: "the people of the sea. . . , the agriculturalists. . . , the mountain people. . . , and the Bedouin of the desert areas" (Oman '91, 1991, p. 26).

The official language of the Sultanate of Oman is Arabic. English is taught as a second language. Other languages such as Balochi, Farsi, Urdu, and Indian dialects are also spoken. These spoken languages are found in the major northern cities such as Muscat and Muttrah.

Islam is the principal religion of the Sultanate of Oman. The Omani people generally belong to one of the following three major Islamic sects: Ibadites, Sunnites, and Shiites. About 75 percent of them are Ibadites, while the rest are Sunnites or Shiites. Also, there are some religious followers of Hinduism in Oman.

The economy of Oman is built around oil. This state of affairs began with the production of oil in 1967, just three years after it was discovered in the sultanate. Oil revenues have helped to fuel prosperity since the mid-1970s. Petroleum now accounts for about 80 percent of the government's revenue and for approximately 40 percent of the country's gross domestic product (GDP) (Oman, 1991). Nonetheless, the Omani government is attempting to diversify its economy by developing such traditional industries as agriculture and fishing as well as new industries such as manufacturing in order to reduce the nation's dependency on oil.

Although formal education has existed in the Sultanate of Oman for some time, notable progress really began since Sultan Qaboos Bin Said Al-Said assumed power in 1970. The number of schools has increased from three boys' schools in Muscat, Muttrah, and Salalah with a total of 909 students in 1970 to 800 state schools in 1990–1991 with an estimated total of 351,217 students (Oman '91, 1991). About 47 percent of the total number of students were females. In addition to state schools, there were 58 private schools with a total of 7,831 students by the end of 1990. Technical, agricultural, and craft training have been developed at the intermediate and secondary levels of education. In 1986, Sultan Qaboos University at Al-Khoudh, which hosts six colleges, became the nation's first university and opened to both sexes. Adult education was also established in 1974. By 1987–1988, there were 248 governmental literacy centers attended by 10,625 students (20 percent males and 80 percent females) plus 209 adult education centers attended by 10,916 students (42 percent males and 58 percent females) (Oman, 1992). Overall, this educational campaign helped to improve the literacy rate to such a degree that it rose to about 38 percent (*Britannica,* 1990).

The administrative system of the state under Sultan Qaboos consists of the Diwan of the Royal Court, the Ministry of Palace Office Affairs, the Cabinet of Ministers and Secretariat of the Cabinet, the Specialized Councils, Governorate of Muscat, and the State Consultative Council (Oman '91, 1991). Oman is divided into 59 *wilayats* (regions), each headed by a *wali* (governor) under the jurisdiction of the Ministry of Interior. The sultan rules with the advice of an appointed cabinet. This arrangement represents the executive branch of the government. The legislative branch is composed of the State Consultative Council, and legislation is made by decree.

PRINT MEDIA

Newspapers

No newspaper was published in Oman prior to 1971 (Oman '91, 1991). The first Omani newspaper, entitled *Al-Watan* (*The Nation*), was founded that year. By 1993, there were a total of four daily newspapers in the Sultanate of Oman. They are *Al-Watan, Oman, Oman Daily Observer* and the *Times of Oman. Al-Watan* and *Oman* are published in Arabic. *Oman Daily Observer* and *Times of Oman* are published in English. The circulations of the Arabic-language newspapers are somewhat higher than the English. The circulations of *Al-Watan* and

Oman are about 23,500 and 20,000, respectively. Meanwhile, the circulations of *Oman Daily Observer* and *Times of Oman* are roughly 10,000 and 15,000, respectively. The orientation of these newspapers is political. They contain sections such as news, business, sports, features, leisure, and classified. Furthermore, advertisements (Arabic and English) are included in the newspapers.

Magazines

The first Omani magazines were established in the 1970s. *Al-Usra* (*The Family*), which was founded in 1974, was among this initial group (Oman, 1990). By 1991, there were about 24 magazines that were catering to different interests, ages, sexes, educational levels, and occupations. These magazines are published weekly, biweekly, monthly, bimonthly, quarterly, semiannually, or occasionally, as shown in Table 13.1. Most of the magazines tend to be published in Arabic.

Furthermore, the types of magazines can be classified into two categories: consumer and nonconsumer. Consumer magazines are "those readily available to the public by subscription—to be received through the mail—or by direct purchase at newsstands" (DeFleur & Dennis, 1991, p. 129). Nonconsumer magazines include sponsored magazines and business magazines. Sponsored magazines are "internal publications of particular organizations, unions, and other groups, including . . . employee magazines" (DeFleur & Dennis, 1991, p. 130). Business magazines "cover particular industries, trades, and professions, and go mainly to persons in those fields" (DeFleur & Dennis, 1991, p. 129). As shown in Table 13.2, consumer magazines include *Al-Adwah* (*The Lights*), *Al-Akidah* (*The Faith*), *Al-Bara'em* (*Blossoms*), *Al-Nahda* (*Renaissance*), *Al-Shabiba* (*Youth*), *Al-Siraj al-Adabeeah* (*Literary Light*), *Al-Tijaree* (*The Commercial*), and *Al-Usra* (*The Family*). These magazines deal primarily with economic, political, social, family, sports, tourism, and literary issues. Sponsored magazines may count among their ranks *Al-Ghurfa* (*The Chamber*), *Al-Harass* (*The Guard*), *Al-Jareeda Rasmeeah* (*The Official Gazette*), *Al-Omaniya* (*Omani Woman*), *Al-Shurta* (*The Police*), *Jund Oman* (*Soldiers of Oman*), *Muscat, Nusoor Oman* (*Eagles of Oman*), and *Risalat al-Masjid* (*Messages of the Mosque*). These magazines cover a wide range of issues such as business, law, society, religion, municipality, and national security. The remainder of the Omani magazines come under the category of business magazines and include *Akhbar Shurkatna* (*PDO News*), *Al-Idaree* (*The Administrator*), *Al-Markazi* (*The Central Place*), *Al-Mawared at Tabeey'iyah* (*Natural Resources*), *Al-Mazari'* (*The Farmer*), *Nashrat al-Fahal* (*Fahal News*), and *Rusayl*. This group of magazines encompasses business affairs that deal with agriculture, economics, natural resources, petroleum, administration, and other industries. The top three consumer magazines in Oman are *Al-Usra* (12,000 circulation), *Al-Adwah* (10,000 circulation), and *Al-Nahda* (10,000 circulation). The circulation of the sponsored magazine *Al-Omaniya* is rather high at 13,500.

Table 13.1
Omani Magazines: Period of Publication, Language, and Circulation

Magazine	Period	Language	Circulation
Akhbar Shurkatna (PDO News)	Quarterly	Arabic	NA
Al-Adwah (The Lights)	Bi-weekly	Arabic	10,000
Al-Akidah (The Faith)	Weekly	Arabic	10,000
Al-Bara'em (Blossoms)	Weekly	Arabic	1,800
Al-Ghurfa (The Chamber)	Quarterly	A & E	NA
Al-Harass (The Guard)	NA	Arabic	NA
Al-Idaree (The Administrator)	Quarterly	Arabic	NA
Al-Jareeda Rasmeeah (The Official Gazette)	Bi-weekly	Arabic	NA
Al-Markazi (The Central Place)	Bi-monthly	A & E	NA
Al-Mawared at-Tabeey' iyah (Natural Resources)	Monthly	A & E	NA
Al-Mazari' (The Farmer)	Weekly	Arabic	NA
Al-Nahda (Renaissance)	Weekly	Arabic	10,000
Al-Omaniya (Omani Woman)	Monthly	Arabic	13,500
Al-Shabiba (Youth)	Weekly	Arabic	NA
Al-Shurta (The Police)	Quarterly	Arabic	NA
Al-Siraj al-Adabeeah (Literary Light)	NA	Arabic	NA
Al-Tijaree (The Commercial)	Monthly	A & E	NA
Al-Usra (The Family)	Weekly	Arabic	12,000
Jund Oman (Soldiers of Oman)	Monthly	Arabic	NA
Muscat	NA	Arabic	NA
Nashrat al-Fahal (Fahal News)	NA	Arabic	NA
Nusoor Oman (Eagles of Oman)	Semi-annually	Arabic	NA
Risalat al-Masjid (Messages of the Mosque)	Occasionally	Arabic	NA
Rusayl	Quarterly	A & E	NA

Sources: Oman: Introductory Survey, 1992, p. 2127; Publications, 1992.

A & E = Arabic and English.

NA = Not available.

Table 13.2
Omani Magazines: Focus and Ownership

Magazine	Focus	Owner
Akhbar Shurkatna	Petroleum	P.D.O.
Al-Adwah	Economic, Social & Political	Private
Al-Akidah	Political	Private
Al-Bara'em	Family	Private
Al-Ghurfa	Business	Oman Chamber of Commerce & Industry
Al-Harass	Guard	Royal Guard of Oman
Al-Idaree	Administration	Institute of Public Administration/ Diwan of Royal Court
Al-Jareeda Rasmeeah	Legal	Legislative
Al-Markazi	Economic	Central Bank of Oman
Al-Mawared at-Tabeey'iyah	Natural Resources	Ministries Agriculture, Fisheries, Petroleum, & Minerals
Al-Mazari'	Farms	Ministries Agriculture & Fisheries
Al-Nahda	Political/Social	Private
Al-Omaniya	Social	Omani Women's Assoc.
Al-Shabiba	Sports/Social/Tourism	Private
Al-Shurta	Police	Royal Oman Police
Al-Siraj al-Adabeeah	Literary	Private
Al-Tijaree	Economic	Private
Al-Usra	Socio-economic	Private
Jund Oman	Military	Ministry of Defense
Muscat	Municipality	Muscat Municipality
Nashrat al-Fahal	Petroleum	P.D.O. llc
Nusoor Oman	Military	Royal Air Force of Oman
Risalat al-Masjid	Religious	Diwan of Royal Court
Rusayl	Industrial	Rusayl Industrial Estate Authority

Sources: Oman: Introductory Survey, 1992, p. 2127; Publications, 1992.

As indicated in Table 13.2, Omani magazines are owned by both private and government institutions.

ELECTRONIC MEDIA

Radio

Oman possessed no radio broadcasting station before 1970 (Oman '91, 1991). Within a week of Sultan Qaboos's accession to the throne, a small radio broadcasting station of only 1 kilowatt (medium wave) was installed at Bait al-Falaj. This radio station was able to broadcast throughout the greater Muscat vicinity, a northern metropolis in the Sultanate of Oman. Another radio transmitter of 1 kilowatt (medium wave) was set up in Salalah, a major southern city, and began broadcasting (from 7:00 P.M. to midnight) in 1971. In 1972, a new radio station of 10 kilowatts (medium wave) was established at Bait Al Falaj. The number of broadcasting hours were increased to 14 hours per day and 18 hours on holidays (Oman '91, 1991). A year later, the Salalah radio station was also expanded to 10 kilowatts for medium wave. The number of broadcasting hours were increased to 8, from 4:00 P.M. to midnight. In 1974, broadcasting commenced on a 100-kilowatt medium wave radio transmitter for the northern radio station. The transmitter was relocated at Asseeb, north of the capital Muscat. In 1975, a 50-kilowatt shortwave station began broadcasting from Muscat. The Salalah radio station also enjoyed expansion in 1975. Growth was provided by a 50-kilowatt medium wave radio transmitter and soon expanded to a 100-kilowatt medium wave transmitter. In 1977, the number of broadcasting hours of Salalah radio were increased to 14, which included morning hours from 6:00 A.M. until noon in addition to the regular broadcasting hours of 4:00 P.M. until midnight (Al-Khusaibi, 1985). Subsequently, additional transmitters were placed in many sections of the Sultanate of Oman in order to strengthen the broadcasting system and to relay broadcasting to the entire nation. In 1979, the Muscat and Salalah radio stations were linked by space satellite and became Radio Oman, using a 150-kilowatt medium wave transmitter and broadcasting at alternate times.

In 1981, FM (Frequency Modulation) broadcasting was established in Musandam in order to reach the farther northern part of the country. Additional FM broadcasting was launched from the Muscat radio station in 1982. This FM capability broadcasts in English from 1:00 P.M. to 9:00 P.M. daily (Al-Khusaibi, 1985).

Broadcasting is transmitted from both radio stations at alternating times of the day in order to make full use of each radio facility. Muscat radio station broadcasts in English and Arabic languages, while the Salalah unit broadcasts in Arabic and Dhofari languages (Oman, 1992). The English-language broadcast runs for 15 hours per day. The Arabic-language broadcasts are aired by both stations for a combined total of 19.5 hours per day (Oman '91, 1991). During the Holy Month of Ramadan, Arabic broadcasting is usually extended on the average to 21.5 hours per day (Omani Ministry of Information, 1990). The 1989 UNESCO (United Nations Educational, Scientific and Cultural Organization) report estimated that there were 932,000 radio receivers in use across the country (Oman, 1992). This calculates to one radio set for every two listeners in Oman.

The types of Arabic radio programs are mainly news, religion, development, culture, education, science, children, youth, family, and entertainment (Omani Ministry of Information, 1990). Most of these programs are locally produced. The English-language radio offers music, nonmusical programs, and news. Commercials are included during both Arabic and English radio broadcasting.

Television

The advent of this technology did not arrive in Oman with the construction of a black and white television station. Instead, it began when the first color television station, which was built at Qurm outside Muscat, was opened in 1974 (Oman, 1992). The color system of Omani television is based on the German phase alternate line (PAL). PAL (scans at 625 lines) is the "electronic scanning and color system used in western European and some other parts of the world" (Gross, 1993, p. 488). A year later, another color television station (PAL) was opened in Salalah to cover the Governorate of Dhofar (Oman, 1992; Oman '91, 1991). In 1979, the two television stations in Muscat and Salalah were linked by space satellite in order to be able to transmit from both stations, thereby reaching a large audience. In addition to the solar relay stations that have been instituted throughout Oman, 12 television relay transmitters have been installed in order to expand TV signals and improve reception. Five of these relay transmitters were installed in Muscat, 3 in Salalah, and the remaining 4 in Nizwa, Sur, Saham, and Buraimi.

On the average, television airs programs for about 11 hours per day. During the weekdays (Saturday through Wednesday), it broadcasts 10 hours per day. Over the weekend (Thursday and Friday), television service is extended to 11 and 15 hours each (Omani Ministry of Information, 1990). Television broadcasting usually starts at 3:00 P.M. during the weekdays and at 10:00 A.M. during the weekend. For the month of Ramadan, television broadcasting hours are increased to an average of about 14.5 per day. Like radio, there is about one TV set per two viewers. This figure is based on the UNESCO report of 1989, which estimated that there were 1.1 million television receivers in use (Oman, 1992).

The types of television programs are similar to those found on radio: news, religion, development, culture, education, science, children, youth, family, and entertainment (Omani Ministry of Information, 1990). Although Omani television broadcasts in Arabic, the daily news is provided in the Arabic language at 9:00 P.M. and in the English language at 10:00 P.M. As far as the rest of the programs are concerned, some are produced by Omani television studios and some are imported from either Arab countries such as Egypt or non-Arab countries such as the United States and India. The imported programs include movies, dramas, comedies, documentaries, events, and so on. Examples of American imported programs are "*Attitudes, Beyond 2000, Donahue, Hill Street Blues, St. Elsewhere, Life Styles of the Rich and Famous, Santa Barbara, The Bold & The Beautiful,* and *The Wonder Years*" (*Times of Oman,* 1993). The imported programs from non-Arab countries are either dubbed or subtitled in Arabic. Moreover, Oman exchanges television programs with the Gulf states of Egypt, Jordan, and Tunisia (Al-Khusaibi, 1985).

Commercials were introduced on local television in 1987. There are two types of commercials: Arabic and foreign. Arabic commercials are produced in Oman, while foreign commercials are dubbed in Arabic. Usually, commercials are aired either before or after the program in order to avoid interrupting it.

Cable Television

There is no cable television in Oman. However, imported cable programs such as CNN (Cable News Network) News and Music Television (MTV) do appear in the television broadcast lineup.

NEW TECHNOLOGIES

The new technologies of mass media are rather recent additions in the sultanate when one considers that ''Oman owned no media before 1970, i.e., no radio, no television and no newspaper'' (Oman '91, 1991, p. 47). Oman uses satellite earth stations, two Indian Ocean International Telecommunication Satellite Consortium (INTELSAT) satellites, one Arab Satellite Communications Organization satellite, and eight domestic units (Oman, 1991).

Oman employs the latest technologies offered by the global telecommunications industry. Communication technologies such as telex, data transmission, and coastal radio stations are already in use. Expansion of the existing fiber optic transmission network is planned, and new links will be established to interconnect various parts of the sultanate (Oman '91, 1991). Additional services are scheduled to be introduced in the near future such as a paging system, data packet services, and teletex. ''A new earth station, which will be linked to the national network by fiber optic cable, will be installed to operate via the Atlantic Ocean Satellite'' (Oman '91, p. 142).

The videocassette recorder (VCR) is relatively new in Oman, although it has been adopted quite rapidly. For example, it was estimated that about 75 percent of the Omani homes were equipped with VCRs in 1986 (Boyd, Straubhaar, & Lent, 1989). In 1989, the country showed that it can skillfully balance its attraction for such new technology by opening the Oman Center for Traditional Music. The center houses videotapes, sound recordings, still photographs, and color slides (Oman '91, 1991).

MOTION PICTURES

Although there is no motion picture production in Oman, a few movie theaters have been constructed during the last 23 years. They are found in large cities such as Muscat and Salalah. These movie theaters are mostly attended by expatriates such as Americans, the British, and Indians. The films shown in those theaters can be categorized into two groups: foreign and Arabic. Foreign films, which are mainly imported from the West and India, are subtitled in Arabic. Arabic films are imported from Egypt. The movies are monitored and censored by the Ministry of National Heritage and Culture for bad language, sex, and violence.

MEDIA OWNERSHIP

The Omani print media are owned and operated by the government, quasi-government, and private sectors. Omani newspapers, for instance, are owned and operated by both the government and private sectors. *Oman* and *Oman Daily Observer* are owned and operated by the Omani government, while *Al-Watan* and *Times of Oman* are privately owned and operated. Also, Omani magazines are owned and operated by the three sectors (see Table 13.2). Consumer magazines are privately owned and operated and constitute about one-third of the total magazines published in Oman. The quasi-government sector runs four business magazines (*Akhbar Shurkatna, Al-Markazi, Nashrat al-Fahal,* and *Rusayl*) and two sponsored magazines (*Al-Ghurfa* and *Al-Omaniya*). These represent about 25 percent of the Omani magazines. The rest of the magazines are basically owned and operated by the government.

The electronic media of Oman are owned and operated by the government (Oman: Ministry of Information). When this technology was in its nascent stage in Oman, the government had to rely on non-Omanis to run such media. Since then, the government has made a concerted effort to train its nationals to run the electronic media. By 1991, about 90 percent of the 450 staff members of the television stations in both Muscat and Salalah were Omanis. Also, the Omani News Agency is owned and operated by the government (Ministry of Information).

MEDIA REGULATION

Omani media appear to enjoy a greater degree of freedom than similar media in many other countries. There is no censorship in the news, and journalists apply good taste in their reportage. Moreover, there is "relative freedom on social and economic issues" (Bahbah, 1989, p. 196). "There is no license fee for broadcast receivers in Oman" (Boyd, 1982, p. 163). Overall, the Ministry of Information and the Ministry of National Heritage and Culture both oversee regulations of the media. The Ministry of Information, in particular, deals with electronic and print media. The Ministry of National Heritage and Culture monitors the videocassette material.

EXTERNAL MEDIA SERVICES

Radio Oman reaches most of the Arab countries (such as those in the Gulf area, north of the Arabian Peninsula, Jordan, Egypt, Tunisia), East Africa, China, France, southern Europe, and the United States. Arab countries in Africa receive about 19.5 hours (from 6:00 A.M. until 1:30 A.M.) of the daily Omani broadcasting (Al-Khusaibi, 1985). Although Radio Oman broadcasts in Arabic, it also transmits in English to non-Arabic-speaking countries. The Omani international broadcasting is based on agreements (time, frequency, and so on) with the International Telecommunications Union (ITU), a United Nations organization. In addition to broadcasting, Omani newspapers and magazines are circulated regionally in the Gulf states.

NEWS AGENCIES

There is one news agency, called the Omani News Agency, which is located in Muscat. This agency was established in 1986, and it carries news about Oman and the region to many countries worldwide (Oman '91, 1991). Omani newspapers deal with international and national news. Similar coverage is observed in the broadcast media. In a recent study, the content of the nine o'clock Arabic-language TV news during a five-day period was analyzed (Al-Habib, 1990). It was found that television news consisted of two major segments, domestic and international. The domestic news was the leading segment and consumed about 40 percent of the total news program. A large percentage of the domestic coverage was soft news that stressed mainly technology and social services. The international coverage dealt mainly with hard news that covered political issues and news about other Arab countries.

THE ROLE OF MEDIA IN NATIONAL DEVELOPMENT

Oman has made great strides toward using the media for informational, educational, and entertainment purposes in spite of the fact that it has been less than a quarter of a century since modern mass media began to grow in this country. This growth is partially revealed when examining the variety of broadcast media programs as shown in Table 13.3. For example, about 74 percent of the radio programs are devoted to entertainment, religion, and news, while those same types represent about 54 percent of all television programs. The balanced programs displayed in Table 13.3 provide "information and guidance in such matters as health, education, agriculture, industry, family affairs, and child care in close cooperation with the relevant ministries" (Oman '91, 1991, p. 49). Moreover, the English-language radio programming furnishes approximately 47 percent of its output in the form of light and popular music, 33 percent in classical music, and 20 percent in nonmusical programs in English (Oman '91, 1991).

The Omani print media has shown a similarity in task to those of the broadcast media inasmuch as it informs, educates, and entertains. This similarity becomes apparent when considering magazines in particular. Omani magazines deal with various subjects such as society, politics, economics, and so on, as shown in Table 13.2.

Table 13.3
Omani Radio and Television Programs

Type of Program	Radio %	Rank	Television %	Rank
Entertainment	52.0	1	27.9	1
Religious	11.3	2	13.7	2
News	10.5	3	12.7	4
Cultural	7.0	4	5.6	8
Educational & Scientific	6.5	5	10.1	5
Development	6.0	6	7.7	7
Family	2.7	7	0.6	9
Children	2.2	8	12.9	3
Youth	1.9	9	8.9	6

Source: Omani Ministry of Information, 1990, pp. 5–21.

CONCLUSION

Besides its international significance as an oil producer, the Sultanate of Oman is rich historically, geographically, and culturally. Although the history of Oman goes back as far as 12,000 B.C., the history of the mass media in this land is less than a quarter of a century old.

Communicative trends in Oman suggest a desire to expand the current services and to adopt the latest in technology. For instance, in 1989, a new comprehensive complex that contains a radio station and studios was opened at Al-Qurm. In 1990, Oman signed an agreement with a French group for the further extension of television and radio facilities. The project involves the establishment of 16 main stations for television and radio and 75 relay and strengthening stations that will be linked with the 16 main stations. The project will cost RO25,645,641 (in Omani rial) and will be completed in 32 months (Oman '91, 1991, p. 49). If the ongoing progress in the mass media indicates anything, it is that the Omanis have learned how to adroitly steer a course that accepts change in the future while maintaining a firm grasp on one's heritage.

REFERENCES

Al-Habib, A. I. (1990, April). *A content analysis of TV news in Saudi Arabia and Oman.* Paper presented at the annual convention of the Association for Education in Journalism and Mass Communication, Minneapolis, MN.

Al-Khusaibi, S. B. N. (1985). *The use of traditional music in the development of mass media in Oman.* Beverly Hills: University of Beverly Hills.

Bahbah, B. (1989). Trends in the Middle East. In E. Barnouw & G. Gerbner (Eds.), *International encyclopedia of communications* (Vol. 3, pp. 195–197). New York: Oxford University Press.

Boyd, D. A. (1982). *Broadcasting in the Arab World: A survey of radio and television in the Middle East.* Philadelphia: Temple University Press.

Boyd, D. A., Straubhaar, J. D., & Lent, J. A. (1989). *Videocassette recorders in the Third World.* New York: Longman.

Britannica book of the year. (1990). Chicago: Encyclopedia Britannica.

DeFleur, M. L., & Dennis, E. E. (1991). *Understanding mass communication* (4th ed.). Boston: Houghton Mifflin Company.

Gross, L. S. (1993). *Telecommunications: An introduction to electronic media* (4th ed.). Dubuque: William C. Brown.

Oman. (1985). *World book encyclopedia.* Chicago: World Book.

Oman. (1988). *Worldmark encyclopedia of the nations: Asia & Oceania* (7th ed.). New York: Worldmark Press.

Oman. (1989a). In T. D. Snyder (Dir.), *Digest of education statistics 1989* (25th ed., pp. 740–741). Washington, DC: U.S. Department of Education.

Oman. (1989b). In A. S. Banks (Ed.), *Political handbook of the world 1989* (pp. 454–456). Binghamton: SUNY.

Oman. (1989c). *World communication and transportation data.* Santa Barbara: ABC-CLIO.

Oman. (1990). *The Middle East and North Africa 1991.* London: Europa.

Oman. (1991). *The world factbook 1991.* Washington, DC: Central Intelligence Agency.

Oman. (1992–1994). *The world media handbook.* New York: United Nations.

Oman '91. (1991). *Omani Ministry of Information.*

Oman: A new dawn. (1983, May–June). *ARAMCO World,* pp. 2–40.

Oman: Facts and figures 1986. (1987). Muscat: Development Council, Technical Secretariat.

Oman: Introductory survey. (1992). *The Europa world year book 1992.* London: Europa.

Omani Ministry of Information. (1990). *Oman* (pp. 1–21, 5–21).

Publications (1992). Oman: Ministry of Information.

Times of Oman. (1993, April 18). Ruwi, Oman, p. 10.

14

PAKISTAN

Mazharul Haque

INTRODUCTION

Approximately 310,402 square miles (803,943 square kilometers) including Jammu and Kashmer, the Islamic Republic of Pakistan is located in the northwestern part of the Indian subcontinent. It is bordered by Afghanistan and Iran to the west and India to the east, with a short frontier with the People's Republic of China in the far northeast and the Arabian Sea to the south.

It has an estimated population of about 120 million and is composed of four provinces or political units: the North West Frontier Province (NWFP), Punjab, Sindh, and Baluchistan. The area called Azad Kashmir (Free Kashmir), which includes Jammu and Kashmir and has a predominantly Muslim population, has a rather undefined status. This area and other ''Northern Areas'' comprising 32,200 square miles (83,400 square kilometers) are administered as de facto dependencies by the government of Pakistan (''Pakistan,'' 1992, p. 586).

While Urdu is the official language, only about 9 percent of the population, predominantly immigrants from India, known as Muhajirs, are native Urdu speakers. Punjabi is spoken by 65 percent of the population; Sindhi and Pushtu are spoken by 11 percent each, while Baluchi/Brahui and Gujrati are spoken by the remainder. English is widely used in the country in government, business, and higher education.

Islam is the state religion professed by 97 percent of the population. About 70 percent of the Muslims are Sunnis; the remainder are Shiites. Other religions are Christianity and Hinduism.

In 1990, according to the World Bank estimates, the gross national product (GNP) was $42,649 million, equivalent to $380 per capita (''Pakistan: An Introductory Survey,'' 1992, p. 2134). During the decade of the 1980s, it was estimated that GNP increased in real terms, at an average annual rate of 6.3 percent, while GNP per capita grew by 2.9 percent per year. During the same period, the population grew at an annual rate of 3.3 percent, perhaps the highest rate of population growth in South Asia (p. 2134).

The share of agriculture to gross domestic product (GDP) was 26 percent in the year 1990, employing slightly over half the work force. The north and west are covered by great mountain ranges, but the country also consists of a fertile plain watered by five big rivers. The main cash crops are cotton and rice, with cotton and cotton-based products accounting for over a third of the nation's export earnings. Fishing and leather products also provide export revenues. Industry including mining, manufacturing, power, and construction employs about 20 percent and accounts for about 26 percent of GDP. Manufacturing alone contributes about 18 percent to GDP and employs about 13 percent of the work force. Even though the national government has adopted a policy to encourage private industry since the late 1970s, the public sector is still dominant, especially in large industries.

The seventh Five-Year Plan (1988–1993) and the past two Five-Year plans placed heavy emphasis on creating a larger role for the private sector in industry. More than 100 state-owned enterprises were offered for sale, including banks and telecommunication corporations. The same policy was also extended to government media properties as well.

The constitution of the country guarantees universal free primary education as a right, yet fewer than half the children in Pakistan actually receive it. In the early 1990s, the total enrollment at primary and secondary schools was only about 29 percent of all school-age children, and about 49 percent of children aged five to nine were enrolled at school. Present government policy stresses vocational and technical education, with an emphasis on disseminating Islamic values and ideology. According to the United Nations Educational, Scientific and Cultural Organization (UNESCO) estimates, the rates of adult illiteracy stand at 65.2 percent, with 52.7 percent for males and 78.9 percent for females. There are 22 universities in the country; however, development expenditure on science and technology, education, and training is estimated at only 1.6 percent (''Pakistan: An Introductory Survey,'' 1992; ''Pakistan: Islamic Jamhuriya e Pakistan,'' 1992).

Pakistan as a state came into existence in August 1947 when India was partitioned under the provisions of the Indian Independence Act by the British colonial rulers. Pakistan is the only country of the twentieth century, with the exception of Israel, whose creation was based on the demand by a religious community to have a state of its own (Nyrop, 1984). Indeed, this demand created a bifurcated country with Muslim majority areas in the Indian subcontinent: East Pakistan and West Pakistan. Linguistic and racial differences, different cultural traditions, and a political and economic structure perceived as inequitable by the East Pakistanis who constituted 54 percent of Pakistan's population led to a secessionist movement by East Pakistan. In 1971, East Pakistan became the independent country of Bangladesh.

Except for brief periods, Pakistan for most of its history has been ruled by military governments. Between 1947, the year Pakistan came into being, and 1973, Pakistan adopted three permanent and four interim constitutions. In 1985, the constitution of 1973 was restored with the exception of some key provisions. The constitution provided for a bicameral federal legislature, a 237-member National Assembly, and an 87-member Senate. The National Assembly is elected for a five-year term, and the Senate for a six-year term. The constitution, as amended in 1986, consolidates Islam as the basis of law and obliges the government to enable the people to order their lives in accordance.

PRINT MEDIA

Newspapers

The forerunner of the newspaper in the Indian subcontinent was the newsletter. The Ghaznavide Muslim rulers introduced the handwritten newsletter toward the end of the tenth century. During the reign of the last great Mughal emperor, Aurangzeb, the news writers known as "Waquai-Nawees" were regarded as the "eyes and ears of the emperor" (Hasan & Khurshid, 1988, p. 68). The newsletter existed in the Mughal courts until the Sepoy mutiny of 1857, known in the subcontinent as the first War of Independence. Newsletters then became extinct, and the printed "newsheet" took their place (p. 68).

James Angustus Hickey, a former employee of the British East India Company, started the first newspaper in the subcontinent of Indo-Pakistan in 1780, a weekly known as the *Bengal Gazette.* It was a two-sheet paper, about 12 by 8 inches, with three columns printed on both sides. It contained advertisements, stories lifted from English newspapers, and local gossip and scandals about the British community in Calcutta. Initially, the paper was nonpolitical, targeted to merchants, traders, and the nonofficial Europeans in Calcutta, but soon it started to attack colonial officials. A couple of years after, the newspaper was silenced by the government.

During the eighteenth century, there were three newspaper centers in the subcontinent under the rule of the East India Company: Calcutta, Madras, and Bombay. Later, newspapers began to be published in other cities, with the regions making up Pakistan having only a few newspapers. During the first half of the nineteenth century, Lahore, the most important city of the most populous province of Pakistan, had one English newspaper and four Urdu newspapers. Peshawar, the largest city in the North West Frontier Province, had two Urdu newspapers during the same period. The contents of the paper published in all these cities consisted of foreign news, parliamentary debates in England, social news, letters to the editor, poet's corner, and months-old stories extracted from English newspapers.

The introduction of the lithographic printing method, during the first half of the nineteenth century, combined with the recognition of Urdu as the court language, contributed to the growth of the Urdu-language press. The Urdu papers tried to promote education and literature. At the trial of the last Mughal ruler, Bahadur Shah Zafar, the British prosecutor allegedly blamed the conspiracy of the press and the palace for the great Sepoy mutiny in India in 1857. The press he was blaming had a total circulation of 5,000 in the subcontinent with a possible readership of about 50,000. One of the most important Urdu newspapers, *Koh-i-noor* of Lahore, had a circulation of only 350 copies at its peak (Hasan & Khurshid, 1988, p. 86).

Historians of the press in Pakistan claim that Sir Syed Ahmed Khan, a nineteenth-century social reformer and the founder of the Aligarh Movement, also laid the foundation of a Muslim press that had the social and cultural mission of trying to transform Muslim life and thinking by acquainting them with European civilization (Yousaf, 1992). The two periodicals he started, *Tahzib-ul-Akhlaq* (*Cultural Reforms*), in Urdu, and a bilingual publication entitled *Scientific Society Magazine,* had a significant impact on Muslim opinion leaders. The Muslim press that followed Syed Ahmed's lead during the early twentieth century emphasized the need for the Muslims to reform their society, learn sciences, modernize education along European principles, and secure a greater share of the public employment.

Four important political figures, Hasrat Mohani, Muhammed Ali, Abul Kalam Azad, and Zafar Ali Khan, took to journalism with the goal of removing apathy and creating political awareness among Muslims. As the struggle for independence intensified, new Muslim newspapers began to emerge, and the press increasingly became polarized into nationalist and separatist factions. The nationalist press advocated a joint Hindu-Muslim struggle against the British. The separatist movement gained momentum and blossomed into a full-scale movement for a Muslim homeland that culminated in the creation of Pakistan.

During the closing phase of the Pakistan movement, a number of newspapers were born. These newspapers, *Morning News* of Calcutta, *Nawai-Wagt* (*The Current News*) of Lahore, *Jang (*The Struggle) and *Anjam* (*The Outcome*) of Delhi, and the *Dawn* of Karachi, had a very significant role in mobilizing public opinion in favor of Pakistan. The tradition of affiliation with political parties and factions, set during the struggle for independence, continues for the Pakistani press. Except for a few independent newspapers, most have direct affiliation with a political party or group and therefore reflect their views and interests. Even independent newspapers are subject to influence and manipulation by government and other interests because of government licenses, perks, privileges, and other business interests.

According to the latest available figures, there are 271 dailies in Pakistan, published in four languages, with a combined circulation of 1.5 million copies in a nation of 120 million people. The low literacy rate creates the phenomenon of newspaper listenership. An educated newspaper reader reading to a number of listeners is a common sight (Saeed, 1992). A Business Research Bureau survey in 1987 indicated that 28 percent of the adult males were regular readers and 23 percent read occasionally. The urban-rural split in readership is 18 percent and 10 percent (Orient Advertising, 1991, p. 42).

There are four main press groups in Pakistan. Jang Publications own the *Daily Jang, The News, The Daily News,* and *The Weekly Akhbar-e-Jahan* (*The News of the World*). The *Jang (The Struggle)* in Urdu is published in five major cities, Karachi, Lahore, Rawalpindi, Quetta, and London, with a combined circulation of 750,000. The Herald Group owns the *Dawn,* the *Star,* the *Watan* (*Nation*) and the monthly *Herald.*

The *Dawn* published in English and Gujrati is one of the most influential newspapers in the country. The newspaper was launched in Delhi, India, by the founder of Pakistan, Mohammad Ali Jinnah, as a weekly in 1930, to put forth the Muslim point of view and to fill a vacuum created by a lack of Muslim-owned English newspapers. The paper was moved to Karachi, the capital of Pakistan in 1947, when the country came into being. Since then the newspaper has enjoyed the reputation of being one of the best dailies in the nation. Currently, the English edition has a circulation of about 80,000.

The Nawa-i-Waqt (The Current News) Group owns the *Nawa-i-Waqt* and the *Nation.* The *Nawa-i-Waqt* is published from four cities, Lahore, Karachi, Rawalpindi, and Multan, with a combined circulation of 400,000. This prestigious Urdu newspaper was started in 1940 as a weekly but was converted to a daily in 1944. Not only was it a powerful advocate of the Muslim cause during the peak of Pakistan movement in the 1940s, but it is also given credit for pioneering a new style of Urdu journalism characterized by simplicity in style, sobriety, and objectivity (Hasan & Khurshid, 1988, p. 115).

The National Press Trust, a government-controlled publishing group, was the largest, owning the *Pakistan Times,* the *Mashrig* (*The East,*) *Imroze* (*The Current News*), *Morning News,* and *Akhbar-e-Khawateen* (*The Women's Magazine*). However, the government has decided to divest itself of all newspapers except the *Pakistan Times. Imroze* ceased publication in 1991. The *Pakistan Times* is published in Lahore and Rawalpindi and has a combined circulation of about 50,000. The *Times* was started as a daily in 1947 in Lahore to propagate the views of the Muslim League in the Punjab. The newspaper initially enjoyed a certain authoritative quality, but in recent years, it has lost much of its credibility.

In Pakistan, the major newspaper centers are Karachi, Lahore, and Rawalpindi-Islamabad, but there are other cities where newspapers are published: Quetta, Peshawar, Hyderabad, Multan, and Faisalabad. Newspapers are published in several languages: English, Urdu, Sindhi, Gujrati, and Pushto. By one count, there are 128 English newspapers in the country, but they reach only 2 percent of the population. The English press is disproportionately influential in political, academic, and professional circles (''Pakistan: An Introductory Survey,'' 1992, p. 2145). The principal English dailies include *Business Records, Baluchistan Times, Dawn, Frontier Post, Morning News, The Muslim, The News, The Nation, Pakistan Observer, Pakistan Times,* and *Sind Observer.*

Of the 11 major English dailies, Karachi and Lahore have 4 each. Some newspapers have both Karachi and Lahore editions. Of the major Urdu dailies, Karachi and Lahore have 6 each, followed by Peshawar and Quetta with 4 each; Multan has 3; Rawalpindi, 2. Some of the largest newspapers, such as *Jang, Mashrig,* and *Nawa-i-Wagt,* publish multiple editions in the largest cities.

The principal Urdu dailies include *Awaz* (*The Voice*), *Adl* (*Justice*), *Amn* (*Peace*), *Al Falah, Atemad* (*Trust*), *Business Report, Intikhab* (*The News of Choice*), *Jang* (*The Struggle*), *Jasarat* (*Courage*), *Markaz* (*The Central News*), *Mashrig* (*The East*), *Musawat* (*Equality*), *Nawa-i-Wagt* (*The Current News*), *Pakistan, Sarhad* (*The Frontier*), *Savera* (*The Dawn*), *Sayadat,* and *Zamana* (*The Times*).

There are about 30 newspapers and periodicals in Sindhi. The major Sindhi dailies are published in Karachi and Hyderabad. Three dailies, *Awami Awaz* (*The Voice of the People*), *Hilal-e-Pakistan* (*The Banner of Pakistan*), and *Jago* (*The Call to Rise*), are published in Karachi, while *Aftab* (The Sun), *Ibrat* (*The Lessons*), *Mehran, Sindh News,* and *Sindhu* are published in Hyderabad. Three dailies are published in the Gujrati language, all in the city of Karachi: *Dawn, Millat* (*The People*), and *Watan* (*The Nation*). The major Pushtu daily *Wahadat* (*The Unity*) is published in Peshawar, but some Pushtu newspaper/periodicals are also published in Baluchistan. Newspapers published in other regional languages include Punjabi, Baluchi, and Brahui.

Some evening newspapers in English and Urdu publish in Karachi. The major English evening papers are *Daily News, The Leader, The Parliament, The Star,* and *Today News;* the major Urdu evening dailies are *Aghaz* (*The Beginning*), *Evening Special, Qaumi Akhbar* (*The National Newspaper*), and *Today Special.*

Magazines

Some press historians cite Hickey's weekly *Bengal Gazette* (1780) as a forerunner of magazine journalism (Yousaf, 1992, p. 320). However, it was Sir Syed Ahmed Khan who laid the foundation for the Muslim magazine press through his publications *Tahzib-ul-Akhlaq* (*Cultural Reforms*) and *Scientific Society Magazine* (1870–1877). Syed Ahmed Khan was possibly influenced on his trip to England by *Tatler* and *Spectator* magazines published by Richard Steele and Joseph Addison. He was followed by other magazine publishers, namely, Zafar Ali Khan, Maulana Azad, Maulana Jauhar, Abdul Majeed Salik, Maulana Hasrat Mohani, and Maulana Ghulam Rasul, among others. These were strong individuals with a political and cultural message to disseminate to their Muslim readers, and their magazines reflected a personalized brand of journalism.

In 1988, a total of 1,644 periodicals were published in the country, of which

368 were weeklies and twice-weeklies; 126, fortnightlies; 776, monthlies; and 374, quarterlies (''Pakistan: An Introductory Survey,'' 1992, p. 2145). *Pakistan Advertising Scene* mentions that, according to government sources, over 2,000 periodicals were published in the country in 1989 in Arabic, Brahui, Baluchi, Gujrati, Punjabi, Pushto, Sindhi, Urdu, and English (Orient Advertising, 1991, p. 40). By far the largest number of periodicals are published in Urdu (about 1,800), followed by English (about 400). As in the case of the dailies, over 90 percent of the periodicals are concentrated in the two most populous provinces of the country, the Punjab and Sind. The periodicals are believed to have a combined circulation of about 2 million. About 16 percent of the male adults are regular readers of periodicals (p. 41).

In recent years, a trend toward special interest periodicals has occurred. There are magazines that are devoted to women's interests, armed forces, current affairs, economy, fashion, broadcasting, politics, children, adventure, detective stories, show business, sports, banking, marketing, medicine, management, public administration, religion, agriculture, textiles, labor, computers, and satellites.

Akhbar-e-Jahan (The News of the World) is the largest independent illustrated weekly family magazine in Urdu, with a circulation of 278,000. *Akhbar-e-Khawateen (The Women's Magazine)* is the largest weekly women's magazine in Urdu, with a circulation of 40,000. Among other notable weeklies are *Amal* (*Action*), a trilingual magazine published in Urdu, Pushtu, and English; *Hilal* (*The Crescent*), an illustrated Urdu magazine for the armed forces with a circulation of 80,000; *Memaar-i-Nau* (*Labor News*), an Urdu magazine for labor; the *Muslim World,* an English current affairs magazine; *Noor Jehan Weekly,* an Urdu film journal (circulation 16,000); *Pakistan and Gulf Economist* (circulation 22,000); *Takbeer* (*The Call*), an Urdu magazine (circulation 50,000); and *Viewpoint,* an English journal devoted to political issues. Other Urdu weeklies of note are *Zindagi* (*The Life*)*; Hurmat* (*Respect*)*; Chatan* (*The Pinnacle*); and *Lail-o-Nahar* (*News Magazine*), a magazine modeled on the U.S. news magazine *Time.*

In Pakistan, a monthly magazine format known as *digest,* inspired by the American *Reader's Digest,* has become very popular. A magazine called *Urdu Digest,* started in 1960, led the field. A digest typically contains articles on social, cultural, political, and economic trends and events, in addition to poems, original short stories, and translations of stories from foreign publications. Some of the notable digests are *Pakistan Digest* (English), *Khawateen Digest* (*The Women's Digest*) (Urdu), *Qaumi Digest* (*The National Digest*) (Urdu), *Sabrang Digest* (*Rainbow Digest*) (Urdu), and *Sayyarah Digest (*The Satellite Digest) (Urdu).

Some of the children's magazines are *The Phool* (*The Flower*), *Taleem-o-Tarbiat (Education and Training), Bachhon Ka Hamdard (A Friend of the Children), Nau Nihal* (*The Toddler*), and *Bachhon Ka Digest.*

Cultural magazines published monthly are *Mirror, Herald, Akhbar-i-Khawateen,* and *Akhbar-i-Jahan.*

Religiously oriented magazines include *Islamic Studies, Iblagh, Khuddam, Tarjuman-u-Quran* (*The Interpretation of Quran*), *Al-Haq* (*The Truth*), *Al-Hadith, Talua-Islam* (*The Rise of Islam*), and *Dars-i-Quran* (*The Lessons of Quran*).

And literary magazines include *Fanoon* (*The Arts*), *Auraq* (*The Pages*), *Sawera* (*The Dawn*), *Nagoosh* (*The Maps*), and *Naia Daur* (*The New Age*).

ELECTRONIC MEDIA

Radio

In the territories constituting Pakistan, the first radio station was set up in Lahore in 1928. The small station, with its signal reaching a radius of about eight miles, was in operation for about six years and was closed for a lack of funds. In 1936, a small radio station was started with assistance from the Marconi Company. A Department of Broadcasting was also created by the government in the 1930s to run a medium wave radio station. When Pakistan came into existence in 1947, a radio station at Karachi was established. In 1949, two powerful shortwave transmitters were procured by the government broadcasting service, creating a central broadcasting service to air programming in Urdu, Bengali, and English.

The national radio broadcasting network comprises 23 radio stations, located at Abbottabad, Bahawalpur, Dera Ismail Khan, Faisalabad, Gilgit, Hyderabad (2 stations), Islamabad, Karachi (2 stations), Khairpur, Khuzdar, Lahore (2 stations), Multan, Peshawar (2 stations), Quetta (2 stations), Rawalpindi, Skardu, Sibbi, and Turbat. In an underdeveloped country, such as Pakistan, with a low literacy rate of about 35 percent, radio remains the most widely used medium. There were an estimated 10.2 million radio receivers in the country in 1989 (''Pakistan: An Introductory Survey,'' 1992, p. 2149). Approximately, 70 percent of the households in the nation own radio receivers.

The administration of radio broadcasting is entrusted to the Pakistan Broadcasting Corporation (PBC). The corporation is run by a board of directors appointed by the federal government. It airs 270 hours of programming in its home service in 21 languages. The national network broadcasts most of its programming in the national language, Urdu. However, the local stations air programming in regional languages as well. The PBC network covers almost the total population of the country. Despite the increase in the number of radio stations in the country, some surveys indicated a decline in radio listening, from 70 percent of the population in 1979 to 40 percent in 1989 (Saeed, 1992, p. 17).

According to a PBC report, music programming ranks first with 48 percent of the total time, followed by religious programming with 12.5 percent; news and current affairs at 11 percent; rural and farm broadcasts at 10 percent; women, children, and labor at 5 percent; literature, science, and education at 4 percent; youth/students at 3 percent; national campaigns at 2.5 percent; armed forces at 2 percent; and plays, features, and sports also at 2 percent (Orient Advertising, 1991, p. 65). A PBC survey also reports that listeners indicated their top preference for light music (65 percent), followed by news and current affairs (39.5 percent), religious affairs (28.6 percent), plays (25.9 percent), sports (24 percent), women's programs (15.4 percent), children's programs (14.7 percent), agricultural broadcasts (12 percent), and students/youth programs (9 percent) (p. 71).

Radio broadcasting is financed through a radio receiver license fee, advertising, and government subsidy. Owing to a decline in radio listening in recent years, advertising revenues have gone down significantly. Therefore, the government has had to increase its subsidies to cover the operating costs of the broadcasting service.

Television

The decision to introduce television to the country was made by the Ayub government in 1963. A television corporation was established to run television as a commercial venture, with the majority of shares owned by the government. The government also invited foreign firms to participate in the project, because, in its view, not only could the foreign companies provide the needed technical expertise, but through their equity participation, they could also reduce the strain on limited foreign exchange resources (Hasan & Khurshid, 1988, p. 260). Under an agreement with the government, the Nippon Electric Company (NEC) of Japan set up two pilot stations in 1964, one in Lahore, the other in Dhaka. NEC brought 600 receivers into the country and distributed 400 receivers to community centers, college dormitories, clubs, and restaurants for communal viewing. The facilities at the stations were minimal for program production, but soon television as a medium gained popularity, and the service expanded.

Pakistan Television (PTV) provides television coverage to 87 percent of the population through its network of 28 rebroadcast stations and 5 program production and transmission stations at Lahore, Islamabad, Karachi, Peshawar, and Quetta. There are two television channels in the country, the state-owned PTV and Shalimar Television Network (STN). In 1989, the government of Pakistan set up a privately owned, commercially run second channel known as People's Television Network (PTN), which was subsequently renamed STN. It offers Cable News Network (CNN) programming, foreign programming from other sources, and local productions.

Like radio, the PTV is financed by a combination of television receiver license fees, advertising, and government subsidies. Over 40 percent of television receiver owners in the country fail to pay the yearly license fee (Slote, 1989). Currently, there are about 2 to 4 million television receivers in the country, but the number is projected to increase by 10,000 every year (Islam, 1991, p. 38).

Since Pakistan Television Corporation is a revenue-earning and profit-making organization, it is in a position to meet a major portion of its development expenditure through self-financing. For major capital-intensive projects, such as opening a second channel for the PTV, the government provides funding from the Public Sector Development Program.

STN has been fairly successful since its beginning in 1989, claiming a significant share of the viewing public and advertising revenues by providing entertainment-oriented programming. An analysis of PTV programming in 1989–1990 showed that foreign feature films and sports as a category ranked first, with 16.39 percent of the total broadcast time, followed by 18 other categories: news (12.58 percent), religion (7.96 percent), plays (7.70 percent), announcements (7.69 percent), current affairs (6.79 percent), repeat programs (6.71 percent), feature (5.98 percent), sports and festivals (5.30 percent), World Cup cricket (4.53 percent), music (4.46 percent), commercial (4.21 percent), children's programming (2.52 percent), quiz (1.59 percent), education (1.58 percent), youth (1.10 percent), poetry (0.76 percent), women's programming (0.58 percent), and Urdu feature films (0.576 percent) (Orient Advertising, 1991, p. 57).

By the end of the 1980s, at least 40 percent of the television viewers in the country had access to videocassette recorders (VCRs) or players. There are an estimated 150,000 video rental stores, mostly in the urban areas, renting out videocassettes of local and foreign films (mostly Indian) for 25 to 75 cents (Akhtar, 1992, p. 82). During recent years, satellite receiving dish antennas have become fairly inexpensive ($400 to $500), a price even lower than that of a color television receiver or a VCR. Through a broadcast satellite, the viewing public has access to BBC (British Broadcasting Corporation)-WSTV, MTV (Music Television), Prime Sports, and other programming provided by the Hong Kong–based Star Television company. In the future, Pakistani television channels are likely to face strong competition from signals provided by satellite television.

MOTION PICTURES

Cinema has been a popular mass entertainment medium in Pakistan since the beginning of the country, primarily because of a dearth of other inexpensive sources of entertainment. However, its popularity has declined in recent years to a point that, in 1990, the industry suffered the highest loss in its history. Very few of the 93 films released during the year recouped the money invested in their production. According to one report, there were 516 cinema houses in Pakistan in 1990, with Punjab accounting for 309, followed by Sindh with 154, NWFP with 43, and Baluchistan with 10 (Saeed, 1992, p. 25). The population-to-cinema ratio is declining, especially in urban areas, due to a relative loss of interest among the educated and well-off Pakistanis for formula-based, poor-quality films produced for the local mass market. Rural audiences continue to patronize the cinema in larger proportions because of a shortage of alternative entertainment.

The quality of Pakistani films is also believed to have suffered because of the government policy of a protected market by banning importation of Indian films. The strict government policy of censorship, high illiteracy rate in the population, and low tolerance in the culture for controversial and untraditional themes may have limited the ability of creative filmmakers to be innovative and challenging.

In Pakistan, during the 1980s, the film industry produced about 80 films a year on an average. Forty-eight percent of the total were made in Punjabi, followed by 30 percent made in the national language, Urdu, about 17 percent in Pushtu, and 5 percent in Sindhi. Between 1984 and 1989, 483 films were made in Pakistani languages; but during the same period, 458 films were imported into the country. The proportion of regular moviegoers (once a month) among male adults is only 9.3 percent; among females and children, it is believed to be even lower (Saeed, 1992, p. 25; Orient Advertising, 1991, p. 81).

MEDIA OWNERSHIP

In Pakistan, radio broadcasting is conducted by a public corporation under the control of the Ministry of Information and Broadcasting. Radio and television broadcasting are provided as a public service by the government, financed through a combination of receiver license fees, the sale of advertising time, and government budget appropriation. But in recent years, a privately owned, commercially run system (Shalimar Television Network) has also been created.

The major newspapers and magazines are published by a handful of private publishing houses. The government-owned National Press Trust has owned and controlled 11 major publications since 1964. But in November 1991, the government made a decision to divest itself of all the publications, except for a major newspaper, *The Pakistan Times.*

The film industry is privately run, but the federal government has a Department of Films and Publications under the Ministry of Information and Broadcasting that produces newsreels and documentary films portraying various aspects of national life with a fairly heavy propaganda overtone. These are made mostly in Pakistani languages, but some are also made in foreign languages for exhibition abroad. The provincial governments also produce newsreels and documentaries for exhibition in the provinces.

MEDIA REGULATION

Article 19 of the Pakistani Constitution provides for free speech and expression, yet it allows for restrictions of these rights for a variety of reasons. The government enjoys unlimited power in curbing press activities. Under the laws, a person in possession of a printing press or desirous of publishing a newspaper must obtain a permit, which the government may refuse for reasons involving moral turpitude, insufficient financial resources, inadequate educational qualifications, and activities prejudicial to defense, foreign relations, or public order.

The government license once granted may become null and void if the publisher changes the language, place, or periodicity of the publication. Even failure to publish regularly may void the license for publication, requiring a fresh permit. The laws allow for various forms of punishment including forfeiture of the published material, and the security deposits a publisher is required to furnish to the government, along with closing down a publication. In 1978, the military government awarded fines, rigorous imprisonment, and floggings to journalists who launched a countrywide movement against government orders that allowed banning and fining of newspapers (Niazi, 1986).

In 1979, press censorship was imposed, and publication of opposition papers was suspended. In 1985, with the restoration of the constitution and repeal of martial law, the principle of freedom of the press was restored; subsequently, the government adopted a more liberal press policy.

In addition to the regulatory framework of the government, the press is also subject to extralegal formal and informal actions of the government. But equally important, the press is subject to intimidation by the political parties, religious groups, and various other interest groups as well. Journalists have been murdered, kidnapped, and beaten; newspaper offices have been ransacked and burned, and distribution of newspapers has been stopped forcibly in recent years. There have also been numerous reports of mob violence and police brutality against reporters and photographers. This form of intimidation of the press by various interest groups leads to self-censorship and what is referred to in Pakistan as censorship in the street (''Penalties of Truth,'' 1991; Niazi, 1992).

Since the electronic media of radio and television are government agencies, the contents of broadcasts are subject to more stringent and direct control of the government. There are detailed codes that broadcasters are required to follow. For regulating the film industry, the government has a Central Board of Film Censors in Islamabad, with two regional offices in Lahore and Karachi. Every film needs to be certified by the board as fit for exhibition before it can be publicly screened. A film is regarded unsuitable for exhibition if it

> directly or indirectly, undermines Islam, or disparages any other religion; brings into contempt any aspect of national ideology or objectives; distorts historical facts such as maligning Pakistan, its traditions or heroes, or fans racial, sectarian, parochial, linguistic or class hatred. (Akhtar, 1992, p. 87)

In judging films, the censor board is supposed to consider what impression a film is likely to create on an average viewer, which includes ''children and young persons of immature judgment and impressionable age'' (p. 87). The breadth and vagueness of standards for certification of a film are striking, and since the board is supposed to consider what is suitable for children and impressionable young people before certifying a film, mature adults may be limited to seeing what is suitable for children.

EXTERNAL MEDIA SERVICES

Radio Pakistan broadcasts nearly 300 hours of programming in its home service, but it also broadcasts 20 hours every day on its external service in 15 foreign languages, such as Arabic, Farsi, French, Gujrati, Hindi, Dari, English, Bengali, Indonesian, Swahili, Tamil, and Turki. The radio also has a World Service on which it broadcasts 10 hours of programming in Urdu and English, featuring drama, music, and news. The radio has a transcription service, which produces cultural programming in a number of languages and makes them available to broadcast stations all over the world. Pakistan Television also broadcasts news programs in Arabic. As a part of the Asiavision news exchange arrangement, PTV supplies news stories and documentaries to television stations in other countries as well. Similarly, the government's Department of Films and Publications produces newsreels and documentaries for distribution in foreign countries. Pakistani films are exhibited in countries of the Middle East and other parts of the world; they are also available in videocassettes in countries where there are concentrations of people from the Indian subcontinent. Pakistan not only invites foreign countries to participate in film festivals held in the country but also participates in foreign film festivals.

NEWS AGENCIES

There are four domestic news agencies. The government owns the largest agency, the Associated Press of Pakistan (APP); the other three, Pakistan Press International (PPI), United Press of Pakistan (UPP), and Independent Press of Pakistan (IPP), are privately owned. APP and PPI have a network of correspondents and stringers inside the country and in many parts of the world; they also have news exchange arrangements with some of the major global news agencies. The UPP and IPP are local agencies. The former covers local news only, while the latter provides service in two languages, Urdu and English.

THE ROLE OF MEDIA IN NATIONAL DEVELOPMENT

Pakistani media, like media in most developing nations, emphasize their role in the socioeconomic development of the nation. The electronic media, owned and operated by the government, stress the need to provide authentic cultural expression and to promote Islamic ideological values. The Educational Television (ETV) division produces programming in collaboration with Allama Iqbal Open University. ETV also broadcasts literacy programs. Radio programming, targeted to farmers, youth, and women, is designed to reach them with development-oriented messages. Even some commercial films have consciously projected messages containing such values as "selflessness, patriotism, respect for parents, teachers and elders, and regard for the handicapped" (Saeed, 1992, p. 26). Film producers have worked on messages relating to the problem of fast increasing population. The print media recognize the same ideological and cultural role. But, in reality, critics point out that newspapers and magazines play up sex, violence, and crime to boost their sales. Imported Western television programming, though popular among the educated, is alleged to violate Pakistani traditional, cultural, and social norms based on Islamic values and way of life. Films have been notorious for crude exploitation of violence and sex, giving rise to demands among conservative and traditional segments of the population for stricter censorship rules.

CONCLUSION

The media, in Pakistani society, seem basically to fit an authoritarian mode of regulation. The electronic media are completely under government control, with little latitude and autonomy for information dissemination on an independent basis. These media, therefore, have suffered from a lack of public credibility. The foreign radio services, such as BBC World Service and Voice of America (VOA), have historically filled the information vacuum. Their enormous popularity, especially in times of a crisis, suggests a hunger among Pakistanis for reliable but unavailable information about controversial political issues. The print media enjoy relatively greater freedom from government interference and dictates. But historically, under different military and political regimes, the print press has had to work under various forms of restrictions, such as precensorship and press advisories.

Technically, the media have made significant progress in the past decades. During brief but shaky periods of democratic governments, the press has enjoyed relative freedom. Government regulation is only part of a broader picture in a society that has little tradition of tolerance for expression of controversial ideas and opinion.

REFERENCES

Akhtar, R. (1992). Mass media. In *Pakistan year book 1991–1992.* Karachi-Lahore: East-West Publishing Company.

Hasan, M., & Khurshid, A. S. (1988). *Journalism for all* (3rd ed.). Lahore: Etisam Publishers.

Islam, M. (1991, August 8). Market report on television. *Economic Review, 22,* 37–38.

Niazi, Z. (1986). *The press in chains.* Karachi: Royal Book Company.

Niazi, Z. (1992). *The press under siege.* Karachi: Karachi Press Club.

Nyrop, R. A. (Ed.). (1984). *Pakistan: A country study.* Area Handbook Series (5th ed.). Washington DC: U.S. Government Printing Office.

Orient Advertising (Pvt) Ltd. (1991). *Pakistan advertising scene.* Karachi: Orient Advertising Ltd.

Pakistan. (1992). In *Political handbook of the world.* Binghamton, NY: CSA Publications.

Pakistan: An introductory survey. (1992). In *The Europa yearbook 1992* (Vol. 2, pp. 2130–2155). London, England: Europa Publication, Ltd.

Pakistan: Islamic Jamhuriya e Pakistan. (1992). In *Statesman's yearbook* (pp. 1057–1066). New York: St. Martin's Press.

Penalties of truth. (1991, April 6). *Economist*, p. 33.

Saeed, A. G. (1992, August). *Media and values.* Paper presented at the workshop on Media Education in South Asia, New Delhi, India.

Slote, A. R. (1989, August 5–11). Revenue loss: Unlicensed television sets. *Pakistan & Gulf Economist*, pp. 46–47.

Wolseley, R. E. (1964). *Modern journalism in India* (2nd rev. ed.). New York: Asia Publishing House.

World radio and television handbook (Vol. 47). (1993). New York: Billboard Publications Inc.

Yousaf, M. M. (1992). *A-One exploring journalism* (3rd ed.). Lahore: A-One Publishers.

15

PALESTINE

Orayb Aref Najjar

INTRODUCTION

Historical Palestine lies on a major overland route between the three continents of Africa, Europe, and Asia. Its area is approximately 10,000 square miles, bordered by Syria in the north, Jordan on the east, the Mediterranean on the west, and Egypt in the southwest. Palestine's central location between continents accounts for its being coveted by a succession of conquerors. The Ottomans ruled Palestine between 1517 and 1917, the British between 1917 and 1948.

Both Palestinian Arabs and Jews claim the country. Hostilities between them, as well as the Arab-Israeli war of 1948, led to the expulsion and/or migration of 840,000 Palestinians from historic Palestine, according to Audeh, Ethelson, and Power (1990). A study by the Center for Policy Analysis (1991) estimated the Palestinian population worldwide at 5,780,422 in 1991. The largest Palestinian concentration is in Jordan (32.6 percent); the second is in the West Bank, including Arab East Jerusalem (18.6 percent); the third is in Israel (12.6 percent); and the fourth is in Gaza (10.8 percent). Palestinians can also be found in Lebanon (5.7 percent of the total Palestinian population), in Syria (5.2 percent), in the remaining Arab countries (7.2 percent), and in the rest of the world (7.3 percent).

Palestinians are an Arabic-speaking people who are mostly Muslim. Estimates on the number of Christians in the West Bank range from 3.5 percent of the population (Burell & Landau, 1992) to 15 percent (Cobban, 1991). Six percent of the population of the East Bank (both Jordanian and Palestinian) are Christian (The Economist Intelligence Unit, 1992).

The West Bank depends on Israel for as much as 61 percent of its employment. Most of those jobs are in labor such as construction and agriculture. Over one-fourth of the labor force is employed in agriculture (Druri & Winn, 1992). There are few jobs for educated Palestinians, and many are forced to emigrate (Graham-Brown, 1983).

The West Bank has 1,253 schools, 14 technical colleges, 16 community colleges, and 5 universities. Gaza has 1 university. The combined university enrollment of Gaza and the West Bank is 16,000 (Baramki, 1987). University education is mostly in Arabic, although science and some social science courses are taught mostly in English. Because of dispersion, Palestinian education lacks a unified cultural base, leaving it up to individual Palestinians and to their cultural institutions to develop a sense of community and identity wherever they live (Tahir, 1985). Palestinians unilaterally declared their independence from Israel on November 15, 1988, but the West Bank and Gaza have remained under military occupation. In 1993, the Palestinians and Israelis began a series of negotiations concerning the city of Jericho and Gaza.

PRINT MEDIA IN THE WEST BANK

Palestinians debated the wisdom of publishing under occupation. Members of one camp argued for publication to fill the void in printed news and to educate a new cadre of readers and writers. The second camp argued that publishing would provide Israel with intelligence it could not get elsewhere about the Palestinian community, would normalize the occupation, and would move resistance against occupation from street confrontations to intellectual discussions in the press (A. Khalili, personal communication, June 24, 1989).

When *Al-Quds* (*Jerusalem*), formerly *Al-Jihad* (*Struggle*), was published 15 months after the occupation of the West Bank, some Palestinian political figures and former journalists boycotted it, but the opposition reconsidered and started publishing in 1972. By 1987, Palestinians got licenses for 22 newspapers, some weekly and some daily, 22 magazines, and 40 press services (Abu Ayyash, 1987; a list of those and other publications can be found in Najjar [1992a]). Israelis closed down some publications permanently and restricted the distribution of others. Yet despite those measures, East Jerusalem continues to have an active, diverse political press that both the Israelis and Palestinians consider important for transmitting the Palestinian point of view to people in the occupied territories, to the Palestinian Liberation Organization (PLO) in the diaspora, as well as to Arabs and others interested in the Palestinian point of view (Bahbah & Kital, 1985). Palestinians unabashedly define their press as a committed political press (Sahafah Siyasiyyah Multazimah) that is a tool for liberation.

NEWSPAPERS

Before 1993, the West Bank had four Arabic dailies and one Arabic and one English weekly, all published in East Jerusalem. Palestinians also published a Hebrew newspaper. West Bank publications ranged from leftist, to Islamic or Christian, to publications sympathetic to various PLO groups or to Jordan, and to those that identify themselves as independent. At the end of the Gulf War, the Gulf states withdrew their financial support of the PLO, which adversely affected the PLO-supported papers on the West Bank. Hence, in 1993, the number of Arabic dailies declined from four to two, and the only Hebrew newspaper published by Palestinians was closed.

Al-Quds (*Jerusalem*), a daily, was founded on November 19, 1968. The paper's publisher defines *Al-Quds* as an independent commercial paper. The paper was thought of as pro-Jordanian until about 1983. Because the paper uses moderate language even when it criticizes its enemies, the Israeli authorities were less strict with *Al-Quds* than they were with other publications until 1982 when the paper was seen as moving away from Jordan. By the time the Intifada started, *Al-Quds,* which enjoys the largest circulation in the occupied territories, was censored as strictly as other publications. Before the Lebanon war, *Al-Quds* had a circulation of 30,000 copies. Its circulation peaked at 50,000 in December 1987 (M. Abu Zalaf, personal communication, July 30, 1989). Although distribution estimates vary, the owners of *Al-Quds* claim to continue distributing 30,000 to 50,000 copies.

Al-Fajr (*The Dawn*), a daily, was founded on April 5, 1972. The paper expressed the point of view of the Left between 1974 and 1976. Later, the publisher of the paper, a Palestinian-American, hired either independent editors or editors who were sympathetic to the Fateh branch of the PLO to prevent the paper from leaning toward the Left. The paper has extensive coverage of PLO affairs but also advises the PLO on the affairs of the occupied territories. The 1986 figures place the circulation between 3,000 and 8,000 (Committee to Protect Journalists [CPJ] and Article 19, 1988). After 22 years, the paper was closed on July 23, 1993, for financial reasons (M. Manasrah, personal communication, August 29, 1993).

Al-Sha'ab (*The People*), a daily, was founded on July 23, 1972. Perceptions of the political orientation of the paper have varied. Said to have ties to Egypt, to Communists, to Syria, and to the PLO, it is nationalist in orientation. Two of its editors were deported: Ali al-Khatib in 1974 and Akram Haniyyeh in 1986. *Al-Sha'ab*'s offices and printing press have been firebombed, and at least one attempt was made on the life of its publisher, Mahmoud Ya'ish (M. Ya'ish, personal communication, June 18, 1989).

Prior to its closure on February 9, 1993, *Al-Sha'ab* sold between 1,500 and 3,000 copies (CPJ and Article 19, 1988). According to M. Manasrah (Personal communication, August 29, 1993), the paper was closed when the PLO stopped funding it because its circulation had sharply declined to 200 copies.

Al-Talia (*The Vanguard*), a weekly, was founded on February 27, 1978. This Communist newspaper was prevented from distributing in the occupied territories with the exception of Jerusalem after a few days of publication (S. Ayyad, personal communication, January 28, 1992). The paper once printed 6,000 copies. With the start of the uprising in December 1987, the weekly prints only about 3,000 when there are curfews and 4,000 copies when the West Bank is relatively quiet (M. Manasrah, personal communication, July 23, 1989). The weekly sends 1,300 to 2,000 copies to Europe and the United States (I. Aruri, personal communication, July 25, 1989). *Al-Talia* holds fund-raisers to generate its budget.

Al-Nahar (*The Day*), a daily, was founded on March 7, 1986. In 1987, this pro-Jordanian paper sold 8,500 copies (CPJ and Article 19, 1988). The paper is supported by advertisements and is also partly funded by Jordan and the PLO. According to M. Manasrah (Personal communication, August 29, 1993), the paper distributed about 13,000 copies daily in 1992 and about 2,500 in 1993.

Arabic-Language Magazines

Before the Gulf War, there were six magazines in the occupied territories. After the war, two were closed, and the others were adversely affected by the lack of funding.

Al-Bayader Assiyasi (*Political Threshing Floor*) started as a monthly literary magazine on March 1, 1976, under the name of *Al-Bayader Al-Adabi* (Literary Threshing Floor). It changed its name and content on April 1, 1981, and is a weekly that publishes news and political commentary, as well as investigative reports on political and cultural issues. According to its owner, Jack Khazmo, the magazine had a circulation of 10,000 copies. He noted that his publication was funded through advertisements and from the sale of the magazine abroad (J. Khazmo, personal communication, July 18, 1989). This magazine ceased publication on May 28, 1993 (Z. Abu Zayyad, personal communication, August 30, 1993).

Al-Kateb (*The Writer*) was founded on November 1, 1979, as a monthly but became a quarterly in February 1993. The magazine was not allowed to circulate in the West Bank, except for Jerusalem, for the first 13 years of its publication. The ban, however, was lifted in October 1992 (1993). *Al-Kateb* depends on its readers and on the Communist Party for financial support and distribution. The magazine has a circulation of 500 copies (M. Manasrah, personal communication, August 29, 1993). This literary and political magazine is an important source for political debates on education, labor, and women's issues. Some of the most heated and literate debates on women's rights were published in this magazine, which mentioned its interest in women's development in its first issue. In 1992, *Al-Kateb* had two women on its seven-member editorial board. Female journalists constitute 8 percent of the membership of the Arab Journalists Association.

Al-Kateb is a shoestring operation that depends on its readers and on Communist Party activists both for financial support and for volunteer work in distribution. One Israeli source estimates its distribution at 600 copies (Shinar, 1987). *Al-Kateb* is allowed to distribute in Jerusalem but not in the rest of the West Bank or in Gaza and, like *Al-Talia,* is clandestinely sold all over the occupied territories.

Al-Usbu' al-Jadid (*The New Week*) was founded on March 31, 1978. This magazine appeared irregularly until April 20, 1982, then was reissued on November 23, 1988, as a bimonthly and then as a biweekly. It was given a permit to distribute in the West Bank in October 1991 and in Gaza on January 1, 1991. *Al-Usbu'* is seen as sympathetic to Fateh, the largest constituent group of the PLO. According to Palestinian journalist M. Manasrah (Personal communication, August 29, 1993), *Al-Usbu*'s circulation was about 1,000 copies when, in July 1993, the PLO stopped subsidizing it.

Huda al-Islam (*Guidance of Islam*), a monthly magazine, was founded in October 1982 (S. Ayyad, personal communication, January 28, 1992). The magazine, which appears ten times a year irregularly, is funded by the Jordanian Ministry of Religious Affairs. It prints 10,000 copies, half of which are distributed free of charge (Abdul Fattah, 1984).

Al-Liqa' (*The Meeting*), a quarterly, was founded on May 1, 1985. This 50-page Christian magazine is a general interest publication that deals mostly with Christian community affairs.

Nida' al-Mara'a (*Women's Call*) was founded on May 1, 1991. This 80-page monthly magazine was unable to obtain a license, so it appears under the onetime publication rule (a loophole that exempts it from obtaining a license and from precensorship). It is published by the Women's Study Center. Every one of the four women's organizations publishes several "onetime" magazines, under different names, several times a year, listed in Najjar (1992a).

Palestinian Publications in English

Al-Fajr (*The Dawn*), a weekly newspaper, was founded on April 23, 1980. *Al-Fajr* translates short news items from Arabic newspapers. The paper's reporters write its features. The paper's distribution is restricted to the West Bank (with the exception of East Jerusalem), but Israeli distributors and hotels refuse to carry it, and teenagers attempting to sell it have been assaulted. The paper is sent to subscribers in Europe and the United States.

Underground Palestinian Publications

The most famous paper is *Al-Watan* (*The Homeland*), published by the Communist Party. Written references to the paper suggest that it was quite active in the early 1970s (Dakkak, 1983), and it continued to publish at least until September 1988 (Schiff & Ya'ari, 1990). The Palestine National Front (PNF) also printed an underground paper called *Falastin (Palestine).*

Palestinian Publications in Hebrew

Gesher (*The Bridge*), a Hebrew bimonthly, was founded on June 15, 1986. The paper is distributed only in Israel and East Jerusalem (S. Ayyad, personal communication, January 28, 1992).

Israeli-Sponsored Arabic Publications

Al-Anba' (*The News*), a daily, was published from October 24, 1968, to January 31, 1985. *Al-Mira'a* (*The Mirror*) published from October 1, 1982, to December 1982 (S. Ayyad, personal communication, January 28, 1992). This paper was the organ for the Village Leagues, an organization created by Israel in the early 1980s in an attempt to provide an alternative leadership to the PLO. The paper was distributed free of charge from the headquarters of the Village Leagues in the city of Ramallah (Shinar, 1987). Israeli authorities stopped its publication as a prelude to dissolving the Ramallah Village League Union (Lothan, 1983).

The PLO and Communication

The issue of whether the PLO or Jordan represents Palestinians was resolved in the PLO's favor, when the Rabat Arab Summit Conference endorsed the PLO as the sole legitimate representative of the Palestinian people on October 28, 1974. Although Palestinians have no national elected leaders on the West Bank and Gaza, they have developed a network of grassroots organizations that oversee education, journalism, health, and union affairs.

The highest body of the PLO is the Palestine National Council (PNC) (483 elected members), often called the Palestinian parliament in exile (Shahin, 1993). The council includes representatives of commando organizations; independents; representatives of trade, women's, teachers', engineers', and artists' unions in various countries; as well as Palestinian representatives from Jordan, the West Bank, the Gulf states, and Western countries. The 18-member Palestine Executive Committee deals with daily affairs and oversees several departments whose function is to protect and disseminate Palestinian culture (Center for Policy Analysis, 1991).

The PLO Print Media

The Palestinian publications that appeared between 1948 and 1959 stressed humanitarian concerns and described the problems and needs of Palestinian refugees. Most publications were irregular and often lacked trained staff. After 1959, Palestinian publications redefined the Palestinian-Israeli conflict from a refugee issue to an issue of national liberation. Various Palestinian groups established their own papers.

The PLO has a Bureau of Information that is headed by the chair from the information office of the organizations represented in the PLO, along with the directors of those offices. The bureau oversees the activities of the Unified Information Department; the Palestine News Agency (WAFA), established in 1972 in Beirut; the Palestine Cinema and Photography Department; the radio stations; and *Filastin al-Thawra,* the central publication of the PLO. Below are some of the main publications of the groups that constitute the PLO.

Al-Huriyyah (*Freedom*), a monthly magazine, was founded in 1959. *Al-Huriyyah* was originally a publication of the Popular Front for the Liberation of Palestine (PFLP). Later, this weekly publication that appeared in Beirut was taken over by a more leftist group within the PFLP, which in late February 1969 was reorganized by the PLO as a separate group, the Popular Democratic Front for the Liberation of Palestine (PDFLP). The ideological rift led PFLP members to found their own publication, *Al-Hadaf.* Further accentuating the split between the two groups was the fact that the PDFLP accepted money from Syria, and the PFLP from Syria's rival Iraq (Quandt, Jaber, & Lesch, 1974).

Al-Hadaf (*The Target/Goal*), a weekly magazine, was first published by the PFLP in Beirut in 1969 (''Periodicals,'' 1971). Like *Al-Huriyyah,* it is now published in Cyprus.

Fateh (*Palestine National Liberation Movement*) started in 1969 as a weekly bulletin in Beirut, then developed into a bimonthly magazine published in Tunis (''Periodicals,'' 1971, p. 136; K. Foutah, personal communication, January 7, 1992).

Filastin al-Thawra (*The Palestinian Revolution*) was established in June 28, 1972, in Beirut and became a daily on June 7, 1976. The PLO decided to unite all of its organs as of June 5, 1972, and to use *Filastin al-Thawra* as the central organ of the PLO. But despite brief periods of unity, roughly until 1981, the various PLO groups chose to retain their own publications whose articles often contradicted the main PLO line (*Palestinian Encyclopedia,* 1984).

Shu'un Filastiniya (*Palestinian Affairs*), a monthly, was founded in March 1971. This journal is published by the Research Center, established in 1965 to document information pertaining to the Palestine question and to supply various PLO departments as well as researchers everywhere with information about Palestinians (Mussalam, 1988).

Al-Karmil ([Mount] *Karmil*), a quarterly journal for cultural affairs, was founded in Beirut in the fall of 1981 by the General Union of Palestinian Writers and Journalists. It is now published in Cyprus.

ARABIC PUBLICATIONS IN ISRAEL

The mission of Arab publications has changed over time. Between 1948 and 1966, Arabs in Israel were still under military rule, and Israel did not import publications from the Arab World. Journalists sought to create a local literature/journalism that preserved the Arab identity and fostered pride in the Arab heritage.

The lifting of Israeli military rule in 1966, as well as the reunion of those Palestinians with the people of the West Bank and Gaza in 1967, and the importation of some mostly nonpolitical publications from the Arab World decreased the cultural isolation of Palestinians with Israeli citizenship. Their press continued to deal with cultural issues, but most of the publications adopted a more confrontational nationalist style than before the 1973 war. The press began to see itself both as an advocate for the rights of Arabs inside Israel as well as a vigorous voice for Palestinians of the occupied territories. Some publications, like *Al-Aswar,* openly advocate the recognition of an independent Palestinian state under the leadership of the PLO. Below is a review of the publications currently published by Arabs in Israel. Most are independent. When they are not, the political orientation of publications that belong to different groups is indicated. Circulation figures are estimates and were obtained from the publications mentioned. The rest of the information is from Antoine Shulhut (Personal communication, February 14, 17, 21, 1993).

Daily Newspapers

In contrast to the West Bank, there is only one daily Arabic newspaper in Israel, founded before the establishment of the State of Israel. *Al-Ittihad* (*Unity*), a daily, was founded on May 14, 1944, as the mouthpiece of the Arab Communist Party in Israel. It is published in Haifa and has a circulation of 10,000.

Weekly Newspapers

Al-Sinnarah (*The Hook*) was founded in 1982. It is published in Nazareth and has a circulation of 25,000.

Kul al-Arab (*All Arabs*) was founded in 1986 and is published in Nazareth. It has a circulation of 25,000.

Al-Bayareq (*The Banners*) was founded in October 1992. It is published in Baqa al-Gharbiyyeh and has a circulation of 3,000.

Sawt al-Hagg Wal Huriyyah (*The Voice of Truth and Freedom*) was founded in May 1990 as the mouthpiece of the Islamic movement. It is published in the town of Umm al-Fahm and has a circulation of 25,000.

Cultural Monthly Magazines

Al-Jadid (*The New*) was founded in January 1951. It is published in Haifa and has a circulation of 3,000.

Al-Mujtama' (*Society/Community*) was founded in 1970. It is published in Nazareth and has a circulation of 2,000.

Al-Mawakeb (*The Processions*) was founded in 1983. It is published in Nazareth and has a circulation of 3,000.

Kana'an (*Canaanite*) was founded in May 1991 in the village of Taybeh by the Center for the Revival of Arab Culture in Taybeh. It has a circulation of 2,000.

Al-Thaqafah (*Culture*) was founded in January 1993. This literary monthly is published in Haifa.

Periodicals

Al-Sharq (*The Orient*) was founded in 1970. It is published in Shafa Amr and receives funding from the Israeli Department of Arab Culture and from the Histadrut (Labor Federation). It has a circulation of 2,000.

Al-Aswar (*The Walls*) was founded in 1990. It is published in Acre and has a circulation of 2,000.

Ida'at (*Spotlights*) was founded in December 1992 by Palestinian poet Samih al-Qassem. It is published in al-Ramah and has a circulation of 2,000.

ELECTRONIC MEDIA

Radio

The British introduced radio to Palestine in 1936, and it broadcast in English, Hebrew, and Arabic (*A Survey of Palestine,* 1991). But the radio itself could not become the voice of Palestinians under the British Mandate, or under Jordan after the unification of the East and West Bank in 1950 (Abu Shanab, 1988). Palestinians did not have access to radio broadcast stations until the establishment of the PLO.

The number of Palestinian stations that came on and off the air in various Arab countries is too numerous to list here, but a review of the main Palestinian stations suggests that Palestinians placed great importance on oral communication and strove to replace stations that were closed.

The first Arab leader to create a daily 15-minute segment about Palestine was President Gamal Abdel Nasser of Egypt, who saw the move as part of his duty as the leader of the Arab World. In 1954, the *Palestine Service of Radio Cairo* was run by Egyptians who interviewed Palestinians and invited them as guests to the program. Iraq followed the Egyptian example with a 15-minute *Palestine*

Program starting in August 1962; Iraq's rival Syria followed with a 5-minute *Palestine Broadcast* in August 1964. Kuwait broadcast a daily half-hour Palestine *Corners* on Radio Kuwait between 1970 and 1974 (Abu Shanab, 1988).

The first PLO station run by Palestinians broadcast on March 1, 1965, by renting from Egypt two hours a day. The station differed from Palestine *Corners* in various Arab radio stations in that it was staffed by Palestinians and was less pressured than the others to follow the political line of the countries from which it broadcast. But the relative independence of the station lasted only until 1967. The Egyptian government assigned an Egyptian censor to the station from September 1967 until the spring of 1969. On July 28, 1970, Egypt closed the station. Also discontinued at that time was *The Voice of al-Asifa* (*The Voice of the Storm*), which ran for an hour a day and had been available to the PLO in May 1968 (Abu Shanab, 1988). Algeria allowed the PLO to broadcast in September 1970 for one hour a day while the PLO was in armed confrontation with Jordan (Soley & Nicholes, 1987). The Egyptian government allowed the *Voice of Palestine,* a PLO radio program stopped earlier, to be broadcast again from Cairo on March 8, 1971. However, in September 1975, when Palestinian broadcasters verbally attacked the Israeli-Egyptian Sinai Agreement, the program was halted again (Abu Shanab, 1988).

The PLO received a portable transmitter from the People's Republic of China and used it to broadcast from Syria on August 6, 1970, under the name of *Voice of the Storm.* The broadcasts condemned Egypt's negotiations with Israel (Browne, 1975). The Syrians destroyed the PLO station in Syria in 1976, following Syrian-Palestinian fighting in the Lebanese civil war. But the PLO's program in Egypt was reopened in June 1976 after the Syrian intervention in Lebanon but closed again on November 19, 1977, after President Sadat announced his intention to visit Israel. The station was moved to Beirut (Abu Shanab, 1988).

On June 5, 1972, the PLO Central Committee announced the unification of all PLO information services and the adoption of the name of *Voice of Palestine–Voice of the Palestinian Revolution.* But the new name could not hide the serious ideological divisions among the various groups that often worked at cross purposes from each other (Abu Shanab, 1988).

In the 1980s, the PLO broadcast from Algiers, and Sana, Yemen. Baghdad's powerful transmitter was better able to reach the occupied territories, but Iraq controlled broadcasting time, generally limiting it to between 7:00 P.M. and 9:00 P.M. local time (Bookmiller & Bookmiller, 1990).

Al-Quds (Jerusalem) Radio began broadcasting on January 1, 1988, less than a month after the outbreak of the uprising. The radio was run by the Popular Front for the Liberation of Palestine—General Command and depended on the Palestinian press for some of its news. The radio broadcast from southern Syria on a high-frequency medium wave (702 kilohertz) throughout the day, but its heaviest transmission period was during the early evening hours (Bookmiller & Bookmiller, 1990). Israel destroyed the radio station in 1988. Palestinians got a new transmitter and were preparing to resume medium wave broadcasting a week later when Israelis bombed and destroyed the building on January 19, 1990 ("Three Die," 1990).

In addition to stations that targeted Israel, some were employed by various factions when inter-Palestinian rivalries were at their most intense (Soley & Nichols, 1987).

The role of the radio programs goes beyond broadcasting patriotic songs, poetry, and coded messages to fighters. The programs are a good recruitment tool for the Palestinian movement.

Television

Palestinians do not control any television stations, although a large number of the employees of Jordan Television are Palestinian. The Buntstift Foundation, a political foundation affiliated with the Green Party in the Federal Republic of Germany and financed by the German Ministry for Economic Cooperation, recently cooperated with the Arab Journalists Association (AJA) to support the Palestinian people in setting up an independent media structure. Nine Palestinians had completed the first three-month intensive television training course in October 1992 and a two-month intensive course starting in February 1993 (AJA and Buntstift Foundation, 1993). There is no cable television in the West Bank, and new technologies have not yet been tapped there.

MOTION PICTURES

The first Palestinian film ever produced was a 20-minute documentary, shot in 1935, about the visit of King Abdul Aziz al-Saud to Palestine. Because of the political fortunes of Palestine, the documentary remained the film type of choice in Palestinian cinema and, later, video.

The first film of Fateh, which established the first film unit, was about the aftermath of the al-Karamah battle in 1968. The unit produced fifteen 16-mm films dealing mostly with the Palestinian reaction to various political events. The films were shown in refugee camps and in commando bases. Other groups in the PLO, namely, the Popular Front for the Liberation of Palestine and the Democratic Front for the Liberation of Palestine, also produced some films (Abu Ali & Abu Ghanimah, 1975).

Individual Palestinian filmmakers who have studied film production abroad and live there also produce films that are often shown at film festivals. Between June 20 and 27, 1992, 30 films were shown during the Palestinian Film Week held in Jerusalem, most documentary in nature.

Between 1980 and 1991, at least 18 more Palestinian films were produced. A Palestinian film and video company called Jerusalem Television Production was established on the West Bank in early 1990. The company concentrates mostly on developmental and educational issues. It coproduced with the British

Broadcasting Corporation (BBC) a video about the religious movement and coproduced with the Council of Middle East Churches a program about "Health and the Occupation" ("Ambitions and Accomplishments," 1992).

Movie theaters in the West Bank were closed with the advent of the uprising of December 1987. Movie attendance had been dropping steadily, both because of strict censorship of films and due to competition from video stores. Prolonged Israeli curfews aid video rentals. Stores take account of curfews and emergencies in their lending policies.

Although most films produced by the PLO are in Arabic and are for domestic consumption, some of the films produced by independent filmmakers (funded either by the PLO or by Palestinian private sources or international organizations) are shown with subtitles at film festivals abroad or during special functions related to Palestinians.

Palestinians once imported foreign films, but the drop in movie attendance has canceled such imports.

MEDIA OWNERSHIP AND FINANCIAL SUPPORT PATTERNS

Palestinian media ownership is either private or political. Only one newspaper in the West Bank, *Al-Quds,* refers to itself as a business. It is common knowledge that the PLO supports several papers, including Communist, Islamic, and pro-Jordanian publications. Radio stations are run by various PLO groups, while film and video production is funded either by private organizations or through the PLO.

MEDIA REGULATION

Regulation of Palestinian media varies by location. In the West Bank, Israeli censorship of the press, books, film, and the theater is done under the 1945 Defense Regulations instituted by the British during their mandate to curb Arab and Jewish nationalism. In practice, publications are required to take everything they intend to publish to the Israeli censors three times a day. About 25 percent of the material is censored (Benvenisti, 1986). Publications as well as editors are regularly punished for not submitting materials to the censor. Journalists are subject to arrest for incitement when found covering confrontations between the army and Palestinians. Journalists have been placed under house or town arrest. Some have been deported or imprisoned.

Israeli authorities have closed a number of printing presses and press services.

The Arab press published in Israel is not as heavily censored as the press of the West Bank. Thus, some West Bank journalists publish articles rejected by the censor in newspapers like *Al-Ittihad* or *Al-Sinnarah.* But distribution laws prevent the distribution of those papers in the occupied territories with the exception of Jerusalem.

Palestinian media under the PLO are not formally regulated, but journalists follow the line of the PLO faction to which their publication belongs. Dissent is possible.

EXTERNAL MEDIA SERVICES

There are no foreign-language broadcast services. In 1987, *Al-Quds* started an international edition of its daily paper, but this Arabic paper is flown to London daily to serve the Arab community there.

The PLO publishes material in various languages, but none of the newspapers and magazines have appeared regularly (''Periodicals,'' 1971, pp. 136–151). Most of its external services deal with onetime painting, photo, or embroidery exhibits used to acquaint people with Palestinian culture.

NEWS AGENCIES

Palestinians depend on international news agencies for their international news. While *Al-Quds* uses various Western and Arab news agencies, other papers depend mostly on Agence France-Presse for their news. To save on subscription fees, newspapers and magazines depend heavily on regional and international radio. The radio used most often is Radio Monte Carlo (''General Manager,'' 1990) because it pays special attention to Palestinian news and uses the Palestine Press Service as a source.

Palestinians in the occupied territories use the Palestine Press Service, established in 1978, both to gather news for their own use and to serve the foreign press corps. Palestinians have a symbiotic relationship with the Israeli press. Reporters who cannot publish the news they gather leak it to the Israeli press and then publish items a day later as translations from the Israeli press.

The PLO established the Palestine News Agency (WAFA) in 1972. It moved from Beirut to Tunis in 1982. The news agency sends daily bulletins in Arabic and English to newspapers, embassies, and PLO information offices around the world.

THE ROLE OF MEDIA IN NATIONAL DEVELOPMENT

Because of the occupation, the most important role for the media has been in consolidating Palestinian nationalism. The media do so by defining the people, their land, and their leaders. The press relates lessons from the Palestinian past and projects a vision of the Palestinian future and, as such, is an instrument of Palestinian nationalism. Because of its adversarial role to the occupation, the press has often been reluctant to criticize national institutions or to do investigative articles on how development aid has been used. Women's and health groups use video for educational purposes and to encourage discussion of political and social issues.

CONCLUSION

Before the Gulf War, the Palestinian press was leaning toward specialization and attempting to address audiences and topics like the handicapped of the uprising, children, women, and economic issues. But censorship restrictions and the lack of trained journalists have impeded the development of many of those topics, as well as the new publications trying to address them. But nothing has hurt the press more than the drying up of outside sources of funding. The 1993 closure of several West Bank publications has left scores of unemployed journalists and closed down local press agencies that used to feed them (*Al-Talia,* 1993, July 29). That closure is expected to lead to two developments: (1) a closer cooperation between unemployed press agency correspondents of the West Bank and Arab newspapers in Israel and (2) an attempt by Arabic publications in Israel to gain readers in the occupied territories. For instance, *Al-Ittihad* of Haifa has attempted to obtain a permit to distribute there (M. Manasrah, personal communication, August 29, 1993).

The Arab Journalists Association, founded in 1981, has helped journalists by negotiating salaries with publishers and by offering professional courses.

Despite censorship restrictions and professional and economic hardships, the Palestinian press has been a success story in terms of documenting Palestinian life, stressing self-determination, and rejecting occupation. Even with the recent closures of major publications, there are some encouraging signs, however. Despite those tensions, both *Al-Talia* and *Al-Kateb* have opened up their pages to opposing points of view. Furthermore, there are frequent calls for the need for Palestinians not to confine themselves to the discussion of the technical aspects of television production but to discuss its philosophy. In a column in *Al-Talia* on July 22, 1993, editor Issam Aruri wrote:

> There are fears that the future [Palestinian] authority will not make room for dissident opinions; thus, killing this important tool by turning it into the arm of the state, regardless of its type and composition. If we are not vigilant, we will meet the same fate as the one-opinion papers, and the one-party states. (Aruri, p. 12)

The fact that such issues are being debated means that perhaps the future Palestinian television will speak with more than one voice, and that would be a departure from the norm as practiced in other Arab countries.

REFERENCES

Abdul Fattah, A. (1984, March 28). Palestinian magazines: Platform for literary expression and political analysis. *Al-Fajr* (in English), p. 8.

Abu Ali, M., & Abu Ghanimah, H. (1975). *About Palestinian cinema.* Tripoli: Libya, United Information Publications [of the PLO].

Abu Ayyash, R. (1987). *The press of the occupied territories* [In Arabic]. Jerusalem: Dar el-Awda, Palestine Press Service.

Abu Shanab, H. (1988). *The Palestinian media* [In Arabic]. Amman, Jordan: Dar al-Jalil.

After 13 years of publication. (1993, February). *Al-Kateb,* p. 55.

AJA and Buntstift Foundation. (1993, May 10). Palestinian TV is for Palestinians. *Al-Fajr* (English), p. 5.

Ambitions and accomplishments: The first company of its kind in the occupied territories. (1992, December 21). *Al-Quds al-Arabi.*

Aruri, I. (1993, July 22). A hope laced with dangers. *Al-Talia,* p. 12.

Audeh, I., Ethelson, S., & Power, J. (1990). In K. Boullata (Ed.), *The Palestine story: Facts about Palestinians.* Washington, DC: Palestinian Center for the Study of Nonviolence.

Bahbah, B., & Kital, S. (1985). Perspectives in conflict: The role of the Palestinian media in the West Bank, the Gaza Strip, and East Jerusalem. *Journal of Communication, 35,* 16–25.

Baramki, G. (1987). Universities under occupation. *Journal of Palestine Studies, 17*(1), 12–20.

Benvenisti, M. (1986). *Conflicts and contradictions.* New York: Villard.

Bookmiller, N. K., & Bookmiller, R. (1990). Palestinian radio and the Intifada. *Journal of Palestine Studies, 19*(4), 96–105.

Browne, D. (1975). The voices of Palestine: A broadcasting house divided. *The Middle East Journal, 29*(2), 133–150.

Burrel, D., & Landau, Y. (Eds.). (1992). *Voices from Jerusalem: Jews and Christians reflect on the Holy Land.* New York: Paulist Press.

Center for Policy Analysis. (1991). *The Middle East and North Africa 1992* (38th ed.). London: Europa Publications Limited.

Cobban, H. (1991). *The Palestinian Liberation Organization.* Cambridge: Cambridge University Press.

Committee to Protect Journalists [CPJ] and Article 19. (1988, October). In *Journalism under occupation: Israel's regulation of the Palestinian press.* New York: CPJ.

Dakkak, I. (1983). Back to square one: A study in the re-emergence of the Palestinian identity in the West Bank 1967–1980. In A. Scholch (Ed.), *Palestinians over the Green Line: Studies on the relations between Palestinians on both sides of the 1949 Armistice Line since 1967.* London: Ithaca.

Druri, R. T., & Winn, R. C., with Michael O'Connor. (1992). *Plowshares and swords: The economics of the occupation in the West Bank.* Boston: Beacon Press.

The Economist Intelligence Unit. (1992). EIU Country Profile 1992–93. *Jordan.* London: Business International.

General manager of Radio Monte Carlo: We are the first broadcasting service in all the Arab area. (1990, September 19–25). *Al-Majallah,* pp. 56–60.

Graham-Brown, S. (1988). Impact on the social structure of Palestinian society. In Aruri (Ed.), *Occupation: Israel over Palestine* (pp. 223–254). Belmont, MA: AAUG Press.

Lothan, A. (1983, October 7). Inconvenient peace. *The Jerusalem Post,* p. 7.

More Palestinians join the army of the unemployed. (1993, July 29). *Al-Talia,* p. 12.

Mussalam, S. (1988). *The PLO: The Palestine Liberation Organization, its function, its structure and its mission.* Brattleboro, VT: Amana Books.

Najjar, O. (1992a). *Portraits of Palestinian women.* Salt Lake City: University of Utah Press.

Najjar, O. (1992b). Power and the Palestinian press: Israeli censorship on the West Bank, 1967–1991. (Microfilm number: 9310220).

Palestinian Encyclopedia. (1984). Milan, Italy: Encyclopedia Palestina Corporation, Stampa Press.

Palestinian Film Week: A festival of the joy of creativity. (1992, July). *Al-Kateb,* pp. 83–91.

Periodicals and pamphlets published by the Palestine Commando Organizations. (1971). *Journal of Palestine Studies, 1*(1), 136–151.

Quandt, W., Jaber, F., & Lesch, A. (1974). *The politics of Palestinian nationalism.* Berkeley: University of California Press.

Schiff, B. (1989). Between occupier and occupied: UNRWA in the West Bank and the Gaza Strip. *Journal of Palestine Studies, 18*(3), 60–75.

Schiff, Z., & Ya'ari, E. (1990). *Intifada: The Palestinian uprising—Israel's third front* (I. Friedman, Ed. and Trans.). New York: Simon and Schuster.

Shahin, M. (1993, January 8). The PLO and Hamas. *Middle East International* [London], pp. 7–8.

Shinar, D. (1987). *Palestinian voices: Communication and nation building.* Boulder: Rienner.

Soley, L., & Nichols, J. (1987). *Clandestine radio broadcasting: A study of revolutionary and counterrevolutionary electronic communication.* New York: Praeger.

A Survey of Palestine. (1991). Washington, DC: Institute for Palestine Studies, p. 114.

Tahir, J. (1985). An assessment of Palestinian human resources: Higher education and manpower. *Journal of Palestine Studies, 14*(3), 32–53.

Three die in Israeli bombing raids on Lebanon. (1990, January 20). *The News and Observer* (Raleigh, NC), p. 8A.

16

QATAR

Mohamed M. Arafa

INTRODUCTION

The State of Qatar lies halfway along the west coast of the Arabian Gulf, east of the Arabian Peninsula, which extends northward covering an area of about 7,108 square miles (11,437 square kilometers). The territory of the State of Qatar includes a number of islands in the coastal waters of the peninsula. The most important of these islands is the Hawar Archipelago, including Shar'ouh, Al-Ashat, Al-Safliliya, Al-Aliya, Janan, Al-Bashiriya, and Halul. Bahrain is some 18 miles (29 kilometers) to the west of the Qatari peninsula, and the United Arab Emirates bounds the base of that peninsula. Saudi Arabia shares a relatively short border with Qatar at the southwest of the Qatari peninsula. The land of Qatar is mostly flat and rugged, with some hills and sand dunes, which reach an altitude of 40 meters above sea level in the western and northern parts of the country. The capital city of Doha is a burgeoning modern city, while vast desert areas are now irrigated by wastewater and crisscrossed by pipelines transporting oil from producing fields in Dukhan to modern refineries or crude oil terminals at Umm Said. Giant desalination plants extracting fresh water from the Gulf have made water shortage seem an old memory and cultivation of relatively large areas in the country possible.

Qatari nationals are the descendants of ancient Arabian lines of kinship, due to Qatar's location and proximity to the Arabian Peninsula, on the one hand, and to the close historical and cultural heritage the state shares with the rest of the states of the Arabian peninsula, on the other. The Arab tribes who migrated from the other neighboring areas during the seventeenth and eighteenth centuries form the bulk of the present Qatari nationals. The present population is estimated (1992) at 400,000 in winter and 175,000 during the summer months. About 70 percent of the Qatari population live in the capital city of Doha.

Arabic is Qatar's official language. English is widely spoken by expatriates living in the country. Islam is the country's official religion, and Islamic jurisprudence is recognized as the basis of its legal system. Qatar has an oil-dependent economy: 90 percent of the country's revenues come from exporting oil and natural gas. In fact, it was the gradual increase of oil revenues that helped lay the foundation of the state, beginning in 1939 when oil was found in Zekrit on the west coast of the Qatari peninsula. However, events leading to World War II delayed oil exploration until 1949 (Ministry of Information, 1991, pp. 117–121). Increase in oil revenues has led to the transformation of the country's social and economic structures, which, up to that time, had relied on fishing, pearling, and camel herding for a living.

Education and human services have been among the first fields to benefit from increased oil revenues. Since the establishment of the first government primary school in 1952, the number of students has expanded from 550 (all male) in 1956 (Al-Ibrahim, 1985, p. 17) to 61,914 enrolled in 132 government and foreign private primary, preparatory, and secondary schools in 1991 (Ministry of Information, 1991, pp. 59–66). In 1973, a college with separate branches for men and women was established, then transformed into a full university that in 1992 consisted of seven different colleges for Education, Engineering, Sciences, Polytechnique, Law and Islamic Studies, Administrative Sciences and Economics, and Humanities and Social Sciences, including a Unit of Mass Communications within the Arabic Department.

On September 3, 1971, Qatar became an independent sovereign state when the present ruler, Sheikh Khaifa Bin Hamad Al-Thani, then the heir apparent, declared the abrogation of the Treaty of Protection signed with Great Britain in 1916. The country is governed by the Provisional Constitution of 1970, which entrusts the amir with full control and stipulates hereditary rule. The amir also presides over the Council of Ministers, issues and ratifies all laws and statutes, commands the armed forces, and appoints the members of the Advisory Council by amiri decrees. Other state political organs include the Council of Ministers and the Advisory Council. The Councils' duties include debating major policies, drafting laws, and preparing state budgets, as well as expressing opinions regarding major issues facing the nation and presenting these opinions in the form of recommendations or wishes without intervening in the works of executive and judicial authorities.

COMMUNICATION PHILOSOPHY

Qatar's media philosophy can best be described as a combination of at least three media theories: development, social responsibility, and authoritarian. It borrows from development theory the notion that media should accept and help carry out the development policies and tasks defined by the Ministry of Information created in April 1972 and aimed at "building and developing the country and the citizens" (Ministry of Information, 1991, p. 80), and the tenet that media should give priority to contents that link Qatar to other Gulf, Arab, and Muslim (all developing) countries that are geographically, politically, and culturally close to it.

The social responsibility components of Qatari philosophy are represented (1) by the notion that media in Qatar (both private print and national broadcast media) should balance their aspirations to freedom with their obligations to their society and (2) by the creation of the Qatari Public Commission for Improving the Quality of the Press to review the performance of privately owned newspapers and magazines every three months and to present its findings to the publishers and editors of those publications to be used as a guide.

A few authoritarian principles are embraced in the present Qatari Press and Publication Law, which has been in effect since its promulgation in 1979. Among these principles are: (1) Media should not in any way criticize the amir, (2) they should not publish anything that could undermine the established order or endanger the political regime, and (3) authorities have the right to impose censorship to ensure media adherence to those rules and principles (Ministry of Information, 1979, pp. 33–41).

PRINT MEDIA

Contrary to the general rule, Qatari print media did not evolve as a result of individual and societal communication needs. They, rather, grew out of a specific national policy and the desire of some individuals for participation in the public life of their society through publishing a newspaper or a magazine. Given their ethnic background, these individuals did not have a chance for such participation through the normal political and economic channels.

Print as well as electronic media first emerged in Qatar because of a plan to build a modern state in which media could play a twofold role. First, their active participation could aid the nation-building process; second, their mere existence could be a proof of the level of modernity the state is reaching.

Newspapers

The *Gazette* (*Al-Jareedah Al-Rasmyah*), Qatar's first publication on January 2, 1961, carried the amiri decrees, official announcements, and state laws. Although it was not published on a regular basis, the *Gazette* was the first and closest publication to any journalistic form Qatar had ever had. Qatar's *Gazette* is still published in 1994 almost in the same form and for the same purpose.

Dailies, however, were started in Qatar as small privately owned publications.

In 1994 there are three Arabic dailies—*Al-Arab, Arrayah* (*The Flag*), and *Al-Sharq* (*The Orient*)—and an English daily, *Gulf Times.*

Al-Arab was the first newspaper published in Qatar. It was started on March 6, 1972, by Abdel Allah Hussein Naama, a Qatari citizen known among newsmen as the "Dean" of the Qatari press. Naama had had some experience in the press business publishing a general interest weekly magazine, *Al-Orobah,* in 1970, though he had brought the first printing press to Qatar in 1955. In 1972, Naama decided that the time was right to start a political independent newspaper even before acquiring the proper printing facilities (Muhammad & Saif El-Din, 1984, p. 48). *Al-Arab* continued to appear as a weekly tabloid until February 22, 1974, when it converted to a broadsheet daily newspaper. *Al-Arab* increased the number of the pages of its daily edition from 6 pages to 8, then 16. In 1994 *Al-Arab* is published by a rather modern publishing house, claiming 9,000 readers, compared with the 800 readers it attracted during its early years. It has recently gained some readers in neighboring Bahrain and the eastern region of Saudi Arabia.

During the second half of the 1970s, a group of Qatari businessmen and intellectuals felt the time was ripe to publish a modern daily paper that could at once serve the increasing Qatari readership and make a profit. They recruited accomplished journalists from Egypt, Lebanon, Syria, and Sudan and launched *Arrayah* newspaper on May 10, 1979 (Al-Ibrahim, 1985, p. 63). The intention was to publish a weekly paper, soon to be converted to a daily, that could compete with the numerous Arabic (Egyptian, Lebanese, Kuwaiti, and Saudi) newspapers, which found an expanding market in Qatar.

Arrayah, which presented itself as an independent political daily, interested in projecting the Qatari viewpoint regarding the major Arab, Islamic, and international issues and problems, enjoyed the strong support of the Qatari government. After all, the chairman of its board is a prominent member of the ruling family, and its publication coincided with Qatar's growing interest and involvement in Arab and international affairs. Because of the diversity of both its editorial staff, which consisted mostly of Arab expatriates, and its readership, the paper rapidly surpassed local interests and took on regional and Arab dimensions.

On January 27, 1980, *Arrayah* began to publish daily, after broadening the scope of its news coverage, with sections on local, Gulf, Arab, and international affairs. It has attracted some prominent Arab writers to freelancing. In 1993, quite a few Qataris are responsible for some of its editorial sections. It claims a circulation of 10,000 copies, of which about 2,000 are distributed in Saudi Arabia and Egypt and the rest are sold locally. Toward the end of 1992, the Gulf Publishing and Printing Organization, which publishes *Arrayah,* moved to a new, modern building with modern printing facilities and introduced computerized journalism in Qatar.

The third Arabic daily in Qatar is *Al-Sharq.* It was first published toward the end of 1985 by Al-Watan Printing and Publishing House under the name *Al-*

Khaleej Al-Youm (Gulf Today). Eighteen months later, the daily, which was not very successful, changed owners. In September of 1987, Al-Sharq Printing, Publishing & Distribution House came into being. The editor of *Al-Sharq* (1991), an experienced Qatari journalist, was determined to make his newspaper all things to all readers: Qatari nationals and Arab expatriates, men and women, professionals and nonprofessionals. So he made sure that the paper provided diversified contents to reflect the description it carried under its title: ''A Political, General Interest Newspaper.''

In 1993 *Al-Sharq,* which claimed a circulation of about 10,000 copies, depended on its own staff (mostly Egyptian, Sudanese, and Jordanian expatriates and a few Qataris) for local news, feature stories, and most editorials. Government, Arab, and international news comes mostly from the wire services and a few correspondents in major news capitals: Washington, Moscow, London, and Cairo. The paper also acquires, by special agreements, the right to print articles written for other Arab big dailies (such as *Al-Ahram* of Egypt) by prominent Arab journalists and writers. For a relatively young publication, *Al-Sharq* has built a reputation among local readers for its color printing and the supplements it prints on various national occasions.

The only other daily published in Qatar is the English tabloid *Gulf Times.* It made its first appearance on December 10, 1978. The newspaper was intended to serve the growing expatriate communities, mostly from India, Pakistan, the United Kingdom, the United States, and a few other Western countries, who had no local publications to read except a bimonthly magazine called *This Is Qatar,* published by a public relations firm.

Like most other local dailies, *Gulf Times,* which had a mainly British editorial staff, started as a weekly but converted to a daily tabloid on February 22, 1981. It has gained some Qatari readers with the return of Qatari young men and women from study abroad, mostly in Great Britain and the United States. During its early years, it printed 5,000 copies on the average. In 1993 the paper, which is published by the Gulf Publishing and Printing Organization, claims it circulates around 8,000 copies.

There are three weekly papers in Qatar. The first is *Al-Dawry* (*The League*), first issued on April 16, 1978. It is a sports newspaper, privately owned but subsidized by the General Organization for Youth and Sports. *Al-Dawry* has had a very limited circulation, never surpassing 1,500 copies. In March 1991, the publisher, who does not have any printing facilities, converted the paper into a weekly magazine. The magazine, however, has only appeared monthly since its conversion.

The second weekly is called *Shabab Al-Yom (Youth Today*) and began publication by Al-Sharq Printing, Publishing & Distribution House on September 14, 1991. It presented itself to the readers as a sports and human interest newspaper. It has been the closest form in the Qatari press to what was called the sensationalist yellow journalism of the late nineteenth century in the United States. Although its editorial staff insist that their paper is informative, readership see it as "more entertaining than informative" (Qatari Commission for the Study of Local Press, 1992, p. 13).

Because of its novel reporting, layout, and colored pictures, *Shabab Al-Yom* initially created a lot of excitement, selling about 9,000 copies in Qatar, Saudi Arabia, and Egypt. In 1994, its novelty is fading, and circulation is steadily decreasing.

The third nondaily in Qatar is again another sports paper called *Qus Qozah (Rainbow),* started in February 22, 1990. It is a small publication that has not been able to publish regularly despite the fact that its license requires that it be weekly.

Magazines

For a population of 400,000, Qatar has a large number of weekly and non-weekly magazines (14 publications). It even had a larger number of magazines a decade ago (17). While the government has left the newspaper business to private initiatives, this has not been the case with magazines. In addition to privately owned magazines that it has steadily supported, the government has published its own. Encouraged by the fact that magazines do not require large editorial staff, in addition to some other political motives, the government, which has not had its own printing press, has published quite a few magazines.

Government External Magazines. The government has published one general interest and four specialized external magazines. In November 1969, the Ministry of Information issued *Al-Doha* monthly magazine. It was a cultural or literary magazine that in addition to literary articles and book reviews published special sections on education, communication, fine arts, and poetry in the Arab World. Some researchers estimated its circulation at 85,000 copies (Al-Ibrahim, 1985, p. 60), with an average of five readers passing each copy along.

Al-Doha ceased to issue in August 1986, following the drastic plunge of oil prices. The Ministry of Information, however, is thinking of resuming the publication of *Al-Doha,* which was sold at a very low price all over the Arab World.

The second official specialized publication is *Al-Tarbiya* (*Education*), started in December 1970 by the Qatar National Commission for Education, Culture and Science. It was published monthly until 1972, when it began issuing bimonthly. Recently, it was converted to a quarterly education journal. In addition to scientific research, studies, and articles on education, culture, and communication, *Al-Tarbiya* carries news, news reports, and interviews on education in Qatar. It contains a section in English and circulates about 5,000 copies in Qatar and the Arab World.

Majalat Al-Khaleej Al-Jadeed (*New Gulf Magazine*) was the only general interest magazine. A monthly that came out of the Ministry of Information in March 1976, it ceased to issue in February 1983. Circulation never surpassed 5,000 copies around the Arab World (Muhammad & Saif El-Din, 1984, p. 163).

Probably the most successful sports magazine to ever publish, not just in Qatar but in the whole Arab World, was *Al-Saker* (*The Falcon*). The magazine began publication by the Ministry of Defense in March 1977 while Qatar was hosting a Middle Eastern military sports conference. It continued issuing monthly, giving priority to big spectator sports in the Arab World such as soccer and basketball and showing just a marginal interest in military sports such as archery, equestrian events, and riflery. *Al-Saker* started to issue weekly on January 5, 1982, covering sports events and big soccer games around the Arab World. By the end of the first year of its weekly publication, *Al-Saker* did sell about 100,000 copies all over the Arab countries and for Arab readers around the world (Personal interview, November 3, 1992). In August of 1986, the same government decision to close down *Al-Doha* ended the life of *Al-Saker.*

The fourth government magazine was a monthly called *Al-Omah* (*The Nation*), first published in November 1980 by the Department of Religious Affairs. It covered a wide range of interests: economic, political, literary, and even medical concerns of the Muslim reader. It claimed a circulation of 90,000 copies. Like other government magazines, *Al-Omah* was closed down in August 1986.

Internal Magazines. Aside from external magazines, the government has published seven internal or business magazines. The Public Relations Department of Qatar Petroleum and Gas Corporation published two monthlies in 1976: *Diaruna Wal-Alam* (*Our Home and the World*), an oil business magazine that ceased to issue in the mid-1980s, and *Al-Mesha'al,* a firm magazine that continues to issue today. Qatar National Museum published a specialized quarterly called *Al-Rayan* in 1978. It printed 3,000 copies and ceased to issue in the mid-1980s. The Ministry of Public Health began publishing *Al-Seha: Qatar Medical Journal* in English in 1980. It reports on medical research in Qatar as well as abroad and is available to physicians and medical staff on a quarterly basis. The other three internal magazines are *Tejarat Qatar,* the official publication of Qatar's Chamber of Commerce, first issued in 1981; *University Journal,* first published in 1981 by the University of Qatar; and *Majalat Al-Sheon Al-Baladiyah* (*Department of Municipalities*), first printed in 1983. Most of these internal magazines are of a public relations nature, and all of them circulate to employees and interested readers free of charge.

The majority of private magazines come out of printing companies that try to supplement their incomes by publishing a magazine or two, rather than from publishing companies with their own printing presses.

The first effort by an individual to start a magazine in Qatar was made on February 5, 1970, when the owner of Al-Orobah Printing Press issued *Al-Oroba* weekly general interest magazine. It was a small publication produced by four professionals and circulated only 400 copies. With time, the magazine has enlarged its staff, broadened its coverage, and as a result, attracted more readers. In 1993 *Al-Orobah* claimed a circulation of 5,000 copies.

The second general interest weekly magazine to publish in Qatar was *Al-Ahed,* issued by Al-Ahed Press and Publishing Organization on July 9, 1974. *Al-Ahed* included essays, book reviews, poetry, and other literary content. Its circulation reached its highest level in the early 1980s (15,000 copies), but has since been declining.

Other noteworthy general interest magazines are *Al-Fajer, Akhbar Al-Osbou'e* and *This Is Qatar.* The first issue of the short-lived *Al-Fajer* appeared in January 1975 and the last in December 1976. *Akhbar Al-Osbou'e,* started toward the end of 1985, has had economic problems of late. Like all general interest private magazines in Qatar, *Akhbar Al-Osbou'e* does not seem to be able to attract enough advertisers to cover the rising cost of production. Although initially intended to be a general interest magazine in English, *This Is Qatar* could not attract enough readers. This monthly, which was first published in March 1978, has gradually narrowed its scope, focusing of late on tourism and commercial matters in Qatar.

There are five specialized magazines: an economic weekly, first issued in January 1980 (*Swaq Al-Khaleej*); a woman's monthly (*Al-Jawhara*), started in 1977; a children's weekly (*Masha'el*); a monthly focusing on construction and development; and a computer magazine, started in 1991, that has not been able to maintain regular publication. Qatar's private magazines, in general, are small publications that live on and for government subsidies.

ELECTRONIC MEDIA

Radio

The government of Qatar started experimental transmission of radio broadcasting on March 15, 1968. Two months later, a radio station was inaugurated, and the Voice of Qatar was aired on June 25, 1968. This new radio service started with an average of five hours of Arabic programs aired on a medium wave from a 10-kilowatt transmitter (Al-Ibrahim, 1985). Two years later, the transmitter was replaced by a 100-kilowatt shortwave transmitter. Airing hours were expanded, allowing for a relatively wider variety of programming.

Station facilities have steadily developed in the last two decades. In 1993, Radio Qatar uses 11 large transmitters: Al-Arish has medium wave 750-kilowatt and shortwave 500-kilowatt transmitters; the Al-Khaisa transmission plant has five medium wave transmitters with different powers and a shortwave 250-kilowatt power transmitter; and the Al-Markheya facility consists of three medium wave and shortwave transmitters (Al-Ibrahim, 1985, p. 46). The Qatar radio service, which started with only 2 studios, has steadily expanded its production facilities. In 1982, a new radio complex was built consisting of 15 radio studios.

Qatar radio's signal can be received by listeners in all the Gulf region, most of the Arab World, as well as parts of Europe and Asia. According to the 1991 media survey carried out by the Audience Research Unit of the Ministry of Information, 95.38 percent of the adult population in Qatar listen to Qatar Broadcasting Service regularly.

Daily airing hours have been extended from 5 hours in 1968 to 46 hours in 1993, broadcast on six medium wave and shortwave AM (amplitude modulation) and FM (frequency modulation) programs (or rather channels), using four different languages—Arabic, English, French, and Urdu.

The First Program (or the Main Program) is the major broadcast service of Radio Qatar. It airs some 20 hours a day but was on the air around the clock during the second Gulf War. In addition to music, news bulletins, and briefs, the programming of this Arabic program includes religious programs, government announcements, education features, drama, sports, and live coverage of big soccer games. The Second Program is an English broadcast service that features Western music, newscasts, drama, short features, and educational programs. It broadcasts on two separate FM and medium wave AM transmitters. The bulk of its programs are imported, especially from the United Kingdom. A small portion of its programs are locally produced. Some 36 percent of listeners to Radio Qatar tune in to this English program on a regular basis.

The other four programs are the Folk Program, featuring folklore music and programs using the local dialect; the Urdu Program, airing three hours a day to serve the Urdu-speaking residents; Hona Al-Doha (Here Is Doha), broadcasting four hours of Arabic music and concerts daily using a high-powered 4 by 30–kilowatt FM transmitter; and the French Program, which airs two hours a day.

Radio Qatar draws large audiences from neighboring Saudi Arabia, the United Arab Emirates, Bahrain, and Iran.

Television

For quite a few years, Qataris tuned in to television programs coming from neighboring countries Saudi Arabia (ARAMCO [Arabian American Oil Company] TV), Kuwait, and Iran because Qatar had no television service of its own until August 15, 1970, when the government launched a daily four-hour monochrome transmission (Marzook, 1988, p. 13). This initial television service used two low-powered 5-kilowatt transmitters (Ministry of Information, 1982, p. 102). Four years later, new color transmission facilities were in place, a new three-studio complex housing modern equipment was built, two 220-kilowatt power transmitters were installed, and a new phase of Qatar Television's development began. As a result of these developments, airing hours were increased to seven daily, allowing for a wider variety of programs, and Qatar Television National Program was transmitted on two channels (9, 11) instead of just one.

In the late 1970s, two large television studios were added, and a 600-kilowatt transmitter was ready for use. In 1982, a Second Program (Channel 37) was started, broadcasting an average of three hours daily. Its daily schedule included some instructional programs produced by the Ministry of Education, as well as an educational program or two. Aside from occasional airing of live coverage of local and international soccer games, soap operas have dominated the daily schedule of the Second Program.

In 1993, Qatar Television broadcast a little over 20 hours on weekdays and 28 on the weekends. The schedule of the Arabic Program (Channels 9 and 11), on an average day, includes four slots for drama (usually three Arabic serials, quasi-soap operas, and a late-night movie), three news bulletins (midafternoon, prime time, and before sign-off), and three hours of sectorial programs (including two hours of children's programs and cartoons and three to four hours of educational or cultural programs). As for the English Channel, animated cartoons and religious programs take up most of the daytime programming, while comedy shows (*Cosby Show, 227,* and *Golden Girls* are the most popular ones), variety shows, soap operas, and American and Indian movies dominate programming at night. The only newscast on this channel is aired at 8:30 in the evening.

Locally produced programs do not amount to more than 25 percent of the total programming of Qatar Television. The bulk of imported Arabic television programs (dramas in particular) come from Egypt, Syria, the United Arab Emirates, Kuwait, and Jordan, with Egypt being the largest provider. American—and, to a much lesser extent, British and Indian—productions constitute the majority of foreign programs broadcast on Channel 37. Educational programs from a variety of sources such as Japan, the Netherlands, and Sweden are occasionally broadcast with English or Arabic subtitles.

Although it is a national medium, owned, controlled, and run by the government, Qatar Television does accept and air commercials on both the Arabic and English channels. Like all other content, commercials are tightly censored in order to block out culturally and politically unfavorable images and ideas.

Cable Television

A special arrangement between the American Cultural Center (which receives Cable News Network [CNN]) and Qatar Television early in 1991 made it possible for viewers to receive CNN International on the local TV. The reception of CNN, which at any time, day or night, could go live with breaking stories on the Gulf War, was an eye-opener on the telecommunications possibilities. As soon as the guns went silent in late February 1991, CNN was taken off the air. But viewers had already been made aware of the importance of having clear reception of satellite television channels without putting up a satellite dish, which is still expensive and risky, since the government does not allow it.

In the meantime, neighboring Bahrain has continued to connect one of its local channels to CNN International for an average of three hours daily. A considerable number of Qatari viewers who had developed an attachment to CNN have started to tune in to Bahrain Television. Then came the Egyptian Satellite Channel, which, by a special agreement, can be received on Bahrain Television, followed by the Saudi-sponsored Middle East Broadcasting Corporation (MBC) satellite channel emanating from London.

Interested in keeping the Qatari audience tuned in to Qatar Television, the government studied options regarding these threatening satellite TV channels.

An agreement was signed, in October 1992, between Qatar Public Telecommunications Corporation and an American cable TV company for operation in March 1993. The first phase of the system will cover the capital city of Doha, which houses about 70 percent of the population. Q-Tel will receive the TV signals through its three earth satellite stations and retransmit them on microwave circuits (not by cable) to subscribers who will be able to receive 20 channels as a basic package. Subscribers with the help of different decoders could receive three or four times that number of channels as long as they pay the extra charge. The basic package will, of course, include Qatar's two programs, all other GCC (Gulf Cooperation Council) States TV Channels (10), the Egyptian Satellite Channel (ESC), the Saudi-sponsored channel (MBC), CNN, British Broadcasting Corporation (BBC), ESPN, an Indian program, a Pakistani channel, and Islam Vision, a religious network that will emanate from Masqat (Oman).

NEW TECHNOLOGIES

During the late 1970s, videocassette recorders (VCRs) were status symbols for a few rich families in Qatar. Today, almost every household in Qatar has at least one VCR next to the TV set. VCRs, however, are not commonly used as devices for time-shifting (a common use in the Western world) but rather as a way of viewing prerecorded imported Arabic, English, and Indian movies and plays. There are about 20 videocassette shops and 220 video clubs in the country, selling and renting desired movies and plays at very affordable prices.

The Arab Satellite Earth Station, commissioned in 1986 to communicate with the Arab Satellite Communications Organization (ARABSAT), linked with communications satellites orbiting over the Indian and Atlantic oceans and thus formed an integrated satellite communications network. This station enabled Qatar to exchange television and public information programs with a number of Arab countries. Special channels for such services (including telephone, telegram, and telex) have been opened with the United Arab Emirates, Oman, Kuwait, Jordan, Tunisia, and Yemen. In addition to this station, Doha 2 Earth Satellite Station, a 330-channel earth station, exchanges telephone and television signals with countries such as the United States and Canada equipped with similar facilities, linked to communications satellites over the Atlantic Ocean (Ministry of Information, 1991, p. 3).

MOTION PICTURES

Qatar is yet to have any film production facilities. Even documentaries occasionally sponsored by the government have been produced abroad. Movie theaters, however, were introduced to Qatar in 1950 when the Shell Oil Company built its own movie theater in Dukhan to provide its employees (almost exclusively expatriates) with the only form of entertainment available in Qatar at that time. Other oil companies followed suit. By the end of the 1960s, there were seven movie theaters in the country showing English, Indian, and a few Arabic movies not just to the expatriate community but to a growing local audience and a considerable number of Saudis who came from the eastern part of the kingdom for an evening of entertainment not available to them at home.

In the mid-1970s, when Qatar's government assumed full ownership and management of all oil operations previously carried out by foreign oil companies, a stock company, Qatar Cinema Company, was formed with the purpose of controlling, through ownership and management, all aspects of operating the existing movie theaters. Qatar Cinema Company renovated three of the five movie theaters it had acquired, got rid of two, built two more, and modernized their projection equipment.

The advent of television and the VCR penetration of most Qatari households during the 1980s, however, have brought in-theater attendance down drastically. In 1993, there are five operating movie theaters in Qatar with an average of 300 seats each. They show mostly Indian, American, British, and Egyptian movies to an in-theater audience consisting overwhelmingly of young Asian expatriates and a few young Qatari nationals.

There has always been tight censorship of any film before being shown to any public or private audience in Qatar. Ever since the Press and Publications Law No. 8 of 1979 was passed, and in accordance with the Department of Information Affairs of the Law No. 20 of 1990, this department has resumed the responsibility of "censoring local and foreign artistic productions" (Ministry of Information, 1991, p. 81) and licensing theaters, bodies, and shops selling and circulating these artistic productions.

MEDIA OWNERSHIP

Private ownership of print media has been the predominant pattern of ownership in Qatar. The government has never owned a political magazine except for the short-lived *Al-Khaleej Al-Jadeed* general interest magazine owned by the Ministry of Information. Despite being private enterprises, print media in Qatar are openly subsidized by the government. This open subsidy is not just a channel of government influence over print media; rather, in many cases, it is a lifeline for these magazines without which they cannot survive.

As for electronic media, both radio and television are owned and operated by their respective departments that are administrative units of the Ministry of Information. Even the forthcoming cable television service is a franchise owned by Q-Tel, a public corporation owned directly by the government.

MEDIA REGULATION

Print media in Qatar are regulated by the Press and Publications Law No. 8 of 1979. This law requires licenses to be issued from the Ministry of Information prior to the printing or circulation of any publication in Qatar.

While mandating that the owner/publisher of any newspaper or magazine be a Qatari national, the law allows, in some cases, for a citizen of another Arab country to hold the position of editor in chief, provided he or she resides in Qatar. Articles 24 and 25 state that government authorities (Council of Ministers and/or Ministry of Information)

> may suspend for a maximum of a year, and/or confiscate and/or close down any publication whose editing policy contradicts "the national interests" or serves the "interests of a foreign country," or receives any financial support from any foreign entity, if such violations are proven.

In addition to these provisions, censors have been stationed in all mass media organizations in Qatar since the beginning of the Iraq-Iran War in the early 1980s. These censors make sure to screen out any content that could violate public order, religion, or morals.

Electronic media are regulated by Law No. 20 of 1990 ordaining the Ministry of Information. This law requires "that radio and television provide the citizen with the political, economic, and social information that could enable him to understand local, regional, and international issues, develop and promote people's understanding [and awareness] within the framework of the vital principles guiding the State's policies, and entertain [their audiences] within the limits of observed religious and traditional values" (Ministry of Information, 1991, p. 80).

EXTERNAL MEDIA SERVICES

Foreign-Language Broadcast Services

Aside from its home radio services in English (the Second Program), French, and Urdu, Qatar offers no foreign-language radio services. The same is true of television, which offers a single home TV service (Channel 37) in English. By contrast, Qataris can receive numerous radio foreign services in English, Persian, Urdu, Hindi, French, and a few other Asian languages. As for television, Qatari viewers, even before the cable TV service, could receive the Persian programs of Iran and CNN International and BBC services from Bahrain Television, the United Arab Emirates TV channels (2), and two Saudi channels whenever climatic conditions allow it.

Foreign-Language Newspapers and Magazines

While only producing two small publications in English, *Gulf Times* and *This is Qatar,* Qatar imports, through a few bookstores and distribution companies, many foreign-language newspapers and magazines to satisfy the needs of various expatriate communities in the country. For the English-speaking sector of the population, the *International Herald Tribune, The Times* (of London), the *Guardian, Time, Newsweek,* and the *Wall Street Journal* are the most commonly read newspapers and magazines. In addition to a few French and German publications, it is not uncommon to find Hindu, Urdu, and Philippino newspapers and magazines on newsstands in a few bookstores and supermarkets in Qatar.

NEWS AGENCIES

With some technical cooperation from Egypt's Middle East News Agency (MENA), Qatar started its own national news agency—Qatar News Agency (QNA)—in 1975. The government was eager to rapidly develop the technical and personnel capabilities of its newborn agency and expand its services in order to secure a strong channel for carrying and disseminating its news and viewpoints locally and abroad. Consequently, QNA, in less than two decades, has developed a network of reporters, offices, and correspondents covering the country, all Gulf states, most Arab countries, and a few important world news capitals in Europe, the Americas, and Asia.

Today, QNA has more than 150 foreign subscribers in addition to 70 local ones. It transmits its news service in four languages: Arabic, English (for most subscribers), Portuguese, and Spanish (for about 80 subscribers in Central and South America and the Caribbean). In addition to news service, the agency offers a weekly news bulletin and a photojournalistic service.

Although the agency does not hold a monopoly on distributing international news stories inside the country, it almost has a monopoly on news coming out of the Emiri Diwan (which houses both the office of the ruler Amir and the cabinet). Qatari media use the services of other regional and world news services such as Reuters, MENA, Agence France-Presse (AFP), and Deutsche Presse-Agentur (DPA) as well.

THE ROLE OF MEDIA IN NATIONAL DEVELOPMENT

Mass media in Qatar was initially started with the purpose of playing a major role in the process of building a modern nation. The planned development of electronic media in particular has projected this fact. The policies and plans of the Ministry of Information are geared toward using media to bridge the development gap created by the fast economic growth resulting from the oil boom in the 1970s and early 1980s, on the one hand, and the lagging concomitant social and cultural changes, on the other. Meetings and directives addressed to programmers and editing policymakers request that they give priority to education and cultural contents over entertaining content. Increased government financial support sometimes serves as a form of positive reinforcement to a private newspaper that publishes an education supplement or starts a new section on health or computers, for example.

CONCLUSION

For a small country, Qatar has rapidly developed a press made possible only by the strong support of the government and the recruitment of relatively well trained journalists from other less affluent Arab countries. Whether Qatari newspapers and magazines will be able to hold ground in the future with the dwindling of government financial support and whether they can attract more Qatari citizens to make a career working for them, especially with the growing pull for the "Qatarization" of media staff, remain to be seen.

The introduction of cable television, in March 1993, not only allows for clear reception of satellite television networks and more liberal philosophies, but puts pressure on the government to ease censorship and other regulations imposed on local print and electronic media. Additionally, this new, tough competition may help improve the quality of local electronic media productions.

REFERENCES

Al-Ibrahim, Y. M. (1985). *The development of media in the State of Qatar.* Unpublished master's thesis, Drake University, Des Moines, IA.

Hicks, R. G. (1977). *A survey of mass communication.* Gretna, LA: Pelican.

Marzook, M. B. (1988). *An investigation of the cognitive and affective need/satisfaction of Qatar university students: The use and gratification approach to television programs.* Unpublished Ph.D. dissertation, State University of New York at Buffalo.

McQuail, D. (1988). *Mass communication theory: An introduction* (2nd ed.). Beverly Hills, CA: Sage Publications.

Ministry of Information. (1979). *Qatar Yearbook.* Doha: Department of Information Affairs.

———. (1982). *Qatar Yearbook.* Doha: Department of Information Affairs.

———. (1991). *Qatar Yearbook.* Doha: Department of Information Affairs.

Mohammad, H. A., & Saif El-Din, O. (1984). *Qatari press: History and evolution* [in Arabic]. Doha: Authors.

Qatari Commission for the Study of Local Press. (1992). Unpublished report. Doha: Qatar.

17

SAUDI ARABIA

Kuldip R. Rampal

INTRODUCTION

The Kingdom of Saudi Arabia, which occupies about four-fifths of the Arabian Peninsula, is bordered by Jordan, Iraq, and Kuwait to the north, by Yemen to the south, by Oman to the south and east, and by Qatar and the United Arab Emirates to the northeast. Saudi Arabia has a long western coastline on the Red Sea, facing Egypt, Sudan, and Ethiopia. Riyadh is the political, and Mecca the religious, capital. Saudi census reports released in May 1993 indicate that the country's population at the end of 1992 was 16.9 million, of whom 27.3 percent were expatriates. Arabic, the official language, is spoken by all of the indigenous population.

Saudi Arabia is the leading exporter of oil and possesses the largest known petroleum reserves. Its economy, therefore, is dominated by petroleum and petroleum-related industry. The country has also made major strides in food self-sufficiency, with agricultural exports a key component of its nonoil exports. The Saudi government has consistently favored a pro-Western, market-oriented economic strategy. Saudis had a per capita income of $6,230 and literacy rate of 62.4 percent in 1990 (*Statistical Yearbook,* 1991).

Saudi Arabia is the center of the Islamic faith, and the country includes the holy cities of Mecca and Medina. Except for some expatriates, virtually all of the inhabitants are adherents of Islam, the official religion. About 85 percent of the population are Sunni Muslims, with the remaining being Shi'a Muslims.

Most of the indigenous inhabitants belong to the strictly orthodox Wahhabi sect.

The Kingdom of Saudi Arabia is almost entirely the creation of King Ibn Saud. A descendant of earlier Wahhabi rulers, he gradually established control over most of the Arabian Peninsula from the 1900s onward and in 1932 proclaimed the Kingdom of Saudi Arabia.

The country is an absolute family monarchy based on Islamic principles, with no constitution or elected assembly. All power is ultimately vested in the king, who is also the country's supreme religious leader. There are no political parties, and legislation is by royal decree. The king rules in accordance with the Sharia, the sacred law of Islam. He also guides the process of consultation and consensus among senior members of the royal family and the Council of Ulama, consisting of the country's senior Islamic scholars, in his decision making. He appoints and leads a Council of Ministers, which serves as the instrument of royal authority in both legislative and executive matters. Decisions of the council are reached by a majority vote but require royal sanction (*Europa,* 1992, p. 2365). The judicial system is largely based on Islamic religious law (Sharia), but tribal and customary law are also applied.

King Fahd issued a decree on March 1, 1992, that provided for the formation of a 60-member Consultative Council by the end of September 1992. Its 60 members would be appointed every four years and would be "chosen by the King from amongst scholars and men of knowledge and expertise." The decree defined the areas on which the council would "express opinions" as including the general plan of economic and social development, annual reports submitted by ministries, international laws and treaties, and the interpretation of laws.

The legislation was hailed as a cautious first move by the Saudi government toward modifying the power of the monarchy, which until then—in theory at least—had been absolute (*Keesing's,* 1992, p. 38839). Appointments to the Consultative Council were completed by early August 1992. The justice minister was appointed as its chairman on September 16, 1992 (Ali Maghrabi, personal interview, May 12, 1993).

Another decree on March 1, 1992, provided for a written constitution, although it also noted that "citizens are to pay allegiance to the King in accordance with the Holy Koran and the Prophet's tradition." In an interview with the Kuwaiti newspaper *Al-Siyasa* of March 28, 1992, King Fahd said that the "prevailing democratic system in the world" was not suitable for the region, and that Islam favored "the consultative system and the openness between the ruler and his subjects" rather than the "free elections," which might be suitable for other countries (*Keesing's,* 1992, p. 38839).

In spite of these moves toward political reform, Saudi Arabia remains an absolute monarchy. The authoritarian political system has, therefore, resulted in a controlled press in Saudi Arabia, especially since 1958 when the government's Publications Department was given the power to censor publications.

PRINT MEDIA

Although private ownership of the press is allowed in Saudi Arabia, such publications must be published by press organizations. These organizations, which took over from small private firms under a royal decree in 1963, are privately owned by groups of individuals experienced in newspaper publishing and administration. In 1993, there were ten press organizations in the country publishing a variety of newspapers and periodicals. Several periodicals are also published by the government.

In accordance with the 1963 Press and Publication Law, most newspapers and periodicals have been published by press organizations, which are administered by government-approved boards of directors. Under this law, all newspapers must be licensed, and a censorship committee reviews and censors all national and foreign publications according to the policies of the state. In addition, a Saudi government policy statement of 1982 requires that all newspapers refrain from criticizing the government, the royal family, or the clergy.

Newspapers

Of the ten daily newspapers in Saudi Arabia, seven are in Arabic and three in English. Six of these newspapers are based in Jeddah, the administrative capital and commercial center; two in Riyadh, the royal capital; and one each in Mecca and Dammam. The leading Arabic-language newspaper is *Al-Riyadh,* which has a circulation of 140,000 during weekdays (Saturday-Thursday) and 90,000 on Fridays. *Okaz* (97,000), *Al-Jazirah* (90,030), *Al-Bilad* (65,000), *Al-Madina al-Munawara* (47,000), *Al-Yaum* (40,000), and *Al-Nadwah* (35,000) are also popular Arabic-language newspapers.

An important Arabic-language newspaper is *Ash-Sharq al-Awsat,* which has a circulation of 100,000. Based in London, the newspaper is also published from New York, Paris, Marseilles, Cairo, Casablanca, Jeddah, Riyadh, and Dhahran. It is published by Saudi Research and Marketing Company, a press organization owned by members of the Saudi royal family. Right-wing in orientation, this newspaper closely reflects government views. It is read throughout the Arab World.

Saudi Research and Marketing also publishes the country's leading English-language daily, *Arab News,* circulation 110,000. Another popular English-language daily is the *Saudi Gazette,* with a circulation of 17,900. This newspaper is published by the Okaz Organization for Press and Publication, which tends to reflect the views of Islamic religious teachers and leaders. *Saudi Review* provides a daily digest of translations into English of Saudi newspaper articles and broadcasts. It is published by a consortium of Saudi newspapers and has a circulation of 5,000. According to the Ministry of Information, another English-language newspaper, *Riyadh Daily,* has been established recently (Ministry of Information, 1992).

Saudi Arabia had a circulation of 39 copies of daily newspapers per 1,000 inhabitants for the year 1988, the latest figures available from the United Nations Educational, Scientific and Cultural Organization (UNESCO) sources. This compared favorably with the average of 33 copies per 1,000 inhabitants in 1988 for all Arab states for that year (*Statistical Yearbook,* 1991). The circulation had climbed to 47 copies per 1,000 people by 1991 (Drost, 1991, p. 434).

The largest weekly is *News from Saudi Arabia,* which is aimed at readers abroad. Published by the Ministry of Information, it has a circulation of 22,000. This publication outlines major events in Saudi Arabia and emphasizes economic and social developments in the country. Another weekly newspaper is the *Arabian Sun,* published by the state-owned Arabian-American Oil Company (ARAMCO) for its staff members.

Magazines

As with newspapers, most periodicals are published by press organizations. Twenty-five magazines and periodicals catering to various reading tastes are produced by such organizations (*The Middle East and North Africa,* 1993, pp. 790–791). There are also a number of popular periodicals published by the government and ARAMCO and distributed free of charge. UNESCO data (*Statistical Yearbook,* 1991) put the total number of periodicals at 58. The 25 publications can be categorized as follows: news, 2; business and commerce, 6; religion, 3; politics, philosophy, and literature, 2; family, 3; women's magazines, 2; tourism, travel, leisure, and sports, 1; popular history and geography, 1; children and young persons, 1; professional journals, 2; and other, 2.

The magazines with the most extensive news coverage are *Al-Majallah,* read throughout the Arab World, and *Al-Yamamah. Al-Majallah,* a weekly current affairs magazines, is owned by the royal family's Saudi Research and Marketing Company. This is a companion publication of the London-based newspaper of this group, *Ash-Sharq al-Awsat. Al-Majallah,* published in Arabic, has a circulation of 116,000. *Al-Yamamah,* published by Al-Yamama Press Establishment in Arabic, is based in Riyadh and has a circulation of 35,000.

The most important and widely circulated business magazine in the kingdom is *Saudi Business,* published by the Saudi Research and Marketing Company. This English-language weekly publication has a circulation of 27,300. Other business-oriented weekly publications are *Saudi Arabia Business Week* and *Saudi Economic Survey,* both in English, with circulations of about 3,000 each. The major Arabic-language business publication is *At-Tijarah,* published monthly by the Jeddah Chamber of Commerce and Industry, with a circulation of 8,000.

Hajj, the most widely read religious periodical, is produced by the Ministry of Pilgrimage Affairs. Founded in 1947, it is published monthly in Arabic and English. This ministry also publishes *At-Tadhamon al-Islami,* a monthly aimed at promoting Islamic solidarity. Another religion-oriented publication is *Al-*

Muslimoon, which looks at Arab cultural life within the framework of religion. It is published by the Saudi Research and Marketing Company. A popular publication devoted to cultural, literary, political, and scientific subjects is *Al-Manhal,* which is published monthly in Arabic.

Two well-known women's magazines are *Ash-Sharkish Elle,* an Arabic-language monthly, and *Sayidati,* a weekly published in Arabic by Saudi Research and Marketing Company. Family-oriented publications include *Al-Mujtama, Arabia,* and *Al-Faysal.* Another prominent publication is *Al-'Arab,* which is devoted to the popular history and geography of the Arabian Peninsula. It is published every two months.

Universities and religious organizations are also involved in publishing. King Abdal-Aziz University in Jeddah publishes *Majallat al-Iqtisad Wal-Idara,* a monthly journal focused on economics and administration. The Islamic University in Riyadh publishes *Al-Da'wa,* which disseminates Islamic missionary literature, legal opinion, and Islamic research studies. The Muslim World League based in the holy city of Mecca publishes *Rabitat al-'Alam al-Islami,* a monthly in Arabic and English (Al-Kahtani, personal interview, Ministry of Information, June 6, 1993).

ELECTRONIC MEDIA

Radio

Radio services were introduced into Saudi Arabia in the 1930s, but the first indigenous program did not begin until 1949. The ultraconservative Muslim religious leaders, the *ulama,* had strongly opposed the introduction of radio in the kingdom. Ibn Saud, the kingdom's founder, won over the *ulama* in the 1920s with a two-way demonstration transmission of readings from the Holy Quran between Mecca and Riyadh.

Today's Saudi broadcasting is equipped with first-class facilities. The state-owned Broadcasting Service of Saudi Arabia (BSSA), a department within the Ministry of Information, holds a monopoly of public broadcasting. BSSA provides its domestic service on 43 medium wave, 25 FM (frequency modulation), and 3 shortwave stations. It also provides external service on 17 shortwave frequencies (*World Radio TV Handbook,* 1992, p. 184). As a result of this vast network, radio programming is available throughout Saudi Arabia.

BSSA operates five radio networks, providing two general Arabic-language services, two religious services, and a foreign-language service in English and French. The general services, known as the General Program and the Second Program, originate from Riyadh and Jeddah, respectively. The Holy Quran service, one of the two religious services, originates from Mecca. The Call of Islam, the other religious service, originates from Jeddah. All of these services are relayed throughout the kingdom. The foreign-language service, broadcast from Dammam on the east coast, is also available in Jeddah.

Both general Arabic-language services begin at 3:00 A.M. and remain on the air until 11:00 P.M. The General Program's offerings are in the areas of religion, culture, folklore, drama, information, education, and health. The Second Program is geared to popular appeal, entertainment, drama, culture, and science. The Holy Quran service begins at 3:00 A.M. and remains on the air until 9:00 P.M. This service presents Koranic readings, recitals, and discussions on the Prophet's traditions. The Call of Islam service is offered from 1:00 A.M. to 3:00 A.M. and for three to four hours in the early evening. This service takes more of an ideological approach to Islam, promoting its doctrine, principles, and concepts. The foreign-language service is on the air from 8:00 A.M. until 1:00 P.M. and from 2:00 P.M. until 9:00 P.M.

There were an estimated 5 million radio receivers in use in Saudi Arabia in 1991, with 338 receivers for every 1,000 inhabitants (*World Radio TV Handbook,* 1992). The most recent available data indicate that total annual broadcasting hours for 1987 were 63,969, which were broken down into the following program categories: news and information, 22 percent; education, 27.5 percent; religion and culture, 38.8 percent; and entertainment, 11.7 percent (*Statistical Yearbook,* 1991).

Because Arabia is the birthplace of Islam and is home to Islam's two holiest shrines in Mecca and Medina, Saudi Arabia considers itself the repository of the Islamic faith. As a result, Saudi Arabia maintains an extensive information dissemination program in and to other countries, especially Islamic nations (Ministry of Information, 1991).

The Riyadh-based Arabic-language network, known as the General Program, is targeted to North Africa and western Europe in addition to the kingdom and neighboring countries. The Jeddah-based Arabic-language network, called the Second Program, is targeted to the kingdom and neighboring countries. The Holy Quran service is targeted to Central and Southeast Asia and Central and North Africa in addition to the kingdom. The Call of Islam service is aimed at North Africa in addition to the kingdom and the neighboring countries (Ministry of Information, 1993).

The Saudi ARAMCO FM Radio, founded in 1957, is a private station, broadcasting music and programs in English for the entertainment of employees of the Arabian-American Oil Company. The network offers pop/country and western music on three stations in the cities of Dhahran, Safaniyah, and Udhailiyah and classical/easy listening music on three other frequencies from the same cities. The network, which is on the air 24 hours, also broadcasts several news broadcasts during the day.

Television

As with radio, there was resistance to the introduction of television in the kingdom by the Muslim religious leaders because the Quran forbids making images of living beings. There was also a fear that television would bring Western influences to the Saudi culture. Head (1985, p. 30) says that King Faisal considered television an essential tool to help combat propaganda from neighboring countries and to assist in national development. Saudi Arabian television went on the air on July 17, 1965. ARAMCO had earlier initiated a television service for its employees in Dhahran in 1957.

The government-controlled Saudi Arabian Television (SATV) operates on a network of 140 stations, including 6 main stations in Riyadh, Jeddah, Medina, Dammam, Qassim, and Abha. The SATV operates two television channels, the first in Arabic and the second in English with some programming in French. Color television was introduced in 1976. Saudi Arabia uses SECAM (Sequence Couleur a Memoire) color standard for its domestic viewers and PAL (phase alternate line) standard to reach other nations in the Persian Gulf. Television signals reached 95 percent of the total area of the kingdom in 1991. There were 4.5 million television receivers in the kingdom in 1991, or 304 sets per 1,000 people (*World Radio TV Handbook,* 1992, p. 403).

The Arabic-language channel is on the air from 7:00 A.M. to 9:30 A.M. and from 2:00 P.M. to 9:30 P.M. Saturday through Wednesday, and from 7:00 A.M. to 9:30 P.M. on Thursdays and Fridays. The program distribution comprised seven categories: religion and culture, 25 percent; news and information, 15 percent; local and Arabic drama, 15 percent; children, 15 percent; variety and musical, 12 percent; sports, 10 percent; and foreign films and series, 8 percent (Ministry of Information, 1991). The programming fare ranges from live broadcasts of the prayer rites in the sacred cities of Mecca and Medina, news about the Arab World, school programs, family dramas, and sports to foreign films. The religion and culture category assumes a primary role because of Saudi Arabia's special place in Islam.

Saudi Arabia imports a substantial amount of programming from other Arabic-speaking countries, especially Egypt, Lebanon, and Jordan, and Western programming from the United States, Britain, and France (Lee, 1988, p. 252). Cairo has been described as "the Hollywood of the Arab World" because of the volume and popularity of films and TV shows, mostly soap operas in Arabic, that it sends throughout the Middle East. Because Saudi Arabia has a far more conservative interpretation of Islam than Egypt or other Arab states, there are strict rules governing the acceptability of foreign programming.

Many of the imported programs are challenging the people's traditional values, on the one hand, and drawing strong opposition from religious leaders, on the other. Forty Saudi women were arrested in 1991 while driving their own cars in a demonstration against the ban on women drivers in the kingdom. A group of ultraconservative religious figures, called the Committee for the Defense of Legitimate Rights, is pressing to further institutionalize the power of the Islamic clergy over Saudi society and restrain the pace of modernization. The committee has demanded further restrictions on entertainment programs on television and radio. A member of this committee advocates severe punishment for the 40 women (*The Strait Times,* May 15, 1993, p. 18). However, despite the strong opposition of religious leaders, television continues to be a very popular medium of communication.

There has been a concerted effort to engage local and regional talent in the development of indigenous program production. The seven nations bordering on the Arabian Gulf formed Gulfvision in 1977, with headquarters in Saudi Arabia, to cooperate in the development and production of programs. It has produced highly popular programs, such as the Arabic version of *Sesame Street.*

In addition to the government-owned television stations, a private noncommercial television station founded by ARAMCO in 1957 is available in the Dhahran area, the center of the oil industry. Known as Channel 3 TV, it is on the air from 6:00 A.M. to 9:00 P.M. The station's programming consists primarily of English-language films to cater to the large expatriate community in this region. Unlike the government-owned stations, Channel 3 operates on the PAL color standard. Saudis living along the east coast can also pick up a variety of stations from the Gulf countries.

Cable Television

The current Saudi government policy does not allow cable television in the country, and the private reception of television programming via satellite dish is also illegal. Satellite dishes, however, are beginning to appear on the rooftops of some of the homes, even though the importation and sale of such equipment for private use are illegal. In an interview, a Saudi government official said that smuggled or illegally imported satellite television equipment is available in the country, with the full package, including installation, costing from $4,000 to $8,000.

The package allows the buyer to receive television broadcasts from Arab states, including a common pan-Arab service, via the ARABSAT (Arab Satellite Communications Organization), in addition to STAR TV from Hong Kong and channels from Turkey, Russia, and western Europe. STAR TV offers Cable News Network (CNN), BBC (British Broadcasting Corporation) Asia, and two entertainment channels. It is estimated that from 3 to 6 percent of Saudi homes have such dishes. The Saudi government apparently tolerates the use of such equipment because it is not widely used and the programming from satellite channels available is mostly informational. The entertainment programming is also not found to be offensive so far (T. Siddik, personal interview, May 19, 1993).

NEW TECHNOLOGIES

Because of the primarily didactic and religious nature of Saudi television programming, videocassette recorders (VCRs) have been highly popular in the country since they appeared on the market in the early 1970s. Wealthy Saudis returning from the West brought back Sony half-inch VCRs to watch TV programs and films that were more entertaining than those offered by the government stations. Some Saudi leaders as a result declared their country the first video society and the first country to demonstrate that the government's gatekeeper role was over (Dunnett, 1990, p. 205). By 1983, there were 450,000 VCRs in Saudi Arabia, placing it ninth among the top ten countries in terms of the absolute numbers of VCRs in use (Head, 1985, p. 227). By 1986, 75 percent of the Saudi homes owned VCRs (Boyd, Straubhaar, & Lent, 1989, p. 66).

Two studies cited by Boyd, Straubhaar, & Lent (1989, p. 89) indicate that series and films imported from the United States and Egypt are especially popular among VCR users in Saudi Arabia. The most popular type of material rented was the thriller, followed by love stories and variety programs such as comedy acts and programs featuring singing and dancing. Kung fu films from the Far East, Indian films, and programs from other Asian countries are also widely available in the country.

In the area of telecommunications, oil-rich Saudi Arabia has invested in the most modern technology available and taken the lead in pushing links among Arab states via communication satellites. It contributed the largest share, 25 percent, of the $100 million cost of ARABSAT, a regional satellite system launched in 1985 to serve the 21-member Arab League. The satellite is operated by ARABSAT, a multinational organization based in Riyadh, Saudi Arabia. It is intended for the exclusive use of member Arab broadcasters, who are linked together through the Arab States Broadcasting Union (ASBU) founded in 1969. The Tunis-based ASBU, with Saudi Arabia as a founding member, was created to strengthen cooperation among broadcasting organizations in the Arab states. The ASBU has become a vital news source for regional events and for Western TV news reports, via satellite links with the European Broadcasting Union and national networks in North America. The ASBU coordinates daily news exchange and weekly exchanges of television programs from member countries via ARABSAT.

Saudi Arabia is also the ninth largest investment shareholder of the International Telecommunications Satellite Organization (INTELSAT), which provides a choice of satellite telecommunications services to users around the world (Dyson & Humphreys, 1990, p. 60). According to the Saudi Ministry of Information, the kingdom has now risen to seventh position in the world, and to second position in Asia after Japan, in the use of satellites.

The country began to switch to fiber optics technology in 1987, when the Swedish manufacturer of telecommunications equipment, Ericsson, was awarded a major contract to lay fiber optics cables in the country. By 1992, about 50 percent of the country's domestic telecommunications traffic was via fiber optics lines and the remaining via a microwave system. The microwave system was established as a substitute to the general network cable lines.

MOTION PICTURES

There are no cinemas in Saudi Arabia because the government prohibits public exhibition of films. All showings, therefore, are organized privately or on a non-profit-making basis. The television service of the Ministry of Information has a film unit that produces films for television. There are no commercial film production companies in Saudi Arabia. Public cinemas are outlawed for several reasons, the most important being that the government feels it would lose control over what would be shown. The religious leaders have been especially concerned about the depiction of women in Western and even Egyptian films that is liable to arouse sexual excitement. Other objections to films include references to Christianity and Judaism, alcoholic beverages, inappropriately attired women, kissing, sex, and excessive violence (Boyd, Straubhaar, & Lent, 1989, p. 57).

The Saudis allow movies to be shown in the large expatriate compounds. ARAMCO, for example, has routinely shown films to its employees for years. Other international firms operating in Saudi Arabia have also been allowed to do the same. The Saudis also allowed private movie rental businesses before the age of the VCR, which charged $50 for a 16-mm projector and film for 24 hours. This was allowed because the showings were not public and the clientele were upscale, influential people including government officials. The movies were also carefully screened for their acceptability before being allowed into the country (Boyd, Straubhaar, & Lent, 1989, p. 58).

MEDIA OWNERSHIP AND FINANCIAL SUPPORT PATTERNS

Private ownership of the press is allowed in the country but not to individuals or families. Under the 1963 Press and Publication Law, each publisher must form a licensed organization according to guidelines set by the law. These concerns are called *press establishments,* and all printing and publishing are placed in their hands. The law stipulates that a press establishment must be made up of at least 15 people experienced in newspaper publishing and administration. They all must be Saudi citizens, and the group must have a minimum capital base as prescribed in the law.

There are ten press establishments in the country. Their names, locations, and publications are: Al-Bilad Publishing Organization, Jeddah (*Al-Bilad,* daily; *Iqra'a,* periodical); Dar al-Yaum Press, Printing and Publishing, Dammam (*Al-Yaum,* daily); Al-Jazirah Organization for Press, Printing and Publishing, Riyadh (*Al-Jazirah* and *Al-Masaeyah,* dailies); Al-Medina Press Establishment, Jeddah (*Al-Medina al-Munawara,* daily); International Publications Agency, Dhahran Airport (publishes material of local interest); Mecca Printing and Information Establishment, Mecca (*An-Nadwah,* daily); Okaz Organization for Press and Publication, Jeddah (*Okaz* and *Saudi Gazette,* dailies; *Child,* weekly); Saudi Publishing and Distributing House, Jeddah (publishers, importers, and distributors of English and Arabic books); Saudi Research and Marketing Company, Jeddah (*Arab News* and *Asharq al-Awsat,* dailies; *Al-Majallah, Al-Muslimoon,* and *Sayidati,* weeklies); and Al-Yamama Press Establishment, Riyadh (*Al-Riyadh,* daily; *Al-Yamama,* weekly). Several periodicals are also published by government-approved religious, cultural, and literary groups. The government itself is involved in a number of publications.

Most of the press is financed by the royalty—attributed to the fact that even though the press establishments are privately owned, most are closely associated with the royal family. One major establishment, the Saudi Research and Marketing Company, is owned by members of the royal family. The state also provides newsprint at subsidized rates. Newsprint consumption in 1989 was 28,000 metric tons, or 2,064 kilograms per 1,000 inhabitants. This was twice the average for Arab states for that year (*Statistical Yearbook,* 1991). Advertising and circulation sales are other sources of revenue.

Other than the ARAMCO radio and television stations in the Dhahran area, the government holds a monopoly in broadcasting. All operating costs of the state-owned broadcasting stations, therefore, have come from the government, although the situation has changed somewhat for television. The Saudi government, noting that advertising has been highly successful on video tapes, began to accept television advertising in 1986 on both channels. However, commercial income provides a very small portion of the system's operating cost. The government continues to provide most of the financing. There is no advertising on radio, and it is financed entirely by the government (*Statistical Yearbook,* 1991).

MEDIA REGULATION

Although other government departments are also involved, control of the media is achieved primarily through the Ministry of Information, which has the national news agency and the broadcasting services under its control and is responsible for applying the censorship regulations.

Press Decree of 1953

Government involvement in the mass media first came in 1953 when King Saud issued a decree to establish a government agency to oversee their functions. The agency, called the General Directorate of Broadcasting, Press, and Publication, was assigned the task of organizing, coordinating, and supervising all mass media in the country. It was also responsible for providing official news to the press and the supervision of both programming and operational aspects of broadcasting (Ministry of Information, 1991).

The General Directorate did not engage in prepublication censorship but kept a close watch on the press against any "offensive" information. Such information would include attacks on the institution of the royal family, mention of the term *Israel* rather than *Arab Palestine,* praise or condemnation of a foreign state in a manner not consistent with the Saudi foreign policy, and infringement of the Islamic religious codes. Any violation of this unwritten code could result in the suspension of the publication involved (Nyrop, 1977, p. 194).

Press Decree of 1958

The General Directorate's Publications Department was given the power of censorship under the royal decree of 1958. The department, with its headquarters in Riyadh, has branches in all major cities in the kingdom and also maintains its operations at airports, seaports, and post offices to scrutinize publications coming from abroad.

The General Directorate of Broadcasting, Press, and Publications was replaced by the Ministry of Information established in 1963 under a royal decree. The creation of this cabinet-level office indicated the importance the government attached to the expanding information activities in the kingdom. Also in 1963, the government promulgated the Press and Publication Law, which imposed still greater controls on the press.

The Press and Publication Law

The 1963 Press and Publication Law continues to apply to the Saudi Arabian press. It states that the press is private and the government has no right to interfere except to protect "general welfare." The phrase "general welfare" has not been defined specifically for purposes of the law, but it is generally understood to mean that journalists may not write anything that is likely to cause friction between the government and citizens or adversely affect "each citizen's duty towards his religion, country and community" (Ministry of Information, 1991).

The law also states that journalists may not criticize the government or any government body, the royal family, heads of friendly states, or the clergy and may not offend Islam or the Islamic law of Sharia or support atheism. Editors in chief are held responsible for the publication of everything in their newspapers, and journalists accused of breach of the regulations are tried by emergency courts.

Under the law, all newspapers must be printed and published by licensed press establishments. These are nominally independent, but the chairs of their boards and editors of individual publications are appointed, and may be dismissed, by the government, which must also approve all other board members. The law also requires that all editorial functions must be supervised by a committee formed from members of the establishment. The government may revoke a license or stop a newspaper from publishing.

A censorship committee, comprising officials of the judiciary, the Publications Department of the Ministry of Information, and the Department of Education, reviews and censors all national and foreign publications according to the policies of the state, including the 1958 censorship decree (Article 19, 1991, p. 388).

Video Legislation of 1980

With approximately half of the population owning VCRs by 1980, the Ministry of Information became increasingly concerned about the control of incoming videotape material. Rules governing video came into effect in February 1980 and were to be enforced by the Ministry of Information.

The legislation provides specific guidelines for those eligible to own and operate a video store. The owner must (1) be a Saudi citizen of at least 18 years of age, (2) be a full-time store operator and not a student, and (3) have no criminal record. The legislation also stipulates that the video store must be on a main road with a visible entrance and away from a mosque. Women are not allowed to enter video rental or sales shops.

The legislation prohibits "material contradicting the Islamic faith or morals or adversely affecting the security of the country." It says the goal of films and tapes should be "the dissemination of culture, knowledge and innocent entertainment." All films and tapes, whether imported or produced locally, are subject to censorship and approval before being made available to the public. The Ministry of Information has the right to cancel a license at any time without mentioning its reasons for doing so (Ministry of Information, 1992).

Regulation of Television

The 1982 information policy, mentioned earlier, also deals with television. The policy prohibits the following: anything that opposes or offends Islam, preaching and advocating of other religions, the customs and rituals of people other than Muslims, the showing of alcoholic drinks or people drinking or referring to it in the dialogue, scenes or words about pork and bacon, religious pictures, and all nude statues. The policy also prohibits scenes of kissing, embracing, adultery, and scenes liable to arouse sexual excitement. It also bans scenes of bars and clubs, drug taking, and dancing except folklore and national dancing in decent clothes.

In the political arena, the policy prohibits everything that contradicts and offends the government or rulers, all political and party principles and slogans that contradict the country's policy, and strikes and demonstrations (Boyd, Straubhaar, & Lent, 1989, pp. 71–72).

EXTERNAL MEDIA SERVICES

Five departments in the Ministry of Information coordinate external media services, with the External Communications Department being directly involved in information dissemination abroad.

Foreign-Language Broadcast Services

The Broadcasting Service of Saudi Arabia offers a daily service from Riyadh for listeners abroad in 11 languages: Bambara, Bengali, English, Farsi, French, Indonesian, Somali, Swahili, Turkestani, Turkish, and Urdu. Target areas for the service's programming are Iran; central, West-central, and East Africa; central, south, and Southeast Asia; Turkey; and eastern and western Europe. This foreign-language service is in addition to the domestic radio services, which are also targeted to listeners abroad. Saudi Arabia also feeds selected domestic television programming to viewers abroad through ARABSAT and ASBU. The ASBU maintains satellite links with the European Broadcasting Union and national networks in North America for further transmission of television programs from Saudi Arabia and other member Arab states.

Conversely, overseas broadcasters have a good listenership in Saudi Arabia. Many urban Saudis are avid listeners of the Arabic-language services of the British Broadcasting Corporation and the Voice of America. The English-language services of these stations, particularly news broadcasts, are also highly popular among the expatriate community from the West and other countries. Other international stations having appeal among the Saudis are Egypt's Radio Cairo and the Voice of Israel.

Foreign-Language Newspapers and Magazines

A variety of printed information, including newsletters, magazines, books, and pamphlets, is made available for foreign readers. *Ash-Sharq al-Awsat,* in Arabic, and *Arab News,* in English, are the most widely read Saudi dailies abroad. The most popular Saudi periodicals abroad, especially in the Middle East, are *Al-Majallah,* the current affairs magazine, and *Sayidati,* the weekly for women. The religious monthly *Hajj,* in Arabic and English, is also widely read in the Muslim world.

About 2,000 newspapers and magazines from abroad are available in the kingdom, with 154 in Arabic and 1,841 in European languages. They include the *International Herald Tribune,* the *Times,* the *Guardian,* the *Economist, Time, Newsweek, Paris Match,* and *Der Speigel.* All imported publications, however, are subject to close scrutiny by Saudi government censors before being admitted. Offensive photographs are either blacked out or covered with plain white paper, and writing found unsuitable is removed from the publication before its distribution (T. Siddik, personal interview, May 19, 1993).

NEWS AGENCIES

Most of the news in Saudi Arabia is gathered and distributed by the government-controlled Saudi Press Agency (SPA) established in 1970. Operating under the jurisdiction of the Ministry of Information, its primary function is to centralize and bring regional and national news to the different channels of information inside and outside the country. The SPA supplies news and features in Arabic and English to both print and broadcast organizations in the country. For international news, the media also rely on other Arab and international agencies, although their copy is subject to censorship to comply with Saudi publication laws.

The SPA is a founding member of the Arab News Agencies Federation, the Gulf News Agency, the Islamic News Agency, and the Non-Aligned News Agencies Pool. The Islamic Press Agency is the second of the two news agencies in Saudi Arabia, with its focus on covering events from the Islamic perspective.

Compliance with the wishes of the royal family and the demands of religious leaders, therefore, are the first considerations of a reporter. In addition, newspapers regularly receive guidelines from the Ministries of Information or Interior on government positions on controversial issues.

Article 19 (1991, p. 388) notes that as a result of such interference the daily press has become repetitive, expressing only official opinions, praising the royal family and with comment on subjects irrelevant to the political and economic life of the country. For reasons such as these, William Rugh (1979) classified the Saudi press as "loyalist." There is no tradition of objective reporting of the news. On any given day, stories reported by the staff of the English-language daily *Arab News,* for example, convey the impression of a society on the move without any problems. The treatment of events outside the kingdom and the Arab World is far more candid. Protecting the interests of Islam and its adherents always comes first, even at the expense of objectivity. Such treatment of issues becomes understandable, however, in view of the fact that the Saudi government is trying to mold the society around a Quranic base.

No international news agency had a bureau in Saudi Arabia as of 1991, although such agencies employed local journalists as stringers. Foreign journalists are allowed to visit Saudi Arabia only in exceptional circumstances. During the Gulf War, for example, the Saudi authorities admitted great numbers of journalists from other countries. Foreign papers critical of Saudi policies, or containing advertisements for alcoholic beverages, or depicting beach scenes are automatically confiscated (Article 19, 1991, p. 388).

THE ROLE OF MEDIA IN NATIONAL DEVELOPMENT

Mass media are used for both curricular instruction and national development in Saudi Arabia, although the use in the former category is limited to closed-circuit television. Because males and females are segregated in Saudi universities, closed-circuit television is used to impart lessons to female students sitting in a classroom separate from the one where the lecture is delivered by the teacher to male students. Female students can put questions to the teacher by using a microphone. The use of closed-circuit television for such instruction is also attributed to a shortage of qualified people to teach at the university level.

Over-the-air broadcasting is not used in Saudi Arabia for any distance education program of the type provided by Britain's Open University, for example. Both of Saudi Arabia's television channels are used, however, to teach Arabic to the expatriate population. Interested persons can tune in to such lessons of 30-minute duration provided two to three times a week. There are no formal requirements of homework or exams that normally go with formal distance education programs.

Saudi broadcasting, especially television, is used considerably more for national development. A variety of campaigns are carried out on the air on a daily basis. They include: Keep environment clean, dispose of garbage properly, keep stereo volume down, respect traffic laws, wear seat belts, donate blood, and reduce electricity consumption. Such campaigns, conducted in the afternoon and during prime time, are done through short public service announcements and longer discussion programs. Development campaigns are initiated by the ministries concerned, who retain public relations companies to produce the message professionally.

CONCLUSION

As anywhere else in the world, the Saudi press is the product of the country's political system. The kingdom has no constitution, parliament, or elected bodies of any kind. As a result, no principle of freedom of the press exists, and there is little opportunity for popular participation in the administration of the country. Not only is the political system an absolute monarchy, ultraconservative in outlook; it is also based on the Quranic law of Sharia. The country's vast religious establishment therefore has a strong influence on the political and social life through its strictest interpretation of the Sharia.

From the Saudi perspective, the primary responsibility of the political and religious establishments is to mold the people around the Quranic way of life because Saudi Arabia is the birthplace of Islam and keeper of the faith for the entire Muslim world. A society based on such a strong religious code understandably does not see political or press freedoms, or secularism, compatible with its mission. As long as the Saudi press respects these basic tenets of the society, it is allowed to operate unhindered.

It is unlikely that the Saudi press situation would change in the near future. The religious Right claims that the Islamic traditions are being eroded because of liberal influences in the Saudi society. It has partly blamed the Western media products for that erosion and is demanding further restrictions on entertainment programming on radio and television. The religious Right also wants to further institutionalize the power of the Islamic clergy over Saudi society through the establishment of Islamic committees in every ministry and government office. The Saudi government appears to be resisting such demands, but it cannot altogether ignore them because religion is the very core of its existence.

REFERENCES

Article 19 World Report. (1991). *Information, freedom and censorship.* London: Library Association Publishing.

Boyd, D. A., Straubhaar, J. D., & Lent, J. A. (1989). *Videocassette recorders in the Third World.* New York: Longman.

Drost, H. (Ed.). (1991). *The world's news media.* Essex, United Kingdom: Longman Current Affairs.

Dunnett, P. (1990). *The world television industry.* London: Routledge.

Dyson, K., & Humphreys, P. (Eds.). (1990). *The political economy of communications.* London: Routledge.

The Europa world yearbook. (1992). Saudi Arabia. London: Europa Publications.

Head, S. W. (1985). *World broadcasting systems.* Belmont, CA: Wadsworth.

Keesing's record of world events. (1992, March). Saudi Arabia: Decree on Consultative Council. Harlow-Essex, England.

Lee, W. L. (Ed.). (1988). Saudi Arabia. In Philip T. Rosen, *International handbook of broadcasting systems.* Westport, CT: Greenwood Press.

Lowenstein, R. (1976). Press freedom as a barometer of political democracy. In H-D Fischer & J. C. Merrill. (Eds.), *International and intercultural communication.* New York: Hastings House.

The Middle East and North Africa. (1993). Saudi Arabia. London: Europa Publications.

Ministry of Information, Kingdom of Saudi Arabia. (1991). *Report of the Saudi Press Agency on the kingdom's mass media.* Riyadh: Ministry of Information.

Ministry of Information, Kingdom of Saudi Arabia. (1992). *Information and communications.* Riyadh: Ministry of Information.

Ministry of Information, Kingdom of Saudi Arabia. (1993). *Radio broadcast schedule: Nov. 1, 1992–March 7, 1993.* Riyadh: Ministry of Information.

Nyrop, R. F. (1977). *Area handbook for Saudi Arabia.* Washington, DC: U.S. Government Printing Office.

Rugh, W. (1979). *The Arab press* (2nd ed.). Syracuse, NY: Syracuse University Press.

Saudi Government Acts to Rein in Muslim Dissidents. (1993, May 15). *Strait Times,* p. 18.

Statistical yearbook. (1991). UNESCO. Paris: UNESCO.

World radio TV handbook. (1992). New York: Billboard.

18

SYRIA

Arvind Singhal and Vijay Krishna

INTRODUCTION

Although Syria only gained its independence from France in 1946, it is one of the oldest inhabited lands in the world. Its history and geography are closely intertwined with those of Lebanon, Jordan, Iraq, and Palestine. These modern nation-states, created as a result of the defeat of the Turkish Ottoman Empire in World War I, were previously part of what was commonly referred to as "Greater Syria."

The Syrian Arab Republic covers an area of about 71,500 square miles and is slightly larger than the state of Oklahoma in the United States. The country lies south of Turkey and west of Iraq. Syria's southern frontier is bordered by Jordan, and to its west are the Mediterranean Sea, Lebanon, and Israel. From the perspective of military and trade, Syria occupies a highly strategic geographic location. The three continents of Asia, Africa, and Europe converge here; in addition, Syria serves as a crossroad between the Caspian Sea, the Indian Ocean, the Black Sea, and the River Nile. Consequently, Syria is a melting pot of diverse cultures, religions, and beliefs. Damascus is Syria's capital city.

In 1992, Syria's population was about 13 million and growing rapidly at a rate of 3.8 percent per year. Thanks to improved health facilities, the average life expectancy in Syria has climbed to about 65 years. If the present growth continues, the Syrian population will double by the year 2010. In 1992, some 50 percent of the Syrian people were under the age of 15.

The official language of Syria is Arabic. Nearly all Syrians speak Syrian

Arabic, a dialect with a slightly different pronunciation, even though it has many cognates in common with modern standard Arabic. Kurdish is spoken in the extreme northeastern part of Syria where the nation's Kurds reside (near the border with Iraq). The Armenian and Turkoman communities (relatively small in population size) speak Armenian and Turkic languages. Also, as a result of colonial influences, many people in Syria, especially those living in urban areas, can speak French and/or English.

Some 85 percent of Syrian people follow the Islamic faith, which is divided into two sects: the Sunni and the Shi'a. In Syria, as in most of the Arab world, Sunni Muslims represent the largest group, making up about 72 percent of the nation's Islamic population. At present, the Alawites, a subgroup of the Shi'a sect, dominate political activity in Syria. Christians account for about 10 percent of the Syrian population, of which the Greek Orthodox are the majority.

Since the early 1960s, when the Ba'ath Party came to power, socialist policies such as shared landownership and state control of industries have guided Syria's economic development. In recent years, the government has encouraged greater private sector involvement in developing business enterprises, especially in agribusiness, food processing, and pharmaceuticals. Private sector investment is projected to rise steeply to about U.S.$20 billion by 1995 (1991). A new investment law of 1990 encourages the private sector to establish new businesses with foreign capital. The Syrian government spends over 50 percent of its annual budget on the military, a reflection of its ongoing conflict with neighboring Israel. This highly restricts the investment of limited resources in more productive development-oriented enterprises.

In 1992, only about 30 percent of the Syrian work force was involved in agriculture, down from 50 percent in the 1970s. Agriculture is presently second to oil in terms of foreign exchange earnings. Oil production in Syria, which is presently increasing at an annual rate of 17 percent (the highest rate in the Middle East), brought in over U.S.$5 billion's worth of hard currency in 1992, in addition to employing over 25,000 people. Until the 1960s, Syria's industrial sector was primarily agro based; factory workers were employed mainly in making cigarettes, weaving cloth, extracting olive oil, and packing dried fruit. Now Syrian factory workers also manufacture glass, paper, fertilizers, cement, iron and steel, television sets, and household appliances.

Since independence in 1946, the Syrian government has actively promoted literacy. Schools encourage young Syrians to acquire vocational skills needed in industry and in modern agriculture. Also, education is viewed as the primary vehicle of training young citizens in the ideology of the ruling Ba'ath (or literally "Correctionist") Party. Elementary school is compulsory for boys and girls between 6 and 11 years of age although dropouts are a common occurrence. Students have access to higher education at several universities and technical training institutes. The University of Damascus, the University of Aleppo, and Tishrin University in Latakia are premier teaching and research institutions.

Educational costs for its citizens are completely underwritten by the Syrian government.

Syria is officially a republic. Citizens over the age of 18 elect a president who must be a Muslim and who is nominated by the Ba'ath Party, the nation's official political organization. Since 1971, Hafez al-Assad has served as president of Syria. The president, who serves a seven-year term and can be reelected an indefinite number of times, has wide powers that include naming a cabinet, commanding the army, and dissolving the legislature. Syria's legislature, or People's Council, consists of 195 elected representatives who serve a four-year term. Administratively, Syria is divided into 14 provinces, one of which is Damascus. The central government appoints a governor for each province, who is then assisted by an elected provincial council. The provincial governors maintain strong links with the central government in Damascus and help implement the central government's political agenda.

The communication philosophy of Syria, reflected in the broader goals of its mass media system, has roots in Syria's pre– and post–World War I history. A strong undercurrent of nationalism and Pan-Arabism forms the basis of Syria's mass communication philosophy, which is understandable given that Syria's land has been occupied many times: the Turks prior to World War I, the French after World War I, and the contentious Israeli occupation of the Golan Heights. The structure of the Syrian mass media and its functions are focused on promoting Arab culture, patriotism, and nationalism.

Syria's communication philosophy is also influenced by the socialist ideology of its government: the belief that mass media can do good when it is in the hands of the government. The Syrian Ministry of Information (formed in 1960) aggressively implements Syria's communication philosophy. The print and broadcast media in Syria, without exception, are a reflection of the government in power.

PRINT MEDIA

The print media in Syria is strongly influenced by the ruling Ba'ath Party. In a sense, most Syrian journalists are "employees" of the Ba'ath Party, with an explicit or implicit mission to propagate the party's ideology. Most publications have affiliations with either a political or a religious group, although some are published by professional associations and trade unions. Many publications are produced by government ministries.

The history of the Syrian press can be understood in three phases:

- *Phase I (1908–1946).* Until 1908, the Syrian press was strongly regulated by the ruling Turkish Ottoman regime. Then for a decade or so, there was a brief reprieve for the Syrian journalists as certain influential Turks forced the Ottoman regime to loosen its stronghold. After World War I, and before its independence (in 1946), the Syrian press was largely controlled and regulated by the French. Licenses were issued to those publications that favored the ruling French power.

- *Phase II (1946–1963).* After the French colonial rule was lifted in 1946, newspapers became politically active. During this period, the country experienced a ''high degree of political activity'' (Rugh, 1987). The frequent change of power in the government, and the internal competition among contenders for power, was reflected in the press. Almost all newspapers were owned and operated by individuals with strong political affiliations.
- *Phase III (1963 to present).* Since 1963, one wing or another of the Ba'ath Party has ruled Syria (Rugh, 1987). The Syrian press has been largely influenced by the socialist stance of the Ba'ath regime. The structure of the press has been modified according to socialist patterns. The government plays a big role in deciding what news is in the greater public interest. To begin a new newspaper or periodical, one must apply for a government license (Rugh, 1987; Boyd, 1982; *Europa World Year Book,* 1992).

The daily newspapers account for a total circulation of 266,000 (*World Media Handbook,* 1992). The nine major Arabic-language newspapers and one major English-language newspaper are listed in Table 18.1. The major Arabic newspapers are *Al-Ba'ath* and *Tishrin* with circulations of over 75,000. Table 18.2 lists the major Arabic-language periodicals in Syria.

ELECTRONIC MEDIA

Radio

Radio broadcasting began in Syria in 1946 with the formation of the Syrian Broadcasting Organization. Administratively, radio was located in the office of the prime minister until 1959, when it became part of the newly formed Ministry of Information. In 1950, the government boosted the power of the radio transmission system from 13.6 kilowatts to 150 kilowatts, bringing many remote regions of Syria within the reach of a radio signal (Rugh, 1987). In the main cities of Aleppo and Damascus, four medium wave transmitters were established to broadcast radio programs in English, French, Turkish, and Hebrew. Shortwave transmitters were also installed to broadcast Syrian radio programs to other foreign countries. However, until the early 1960s, lack of funds and a lack of government commitment to radio limited radio's expansion in Syria. Unlike Jordan and Egypt, Syria did not have strong, stable political leadership to implement the expansion of radio personnel, transmitters, and studio facilities (Boyd, 1982).

Syria's radio and television services were greatly influenced by its union with Egypt between 1958 and 1961. Many Egyptian radio employees came to Syria, and many Syrian media officials went to Egypt for training. Syrian radio officials learned the Egyptian technique of using radio for propaganda purposes, which proved to be useful when the Egypt-Syria unification pact crumbled in 1961 and

Table 18.1
The Major Daily Newspapers in Syria

Name of Publication	Place of Publication	Time	Language	Circulation
Al-Ba'ath (Renaissance)	Damascus	Morning	Arabic	75.000
Al-Fida (Redemption)	Hama	Morning	Arabic	4.000
Al-Jamahir al-Arabia (The Arab People)	Aleppo	Morning	Arabic	10.000
Al-Orouba	Homs	Morning	Arabic	5.000
Ash-Shabab (Youth)	Aleppo	Morning	Arabic	9.000
Al-Thawra (Revolution)	Damascus	Morning	Arabic	75.000
Al-Wahdah (Unity)	Latakia	Morning	Arabic	10.000
Barq ash-Shimal (The Syrian Telegraph)	Aleppo	Morning	Arabic	6.400
Syria Times	Damascus	Morning	English	12.000
Tishrin (October)	Damascus	Morning	Arabic	75.000

Source: Compiled from data in *World Media Handbook,* 1992; and *Europa World Year Book,* 1992.

also in subsequent years with hostility mounting against neighboring Israel (Boyd, 1982). By 1965, Syria had installed 16 radio transmitters that could broadcast radio programs to the entire nation (Boyd, 1982).

While medium wave broadcasting flourished in Syria, shortwave broadcasting witnessed a decline in the 1960s and the 1970s. A lack of commitment to shortwave broadcasting and poor infrastructural maintenance led to the deactivation of all shortwave transmitters in 1978. In the 1980s, five 150-kilowatt replacement transmitters with sophisticated antenna systems were installed (Boyd, 1982).

In 1992, there were a total of 29 transmitters and 3 million radio receivers in Syria (*World Media Handbook,* 1992). Syrian radio broadcasts programs in 11 languages: Arabic (major language of radio programming in Syria), French, English, Russian, German, Spanish, Portuguese, Hebrew, Polish, Turkish, and

Table 18.2
The Major Arabic-Language Periodicals in Syria

Name of Periodical	Place of Publication	Periodicity	Language
Al-Daad (Literary)	Aleppo	Monthly	Arabic
Al Funoon (The Arts)	Damascus	Weekly	Arabic
Al Iktisaad (Financial)	Damascus	Monthly	Arabic
Al Mara'a Al Arabiah	Damascus	Monthly	Arabic
Al-Maseerah (Progress)	Damascus	Weekly	Arabic
Al-Maukef Al Arabi	Damascus	Monthly	Arabic
Al-Mawkif al-Arabi (The Arab Situation)	Damascus	Monthly	Arabic
Al Thakafah (Cultural)	Damascus	Monthly	Arabic
Al Usbu' Al Adabi (Literary)	Damascus	Weekly	Arabic
Kifah Al Ummal Al Ishtiraki	Damascus	Weekly	Arabic
Nidal Al Fallaheen	Damascus	Weekly	Arabic

Source: Compiled from data in the *World Media Handbook,* 1992; and *Europa World Year Book,* 1992.

Bulgarian. Overseas shortwave broadcasts are targeted mainly to sympathetic expatriate Syrians, who escaped to Europe, North America, and Latin American countries during the Ottoman rule.

Radio broadcasts from the central studios in Damascus are available in Syria, except for a few hours in the early morning. Newscasts, drama, interviews, music, capsules on agriculture, health, and sanitation form the basic radio fare. While mainly designed for the Syrian audience, radio broadcasts are also intended for neighboring states. The content of radio programs is strongly influenced by the Ba'ath Party ideology. Media officials of such countries as Jordan,

Iraq, and Israel continuously monitor Syrian radio broadcasts to gauge possible shifts in Syrian policies that might affect them (Boyd, 1982).

Television

Syria's television system began in 1960 after the country briefly unified with Egypt to form the United Arab Republic (Boyd, 1982). The United Arab Republic forged a contract with the Radio Corporation of America (RCA) to implement a comprehensive television system in Syria. Both Syria and Egypt started their official television broadcasts on July 23, 1960 (Boyd, 1982). During the early years of Syrian television, Egyptian programming dominated nightly telecasts (Boyd, 1982). In fact, after the United Arab Republic collapsed in 1961 (with Egypt and Syria separating), Syrian officials blamed Nasser for having promoted the Syrian television system in order to have an eastern relay for Egyptian television programming (Boyd, 1982). During the 1960s and early 1970s, the facilities for television broadcasting did not expand rapidly in Syria owing to limited budget allocations and the frequent change of government leadership. Four studio facilities were built in Damascus in the 1960s, and television stations were also built in the cities of Aleppo and Homs in the 1960s.

Four major factors contributed to the rapid rise of television in Syria in the 1970s. First, the Ministry of Information with the Directorate General of Radio and Television embarked on an ambitious plan to install transmitters and relay stations in various parts of Syria. One motivation for installing relay stations was the increased availability of television signals from such neighboring countries as Jordan and Iraq. Particularly attractive was the Western entertainment programming broadcast on Jordanian channels (Boyd, 1982). Second, the Syrian Ministry of Industry began its collaboration with Siemens of Germany to assemble TV sets in Syria under the brand name of Syronex and to sell them to Syrian audiences at subsidized prices. At this point, the government also eliminated the television license fee, which also helped spur the sales of TV sets in Syria. Third, the Euphrates Dam was commissioned in Syria in the 1970s, which made possible large-scale electrification of almost every household in Syria, consequently encouraging the Syrian people to adopt television sets. Finally, several expatriate Syrians who worked in the Gulf brought home several thousands of television sets (Khudr, S. Personal Communication, January and March 1993).

By 1989, Syria had an estimated 710,000 television sets in the country (*Europa World Year Book,* 1992), and it was estimated that in 1992 at least 80 percent of all Syrian households owned a TV set. Many of these television sets are black and white, since color transmission only began in the late 1970s. Syrian television signals reach all parts of the country and also spill over into neighboring countries.

In 1992, Syrian television had two major national-level channels. One channel, which began as an experiment in commercial programming for the Damascus area, broadcasts entertainment programming (including imported television shows) in Arabic, English, and French. Such programs as the U.S. serial *Dallas* and many other Egyptian, Jordanian, and Lebanese shows are highly popular with Syrian audiences and achieve high audience ratings. The second channel broadcasts entirely in the Arabic language. Programming on this channel typically begins at 2:00 P.M. and runs until midnight. On Fridays and Saturdays, the programming hours are extended, beginning in the morning and closing at midnight.

Programming on the Arabic channel is mostly government supported, and there is a strong emphasis on such issues as news and public affairs, maintenance of Arab culture, children's programming, and light entertainment. Educational programs are broadcast in the afternoon from 2:00 P.M. to 5:00 P.M. for middle and high school children. The subjects treated on television include Arabic literature, English, French, math, physics, and chemistry. From 5:00 P.M. to 6:30 P.M., children's programs are telecast (including animated cartoons, folk stories), followed by a half-hour news program consisting of international news, national news, and news related to governmental affairs. The news program is quite easily the most important program to both the government and the Syrian viewers, and the television personnel put a great deal of time and effort into producing this program. From 7:00 P.M. to 9:30 P.M., light entertainment programs, including Arabic-language serials, are shown. From 9:30 P.M. to about midnight, feature films and sports programs showing mainly soccer and boxing events are shown.

Television programs on Syrian television are sponsored by both government sources and commercial advertisers. The operating costs of the Arabic-language channel come from the Ministry of Information; so there is virtually no pressure to raise money through the sales of commercial advertisements. Commercial advertisements, however, are increasing in number on Syrian television, even though only 30 percent of the advertising revenue that is raised is retained by the Syrian television system; the remaining 70 percent goes to the Ministry of Finance (Boyd, 1982). A large portion of commercial advertising on Syrian television includes publicity for state-run consumer goods industries.

While the television system in Syria expanded rapidly in the late 1970s and the 1980s, it is unlikely that Syria will build an elaborate national multichannel television system on par with that of some other Arab countries (Boyd, 1982), as national priorities and economic constraints serve as limiting factors. Audience research on viewers' preferences or on the effects of Syrian television is virtually nonexistent.

NEW TECHNOLOGIES

Videocassette recorders (VCRs) are increasingly being adopted and are mainly used for entertainment purposes, including watching films, soap operas, and imported shows. Satellite dishes that can access overseas channels are highly controlled because of national security concerns. Owning a satellite dish requires government permission.

MOTION PICTURES

As in most Arab countries, motion pictures are a highly popular form of entertainment media in Syria. Syria started producing Arab-language movies in the early 1960s, and it produces about 15 to 20 movies a year. However, most Arabic-language movies are imported from Egypt, the "Hollywood of the Arab World," and from India. English and French movies are also screened on a regular basis in theaters in Damascus and other major cities. In most cities, some theaters feature exclusively foreign-language films, while others prefer to feature only Arab-language films. There are about 20 movie theaters in Damascus, a relatively small number when compared with the number of theaters in other major cities of the world. Islamic traditions, which restrict women's movement in public places, limit the numbers of theater-going audiences.

A government agency called the National Organization for Cinema, which is affiliated with the Ministry of Culture and National Guidance, produces documentaries and full-length feature films. Many have won high acclaim in the Arab and Western worlds.

All foreign movies, especially the non-Arab-language movies, have to be cleared by the Censor Board, which is part of the Ministry of Culture and National Guidance. The Censor Board follows strict guidelines to make sure that extreme violence, sex, and obscenities are banned from movies.

Many Syrian artists and technical personnel were educated in the former Eastern Bloc countries. Hence, their filmmaking style is highly influenced by their teachers from those countries. In Syria, the Institute of Theater and Public Art, which is affiliated with the Ministry of Culture and located in Damascus, is one of the few renowned schools that offers courses in acting and film production.

In recent years, the private sector involvement in film production has increased. The top private film producer is Duraid Lahham. A former professor of chemistry, Lahham is a popular movie star and producer of many hit films. His movies are a commentary on the political and social structures of Arab countries. They also deal with Arab culture and stereotypes. Much liked throughout the Arab World, Lahham's movies, some say, have "revolutionized pan-Arabism" (Imadi, 1992).

The movie industry in Syria has prospered in the last 20 years. The movies have shown a great deal of improvement in production techniques. Syria exports movies to other Arab countries such as Egypt, Jordan, and Lebanon.

MEDIA OWNERSHIP

Mass media ownership in Syria is mostly concentrated in the hands of the government, which exercises a high degree of control in running the print, film, and broadcast media and also in formulating policies for such new communication technologies as cable television, fiber optics, and computers. Private sector involvement in the form of commercial support for broadcasting and film production is limited but on the rise. The government strongly believes that the mass media and their messages have an important role to play in the development of the Syrian society and hence regulates it closely.

MEDIA REGULATION

The Syrian government regulates its mass media through a variety of licensing procedures, gatekeepers, and cultural guidelines. The Ministry of Information and the Ministry of Culture and National Guidance play an important role in determining the content of television programs and movies. Government approval is needed for beginning newspapers and owning satellite dishes. Often, certain media are more easy to regulate than are others. For instance, the privately run video industry is very hard to regulate even though strong guidelines about appropriate video content and anti–video piracy laws are in place.

EXTERNAL MEDIA SERVICES

Because of the prevalence of the English and French languages among Syrian elites, Syria's external services division is quite strong. Syrian radio broadcasts in 11 different languages, while television broadcasts in Arabic, French, and English. Major English and French newspapers and magazines are published in Syria on a variety of topics (see Table 18.3). There is a lot of two-way media exchange between Syria and such countries as Egypt, Turkey, Jordan, and Iraq.

NEWS AGENCIES

Syria established its own national news agency, Agence Arabe Syrienne d'Information, or Syrian Arab News Agency (SANA), in 1966 in Damascus. All Syrian media receive their news stories from SANA. This national news agency has agreements with almost all major international news agencies for procurement and supply of news items from within and outside of Syria. Many foreign news agencies such as National News Agency EFE (Spain), Agence France-Presse (AFP, France), Agenzia Nazionale Stampa Associata (ANSA, Italy), Allgemeiner Deutscher Nachrichtendiest (ADN, Germany) Deutsche Presse-Agentur (DPA, Germany), Associated Press (AP, United States), Informatsionnoye Telegrfnoe Agentsvo Rossii (ITAR, Russia), and Telegrafnoe Agentsvo Sovetskovo Soyuza (Tass, Russia) have bureaus in Syria.

THE ROLE OF MEDIA IN NATIONAL DEVELOPMENT

The Syrian government believes that the mass media can play an important role in the education and training of its citizens and contribute to national and regional development. Specifically, the government believes the media can:

Table 18.3
Foreign-Language Periodicals in Syria

Name of Periodical	Place of Publication	Periodicity	Language
Ecos	Damascus	Monthly	Spanish
Flash	Damascus	Monthly	English/French
Le Lien circ. 2,500	Damascus	Monthly	French
Monthly Survey of Arab Economics	Damascus	Monthly	English/French
Revue de la Presse Arabe	Damascus	2 a week	French
Syrie et Monde Arabe (Deals with economic, statistical, and political survey)	Damascus	Mmonthly	French/English

Source: Compiled from data in the *Europa World Year Book,* 1992.

- Promote the political, social, and cultural agenda of the Ba'ath Party in order that an appropriate climate for national development is created.
- Provide nonformal education and training to its citizens in the areas of health and hygiene, agriculture, and child development.
- Enhance Arab pride and promote "Pan-Arabism."

It is fair to say that the Syrian media has been successful in meeting at least some of its stated goals despite the criticism it has received of being a purely political propaganda apparatus.

CONCLUSION

The mass media system in Syria is strongly influenced by the ruling Ba'ath Party and is geared toward sustaining and promoting Arab culture, patriotism, and nationalism.

The print medium is a stronghold of the ruling party with many major publications having affiliations with government organizations. The broadcast media have seen some expansion in the last decade; the number of radio transmitters and television sets have increased rapidly since the 1980s. In accordance with the interests and policies of the government, Syrian radio broadcasts in different languages to reach many neighboring countries. The television industry has prospered in the last decade but at a guarded pace set by the government.

The motion picture industry of Syria has also seen some major changes in the quality and quantity of movies produced, especially since the 1980s. With a rise in the number of talented personnel and the increasing number of private entrepreneurs, the motion picture industry is bound to exert a strong influence in the Arab World.

These improvements in the motion picture industry in the last decade indicate that the ruling socialist Ba'ath Party is not totally opposed to the concept of free enterprise. However, since the government exercises a high degree of control in running the print, broadcast, and film media, and also in formulating policies for such new communication technologies as cable television, fiber optics, and computers, the future of the Syrian mass media in general will be determined by the government's communication philosophy.

REFERENCES

Boyd, D. A. (1982). *Broadcasting in the Arab World: A survey of radio and television in the Middle East.* Philadelphia: Temple University Press.

Europa world year book. (1992). London: Europa Publications Limited.

Rugh, W. A. (1987). *The Arab press: News media and political process in the Arab World* (2nd ed.). Syracuse: Syracuse University Press.

Syria. *Background notes.* (1986). Washington DC: U.S. Department of State, Bureau of Public Affairs.

World media handbook. (1992). 1992–1994 Edition. New York: United Nations, Programme Evaluation and Communications Research.

19

TUNISIA

Abdallah Hidri

INTRODUCTION

The Republic of Tunisia (Al-Jomhourya Attunisia) is a small country of 164,152 square kilometers (63,379 square miles), with an estimated population of over 8 million. Tunisia is located in North Africa, known as the Maghreb, bordered on the north and northeast by the Mediterranean Sea, on the southeast by Libya, and on the west by Algeria. Arabic is the official language, and Islam is the practiced religion.

Tunisia has a literacy rate of 65.3 percent, which ranks high among the Third World countries. Although the government routinely encourages education, particularly in the rural areas, about 25.8 percent of men and 43.7 percent of women are still illiterate.

According to the constitution, the executive power is vested in the president, who is elected for five years and is eligible for reelection for an additional two terms.

The Tunisian population is scattered unevenly. About 41 percent live in rural areas, and the rest are concentrated in large cities, particularly in the north and along the Mediterranean coast. This population imbalance creates major communication problems in terms of print media distribution and broadcast reach. Also, audience measurement is difficult to obtain, especially in the rural zones where the lack of roads, electricity, postal service, and telephone poses serious obstacles to the process.

PRINT MEDIA

The history of newspapers and magazines in Tunisia is closely linked to the political systems of the country. Three major periods have marked the development of print media in Tunisia: (1) the colonial period, (2) the independent period, (3) the modern period.

The colonial period (1881–1956) was characterized by two elements: the French and Italian colonizers and the colonized Muslims. In 1884, for the first time in Tunisia, a press law was passed that allowed foreigners to establish their cultural and political hegemony. That law permitted the publication and distribution of French and Italian press in Tunisia under a liberal system that was rooted in France and Italy. Ironically, the same law hampered the establishment of local, Muslim, and Jewish presses. The result was a clear polarization. While the colonial press defended the origins and values of the French, Italians, and Maltese, the local press was poised to preserve the Arab and Islamic culture, identity, and aspirations. Hence, the local press became a vehicle for the expression of political concerns, questioning the colonial power and influence. Among those newspapers were *Le Tunisian,* published in 1907 by the Young Tunisians movement, and *Al-Amal,* published in 1934 by the Neo-Destour. The Arabic-language newspapers were generally inspired by the Islamic publications in the Middle East.

The independent period (1956–1970) marked a major turning point for the print media in Tunisia. As the sovereign state tried to adjust to the new political reality, the press also began to adjust itself by focusing on issues of national interest. In May 1956, the government created the Secretariat of State for Information to manage the press sector and formulated a new information and communication policy based on a monovectorial approach. The dominance of the party-state was behind such a choice, which significantly restrained freedom of the press. This period also led to discontent.

The modern period began in 1970 when political pluralism emerged in Tunisia. In addition to a government-owned press, a few privately owned publications also emerged. Furthermore, in August 1988, the Tunisian government reformed the country's press code, thereby allowing for more freedom of expression. The new press code, along with privately owned publications, contributed to improvements in news and information, better work conditions for journalists, and democratization of the political process.

The print media in Tunisia may be divided into four categories: (1) the government-owned press, (2) the popular press, (3) the specialized press, and (4) the opposition press.

The government-owned and financially supported press in Tunisia enjoys the highest circulation rate both domestically and internationally, particularly in Europe and the Arab World. Determined to support and explain the views of the state, the official press defends the government policies and political figures. Table 19.1 lists the official publications in Tunisia.

Table 19.1
Official Publications in Tunisia

Title	Periodicity	1st Issue	Circulation	Language
Al-Hourria	daily	3-20-88	30,000	Arabic
Es-Sahafa	daily	1-10-89	25,260	Arabic
Le Renouveau	daily	3-20-88	29,000	French
La Presse	daily	1934	41,800	French
Presse Lundi	weekly	9-18-89	28,600	French
Revue 7 Nov.	monthly	7-25-88	31,000	Arabic
Journal Officiel	bi-weekly	1957	9,500	Arabic & French

Source: Directory General for Information, 1991.

The popular press emerged in the early 1970s, calling into question the information policy promulgated by the government. These independent newspapers appealed to the general population because they focused on venting their aspirations and grievances; consequently, they were widely sought and read. Between 1970 and 1975, the number of independent newspaper licenses issued by the Ministry of Interior reached 105 titles. Of these, 48 were actually published. *Al-Ayam, Al-Massira,* and *Tunis Hebdo* were widely read (Hamdane, 1991). Table 19.2 shows the major independent newspapers, including their circulation figures.

The specialized press (institutional publications) category is closely linked to the activities of the Tunisian institutions. The various government ministries and academic institutions publish and distribute these magazines. Tunisia has known the specialized press since the protectorate regime with the publication of union, commercial, and student press publications that were generally stimulated by the colonial climate. Table 19.3 lists the major specialized magazines published in Tunisia.

The opposition press emerged in reaction to the dominance of the party-state just after independence. On November 7, 1987, a new government that was supportive of political pluralism came into power, giving impetus to the emergence of the opposition press, which provided an equilibrium to the media scene. The major opposition press publications in Tunisia, published weekly in Arabic by several opposition parties, include *Al-Watan, Al-Mustaqbul, Attariq Al-Jadid,* and *Al-Wihda.* These publications, because of mainly financial problems, have a modest circulation and a relatively small readership.

Overall, the official press and the popular press enjoy high visibility in terms of circulation and readership, mainly among the urban populations. Because of

Table 19.2
Popular Publications in Tunisia

Title	Periodicity	1st Issue	Circulation	Lanquaqe
Echourouk	daily	Nov. '88	56,820	Arabic
Es-Sada	weekly	5-13-74	45,000	Arabic
El-Anwar	weekly	8-16-81	116,000	Arabic
Les Annonces	weekly	12-7-77	40,000	Arabic & French
El-Ayem	weekly	12-3-84	30,000	Arabic
El-Akhbar	weekly	2-14-84	36,378	Arabic
Sabah El-Kheir	weekly	6-10-87	48,000	Arabic
Tunis Hebdo	weekly	9-25-73	38,000	French

Source: Directory General for Information, 1991.

geographical distances and lack of an efficient transportation or distribution system, the rural areas experience enormous difficulties in gaining access to the print media.

According to the latest data (Directory General for Information, 1993), 7 dailies, 13 weeklies, 52 monthlies, and 43 irregular newspapers and magazines are published in Tunisia.

ELECTRONIC MEDIA

Radio

In colonized Tunisia, radio began as a private enterprise. The first radio, an amateur station (Dematteis), went on the air in 1924 (Pige, 1966).

On June 17, 1935, two private radio stations, Radio Bizerte and Radio Sfax, using low-power transmitters, obtained licenses to broadcast programs for three to four hours daily. In 1937, two other stations, Radio Tunis and Radio Sousse, went on the air. After World War II, the private stations were requisitioned by La Radiodiffusion Television Francaise (RTF).

With the political change of climate in 1987, advertising was introduced into broadcasting for the first time.

Radio Tunisia's Arabic National Channel is the main station in the country. Five radio stations are affiliated with it: Radio Gafsa, Radio Le Kef, Radio Monastir, Radio Sousse, and Radio Tunis. The National Channel broadcasts 24 hours a day in Arabic on medium waves. It airs four newscasts, 15 to 20 minutes each, at 7:00 A.M., 2:00 P.M., 6:00 P.M., and midnight, highlighting the president's and government's activities. News bulletins are broadcast at the top of

Table 19.3
Specialized Publications in Tunisia

Publisher	Title	Periodicity	1st Issue	Language
Ministry of Justice	*El-Kadha wa Ettachrii*	Monthly	January 1959	Arabic
Ministry of Defense	*Ad-Difaa*	Irregular	1986	Arabic
Ministry of Public Health	*Idees*	Monthly	1985	French
Ministry of National Economy	*Revue de l'Energie*	Trimestrial	--	French
Union Nationale Agriculteurs	*Tounes El-Khadhra*	Monthly	March 1976	Arabic
Ministry of Cultural Affairs	*Al-Hayat Ethakafiya*	Monthly	June 1975	Arabic
ERTT	*Radio et Television*	Weekly	5-15-59	Arabic

Source: Based on figures provided by the Directory General for Information, 1991.

every hour. In general, international news events receive a lower priority, in terms of coverage, than domestic happenings.

Additionally, stations in Ain Draham, Biadha, Gorraa, Kasserine, Sfax, Tunis, and Zaghouan broadcast programs via FM (frequency modulation). The French International Channel broadcasts programs on shortwave and FM frequencies.

Entertainment programs consist of live broadcasts, mainly interviews, call-ins, contests, and music. For instance, the program *Douroub Echems,* broadcast daily at 10:00 A.M., allows call-ins, thus offering an opportunity for the listeners to vent their concerns and difficulties.

Television

Television broadcasting in Tunisia is quite young, dating back to the 1960s. Under a French-Tunisian cooperation, on January 7, 1966, Tunisian television began broadcasting for only two hours (7:00 to 9:00 P.M.) daily. Airtime was equally divided between the Arabic and French languages.

By 1974, domestic television signals could not only cover the entire Tunisian territory but could also penetrate into the neighboring countries of Algeria and Libya. On the other hand, Tunisians can pick up spillover signals from Algerian Radio and Television (RTA), Italy's Channel One (RAI-1), and Libyan Television (PRDC). Other TV programs accessible to Tunisians are the Maghrebi Channel, Canal Horizon pay channel, and France's public channel, France 2.

The Maghrebi Channel, launched on March 20, 1990, is a regional network whose mission is to consolidate the political projects of five Maghreb countries: Tunisia, Algeria, Morocco, Libya, and Mauritania. The channel broadcasts programs only three and a half hours (8:30 P.M. to midnight) per day and only covers metropolitan Tunis, or about 25 percent of the population. Canal Horizon, launched in 1992, is a subsidiary of France's Canal Plus. Tunisia is one of several African countries where Canal Plus started stations, providing a variety of pay-TV programming. France 2 programs have been sent through satellite and are rebroadcast almost in totality on de la Radiodiffusion et Television Tunisienne (ERTT) transmission channel. However, France 2 newscasts are replaced by locally produced newscasts.

Tunisia is at the footprint of several European and other telecommunication satellites. Starting in the early 1980s, Receive only Television Dish or Station (TVRO) dishes made their appearances over the roofs of foreign embassies and then appeared in residential areas (Kallel, 1991).

Arabic Language National Channel (TV-7), inaugurated on November 7, 1992, by President Ben Ali, is the main television channel in Tunisia. This channel, which replaced the National Channel, covers Tunisia and is available, via Eutelsat II, in the Maghreb, Middle East, and Europe. The channel broadcasts eight hours of programming daily (4:00 P.M. to midnight).

Television news is the cornerstone of programming "due to the uppermost role it plays in deepening the sense of civic responsibility, strengthening tolerance, propagating freedom and promoting national dialogue" (Ali, 1991). Hence, from the very beginning, the National TV Channel has been advocating the objectives defined by the state. Although in recent years domestic news coverage has been characterized by a praiseful tone for the ruling party, the state has encouraged the production of analytic and critical programs, thus allowing a relatively increased tolerance margin.

Television newscasts typically consist of political news (60.41 percent), economic news (25 percent), cultural news (1.8 percent), and sports (12.50 percent), including national and international coverage. Overall, information programs consume 21.7 percent of television broadcasting time. Table 19.4 shows the amount of national (domestic) and imported television programs. The focus is on increasing the quality and quantity of domestic productions, relying less on imported programs. National TV production is an intelligent mixture of information, education, and entertainment. The trilogy of information-entertainment-development reflects the essential mission of TV-7.

MEDIA OWNERSHIP AND REGULATION

Although broadcasting in Tunisia began as a private enterprise, the government now owns and operates all radio and television outlets. The Bey's Decree of August 26, 1948, strengthened RTF's direct control of the station by establishing, for the first time, state monopoly of broadcasting in Tunisia through

Table 19.4
National Production Versus Imported

Programs	% National	% Imported	Total
Information	13.9	0	13.9
Magazines	2.15	0	2.15
Social/Economic Programs	7.9	0	7.9
Educational Programs	1.44	1.44	2.8
Cultural Programs	6.95	--	--
Variety	18.8	0	18.8
Movies/Soap Operas	1.08	18.44	19.52
Children Programs	6.84	5.02	11.86
Sports Programs	7.9	1.7	9.7
Religious Programs	3.84	2.51	6.35
Total	69.65	30.19	99.8

Source: Eddaassi, Monia, 1993.

RTF. This control was confirmed by the decree of April 23, 1953. After independence (1957), RTF was renamed Radiodiffusion Television Tunisienne (RTT). Being a monopoly of the state, RTT could not broadcast programs that were not concordant with government policies.

However, private ownership of the print media is allowed. Upon gaining its independence from the French in 1956, and becoming a sovereign republic, Tunisia created the Secretariat of State for Information to manage the press sector. Later, in December 1973, the Higher Council of Information was established as an advisory body whose purpose was to outline effective information and communication policies. In general, the privately owned publications are expected to observe the governmental rules and regulations.

In a 1992 interview (Jelassi, 1992), the RTT director general made the following statement: ''We cannot say censorship is totally nonexistent, but it is limited to a few topics and considerations which are not directly linked to freedom of expression. These topics are of an ethical, religious, legal or moral nature'' (p. 5).

EXTERNAL MEDIA SERVICES

An International Radio Channel, created in 1938, broadcasts 18 hours a day in four languages: French, Italian, English, and German. Its programs consist of news, information, cultural materials, and entertainment. This channel is particularly appealing to the 15- to 20-years-olds.

In addition, Radio Sfax broadcasts programs in Arabic, via shortwave frequencies, for external audiences.

NEWS AGENCIES

Tunis-Afrique-Presse (TAP) is the official news agency in Tunisia. It disseminates national and international news to print and broadcast media throughout the country.

CONCLUSION

Although Tunisia has its share of multiple TV channels, radio stations, newspapers, and magazines and also new technologies, the print media seems to suffer from a number of obstacles including a high rate of illiteracy, especially among women and the rural populations, an inefficient distribution system, and dominant state publications.

While the print media is not readily accessible to the majority of the population, the broadcast media is easily available. Hence, the imbalance between broadcasting and print media contributes to the creation of a culture of the elite. It is claimed that the destitute classes acquire a television set before other, economically better-off classes. In addition, the traditional life-style is under a continuous and massive invasion by sophisticated communication messages and techniques being beamed into homes via broadcast and satellite channels. This creates the paradox of simultaneously using telecommunications means and purely traditional communication techniques for information and education. Research in the field of communications highlighted the seriousness of this phenomenon, therefore suggesting the need to introduce the teaching of media at the secondary school level in order to allow new generations to better handle the challenges created by the new telecommunication technologies.

REFERENCES

Ali, B. (1991, March 20). Excerpt from a speech. Tunis, Tunisia.

Directory General for Information. (1993). *Radio & television reports.* Tunis: Directory General for Information.

———. (1991). *Publications Reports.* Tunis: Directory General for Information.

Hamdane, M. (1991). *Introduction a la presse en Tunisie.* Tunis: IPSI, p. 23.

Jelassi, I. (1992, November 7). *Tunisian Television,* p. 5.

Kallel, S. (1991, June 20). La legislation Tunisienne en mariere de reception des programmes de television par satellite. *A seminar on DBS.* Tunis.

Pige, F. (1966). *Radiodiffusion et television au Maghreb.* Tunis. P. 2.

20

TURKEY

Husamettin Unsal

INTRODUCTION

The Republic of Turkey occupies an area of around 815,000 square kilometers on the Asia Minor and Trachean peninsulas in a location that has constituted a major crossroads for civilization since ancient times. Founded on the ruins of the Ottoman Empire, one of the biggest in history, Turkey is a secular state governed through a multiparty political system. Turkey has a population of 59 million, of which 54 percent live in urban areas, while the remaining 46 percent live in rural areas. With an annual population growth rate of 2.17 percent and an urbanization rate of around 5 percent, Turkey has a growing and rapidly changing population.

Ninety-eight percent of Turkey's population are Muslims. The remaining 2 percent are Christians, Jews, and other religions. Being a mosaic of races and religions, Turkey has separated government affairs from religious affairs with the foundation of the republic and adopted secular principles.

In principle, a liberal economy is the norm in Turkey. However, during the first years of the republic, a strict nationalist economic policy that aimed to build infrastructure and move the economy toward self-sufficiency was adopted. In order to switch from this nationalistic policy to a more market-oriented economy, radical policy changes were undertaken. The liberalization policies adopted during the early 1980s aimed at increasing exports, on the one hand, and privatization, on the other. National income per capita in Turkey was U.S.$2,675 at the end of 1992. Turkey's annual import volume is U.S.$22.8 billion, and the annual export volume is U.S.$14.7 billion.

Turkey is a member of the European Free Trade Association (EFTA) and has been in the process of becoming a member of the European Community (EC) since 1963. However, problems such as economic difficulties and disagreements with Greece on the Cyprus issue have blocked the way for a full membership to EC. Turkey initiated efforts leading to the creation of the Black Sea Economic Cooperation Region (BSECR) in 1992, whose members consist of those countries having coasts on the Black Sea as well as from Caucasian countries. The BSECR offers economic cooperation among its members. Turkey is also one of the founding members of the United Nations and a member of the European Council and the North Atlantic Treaty Organization (NATO). Furthermore, Turkey is the founding member of the Islamic Organization and other subsidiary organizations.

The official language of the Republic of Turkey is Turkish. With its various dialects that belong to the Altaic group of the Ural-Altaic language family, the Turkish language is now spoken by 250 million people in a wide area extending from the Adriatic Sea to the Altai Mountains. Turkey adopted the Latin alphabet immediately after the formation of the Republic of Turkey in 1923. Ninety percent of the population are literate.

Elementary education of five years is obligatory, and there are efforts to extend the obligatory elementary education to eight years. The schooling rate is around 20 percent for secondary education and 9 to 10 percent for university education. The schooling rate in university education rises to 16 percent when the Open University, which broadcasts lectures (telecourses) on national television and has centrally administered exams, is taken into account. Moreover, 25 new universities were opened within the last two years, which brought the total number to 54. When these new universities become fully operational within the next four years, the university-educated rate, excluding the Open University, will exceed 20 percent. Of the 54 universities in Turkey, 3 are Foundation universities, and 2 are High Technology institutes. Turkey has adopted the principle of mixed education, and accordingly, males and females enroll at the same schools. Both sexes have equal rights, and women obtained the suffrage and right for election in 1934.

Turkey is a democratic republic. Although ruled through a single party system during the first years of the republic, Turkey adopted its multiparty system in 1946. Democratic life based on the multiparty system was interrupted in 1960, 1971, and 1980 by military interventions. Nevertheless, because the Turkish Army is loyal to democracy and the system is well accepted by the people, the multiparty Parliament was resumed in 1993. In the spring of 1993, former Prime Minister Suleyman Demirel, an outstanding political personality in Turkey since the 1960s, became the president. Subsequently, Tansu Ciller became the first woman prime minister in Turkey's history. She heads the coalition government between the True Path Party (DYP), a central Right party, and the Social Democratic Populist Party (SHP), a central Left party. This coalition represents the historical compromise between the central Left and central Right in Turkey.

PRINT MEDIA

Newspapers

The printing press came to the Ottoman Empire 250 years after its invention. Due to this delay, which arose from religious conservatism, newspapers were published in Turkey much later than in contrast to Western countries. The first Turkish newspaper, *Takvimi Vekayi,* was published in 1831 in Istanbul. The modern press began in Turkey in 1926 with the adoption of the Latin alphabet and, more important, with the adoption of the multiparty system in 1946.

Today, newspapers are published with freedom of the press under the guarantee of the constitution. Publishing newspapers is possible only with the condition of notification. Twenty-four daily newspapers are published in Istanbul, the center of Turkey's press business, 4 of which are economic journals. Istanbul newspapers are national newspapers, and the majority are distributed throughout Turkey. Some of them are also printed in Germany and marketed in Europe as well. Among these are *Hurriyet, Milliyet, Turkiye, Cumhuriyet,* and *Tercuman.*

In addition to Istanbul newspapers, there are 26 regional newspapers published in Turkey, including 8 in Ankara, 4 in Izmir, 5 in Adana and Bursa, and 4 in Konya. Moreover, there are 290 local newspapers in provinces and towns. The overall circulation of regional and local newspapers varies between 500 and 10,000, while that of national newspapers varies between 100,000 and 1 million.

Published on the principle of free competition, the newspapers are subject to state subsidy through the Press Announcement Department. These public announcements include the announcements of public activities, public tenders, and purchases and provide great contributions to the survival of local and regional newspapers.

The major national newspapers in Turkey and their circulation as of the end of 1992 are as follows: *Sabah* (1,258,000), *Hurriyet* (1,065,000), *Milliyet* (1,117,000), *Turkiye* (356,000), *Meydan* (149,000), *Bugun* (106,000), and *Cumhuriyet* (70,000).

Newspapers in Turkey are published in a highly competitive environment; hence, they routinely employ promotional campaigns to increase their readerships. By mid-1992, the daily circulation of ten major newspapers in Turkey had stagnated around 3 million copies. Thus, at that time, encyclopedias were added to the list of promotional gifts that had formerly included books, houses, cars, trucks, and buses that major newspapers gave to readers through lottery to lure more readers. The announcement by *Sabah,* one among those with the largest circulation, that it would give its readers 2 volumes of the *Encyclopedia Grand Larousse* each month (until the 20 full volumes were completed) in return for 30 coupons cut daily from the newspaper stirred a fierce competition among other major newspapers. *Hurriyet* has begun to give volumes of the *Encyclopedia Britannica,* and *Milliyet,* the *Encyclopedia Grand Larousse.* This promotional campaign has increased the circulation of these newspapers to a great extent; consequently, the total circulation of national dailies had reached 4.3 million by late 1992. The rate of newspaper reading in Turkey is 72 newspapers per 1,000 persons.

Magazines

The magazine publishing business in Turkey also developed alongside newspapers. Owing to the development of modern printing techniques, urbanization, and concomitant specialization, significant expansions are observed in this field. The majority of magazines in Turkey are published by the four major newspaper groups (*Sabah, Hurriyet, Milliyet,* and *Turkiye*). As of 1992, a total of 156 periodicals are published in Turkey. Of these, 7 are published daily, 32 weekly, 5 biweekly, and 101 monthly. Another 11 are published irregularly. The average circulation of political and economic periodicals varies between 10,000 and 45,000 copies. The circulation of monthly women's magazines and various professional journals varies between 3,000 and 55,000.

ELECTRONIC MEDIA

According to the constitution adopted in 1982, "Radio and television stations may only be founded by the state, and their administrations are regulated as a public institution." The law stipulates that broadcasting should be regulated in such a way as to protect the existence and sovereignty of the Turkish state, the indivisible unity of people and country, and the basic quality of the republic as defined in Article 2 of the constitution and to observe the principle of impartiality in the organization of administration, management, and operation of such institution and in any radio and television broadcasts (Article 133). A new Radio-Television Higher Council was formed according to the law concerning the Turkish Radio and Television Institution (TRT) and adopted in accordance with the new constitution. One of the tasks of this Radio-Television Higher Council, which consists of 12 persons and is an autonomous authority above the Radio Television organization, is "the supervision, control, and evaluation of the activities of TRT as well as any radio and television broadcasts and other electronic broadcasts other than TRT."

An intense debate began by the end of the 1980s in spite of these constitutional limitations, with many advocating the deregulation of such broadcasts, the privatization of existing state monopoly over radio and television broadcasting, and the legalization and encouragement of additional private radio and television stations. During these debates, TV broadcasts through satellites from abroad and later radio broadcasts from abroad have proliferated. And since required modifications were not made on the constitution and other applicable laws, such TV and radio stations were de facto in existence, although legally the state monopoly still stood. One of the first actions of the Ciller cabinet, in July 1993, was to change the constitution to legalize private TV and radio stations.

Radio

The first radio in Turkey was founded in 1926, immediately after the formation of the republic, through a privilege granted to a private company. The first broadcast was made in 1927 in Ankara and Istanbul in a little studio using 5- to 7-kilowatt transmitters. In the early 1930s, the government acquired the control of radio stations and carried out their operations through the Prime Ministry until the early 1960s. The radios, broadcasting separately through Ankara and Istanbul transmitters, operated under the strict control of political power. This situation, in part, contributed to the 1961 Military Intervention, and the Turkish Radio and Television Institution was hence created as an autonomous public institution by the 1961 constitution. TRT began its operation in 1964 with the adoption of a special law. However, it became an institution under the strict control of government during the 1971 and 1980 Military interventions through modifications on both the constitution and applicable laws and de facto interventions.

Today, broadcasts are carried by TRT on four channels: popular productions on TRT-1 (AM [amplitude modulation]), cultural productions on TRT-2 (AM), classical music and pop music on TRT-3 (FM [frequency modulation]), and traditional Turkish music and folkloric Turkish music on TRT-4 (FM). TRT also broadcasts a total of 47 hours through different stations in 16 different languages every day throughout the world via the Voice of Turkey on shortwave. These broadcasts are received primarily in Europe, the Middle East, and central Asia as well as in other regions including North America and southern Asia.

Broadcasts transmitted on standard AM frequencies under the control of the government were invaded by private FM radio broadcasts in early 1990. By the end of 1992, almost every province could pick up these private FM stations on the standard receivers. Some of these radios are owned by private television stations, and others are controlled by municipalities. Adana, Ankara, Antalya, Bursa, Canakkale, Eskisehir, and Isparta each have 3 private FM radio stations. Aydin, Balikesir, and Manisa each have 4 FM stations. In addition, there are 9 FM stations in Izmir and Denizli, 16 in Konya, and 21 in Istanbul. Until the July 1993 change in the constitution, legal radio and television broadcasting were under the monopoly TRT. Although these private broadcasts were considered illegal, they could not be stopped.

All public and private radio stations in Turkey receive advertisements. TRT has such resources as the fixed premium from radio and TV sets sold in Turkey and a general share received from the electricity consumption in the country.

However, the major revenues of TRT come from advertisements. After the foundation of private radio and television stations, the share of TRT in the advertisement pie has declined to one-fourth. This has had an enormous influence on the investments and production expenses of TRT.

On the other hand, the only resources of private radio and television stations are their revenues from advertisements. Although radio stations that are very new do not receive enough advertisements to finance operations, they receive support from sponsor productions, from television channels that they promote, or from such public bodies as local municipalities for their productions, which they carry out with limited staff.

Radio stations of TRT produce their programs in various studios in Turkey and broadcast live as well as taped programs. On the other hand, private radio stations conduct their operation mainly through live programs and disco productions consisting of popular music.

Unlike TRT radio stations that have access to the rich resources of the organization's news centers, private radio stations with limited resources base most of their news broadcasts on national news agency sources.

Television

Television—unlike radio, which was adopted a very short time after its invention—was introduced in Turkey quite late. The first black and white television began broadcasting on January 31, 1968, from the TRT training studios in Ankara. Turkey started color broadcasts in 1984.

Holding the monopoly of broadcasting in Turkey in accordance with the constitution before the recent changes, TRT has three channels covering 98 percent of the population. A fourth channel is used for educational purposes; and an international channel (INT-AVRASYA) broadcasts over a wide area in Europe and Asia via satellite. However, since the beginning of 1990, TRT has encountered serious competitors.

In spite of limitations set forth by the Constitution of the Republic of Turkey as well as by the law on TRT, private television broadcasting began via satellites. A corporation partially owned by the son of the president of Turkey began its broadcasts over Turkey on May 7, 1990, via a satellite in Germany. These broadcasts were first received only through special disc antennas but later could be received off the air by standard receivers. While the debate created at the beginning of broadcasts by this TV channel, called InterStar, were continuing, the same group opened another TV channel called TeleOn, followed by Show TV, owned by a banker and operated in France. These were followed later by (HBB) broadcasting from London and Kanal 6, again owned by the president's son, which also broadcast from London. Kanal 6 has also begun to operate a marketing channel called Kanal Market. In line with these developments, Flash TV began broadcasting in Bursa and reached to Istanbul; and (BRD), founded by the Metropolitan Municipality of Istanbul, also began its operations. Other

TV channels, primarily (SATEL) founded by *Sabah* newspaper, are continuing their preparations for broadcasting. Moreover, *Milliyet* and *Turkiye* (Turkey Radio and Television Network [TGRT]) continue their preparation for national broadcasting.

This anarchy in broadcasting in Turkey has led to serious noise problems in frequency bands. The government and Parliament have decided to make the required modifications/amendments to the constitution and to adopt new regulations in order to legalize the existing de facto situation. No solution was possible until July 1993 when the constitutional amendments undertaken by the Ciller government opened the way to legalizing and regulating these broadcasts.

TRT channels under public property as well as the private channels in Turkey accept advertisements and broadcast sponsored productions. As stated in the section on radio, TRT has revenues derived by virtue of law such as fixed premiums from radio, television, and music sets sold in Turkey as well as a share received from electricity consumption. But its major resource is revenue from advertisements. With the acquisition of a great share by private channels, TRT has encountered serious difficulties in continuing the operations of its four channels at the same time. TRT INT-AVRASYA is financed directly through public resources.

The private TV channels finance themselves solely through revenues from advertisements and sponsorships for some productions. Since the total supply of advertisements in Turkey is very limited (advertisement expenses per capita in Turkey are much smaller than those in Europe), it is expected that the number of private TV channels will decline in the future.

TRT channels have an extensive production network and a wide range of human resources. In this respect, the rate of TRT's own productions in its total broadcasts is close to 60 percent. But the productions of private channels are very limited. Their broadcasts consist mainly of programs purchased from independent producers, including soap operas, game shows, and movies imported from other countries. With the increase in the number of channels, there has been a significant increase in the number of locally produced talk shows broadcast by TV channels.

With 24 years of organizational experience, TRT is capable of using a wide news network with links to various international sources. However, in contrast to the official news productions of TRT, private television channels offer audiences the opportunity to watch alternative news sources with their peculiar dynamic news concept.

Cable Television

The cable television, started by Post, Telephone, and Telegraph (PTT) in 1989 within the framework of a project that included channels from Europe and the United States, has been realized as a model with 16 channels. Efforts are being made for the spread of cable TV with a current number of subscribers of more than 60,000 in Ankara, Istanbul, Antalya, Gaziantep, and Bursa. Expected to cover more areas in these provinces in the near future, cable television shall also be put into operation in Adana, Konya, Izmir, and Kocaeli in 1993. Costs for cable TV are U.S.$100 for installation and a subscription fee of U.S.$3 every month.

NEW TECHNOLOGIES

Turkey is one of the most fortunate countries in its region in terms of its access to new technologies. The Turkish PTT adopted digital technology during the 1980s, and the completed telecommunication infrastructure has played an important role in the utilization of new technologies.

PTT uses fiber optics for the development of its infrastructure and especially for the spread of cable television. In addition to COMSAT (Communications Satellite Corporation) and similar satellites, the preparation for the launching of TURKSAT (Turkish Satellite) is under way. Both TRT INT-AVRASYA broadcasts of TRT and the private TV broadcasts from abroad to Turkey are transmitted via satellites.

Videocassette recorder (VCR) penetration in Turkey is among the highest in the Middle East. Similar to TRTs beginning its TV broadcasts in black and white, the preference for Betamax for VCR was a great waste, and the VHS standard adopted by all European and Western countries was late to be adapted in Turkey. VCRs, widely used during a period in which TV broadcasting was carried out solely by TRT, are now seen as a dead investment in many households, which hardly ever use them and prefer TV viewing instead.

MOTION PICTURES

The beginning of Turkish cinema precedes the foundation of the republic in 1945. Turkish cinema was developed with the pioneering works of Muhsin Ertugrul, who studied in the former Soviet Union in the first years of the republic. Experiencing a rapid growth during the 1960s, the number of movies produced had reached to 200 films per year. These films, which were mainly copies from Hollywood-made dramatic films, were followed by cheap sex films. The spread of TV has led to a great bottleneck in cinema beginning from the 1970s, and as a consequence, a great majority of the movie theaters were closed, and the Turkish film industry (called Yesilca) has entered a period of regression. During the 1980s, the average number of annual film productions declined to 20. In spite of this decline in the numbers of films produced, there were significant developments in the quality of films, and Turkish films have begun to receive international awards and recognition.

Film weeks, special programs organized since the middle 1980s, as well as the decreased effects of television have led Turkey to rediscover the cinema. For instance, movie theaters in big cities have been restored, or increased in number, and mainly show the latest Hollywood films. By the early 1990s, American film distributing agencies within Turkey had gained control of almost all cinema operations, and domestic productions began to struggle to find a theater to premiere. Consequently, the Turkish film industry is facing financial difficulties. Film festivals held in Ankara and Antalya provide some financial support for Turkish films. Also, the participation of EURIMAJ, the Ministry of Culture, and television channels as coproducers in film productions comes as a new breath in the development of the Turkish film industry.

Since censorship has largely been abolished as a result of democratization beginning in the late 1980s, there has emerged a freer atmosphere for cinema.

At the end of 1992, there were 96,033 seats in 133 movie theaters. Of these, 53 are located in Istanbul, 13 in Ankara, 10 in Izmir, and the remaining 57 in other cities and towns.

MEDIA OWNERSHIP AND FINANCIAL SUPPORT PATTERNS

All communication facilities in Turkey other than TRT, which is under public control, are privately owned and operated in a truly competitive atmosphere. The revenues of newspapers, radio stations, and television channels are from advertisements and sales. Owners of some press companies are engaged in diverse forms of commercial activities and are thus capable of occasionally transferring resources for the financing of their activities in the communication sector. However, the basic principle is that such activities should be carried out profitably under free competitive conditions.

Although it is assumed that the Press Announcement Department founded in 1960 provides a certain subsidy for newspapers through public announcements, such subsidies provide a minor contribution to major companies. However, such subsidies are a vital resource for the survival of small local newspapers.

Developments observed in recent years in the press sector in Turkey can be regarded as a trend toward monopoly. With a total average daily circulation of 4,300,000, three major groups hold 86 percent of the newspaper market (Sabah, Bugun, Yeni, and Asir, 1,400,000; Hurriyet, 1,100,000; and Milliyet and Meydan, 1,220,000). The magazine market is also controlled by these three groups. The Hurriyet group produces newstalk and entertainment productions for all television channels, while the Sabah group is introducing its own television channel. These groups, while experiencing fierce competition for market share, often arrange joint policies.

The distribution of newspapers is also under the control of these three groups. While the distribution company founded by the Hurriyet and Sabah groups is distributing their own newspapers, the distribution company under the control of the Milliyet group distributes its own newspapers, on the one hand, and shares the distribution of other newspapers with the former. It is almost impossible to find a channel for newspaper distribution that is not under the control of these two companies.

MEDIA REGULATION

Freedom of the press is under the guarantee of the Constitution of the Republic of Turkey. Under the press law, the press is free and cannot be censored. Anyone may publish any newspaper, magazine, or other printed materials by applying to competent authorities. Publications are controlled by the judiciary. However, according to a law adopted during the mid-1980s, the principle is set forth that those publications against the established morals should be controlled. Following this restriction, pornographic publications are either sold in special packages or seized.

TV and radio operated by TRT are governed by a special law. However, there is no law or regulation governing the operation of private radio stations and TV channels, which legally cannot even exist. This legal confusion, which came about because necessary constitutional amendments were made neither before 1991 nor afterward, has led to a freer press against which no major objections have resulted. The knowledge and conscience of the professionals that work for the private stations and channels, most of whom are in fact ex-TRT personnel, have ensured the observance of established morals and Turkish traditions. Nevertheless, one of the most significant issues on the agenda of both the government and the Parliament is the regulation of private radio and television business and the concomitant required modifications to and amendments on the constitution. The recent constitutional amendment that legalizes such private channels also opens the way for government regulations that can monitor their activities.

EXTERNAL MEDIA SERVICES

Transboundary broadcasts in Turkey were begun during the first years of the radio business. During World War II, Turkiye'nin Sesi (Voice of Turkey) entered into significant international polemics. These activities developed and continued during the postwar period. Today, TRT's Transboundary Broadcasts Service broadcasts 47 hours through different stations each day in 16 different languages.

Domestically, TRT-3 broadcasts its news productions six times a day in French, English, and German as well as in Turkish. And the second channel of TRT TV broadcasts its evening news in Turkish and English for 20 minutes each. This program, highlighting daily domestic and international news in English, is especially important for foreign missionaries, tourists, and businessmen.

Newspapers in foreign languages were published in the Ottoman Empire before the arrival of the Turkish printed press. *Istanbul,* published in French in 1875, had survived until 1964. Various minorities living in Turkey have published their own newspapers for years. They include, among others, weekly

Salom, published in Judeo-Spanish and Turkish; *Apoyovmatini* and *Iho,* published in modern Greek six days a week; and *Jamank* and *Nor Marmara,* published daily in Armenian. In addition, *Turkish Daily News* is published in English daily in Ankara and has a circulation exceeding 20,000.

In addition to newspapers published in foreign languages, the monthly *Image of Turkey* and *Middle East Business* can be counted among the periodicals published in English. Moreover, there are numerous bulletins and magazines published by various banks and independent bodies.

NEWS AGENCIES

Almost every broadcast and publication unit in Turkey has its own news-gathering organization. In addition, mass media receive news and information through the various national and international news agencies such as Associated Press (AP), United Press International (UPI), Reouters, and Agence France-Presse (AFP).

The most widespread news agency is the semipublic Anadolu Ajansi, founded during the early days of the republic. Anadolu Ajansi is the most extensive news source in Turkey with its international reporters and connections with international news agencies. Also, since the middle of 1992, Anadolu Ajansi has produced and distributed visual news. In addition to Anadolu Ajansi, there are other independent national news sources including Anka Ajans and Akajans, a news agency of Hurriyet.

THE ROLE OF MEDIA IN NATIONAL DEVELOPMENT

The notion that mass media can make great contributions to the national development in Turkey has been dominant for a long time. Radio and TV programs during their early years were used extensively for education, particularly in rural areas. However, there are no studies or evaluations on the effects and results of these educational productions.

The Open University, based on education by television, was developed by Anadolu University during the mid-1970s and grants diplomas to hundreds of students every year. The textbooks are delivered to students by mail, and the lectures are delivered via TV. Students receive two centrally administered written exams each year. Besides the higher education productions, television is also used for the improvement of teachers through the facilities of Anadolu University. Those teachers who graduated from high school equivalent schools and followed two-year open university programs are regarded as university graduates.

CONCLUSION

Mass media in Turkey shows an explicit double structure. While the urbanized population lives in an intensive communication atmosphere, the rural areas are surrounded by an extensive radio and television network. The lack of regulations in radio and television broadcasting has led to increased public exposure to free radio-television broadcasting.

Fierce competition among the newspapers has made Turkey an encyclopedia-rich country. As a consequence of this encyclopedia race that began in late 1992, more than 3 million houses will be furnished with 20-volume encyclopedias.

The trend toward media monopoly in Turkey is accelerating. There is no legislation or legal restriction that would counteract this trend both in print and in the electronic media.

The collapse of the Soviet Union and the emergence of its subsequent independent republics present new opportunities for the world of communication in Turkey. The preparations for the adoption of the Latin alphabet by five Central Asian republics, similar to the Turkish language, will enable print and broadcast media and films produced in Turkey to reach a population of more than 200 million without encountering a language barrier. Overall, the future prospects for the Turkish mass media are promising.

REFERENCES

Cankaya, O. (1992, December). Turkiye'de TV'nin bugunku durumu. *Marmara Iletisim Dergisi.* Istanbul.

Devlet Planlama Teskilati (DPT). (1992). *1993 Program.* Ankara: DPT.

Fida Film. (1992). *Turkiye'de sinema seyircisi profili.* Istanbul.

Iletisim Arastirmalari Dernegi (ILAD). (1991a). *Basmda tekellesmeler.* Istanbul.

Iletisim Arastirmalari Dernegi (ILAD). (1991b). *Gelecegin radyo TV duzeni.* Istanbul.

Kurumu, B.I. (1992). *1992 Aralik gazete tirajlari raporu.*

Serarslan, M. (1992). *Radyo-TV duzeninde degisimler arayislar ve Turkiye.* Yayinlanmamis Master Tezi.

Topuz, H. (1973). *100 Soruda Turk basini.* Istanbul: Gercek Yayinevi.

21

UNITED ARAB EMIRATES

Anantha S. Babbili and Sarwat Hussain

INTRODUCTION

The United Arab Emirates (UAE)—Dawlat al-Imaaraat al-Arabiyya al-Muutahidah, in Arabic—collectively compose one of the youngest states of the Arabian peninsula established formally as a union on December 2, 1971. Formed after British withdrawal from the Arabian Gulf region, the UAE was known until then by a variety of names such as Pirate Coast, Trucial Coast, Trucial States, and Trucial Oman.

The UAE is a federation of seven individual emirates (Ajman, Abu Dhabi, Dubai, Fujairah, Ras al Khaimah, Umm al-Qawain, and Sharjah), and the federal capital is Abu Dhabi. An *emirate*—a *sheikhdom*—is a federal unit with an independent ruler (*sheikh*) who has considerable autonomy over local affairs. Each emirate has a major city or town that carries the same name as that of the emirate. Table 21.1 lists the seven emirates that compose the UAE federation, together with their rulers, tribal affiliations, geographical area, and population.

The UAE lies to the east of the Arabian Peninsula. It has a 470-mile northern shoreline in the area commonly known as the Lower Gulf, constituting more than one-third of the Arabian coast of the Gulf (Heard-Bey, 1982). The UAE has an area of 32,000 square miles, although figures vary. In the north, the UAE shares a frontier with Qatar, and its immediate neighbors are the Sultanate of Oman to the east (in the area often referred to as the ''Horn of Arabia'') and the Kingdom of Saudi Arabia to the west and south. The UAE's climate is hot

Table 21.1
Salient Facts About the United Arab Emirates

Emirate	Ruler (and Tribe)	Area (Sq km)	Population
	His Highness:		
Abu Dhabi	Sheikh Zayed bin Sultan Al Nahyan (Al bu Falah of the Bani Yas)	67,000	772,000
Dubai	Sheikh Maktoum bin Rashid Al Maktoum (Al bu Falasah of the Bani Yas)	3,900	484,000
Sharjah	Dr. Sheikh Sultan bin Mohammed Al Qasimi (Qawasim)	2,600	302,000
Ras al Khaimah	Sheikh Saqr bin Mohammed Al Qasimi (Qawasim)	1,700	125,000
Fujairah	Sheikh Hamad bin Mohammed Al Sharqi (Sharqiyyin)	1,300	61,000
Umm al Quwain	Sheikh Rashid bin Ahmed Al Mualla (Al Mualla or Al Ali)	777	26,000
Ajman	Sheikh Humaid bin Rashid Al Nuaimi (Al bu Khurayban)	259	74,000

Sources: The United Arab Emirates, 1991, p. 185; Kay, 1991.

and humid (May to September), and winters are usually mild. Rainfall is sparse, and annual precipitation ranges from four to eight inches (100 to 200 mm).

Two geographical features—the ocean and desert—have long dictated the way of life in the UAE. Prior to the discovery of oil, the mainstays of the economy were pearling, fishing, and commerce. With its strategic location along the world's major shipping routes (in the lower Arabian Gulf and going out through the Gulf of Oman to the Indian Ocean), with over a dozen ports and five international airports, the UAE has established itself as a center of international business and trade.

The UAE's inhabitants are Arabs, and the official language is Arabic, although English is used widely. The indigenous population is outnumbered by non-Arab immigrants from India, Pakistan, Bangladesh, and Iran. In 1985, the total population was 1,622,464, with a major portion in its three cities of Abu

Dhabi, Dubai, and Al Ain, an inland oasis city. Although the state religion is Islam, other religions and denominations are free to practice their religions. Besides the dominant religion of Islam, Hinduism, Christianity, and Buddhism are represented in the migrant force.

The UAE has made rapid strides in education. In 1971, there were approximately 28,000 students attending educational facilities confined to urban centers. Although a reliable rate of literacy is unavailable, in 1991–1992, school enrollment grew to 300,000 in government schools and 100,000 in private schools. For citizens wishing to pursue advanced degrees in the Middle East, Europe, and the United States, generous scholarships are provided by the government. With the establishment of The Emirates University in 1977 at Al Ain, demand for foreign education decreased, and the university has now produced over 10,000 graduates (approximately half men and half women) who occupy important positions in the government and private sector. Vocational training is available through a number of technical colleges such as the Dubai Aviation College (linked to Dubai's Department of Civil Aviation), the Emirates Banking Institute, or the Career Development Centre of the Abu Dhabi National Oil Company (ADNOC).

The first constitution was signed on July 18, 1971, by six of the seven emirates that compose the federation. Ras al Khaimah joined on February 1, 1972. The head of state, the president, is His Highness Sheikh Zayed bin Sultan Al Nahyan, ruler of Abu Dhabi. The vice president and prime minister is His Highness Sheikh Maktoum bin Rashid Al Maktoum, ruler of Dubai.

The UAE's main executive body of government is the Supreme Council of Rulers, made up of the president, prime minister, and the rulers of the remaining five emirates that compose the federation. This body elects from among its members the president and the vice president. The president was elected in 1971 and has subsequently been reelected every five years. The president is also supreme commander of the country's armed forces, while the deputy supreme commander is Abu Dhabi's crown prince. Day-to-day affairs of state are handled by the cabinet, headed by the prime minister.

The country's parliament is the Federal National Council (FNC), established on February 13, 1972, and consisting of 40 appointed members drawn proportionately from each emirate (eight members each from Abu Dhabi and Dubai, six each from Ras al Khaimah and Sharjah, and four members from Ajman, Fujairah, and Umm al-Qaiwain). The FNC is headed by a secretary general and is empowered to amend and review legislation, summon ministers, and critically review the work of their ministries.

The FNC fulfills a major Islamic principle—that of *Shura,* or consultation whereby a ruler who wields absolute authority is obliged to consult a small, informal council of members of the ruling family and social and religious opinion leaders called the *majlis.* The practice of *Shura* enables participation in governmental decision-making processes and a system of shared responsibility (Zahlan, 1989).

Regionally, the UAE is recognized as a nonaligned Arab and Islamic country. The UAE was a major initiator of the concept of regional security and led efforts to establish the Arab Gulf Cooperation Council (AGCC), whose member countries include the Kingdom of Saudi Arabia, Bahrain, Kuwait, Qatar, and Oman. According to Nonneman (1988) and the Ministry of Information and Culture, the UAE is a major donor through the Abu Dhabi Fund for Arab Economic Development (ADFAED) established in 1971 (1986 disbursements = $2.1 billion).

COMMUNICATION PHILOSOPHY

The pursuit and propagation of *ilm* (knowledge) is a very important facet of Islamic society, and it is one of the most frequently occurring themes in the Holy Quran. Since early times, oral communication was the preferred mode of communication, given the tribal and nomadic nature of Arab society. However, with the establishment of a modern nation-state, mediated forms of mass communication such as newspapers, radio, and television began to occupy an important place in the country's communication milieu.

The UAE's founders were keenly aware of mass media's potential to foster cultural, economic, and social development. The UAE's communication philosophy continues to be guided by the desire to keep its citizens informed of political, economic, developmental, and sociocultural events in the federation. At the inception of the federation, the press was an important instrument in achieving political socialization and stability. In particular, the UAE's communication philosophy seeks to promote and sustain the regional culture and enhance the flow of information both within the country and with the community of Arab nations. In keeping with these objectives, a healthy mix of media ownership, including government, private, and foreign, has been established in the UAE. Frequent meetings and information exchange by media personnel of AGCC countries are the norm, and some efforts have been made at implementing a media agreement along the line of an economic pact between the UAE and neighboring Arab countries.

PRINT MEDIA

Newspapers

The print media had a modest beginning in the UAE. In the late 1960s, there were no newspapers, and the few newspapers that were available were imported from Europe and India and thus were often dated. Because demand was lacking, there were no incentives to import newspapers on a regular basis. The nearest place where an English newspaper was produced and distributed was the port city of Aden in Yemen, *The Aden Chronicle.*

In 1967, an Indian expatriate, Kawas Motivala, began publishing a small

Table 21.2
United Arab Emirates' Leading Daily Newspapers

Newspaper	Year of publication	Publisher	No. of pages
Arabic:			
Al Ittihad (Union)	1969	Al Ittihad Press and Publishing Corporation	24
Al Khaleej (Gulf)	1970	Al Khaleej House for Printing and Publishing	20
Al Wahdah (Unity)	1973	Al Wahdah Newspapers Establishment	16
Al Fajr (Dawn)	1975	Al Fajr Establishment	16
Al Bayan (Decree)	1980	Al Bayan Establishment	20
English:			
Emirates News	1971	Al Ittihad Press and Publishing Corporation	12
Gulf News	1979	Al Nisr Corporation	22
Khaleej Times	1979	Galadari Establishment for Printing and Publishing	20

Source: Directory of the Periodicals in the United Arab Emirates, 1992, pp. 1–106.

bulletin in English, *The Recorder.* Mechanically reproduced on an office duplicator, its primary content was advertising and information on mercantile shipping with very little news. *The Recorder* was published three to four times a week, and circulation was low because of poor transport. *The Recorder*'s primary readership was a fledgling expatriate community, and some copies of *The Recorder* went to neighboring Oman and Bahrain.

The British withdrawal from the Gulf region and the emergence of the UAE as an independent nation-state provided the impetus for the establishment of print and broadcast media. Aware that the UAE—a product of the merger of several fractious emirs and emirates—was based on a fragile coalition, the founders quickly seized the opportunity to instill and inculcate the much-needed spirit of nationalism by using the press as a powerful agent to enhance and support political integration. Table 21.2 lists the leading Arabic and English dailies.

The first Arabic newspaper in the UAE was the appropriately named weekly *Al-Ittihad* (*Union* or *Federation*) that began publication in October 1969 from Abu Dhabi. It was a well-rounded newspaper and covered political, social, and cultural affairs, with special emphasis given to local news and the development of an industrial infrastructure. It also published supplements on culture, religion, literature, and the arts. Because of the dearth of printing presses in the UAE at that time, the early issues of *Al-Ittihad* had to be printed in Kuwait and Beirut. *Al-Ittihad* ceased printing in April 1972 and resumed publication as a daily soon after.

As the first official Arabic newspaper in the newly formed country with an estimated circulation of 60,000 copies, it was instrumental in helping the government achieve the primary objective of establishing an effective administration. *Al-Ittihad* has an estimated circulation of 75,000 copies.

Several government and privately owned newspapers began publication in the 1970s. Notable among these was the Arabic newspaper *Al-Khaleej* (*Gulf*), established in October 1970 by Sharjah's Al Khaleej House for Printing and Publishing, a private publisher. The newspaper had a shaky start, and *Al-Khaleej* discontinued publication on February 18, 1972. It resumed publication in April 1980. The newspaper, with a circulation of 45,747, is a member of the Audit Bureau of Circulation (ABC).

In August 1973, the government began publishing *Al-Wahdah* (*Unity*) from Abu Dhabi. As a daily, *Al-Wahdah* made a change in editorial policy by expanding its coverage of local and regional events.

In 1975, Abu Dhabi's Al Fajr Establishment initiated *Al-Fajr* (*Dawn*). Reflecting progress made in the UAE's infrastructure and access to information, *Al-Fajr* provides an eclectic mix of news—local, regional, and international—and includes supplements on the arts and women. The newspaper is a member of ABC and has a circulation of 4,284.

The fifth Arabic daily, *Al-Bayan* (*Eloquence*), began publication from Dubai in May 1980. Similar to *Al-Fajr, Al-Bayan* focuses on economic and commercial affairs and local, regional, and international news. Supplements on arts, literature, and book reviews are published, and 1992 circulation was estimated at 70,000 copies.

The first government-owned English newspaper, *Emirates News,* began publication in August 1971 four months before independence. Because it was the country's first English daily, its editorial policy focused more on the developments in the UAE, on events in the Arab World, and on international news. Although circulation figures are not released by the government, the newspaper is available by subscription and includes reports on weather, business, and sports.

In 1979, two prominent, privately owned English dailies, *Khaleej Times* and *Gulf News,* were established. In February, *Khaleej Times* was launched with the slogan "*Khaleej Times* slips the world under your door" and was an instant success, especially among the expatriate population from India, Pakistan, Bangladesh, and Iran.

The editorial policy of the *Khaleej Times* is eclectic, and about 40 percent of the news hole (space left for news and editorial matter after ads have been placed on a newspaper's pages) covers events in India, Pakistan, and Southeast Asia, from which a majority of the migrant work force comes. *Khaleej Times* follows an eight-column broadsheet format and has regular supplements on business and sports and a weekly magazine section entitled "Week End." This newspaper, with an approximate circulation of 50,000, is a member of ABC. *Khaleej Times* is owned by a prominent Dubai family, the Galadaris. The newspaper has bureaus and offices in Abu Dhabi, Bahrain (Manama), Qatar (Doha), the Sultanate of Oman (Muscat and Salalah), India (Bombay, New Delhi, Madras, Bangalore, and Calcutta), Pakistan (Karachi), the United Kingdom (London), and Sri Lanka (Colombo).

Gulf News began publication from Dubai and, as one of the two leading English dailies, has provided keen competition to *Khaleej Times*'s leadership in the Gulf. The editorial policies of *Gulf News* and *Khaleej Times* are similar, and *Gulf News* publishes supplements on finance and business. It also has a daily supplement called the *Gulf News Tabloid* and a popular weekend magazine entitled *Gulf Weekly*. *Gulf News,* owned by the Al Tayer family, has bureaus and offices in Abu Dhabi, Bahrain (Manama), Pakistan (Karachi), India (Bombay), Taiwan (Taipei), and the United Kingdom (London).

Magazines

Table 21.3 lists the leading Arabic and English weekly magazines being published in the UAE. Although there were few printing agencies when the nation was established in 1971, their numbers have grown substantially. With one of the highest mass media densities in the Arab World, the UAE's 5 Arabic newspapers, 3 English newspapers, and a host of weekly, fortnightly, and monthly magazines (total 156, published in Arabic and English) are fulfilling the information needs of the citizens and the multilingual expatriate community. In 1992, a moratorium on new titles imposed earlier by the federal Ministry of Information and Culture, which oversees the UAE's mass media, continued. Although print media exert a strong presence in the UAE, television and radio are gaining popularity steadily.

ELECTRONIC MEDIA

Radio

Broadcast media, like the print media, have a nascent history in the UAE. Broadcast media have experienced a sustained growth, as evidenced in the siz-

Table 21.3
United Arab Emirates' Leading Weekly Publications

Publication	Year	No. of pages	Contents
Arabic:			
Akhbar Dubai	1965	54	Popular periodical, local, and regional news. Ceased publication
Al Ayaam	1969	52	Cultural and political journal concerned with UAE development.
Direo Al Wattan	1971	82	Military affairs.
Heyah (She)	1978	50	Women's interest magazine (former title Samraa).
Al Arabia Azmina	1979-1981	66	Popular periodical. Ceased publication.
Zahratu Al Khaleej	1979	82	Magazine for women, women's issues in UAE, and the Arab world.
Majed	1979	54	Children's magazine for 4-16 year olds.
Al Hadaf	1988	80	Sports magazine, local, and regional.
Riadahwa Al Shabab	1981	50	Sports, youth affairs. Was issued as a supplement for Al Bayan newspaper until Feb. 1981.
English:			
Week End	1986	24	Weekly supplement for the daily newspaper, Khaleej Times.
Gulf Weekly	1979	63	Weekly supplement for the daily newspaper, Gulf News.
Emirates Women	1981	80	Women's interest journal, fashion, What is New, health and beauty, food.

Source: Directory of the Periodicals in the United Arab Emirates, 1990, pp. 12–97.

able ownership of receivers: 521,000 radio and 166,000 television sets in 1990 (Banks, 1991).

Prior to independence, the first attempts to begin radio broadcasting were made by the British in Sharjah emirate on a limited scale. UAE Broadcasting is a government-owned service, operating within a two-tiered structure; the federal government owns and operates the broadcast industries, while allowing individual emirates to undertake their own broadcasting (Dubai, Ras al Khaimah, and Sharjah). Broadcasts are in four languages: Arabic, English, French, and Urdu (Urdu for the large number of expatriate workers from Pakistan, Bangladesh, and India). The flat topography of the country (with the exception of the Hajar mountain range in the east) is particularly conducive to broadcasting. Table 21.4 lists the locations of major transmitters of UAE Radio, which are linked by a UHF (ultrahigh frequency) microwave system.

There are four radio stations, one each in Abu Dhabi (capital), Dubai, Ras al Khaimah, and Sharjah. In 1971, installation and commissioning of modern studios in Abu Dhabi and Ras al Khaimah, and commercial stations in Dubai and Sharjah were completed. Abu Dhabi serves as the main transmitting station and is equipped with a superpower transmitter of a 1,500-kilowatt rating that is used to broadcast the national service. This program is rebroadcast throughout the nation using low-power transmitters (Boyd, 1982).

Abu Dhabi. In 1969, Radio Abu Dhabi was the first station to broadcast Arabic programs; soon after, it came to be known as United Arab Emirates Radio. Broadcast media have identified themselves as the Voice of the United Arab Emirates since 1976 (Boyd, 1982).

Table 21.5 lists foreign service broadcasts including language of broadcast, frequencies (kilohertz [KHz]), meter bands, and time. Foreign broadcasts (AM/FM [amplitude modulation/frequency modulation]) from the Kingdom of Saudi Arabia, Bahrain, Kuwait, Oman, and Qatar are beamed to the UAE along with broadcasts from the Voice of America, Radio ARAMCO (operated by the Arab-American Oil Company in Dhahran, Saudi Arabia), the British Broadcasting Corporation (BBC), and Radio Monte Carlo. A majority of foreign service broadcasts are in Arabic, with the largest segment being directed toward Europe. Prime-time broadcasts in the evening are directed toward neighboring Arab countries.

Dubai. This emirate operates both Arabic and English services. The Arabic service operates for 18 hours a day (6:30 A.M. to 12:30 A.M.), and it is essentially a music service with some news and brief features. More than 50 percent of the staff are Arab expatriates; commercial rates for the Arabic service are slightly higher compared with the English service. Dubai Radio's English service is broadcast on FM between 6:30 A.M. and 12:30 A.M. The disc jockeys are native English speakers, and popular Western music is played throughout the day. Between 9:00 P.M. and sign-off, continuous stereo music is played from prerecorded tapes. Table 21.6 provides a flavor of programming on Dubai FM radio in May 1992 (*Khaleej Times,* 1992).

Table 21.4
Transmitters of UAE Radio, Abu Dhabi

Transmitting station	Power	Wave	Frequency
Maqta	1 x 50	MF	810
	1 x 120	HF	
Sadiyat	2 x 250	MF	729
	2 x 50	MF	657
	2 x 50	MF	1539
Dhabyya	2 x 1000	MF	1314
	4 x 500	MF	
Sharjah	1 x 50	MF	1575
	1 x 5	MF	Standby
Fujairah	2 x 50	MF	972
Abu Dhabi	2 x 1	FM	93.5 MHz
	1 x 1	FM	98.1 MHz

Source: Technical Advisor's Office, Ministry of Information and Culture, P. O. Box 17, Abu Dhabi, UAE.

Note: Studio and transmitters linked through UHF/Microwave system.

FM = Frequency modulation.
MH_z = Megahertz.

Ras al Khaimah and *Sharjah.* These emirates operate a limited radio broadcasting service but are no match for the sophisticated broadcasting facilities and programming of the larger emirates Abu Dhabi and Dubai.

Television

One of the striking features of broadcast media in the UAE is the pervasiveness of television. Given its short history, phenomenal growth, and rate of development, television has integrated itself as an essential part of the UAE's cultural landscape.

Table 21.5
Foreign Service Broadcasts, UAE Radio, 1990–1991

Target area	Language	Frequency (Khz)	Meter band	Time
North America	English	9600	31	2 a.m.- 4 a.m.
	English	6170	49	10 p.m.-12 a.m.
	Arabic	9505	31	4 a.m.- 6 a.m.
	Arabic	6170	49	4 a.m.- 6 a.m.
North-West America	English	15100	19	2 a.m.- 3 a.m.
		13605	21	3 a.m.- 4 a.m.
Far East (toward Japan)	Arabic	15315	19	6 a.m.- 7 a.m.
		21515	13	6 a.m.- 7 a.m.
		21735	13	6 a.m.- 8 a.m.
		25690	11	7 a.m.- 8 a.m.
Far East (toward Australia)	Arabic	21735	13	8 a.m.-10 a.m.
		25690	11	8 a.m.-10 a.m.
North Africa	Arabic	9600	31	6 a.m.-10 a.m.
		13605	21	8 a.m.-10 a.m.
		11985	25	8 p.m.-1:35 a.m.
Europe	Arabic	13605	21	10 a.m.-12 p.m.
		15315	19	10 a.m.-12 p.m.
		17855	16	10 a.m.- 8 p.m.
		21735	13	10 a.m.- 8 p.m.
		25690	11	12 p.m.- 5 p.m.
		21515	13	12 p.m.- 8 p.m.
		11965	25	8 p.m.-1:35 a.m.
		9780	31	8 p.m.-1:35 a.m.
Middle East	Arabic	15315	19	5 p.m.- 7 p.m.
		11815	25	7 p.m.- 9 p.m.
		6170	49	9 p.m.-1:35 a.m.
India and Pakistan	Arabic	9695	31	6 a.m.-10:30 a.m.
		9695	31	8 p.m.-12 a.m.

Source: Technical Advisor's Office, Ministry of Information and Culture, P. O. Box 17, Abu Dhabi, UAE.

Table 21.6
A Day's Programming on Dubai FM

Time	Programming
12:30 a.m.	Chart Music (Classical, New Age)
6:15 a.m.	Holy Koran
6:30 a.m.	Good Morning Dubai with Dave Beatty
8:05 a.m.	Keeping Fit with Nargis Fikree
10:00 a.m.	Morning Delight with Phil Richardson
12:00 p.m.	Mid-Day Special with Phil Blizzard
3 p.m.	The Classical Hour with Linda Floyd
4 p.m.	Good Sounds with Mark Lloyd
5 p.m.	Countdown with Walt Love
7 p.m.	Night Beat with Richard Lee
10 p.m.	The Folk Spot with Tommy Brennon
11 p.m.	Late Night Listening
Various	News (7:30 a.m., 9:30 a.m., 2:30 p.m., 5:30 p.m., 8:30 p.m.)
Various	News Summaries (8:30 a.m., 12:30 p.m., 1:30 p.m., 6:30 p.m., and 7:30 p.m.)

Source: Khaleej Times, 1992.

Note: All programs are subject to change.

Abu Dhabi. The first monochrome television broadcasts were made from Abu Dhabi on August 6, 1969. In 1971, new phase alternate line (PAL) color equipment was installed in Abu Dhabi, and color transmissions commenced on January 4, 1974 (Boyd, 1982).

Dubai. The two-tiered structure of broadcasting in the UAE led to the establishment of commercial television in Dubai, the major port and commercial center in the Gulf. In keeping with its commercial outlook, Dubai television's first broadcasts in 1972 were a commercial monochrome service (Boyd, 1982). Broadcasting in the evening hours, the station carried imported Arabic and Western entertainment programs that were preferred by advertisers and Dubai's expatriate population. Designated Channel 2, its success led to the establishment of two commercial channels broadcasting in Arabic (Program One) and English (Program Two).

Program One broadcasts on Channels 2, 10, 30, 38, and 41, starting at 4:00 P.M. and sign-off at 12:50 A.M. Catering exclusively to Arab audiences, telecasts are produced locally and typically include a mix of humor, sports, documentary film, a serial, news (at 8:00 P.M. and 10:00 P.M.), medical magazine, wrestling, and an Arabic play. Sign-off at 12:50 A.M. is preceded by a recitation of the Holy Quran and playing the national anthem.

Program Two began in June 1978 and is currently broadcast on Channel 33. Targeted primarily at the expatriate community, the telecast begins at 4:00 P.M. and usually ends at 12:15 A.M. Advertising can be purchased to run both within a program and in between programs. However, there is a hefty 50 percent surcharge for the former option (Boyd, 1982). Table 21.7 lists an example of programming from May 1992.

Other broadcasts received in Dubai are from Abu Dhabi (Channels 5, 6, 7, 35, 36, 43, and 48), Sharjah (22, 28, 54, and 57), Bahrain (4), Bahrain (55), and India's national television service, Doordarshan.

Sharjah. This emirate operates a single television channel. Because of its small size and limited budget, it offers limited programming.

Cable Television

Three major cable networks—BBC, STAR TV PLUS, and Music Television (MTV)—operate in the UAE. BBC is the preferred network among Western expatriates, and STAR TV PLUS is the network of choice for Asian expatriates because of its larger quantity of Asian and Southeast Asian content. Prior to and during the Persian Gulf War, Cable News Network (CNN) was the preferred network despite poor reception in Dubai.

NEW TECHNOLOGIES

The Arab countries of the Gulf have seen the highest videocassette recorder (VCR) proliferation rates in recent history. Although exact figures on VCR ownership are not available for the UAE, it was estimated that in 1983, 65 percent of households owning a television set also owned a VCR. Data from 1984 indicate that 75 percent of households owned VCRs (Howell, 1986). Extrapolating from these numbers, it is reasonable to assume that at least 85 percent of households owned a VCR in 1992. The proliferation of VCRs is explained by easy availability because the Gulf countries are some of the largest importers of Japanese audiovisual products and by life-styles that cater to family-centered entertainment at home.

Table 21.7
A Day's Programming on Dubai TV, Channel 33

Time	Programming
4:00 p.m.	Recitation of Holy Quran
4:12 p.m.	Pingu (Comedy)
4:18 p.m.	The Adventures of Tin Tin
4:40 p.m.	Animated Classics
5:04 p.m.	3-2-1 Contact
5:32 p.m.	Get a Life
5:55 p.m.	Horse Racing (Live 1000 Guineas Race)
7:06 p.m.	Star Trek
7:30 p.m.	News Bulletin
7:44 p.m.	Hollywood Stuntmakers
8:08 p.m.	Nasty Boys
9:10 p.m.	Thirtysomething - Closing the Circle
10 p.m.	World News and Weather
10:37 p.m.	Night Court
11:25 p.m.	Studio 5-B Programming
12:15 a.m.	National Anthem and Closedown

Source: Khaleej Times, 1992.

Note: All programs are subject to change.

MOTION PICTURES

Motion pictures remain an important part of the UAE's cultural milieu. Absence of hard data on film imports is likely to mask the popularity of this medium as a form of entertainment. According to an official report by the Ministry of Information and Culture, in 1991 there were 27 cinema theaters. However, listings in daily newspapers reveal that there are at least a dozen theaters each in Abu Dhabi and Dubai, and the total number for the UAE is nearly twice the estimate. A majority of the films shown were Hindi and English films. Also, a majority of the Gulf countries, including the UAE, import motion pictures from Egypt, India, Pakistan, the United Kingdom, and the United States.

MEDIA OWNERSHIP AND REGULATION

The ownership of mass media in the UAE follows a dualistic structure wherein print media are privately owned, and electronic media, including the official news agency, Emirates News Agency (WAM), are government owned.

In the English press, two of the three leading daily newspapers (*Gulf News* and *Khaleej Times*) are privately owned. The third English daily, *Emirates News,* is ''semi-official,'' a catchword for a government-controlled and -subsidized newspaper. In the Arabic press, *Al Ittihad, Al Wahdah,* and *Al Bayan* are government owned.

The stage for government control of print media was set in 1973 when a bill was enacted placing the press under fairly rigid control, common in most Arab countries of the region. From the beginning, official policy was to disseminate information or political messages that were in accord with the UAE's domestic and foreign policies (Nyrop, 1977).

In 1980, the government published the Publication Law, which brought together in a comprehensive format the various laws relating to the press, advertising, and electronic media. The salient point of the law was that all mass media would fall under it, and the authority to adjudicate and review appeals was vested in the national Ministry of Information and Culture. For example, under the law the press cannot criticize the ruling family or the UAE's allies and friendly countries nor carry the names of crime victims. Propagation of religion, dishonest and misleading commercials, one-sided reporting of controversies, and promotion of liquor, sex, or pornography are all prohibited. Punitive measures include fines, cessation of publication, and cancellation of licenses.

Despite their overarching nature, the UAE's Publication Laws are not zealously enforced by the government. Given the guidelines, newspapers tend to indulge in self-regulation. Day-to-day surveillance is not done by the government, although strictures in the form of phone calls from Ministry of Information and Culture officials to concerned print media editors occur.

NEWS AGENCIES

The major news-gathering methods used by the mass media in the UAE are interviews with opinion leaders in the communities and government sources, both human and documents, which are then augmented by international wire services such as the Associated Press (AP), Agence France-Presse (AFP), and others.

CONCLUSION

The mass media industries have experienced a period of steady growth and have entrenched themselves in the political, economic, and cultural landscape of the United Arab Emirates. The UAE's mass media are currently in a phase of consolidation and continue to fulfill the communication needs not only of the indigenous population but also of the expatriate community. Regional cooperation and sharing of information with AGCC countries are also common.

Regarding media industry employment, the mass media industries have inordinately relied on a foreign work force because of the lack of training opportunities. For the Arabic press, newspeople have been hired from countries with older press traditions such as Egypt and Lebanon. News workers for the English press come from Europe, India, and Pakistan. However, this excessive reliance on a foreign work force is changing slowly as local talent becomes available.

Given the political stability that the UAE has enjoyed since its inception, it is safe to predict a continued thriving of the UAE's mass media industries, nurtured and sustained by a pragmatic and benign leadership.

REFERENCES

Banks, A. S. (1991). *Political handbook of the world 1991.* Binghamton, NY: C. S. A. Publications.

Boyd, D. A. (1982). *Broadcasting in the Arab World.* Philadelphia: Temple University Press.

Directory of the periodicals in the United Arab Emirates. (1990). Abu Dhabi: Cultural Foundation National Library.

Directory of the periodicals in the United Arab Emirates. (1992). Abu Dhabi: Cultural Foundation National Library.

Heard-Bey, F. (1982). *From Trucial States to United Arab Emirates—A society in transition.* New York: Longman.

Howell, W. J., Jr. (1986). *World broadcasting in the age of the satellite.* Norwood, NJ: Ablex.

Kay, S. (1991). *Land of the emirates.* Dubai, UAE: Motivate Publishing.

Khaleej Times. (1992, May 23).

Nonneman, G. (1988). *Development, administration and aid in the Middle East.* New York: Routledge.

Nyrop, R. F. (1977). *Area handbook for the Persian Gulf states.* Washington, DC: American University.

The United Arab Emirates. (1991). Abu Dhabi: Ministry of Information and Culture.

Zahlan, R. S. (1989). *The making of the modern Gulf states.* London: Unmin Hyman Limited.

GLOSSARY

ABSP. The Arab Ba'th Socialist Party. The ruling political party in Iraq.

ADN. Allgemeiner Deutscher Nachrichtendiest. A German news agency.

AFP. Agence France-Presse. French news agency.

AGCC. Arab Gulf Cooperation Council. A regional body formed by the Persian Gulf's Arab states.

AM. Amplitude modulation.

ANA. Arab News Agency. Egypt's news agency prior to MENA.

Anadolu Ajansi. The official news agency in Turkey.

ANSA. Agenzia Nazionale Stampa Associata. The Italian news agency.

AP. Associated Press. A commercial U.S. news agency.

API. Agence Photographique d'Information et de Presse. One of the two news agencies in Algeria.

APP. Associated Press of Pakistan. One of the four news agencies in Pakistan.

APS. Algerie Presse Service. One of the two news agencies in Algeria.

ARABSAT. Arab Satellite Communications Organization. A regional system consisting of 22 nations of the Arab League.

ARAMCO. The Arabian-American Oil Company.

ASBU. Arab States Broadcasting Union. Organization for broadcasting cooperation among the Arab states.

Bakhtar. Afghanistan's official news agency.

BBC. British Broadcasting Corporation.

Bezek. The Israel Telecommunications Corporation.

BRTC. Bahrain's Radio and Television Corporation. Distributes CNN International's service in Bahrain.

BSECR. Black Sea Economic Cooperation Region.

BSSA. Broadcasting Service of Saudi Arabia.

BTV. Bahrain Television.

CFI. Canal France International.

Canal Plus. French subscription TV network.

Channel. A frequency used by a radio or TV station or a network.

CLT. La Compagnie Libanaise de Te'le'vision. Lebanon's television company.

CNA. Cyprus News Agency. Cyprus's official news agency.

CNE. Egyptian News Channel.

CNN. Cable News Network. A U.S.-based commercial cable network.

CNN International. The international service of Cable News Network (CNN) based in the United States.

Coverage. An area reached by a particular broadcast signal.

CyBC. Cyprus Broadcasting Corporation. In charge of radio and TV operation and programming.

DBS. Direct broadcast satellite.

DPA. Deutsche Presse-Agentur. A German news agency.

EBU. European Broadcasting Union. Organization of the European broadcasters that operates Eurovision.

EC. European Community. Consists of Belgium, Denmark, Germany, France, Greece, Ireland, Italy, Luxembourg, The Netherlands, Portugal, Spain, and the United Kingdom.

EFE. Spain's National News Agency.

EFTA. European Free Trade Association.

ENAMEP. National Press Distribution Enterprise. Responsible for newspaper distribution in Algeria.

ENPA. National Audio-Visual Production Enterprise. Responsible for Algerian radio and TV productions.

ENRS. National Radio Broadcasting Enterprise. Responsible for radio broadcasting in Algeria.

ENTD. National Telediffusion Enterprise. Responsible for program distribution in Algeria.

ENTV. National Television Enterprise. Responsible for TV broadcasting in Algeria.

EPIC. Industrial and Commercial Public Institution. The main umbrella for broadcast programming and services in Algeria.

ESPN. Entertainment Sports-Network.

ESTV. Egyptian Satellite Television. A regional satellite service for program transmission/distribution.

Eurovision. International news exchange and programs operated by EBU.

External service. Print or broadcast services intended for audiences outside a given country.

FM. Frequency modulation.

FNC. Federal National Council. The UAE's parliament.

FTV. Future Television. An independent television network in Lebanon.

GDP. Gross domestic production.

GMT. Greenwich mean time. Mean solar time that passes through Greenwich, England. Also called UTC (coordinated universal time).

GNA. Gulf News Agency. Bahrain's official news agency.

GNP. Gross national product.

GPC. General People's Congress. The highest political body in Libya.

HBO. Home Box Office. A private U.S. cable service.

IBA. Israel Broadcasting Authority. The official broadcasting body in Israel.

ICP. Israel Cable Programming. A conglomerate in charge of cable TV in Israel.

INA. Iraqi News Agency. Iraq's official news agency.

INMARSAT. International Maritime Satellite Organization. A London-based organization providing satellite communications for seafaring vessels and other mobile units.

INTIFADA. The Palestinian uprising that is thought to have started in Gaza on December 9, 1987.

INTELSAT. International Telecommunications Satellite Consortium.

IPP. Independent Press of Pakistan. One of the four news agencies in Pakistan.

IRANA. International Islamic News Agency. An agency formed by the Islamic countries.

IRNA. Islamic Republic News Agency. The official Iranian news agency since 1979.

IRTO. International Radio and Television Organisation.

ITAR. Informatsionnoye Telegrfnoe Agentsvo Rossii. A Russian news agency.

ITIM. Associated Israel Press Service. Israel's official news agency.

ITU. International Telecommunication Union. A United Nations agency concerned with international telecommunication regulation and policy.

ITV. Independent Television. A privately run television system in Lebanon.

ITV. Israel Television. A television network in Israel.

JANA. Jamahiriyya News Agency. The official news agency in Libya.

JTV. Jordan Television. The television network in Jordan.

Knesset. The Israeli Parliament.

Kol Yisrael. The Voice of Israel. Israel's radio network.

KUNA. Kuwait News Agency. Kuwait's official news agency.

Majlis. The Iranian congress (parliament).

MBC. Middle East Broadcasting Corporation. A London-based satellite service for program transmission/distribution.

MENA. Middle East News Agency. The official news agency of Egypt.

MTV. Music Television. A cable TV channel based in the United States.

NANAP. Non-Aligned News Agency Pool. A news agency formed by the nonaligned nations.

NATO. North Atlantic Treaty Organization.

NCKC. National Company of Kuwaiti Cinema.

Network. Group of two or more broadcast stations interconnected to air programs simultaneously.

NIRT. National Iranian Radio and Television. A national organization responsible for broadcasting prior to 1979.

NNA. National News Agency. Lebanon's official news agency.

Nonaligned nations. Approximately 100 advancing countries that adopted a policy of political independence during the cold war.

NTSC. National Television Standards Committee. The U.S. color broadcast system.

ONA. Omani News Agency. The official news agency in Oman.

OPECNA. OPEC News Agency. An agency whose members are the oil-producing countries (Organization of Petroleum Exporting Countries [OPEC]).

Open university. A British-based institution of higher education whose courses are offered via radio and television.

PAL. Phase alternate line. German color TV system.

Pars News Agency. The official Iranian news agency prior to 1979.

PBC. Pakistan Broadcasting Corporation. The body in charge of radio broadcasting in Pakistan.

Petra. Jordanian News Agency. The official news agency in Jordan.

Pirate channels. Radio or TV stations operated illegally within or without the boundaries of a state.

PLO. The Palestinian Liberation Organization.

PNC. Palestine National Council. The highest body within the PLO.

PPI. Pakistan Press International. One of the four news agencies in Pakistan.

PRDC. The Libyan broadcasting station.

PTI. Press Trust of India. India's news agency.

PTT. Post, Telephone, and Telegraph. A government body (often a ministry) responsible for national telecommunications facilities.

PTV. Pakistan Television. Pakistan's television broadcasting network.

QNA. Qatar News Agency. The official news agency in Qatar.

Quran. Also **Koran** or **Qur'an.** The holy book in Islam.

Ramadan or **Ramazan.** The ninth month of the Islamic calendar, spent in fasting from dawn to dusk.

RCA. Radio Corporation of America.

Reuters. British international news agency.

RAI. Radio Televisione Italiana. The Italian broadcasting service.

RTA. Algerian Radio and Television. Responsible for broadcast media in Algeria prior to 1986.

RTF. La Radiodiffusion Television Francaise. A Tunisian radio and television organization.

RTT. Radiodiffusion Television Tunisienne. The Tunisian radio and television organization.

SANA. Syrian Arab News Agency. The official news agency in Syria.

SATEL. Satellite Television Network.

SECAM. Sequence Couleur a Memoire. The French color system of broadcasting.

Sheikhdom. A state headed by a sheikh (the leader of an Arab family or tribe; also a religious official in Islam).

SHI'A (also Shiah or Shiite). The principal minority sect of Islam, composed of the followers of Ali, the cousin and son-in-law of Prophet Mohammad.

SKY News. A British television news network.

SPA. Saudi Press Agency. The official news agency in Saudi Arabia.

STAR TV. Rupert Murdoch's Hong Kong–based satellite TV service.

STAR TV PLUS. Hong Kong's satellite TV service.

STN. Shalimar Television Network. A commercially run TV network in Pakistan.

TAP. Tunis-Afrique-Presse. The official news agency in Tunisia.

Tass. Telegrafnoe Agentsvo Sovetskovo Soyuza. Russian news agency.

Telecommunication. Distance communication via radio, TV, telephone, telegraph, satellite, and data transmission.

TGRT. Turkish Radio and Television Network.

TRT. Turkish Radio and Television Institution. The body in charge of radio and television in Turkey.

TURKSAT. Turkish Satellite. A satellite transmission planned by the Turkish government.

TV5. A satellite television service based in France.

UAE. United Arab Emirates. A state located in the Persian Gulf region.

UNESCO. United Nations Educational, Scientific and Cultural Organization.

UPI. United Press International. A U.S. international news agency.

UPP. United Press of Pakistan. One of the four news agencies in Pakistan.

URTNA. African National Radio and Television Union. Based in Senegal, it assists member countries in programming.

VCR. Videocassette recorder.

VOA. Voice of America. The official external broadcast service of the United States.

VPIR. Voice and Profile of the Islamic Republic. An Iranian organization responsible for radio and TV broadcasting.

WAFA. The Palestine News Agency, established by the PLO in 1972.

SELECTED BIBLIOGRAPHY

Abu-Nasr, J. M. (1987). *A history of the Maghrib in the Islamic period.* Cambridge: Cambridge University Press.

Adams, M. (Ed.). (1988). *The Middle East: A handbook.* New York: Facts on File.

Anwar, M. A. (1985). *Information services in Muslim countries: An annotated bibliography of expert studies and reports on library information and archives.* London: Mansell.

Barton, F. (1979). *The press in Africa: Persecution and perseverance.* New York: Africana.

Bill, J. A., & Leiden, C. (1987). *The Middle East politics and power.* Boston: Allyn and Bacon.

Boyd, D. A. (1993). *Broadcasting in the Arab world: A survey of the electronic media in the Middle East.* Ames: Iowa State University Press.

Boyd, D. A., Straubhaar, J. D., & Lent, J. A. (1989). *Videocassette recorders in the Third World.* New York: Longman.

Boyd-Barrett, O. (1980). *The international news agencies.* Newbury Park, CA: Sage.

Browne, D. R. (1982). *International radio broadcasting: The limits of the limitless medium.* New York: Praeger.

Cambridge Ancient History (3rd ed.). (1975). Cambridge: Cambridge University Press.

Cambridge History of Islam. (1977). Cambridge: Cambridge University Press.

Dejani, N. H. (1979). *Studies in broadcasting.* London: International Institute of Communications.

Dizard, W. P. (1966). *Television: A world view.* Syracuse, NY: Syracuse University Press.

Drost, H. (Ed.). (1991). *The world's news media.* Essex: Longman Current Affairs.

Dunnett, P. (1990). *The world television industry.* London: Routledge.

Europa world year book. (1992). London: Europa.

Fischer, H. D. (1976). *International and intercultural communications.* New York: Hasting House.

Fortner, R. S. (1993). *International communication.* Belmont, CA: Wadsworth.

Frederick, H. H. (1993). *Global communication and international relations.* Belmont, CA: Wadsworth.

Gerbner, G., & Siefert, M. (Eds.). (1984). *World Communications: A handbook.* New York: Longman.

Head, S. W. (1985). *World broadcasting systems: A comparative analysis.* Belmont, CA: Wadsworth.

Horton, P. C. (Ed.). (1978). *The Third World and press freedom.* New York: Praeger.

Howell, Jr., W. L. (1986). *World Broadcasting in the age of satellite.* Norwood, NJ: Ablex.

International Encyclopedia of Communication (4 volumes). (1989). New York: Oxford University Press.

Islam and Communication. (1993, January). *Media & Society* (special issue), *15*(1).

Katz, E., & Wedell, G. (1977). *Broadcasting in the Third World: Promise and performance.* Cambridge: Harvard University Press.

Kazan, F. (1993). *Mass media, modernity and development: Arab states of the Gulf.* Westport, CT: Praeger.

Kipper, J., & Saunders, H. H. (Eds.) (1991). *The Middle East in global perspective.* Boulder, CO: Westview.

Lenczowski, G. (1980). *The Middle East in world affairs.* Ithaca, NY: Cornell University Press.

Lent, J. (1987). *Global guide to media and communications.* London: K. G. Saur.

Martin, L. J., & Chaudhary, A. G. (Eds.). (1983). *Comparative mass media systems.* New York: Longman.

Merril, J. C. (1991). *Global Journalism: Survey of international communication* (2nd ed.). New York: Longman.

Middle East and North Africa (38th ed.). (1992). London: Europa.

Mowlana, H. (1971). *International communication: A selected bibliography.* Dubuque, IA: Kendall-Hunt.

Mowlana, H. (1985). *International flow of news: An annotated bibliography.* Paris: UNESCO Press.

Mowlana, H. (1986). *Global information and world communication.* New York: Praeger.

Nyrop, R. F. (1977). *Area handbook for the Persian Gulf states.* Washington, DC: The American University Press.

Ochs, M. (1986). *The African press.* Cairo, Egypt: The American University in Cairo Press.

Peretz, D. (1983). *The Middle East today* (4th ed.). New York: Praeger.

Rosen, P. T. (Ed.). (1988). *International handbook of broadcasting systems.* Westport, CT: Greenwood.

Rugh, W. A. (1987). *The Arab press: News media and political processes in the Arab World* (2nd ed.). Syracuse, NY: Syracuse University Press.

Sardar, Z. (1988). *Information and the Muslim World.* London: Mansell.

Satloff, Robert B. (Ed.). (1993). *The politics of change in the Middle East.* Boulder, CO: Westview.

Stevenson, R. L. (1994). *Global communication in the twenty-first century.* New York: Longman.

UNESCO. (1989). *World communication report.* Paris: UNESCO Press.

Wilcox, D. L. (1975). *Mass media in black Africa: Philosophy and control.* New York: Praeger.

World almanac and book of facts. (1993). New York: World Almanac.

World media handbook. (1992). New York: United Nations.

World radio TV handbook. (1992). New York: Billboard.

INDEX

ABOUT THE EDITORS AND CONTRIBUTORS

YAHYA R. KAMALIPOUR is associate professor of mass communication and director of graduate studies, Department of Communication and Creative Arts, Purdue University Calumet, Hammond, IN.

HAMID MOWLANA is professor of international relations and the founding director of the International Communication Program at the American University, Washington, D.C. He is president of the International Association for Mass Communication Research (IAMCR/AIERI).

WALID A. AFIFI is a doctoral student at the Department of Communication, University of Arizona, Tucson.

MOHAMED M. ARAFA is a communication faculty member, Mass Communication Department, University of Qatar, Doha, Qatar.

MUHAMMAD I. AYISH is a communication faculty member, Department of Journalism and Mass Communication, Yarmouk University, Irbid, Jordan.

ANANTHA S. BABBILI is associate professor and chair of the Department of Journalism at Texas Christian University.

SONIA DABBOUS is associate professor of journalism and mass communication at the American University in Cairo, Egypt. She is also assistant editor of *Akhbar El-Youm.*

MOHAMED NAJIB EL-SARAYRAH is a communication faculty member, Department of Journalism and Mass Communication, Yarmouk University, Irbid, Jordan.

MAHMOUD M. HAMMOUD is a communication faculty member at the United Arab Emirates University.

AFAF HAMOD is the Academic Director of Naseem School and a consultant with a communication and advertising agency in Bahrain.

MAZHARUL HAQUE is associate professor of communication at the Radio, Television, and Film Department, University of Southern Mississippi.

ABDALLAH HIDRI is assistant professor of journalism at the Institute of Press and Information Science, Tunis, Tunisia.

KHALID SERHAN HURRAT is a counselor at the Iraq Ministry of Foreign Affairs and a lecturer in communication, College of Arts, University of Baghdad.

SARWAT HUSSAIN is a graduate student in media studies at Texas Christian University.

FAYAD E. KAZAN is a faculty member of arts, Mass Communication Department, Kuwait University.

JOHN E. KESHISHOGLOU is professor and international consultant, School of Communications, Ithaca College, Ithaca, NY.

VIJAY KRISHNA is a doctoral student in the School of Interpersonal Communication at Ohio University.

SAM LEHMAN-WILZIG is professor and chair of the Journalism and Public Communication Division, Bar-Ilan University, Israel.

LISA ISABEL LEIDIG is a policy analyst at the National Telecommunications and Information Administration, U.S. Department of Commerce, Washington, D.C.

ABBAS MALEK is associate professor of communication, Radio-TV-Film Department, Howard University, Washington, D.C.

KARIM MEZRAN is a doctoral student in international studies at the Johns Hopkins University, Baltimore.

ORAYB AREF NAJJAR is assistant professor of journalism, Department of Journalism, Northern Illinois University, DeKalb.

HANA S. NOOR AL-DEEN is associate professor of mass communication at the University of North Carolina at Wilmington.

ELISE K. PARSIGIAN is an adjunct professor in the Department of Social Sciences and Associate Director of the Center for Armenian Research, Studies and Publication at the University of Michigan-Dearborn. She also heads her own consulting company, Communication Solutions, and has authored two books, *Mass Media Writing* and *Proposal Savvy*.

MEHDI MOHSENIAN RAD is a researcher and lecturer in communication, School of Mass Communication, Allameh TabaTabaie University, Tehran, Iran.

KULDIP R. RAMPAL is professor of communication at Central Missouri State University, Warrensburg. He has taught, as a visiting senior fellow in mass communication, at the National University of Singapore.

MOHAMMAD HOUSSAIN RAZI is adviser to international students at Vincennes University, Vincennes, IN. He earned a bachelor's degree at Kabul University, where he also taught journalism from 1964 to 1978.

ZIYAD D. RIFAI is a communication faculty member, Department of Journalism and Mass Communication, Yarmouk University, Irbid, Jordan.

AMIT SCHEJTER is a doctoral student in communication at Rutgers University, New Brunswick, NJ.

ARVIND SINGHAL is assistant professor of communication, School of Interpersonal Communication, Ohio University.

HUSAMETTIN UNSAL is a communication researcher/lecturer and the first general secretary of the Research Association on Communication in Turkey (ILAD).

LAID ZAGHLAMI is a communication researcher and a writer with Algerian Radio and Television.

ISBN 0-313-28535-7

90000>

EAN

9 780313 285356

HARDCOVER BAR CODE